# cyber*sounds*

D1494350

Steve Jones
*General Editor*

Vol. 31

PETER LANG
New York • Washington, D.C./Baltimore • Bern
Frankfurt am Main • Berlin • Brussels • Vienna • Oxford

# cyber*sounds*

## Essays on Virtual Music Culture

*Michael D. Ayers,* EDITOR

LEARNING RESOURCES CENTRE

Havering College
of Further and Higher education

PETER LANG
New York • Washington, D.C./Baltimore • Bern
Frankfurt am Main • Berlin • Brussels • Vienna • Oxford

306.484

AG.

164729

Library of Congress Cataloging-in-Publication Data

Cybersounds: essays on virtual music culture / edited by Michael D. Ayers.
p. cm. — (Digital formations; v. 31)
Includes bibliographical references and index.
1. Popular music—Social aspects. 2. Internet—Social aspects. 3. Music—
Computer network resources. I. Ayers, Michael D. II. Series.
ML3918.P67C93    306.4'8424—dc22    2005013510
ISBN 0-8204-7861-X
ISSN 1526-3169


Bibliographic information published by **Die Deutsche Bibliothek**.
**Die Deutsche Bibliothek** lists this publication in the "Deutsche
Nationalbibliografie"; detailed bibliographic data is available
on the Internet at http://dnb.ddb.de/.

Cover design by Lisa Barfield

The paper in this book meets the guidelines for permanence and durability
of the Committee on Production Guidelines for Book Longevity
of the Council of Library Resources.

© 2006 Peter Lang Publishing, Inc., New York
29 Broadway, New York, NY 10006
www.peterlang.com

All rights reserved.
Reprint or reproduction, even partially, in all forms such as microfilm,
xerography, microfiche, microcard, and offset strictly prohibited.

Printed in the United States of America

For Doug and Elaine—from whom I learned about life and Peter, Paul and Mary

# Contents

# Acknowledgments

To put a collection together is a collaborative effort, to say the least. If it was not for the contributors of this volume that I had the pleasure to work with, this would never seen the light—I don't think I could have asked for an easier bunch of academics to converse about music with. I would like to thank Steve Jones and Damon Zucca, of the University of Illinois-Chicago and Peter Lang Press, respectively, for having faith, patience, and dedication to this project. I would like to thank Martha McCaughey of Appalachian State University— how I got so lucky in convincing you of my merit, I will never know, but will never ponder. I would like to thank the Virginia Tech Department of Sociology and the Manhattan College Department of Sociology for providing my mind much needed stimulus over the years. Donna Gaines, Jonathan Cohen, and Shawn Bosler have all been more than helpful in making a better writer out of me and on top of that, allowing me to write about music. And without the artists that mean so much to us in our day to day lives, this book wouldn't exist: Jeff Tweedy, Ryan Adams, Calexico, Tom Waits, Johnny Cash, Otis Redding, Will Oldham, Radiohead, Pavement, Beth Orton, the Velvet Underground, Bob Dylan, Jerry Garcia, and John Coltrane—you've given me so much joy over the years; let me buy you dinner. To my family and friends, thanks for putting up with me. And lastly, but always first in my life, this book would not be possible without Diedre Schremp—I am forever grateful for her love and support.

# Introduction

## Michael D. Ayers

In April of 2003, I found myself at an NYU student-only Wilco concert at one of New York's midsized clubs, Irving Plaza. The crowd was littered with 18 to early 20-somethings; everyone was jockeying for a position close to the stage, regardless of how familiar some of the audience members were with the band. I inched my way through the close quarters, dodging lit cigarettes and potential "talkers" so I could position myself about 20 feet from the stage, dead center. As the night progressed, the band played with as much intensity as I had seen them in the past, but because of the "youthfulness" of the crowd, lead singer Jeff Tweedy made two comments that caught my attention.

First, he commented on the apparent giddiness of a few female fans in the front row, insinuating that they were playing at a "sweet-16 birthday party." As I felt like I identified more with the "older guys" on stage than my surroundings, I chuckled slightly to myself. But almost immediately following the snide comment, knowing his audience, Tweedy also remarked, "So, did you all download your free EP?" Half the crowd let up a jubilant cheer, while the other half seemed to retreat to a murmur of questions. He continued on with explicit instructions on where to find this: "Go to the band's website, click on 'download free EP,' and you can also print the covers to the album if you like." And it was at that moment I felt as if I had just converged into a cultural space where the digital met the original; the live sound met the studio sounds; the music industry, the artist, and the fans converging into one "happy place" in which art was of utmost importance and any controversy surrounding music existing online had ceased. Or had never been an issue in the first place.

A few months prior, Wilco's label, Nonesuch Records (owned by Time Warner Group, considered to be one of the "Big 4" record labels) scrapped plans to commercially release an EP—and instead "allowed" Wilco to release it for free via the band's website. Anyone could download the album in the compressed mp3 format, print out the CD case artwork, and burn a copy for "on the go" listening. Although it was not quite clear why Nonesuch and the band decided to axe this plan for a commercially available product, this moment provides a clear-cut example of the convergence between artists, capitalists, fans, media, technology, and music itself. Nothing anymore is "separate" in any sense; moreover, all of these entities are interacting with each other. A relationship has slowly been developed, albeit a sometimes dysfunctional one, in which social actors and technology, specifically Internet technologies, have altered the course of how this one art form, music, is created, produced, consumed, worshipped, and ultimately perceived.

I assembled this collection with the hopes of exploring these issues, as I was convinced it was not just me who had been thinking in an academic sense of what was occurring online in regards to music. My own personal history with Internet music has passed the decade mark; with my first high-speed university connection in 1994, I immediately inundated myself with online music subcultures, gaining the latest tidbit of information about my favorite groups, not to mention beginning to amass a "real world" collection of audiocassette tapes of recent performances. As the 1990s progressed, so did the mainstreaming of music in cyberspace. And with a technology that has a global reach, what could be characterized as the Internet Music Revolution reached the far corners of the globe. Ultimately, this volume points not only to this with regard to the contributors' home countries but also in terms of the subject matters that each chapter addresses. Each author not only advances the study of cyberculture and musicology but contributes to a relatively underpublished area of the two disciplines' convergence. Each author demonstrates this collaboration and/or tension that I just described in my narrative about Wilco: There is a unique relationship that has been forged within cyberspace surrounding this art form, and no other art form to date can claim having as much of an impact on as many social spheres.

This volume seeks not only to highlight social issues surrounding music and cyberspace but to serve as a foundation for research. Over the years, cyberculture studies have developed into a unique discipline, drawing on theoretical thought from multiple avenues. Edited collections, academic journals, and poignant case studies have defined issues that cyberspace raises, as well as a methodology for investigating what is commonly thought of as an intangible space. *Race in Cyberspace* (2000), *Cybertypes: Race, Ethnicity and Identity on the Internet* (2002), and *Wired Women: Gender and New Realities in Cyberspace* (1996) raise issues of social inequalities and their manifestation in what was supposed to be a "utopian" medium. Sherry Turkle (1995) and Howard Rheingold (1994) both paved the way for studying virtual communities, in which issues of identity, identity play, and basic human connections that lack face-to-face presence were dissected. Manuel Castells (2000) extensively documents our "world of connections" as the networked society expands into the McLuhanesque "global village," pointing to the vast arrays of social, political, and cybernetic networks that Internet technologies foster. As Castells (2000) articulated and later echoed by the scholars of *Cyberactivism: Online Activism in Theory and Practice* (2003), cyberspace is not devoid of politics or collective action. As these examples have shown in the past, and this volume continues to do, cyberspace is another aspect of the "public sphere" in which different actors and organizations assert themselves as major players, power holders, and a site of social and communal development, or evolution.

This volume asks the same questions that are often raised within any specific junction of social factors and cyberspace. But in doing so, many new issues are brought to the table, and *Cybersounds* attempts to tackle some of these. As popular press accounts like to highlight, there is a distinct rift between the music industry, consumers or fans, and the artists responsible for creative output. Some arenas of the music business embrace the Internet; many do not. Some artists, established as well as underground, look to the Internet for not only a commercial opportunity but also a way to communicate directly with fans. And those fans are also using the Internet in democratic and creative ways that further point to the Internet's innovative capabilities.

What exactly are these new issues? For starters, how will the legal challenges that surround music and the Internet affect music in general? Will artists be more or less willing to create and participate if they are involved within a system that favors copyright clearance over innovation? If the Internet represents a site of disembodied musical consumption (Peterson and Ryan 2004), is there now also a disembodied performer? In other words, if the "networked" society is allowing for disparate locations with no true "central nervous system," then will the need for the performance in a live setting decline? Or will performance start to become decentralized too?

In regards to communities in cyberspace, music has made an impact as well, in terms of being a catalyst for people coming together via different methods in cyberspace. This is not new, as Rheingold (1994) documents the rise of San Francisco's WELL community in the early days of cyber activity. One of the offshoots of the WELL community was a crude forum dedicated to discussing anything and everything Grateful Dead related. Besides mere fan-type discussion, authors here look at how communities produce and organize their own media, how they negotiate politics and the avoidance of being co-opted within the mainstream of their genre, as well as using the decentralized aspect of the Internet to promote their own computer-born music.

Also, the questions of transformation have come up as well. How has cyberspace transformed the ways in which we listen to music? How has it allowed for the creation of new types of music? And with new modes of producing music, how are the older, more "traditional" modes affected?

While these rhetorical questions do get addressed here, they only begin to serve as an entry point for this area of study. As with most Internet research, authors draw on multiple theoretical sources that bring up new issues as well. For example, does cyberspace present another social sphere in which historical anthropological practices take place? Do Pierre Bourdieu's (1984) and Sarah Thornton's (1995) notions of cultural and subcultural capital become an issue online? In other words, do cyber-music communities create the same social hierarchies that are often witnessed in the real world, regarding how much cultural knowledge one has?

In regards to power, music in the online world has pushed the envelope— but have the hegemonic powers remained the same? When discussing the Internet, it is important to keep in context that this medium is not a separate entity. Governments and corporations have not only an insurmountable amount of money invested into cyberspace but they also have just as much control within this media sphere as they do within television, radio, and print. Scholars Lawrence Lessig (2002) and Robert McChesney (1999) both trace how the privatization of the Internet over the last three decades has stifled massive amounts of creativity and innovation. Therefore, how have corporate interests clashed with the public's interest? Or how have corporate interests worked with the artists and the fans in new ways of selling their own product? A recent example illustrates the ways that the music industry has used the Internet to manipulate—or at the very least "advertise"—a new band of theirs.

In the summer of 2004, when Brooklyn-based trio The Secret Machines released their first album on the major label Warner Brothers, the marketing team went the traditional routes that are used to move units: music videos, magazine stories and reviews, as well as "street" marketing in which young people would hand out promotional fliers and buttons at shows that attracted similar audiences. But with all this typical advertising, there was also another route that Warner went: they infiltrated mp3 blogs, or weblogs that primarily discuss music while at the same time providing a free song one could download. Warner took two steps in attempting to co-opt blogs for their own profit: one, they emailed the blog owners and requested them to host one of their songs. They also filled comment sections, where readers can add their own two cents about whatever topic is being "blogged" about, with "discussions" about this new, hip band. But they used different names in order to construct what would appear to be an authentic dialogue between music lovers. Instead, it was discovered that much of the "hype" was originating from one single IP address, which led back to Warner Brothers. Needless to say, the blogging community reported this issue to death, mainly sneering at a corporate attempt to "manufacture" cool.

This narrative might not be anything new, at least in Adorno's (1941) view—whose critiques of the culture industries, although separate from anything having to do with cyberspace, ultimately pointed to audiences of popular music being a manipulated mass. Which then raises the questions of art worlds, in Becker's (1982) sense: How is the music world now organized within and externally of cyberspace? What happens to the work of art once it can be digitally altered, copied, and/or distributed at relatively no cost? And as most would agree, artwork, and music specifically, is a collaborative process—one that involves many actors engaging in different activities. Does cyberspace challenge any of these conventional jobs?

## And the Beat Goes On

I consciously chose not to lump the essays into categories for the reason that I believe they all make strong arguments on multiple ideas, therefore rendering any specific classification of ideas not only useless but also potentially problematic. As you will notice, the authors tend to make subtle arguments about many different issues throughout each essay. Therefore, it is my hope that readers can take away new ideas and issues without being told what a general theme may or may not be.

In chapter 1, Elizabeth A. Buchanan dissects how music in an online environment raises several ethical concerns. She frames her discussion within a legal context, and in doing so, raises the question of how the logic of ethics could exist in the world of peer-to-peer file-sharing networks.

In chapter 2, Markus Giesler takes a unique approach at how swapping music files via peer-to-peer networks actually undergoes a process of "anthropological gifting" in which the customs and norms of this practice are oftentimes called into question. He provides rich qualitative data from ethnographic field observations of the original Napster.

In chapter 3, Andrew Whelan gives a unique look into how amateur electronica musicians use peer-to-peer chatrooms to push their "creations." Central to Whelan's argument is Thornton's (1995) notion of subcultural capital, and in this case, Whelan echoes Thornton's argument that within this subculture, social hierarchies are established. He also provides an insight into how musicians, and not consumers, use p2p as a place for cultural exchange of art.

In chapter 4, Andre Pinard and Sean Jacobs engage in a comparative study of two online hip-hop communities—one that is based around U.S. hip-hop and one that is based on hip-hop from South Africa. Drawing on Anderson's notion of "imagined communities," they examine the ways in which a "virtual diaspora" manifests itself primarily within this African American/African musical genre.

In chapter 5, Adam Haupt compares the practice of sampling in hip-hop and the practice of mp3 distribution; in doing so, he argues that both practices were subversive in nature, in that they were both challenging hegemonic order. Haupt takes the concept of "empire" to focus on how both of these practices were ultimately modified by the major record labels in the sense that they exerted their power(s) to subvert the subverting.

In chapter 6, Michael D. Ayers examines how music and online activism have recently come together. Using the case of DJ Dangermouse's Internet-only release *The Grey Album*, Ayers argues that this one act of creativity that was challenged opened the floodgates to hundreds of "bedroom activists" who utilized the web, primarily through weblogs, to create a quasi-model for active resistance.

In chapter 7, Daragh O'Reilly and Kathy Doherty look at how British band New Model Army uses their website for not only band-fan interactions but also to brand themselves and construct a community through (supposed) shared values. Using primarily qualitative data culled from the band's message board, thi article provides an impressive window into how fans negotiate their interpretations of New Model Army.

In chapter 8, Chris Anderton examines how fans challenge the recording industry by making and trading their own "recordings" of live concerts. Anderton argues that this practice does not take away from the industry profits, but in turn freely markets a band's music. An extensive "code of ethics" is mapped out as well as the way people use Internet technologies to distribute their own "creations."

In chapter 9, Gabriele Cosentino argues that the symbolic cultural icon of the 2000s so far is Apple's iPod. Costentino traces the corporate development of the iPod, and in doing so, he demonstrates that Apple has walked a tightrope-thin line between commercial development with the record industry while remaining true to the "cult of mac" where the ethos of "user friendly" still has underlying meaning.

In chapter 10, Trace Reddell portrays a virtual landscape in which artists and DJs collaborate with each other over large geographical spaces to create new musical works of art, and also how the digital aesthetic in cyberspace allows for new modes of musical creation.

In chapter 11, John Ryan and Michael Hughes draw on Howard Becker's *Art Worlds* (1982) and production of culture models to examine the notion of "authority" in the digital age, and how access to computer technologies has called into question the role of the record producer.

Lastly, Jonathan Sterne takes the central themes presented in this volume and ties them together, offering a modest look into where this area of study can and should head. The issues that I raise here, and that the authors point to in their individual contributions, is a point to begin with—and by no means exhaustive of how these two mediums interact. I am positive that for as many questions answered here, there are several new ones that have taken precedent.

## References to Introduction

Adorno, Theodor W. 1941/1990. "On Popular Music." In *On Record: Rock, Pop, and the Written Word*, edited by Simon Frith and Andrew Goodwin. New York: Pantheon Books.

Becker, Howard. 1982. *Art Worlds*. Berkeley: University of California Press.

Bourdieu, Pierre. 1984. *Distinction: A Social Critique of the Judgment of Taste*. Cambridge, MA: Harvard University Press.

Castells, Manuel. 2000. *The Rise of the Network Society*. Malden, MA: Blackwell Press.

Cherny, Lynn, and Elizabeth Reba Weise. 1996. *Wired Women: Gender and New Realities in Cyberspace*. Emeryville, CA: Seal Press.

Kolko, Beth E., Lisa Nakumura, and Gilbert B. Rodman, eds. 2000. *Race in Cyberspace*. New York: Routledge Press.

Lessig, Lawrence. 2002. *The Future of Ideas: The Fate of the Commons in a Connected World*. New York: Vintage Press.

McCaughey, Martha, and Michael D. Ayers. 2003. *Cyberactivism: Online Activism in Theory and Practice*. New York: Routledge Press.

McChesney, Robert. 1999. *Rich Media, Poor Democracy: Communication Politics in Dubious Times*. New York: New Press.

Nakumura, Lisa. 2002. *Cybertypes: Race, Ethnicity, and Identity on the Internet*. New York: Routledge Press.

Peterson, Richard A., and John Ryan. 2004. "The Disembodied Muse: Music in the Internet Age." In *Society Online: The Internet in Context*, edited by Philip N. Howard and Steve Jones, 223–36. Thousand Oaks, CA: Sage.

Rheingold, Howard. 1994. *The Virtual Community: Homesteading on the Electronic Frontier*. Cambridge, MA: MIT Press.

Thornton, Sarah. 1995. *Club Cultures: Music, Media, and Subcultural Capital*. Middletown, CT: Wesleyan University Press.

Turkle, Sherry. 1995. *Life on the Screen: Identity in the Age of the Internet*. New York: Simon & Schuster.

CHAPTER ONE

# Deafening Silence: Music and the Emerging Climate of Access and Use

## Elizabeth A. Buchanan

### Introduction

The Internet, once thought to be the great domain of free exchange, the medium for the masses, is in a state of redefinition: Is "free" out, "fee" in? Will the Internet continue to grow more as a supra-scale shopping mall and less as an information commons? And, will we be able to easily identify "owners" of the Internet, corporate interests who have bought the rights to control the means of dissemination online? If we look at the state of online music, these questions may be easily answerable.

Was the Napster ruling the defining moment? What did Napster do to the state of music online? Few can argue that the Napster ruling indeed represents a seminal moment in the cultural history of the Internet, and for music in general. The Napster controversy's final resting place, in a U.S. district court in July 2000, effectively "ended" the free-for-all known as file sharing, and with it came a dramatic change in the discourse of ethics and legality vis-à-vis online music. Yes, new technologies, such as KaZaa, Morpheous, and Grokster surged in Napster's demise—different, better, perhaps—offering file sharers new ways to continue their relationships seemingly out of reach from the law. Indeed, despite legal questions and concerns, file sharing is on the rise, much to the dismay of many entertainment industry conglomerates. But *something* has changed, dramatically.

The Napster ruling is just one of many legal conquests that is changing the face of music—and entertainment—in general. In September 2003, the Record Industry Association of America (RIAA) issued lawsuits against 261 individuals that they accuse of sharing more than 1,000 digital music files. Threats of thousands of additional lawsuits hang in the air.

A recent interview with Peter Chernin of 20th Century Fox (Stahl 2003) leaves downloaders of movies feeling the same legal chill in the air as music downloaders have experienced, as he notes the movie industry's "absolute future" is at stake; he calls the battle between the industry and the file sharers an "arms race." Ultimately, the battleground includes the Digital Millennium Copyright Act (DMCA) and the Sonny Bono Copyright Extension Act.

How can the current chilling legal discourse play out with music? Is there a future for online music? Will the divide between true commercial music and its creators—that which is purchased—and underground music and its individual artists—that which is shared—explode beyond reconciliation? Will we witness a fundamental change in how music is created and disseminated, because of the current state of the law in the U.S.? And, is the current reality of online music, downloaders, file sharers, as immoral as the RIAA and others contend? Ultimately, this chapter asks us to consider how ethics and legality can peacefully coexist in the worlds of KaZaa, Grokster, and others. Ethics should be understood as the systematic, philosophical study of moral behavior, of moral decision making, or of how to lead a "good life." Ethics does not necessarily correlate with law; they are distinct insofar as the law provides a structured context to which we look for "reasonable" decisions. The law does not necessarily tell us what is inherently "good" or "bad," "right" or "wrong." The law does not prescribe behavior for the purpose of morality but for the purpose of satisfying a societal requirement. This is an important distinction to consider in light of the discussion throughout this chapter. What is morally right, as discovered through an ethical consideration of the impact of copyright on the common good, differs fundamentally from the directions the laws surrounding copyright are moving. Thus, this chapter will first review copyright law in general, before examining the role of the DMCA and the Copyright Extension Act in particular as they impact the discourse surrounding music. Implications for the future of music, both online and off, are discussed in a framework of ethics and law.

## Copyright: A Balance between Societal and Personal Interests?

If we look briefly at the history of copyright in the United States, we can notice an interesting shift in the ideas of protection and incentives that copyright law affords. In the 1787 Constitution, in Article I, Section 8, the Founders charged the Congress to "Promote the Progress of Science and Useful Arts, by securing for limited Times to Authors and Inventors the exclusive Right to their respective Writings and Discoveries." The Founders' reasoning was straightforward:

protect, and therefore enable, authors and inventors to benefit from their works and they will have incentive to produce more "writings and discoveries." "Science" was to be understood in its eighteenth-century etymology (Pallas Loren 2003): the promotion of *knowledge* and *learning*.

The copyright provision was enacted in 1970 by Congress, which according to the Association of Research Libraries (Masciola 2002) was modeled on the English 1710 Statute of Anne. The Act afforded "American authors the right to print, re-print, or publish their work" for a period of 14 years and to renew for another 14. The law was meant to provide an incentive to authors, artists, and scientists to create original works by providing creators with a monopoly. At the same time, the monopoly was limited in order to stimulate creativity and the advancement of "science and the useful arts" through wide public access to works in the "public domain" (Masciola 2002). The understanding was that after "limited times," the use of those works would become available for general use by the body politic, which use would inspire more writing and invention— and subsequently, more progress. Copyright was then both an individual as well as a social good.

Revisions to the Copyright Act occurred over time, for a variety of reasons. Notably, term length has been a point of much debate. The length of copyright protections was extended in 1831, from 14 to 28 years, with the possibility of adding another 14-year extension. The 1909 Copyright Revision is generally recognized as a critical juncture in copyright history. This revision maintained the 28 years but lengthened the 14-year extension to 28 years. Much discussion ensued about the public's rights vis-à-vis private rights:

> The main object to be desired in expanding copyright protection accorded to music has been to give the composer an adequate return for the value of his composition, and it has been a serious and difficult task to combine the protection of the composer with the protection of the public, and to so frame an act that it would accomplish the double purpose of securing to the composer an adequate return for all use made of his composition and at the same time prevent the formation of oppressive monopolies, which might be founded upon the very rights granted to the composer for the purpose of protecting his interests. (H.R. Rep. No. 2222, 60th Cong., 2nd Sess., 1909, p. 7)

The 1976 Revision took the existing 28-year term, with a 28-year extension possibility to new lengths: The term of protection became life of the author plus 50 years. Some years later, in 1992, with the Amendment to Section 304 of Title 17, copyright renewal became automatic, replacing the renewal process. "The amendment dramatically curtailed the entry into the public domain of works protected by copyright before 1978" (Masciola 2002).

Thus, as time continued, legislation of copyright seemed to be focusing on the "protections" realm, guaranteeing that monopoly safeguard, at the expense of the "incentive" component. The public's interests were increasingly over-looked. The ideas or ideals of a *public domain* or the *information commons,* that knowledge or those resources that are commonly shared, cared for, and respected by all peoples, were progressively deteriorating. The copyright owner, whether that is an individual artist, a corporation, an estate, or other entity, saw his/her/its interests become paramount on a number of levels. Ultimately, the political landscape embraced copyright and its laws and related issues and turned them into political fodder. Moreover, the promotion of knowledge and learning became a secondary consideration, while the monetary assumed prominence.

But wait. Things get worse—or better, depending on one's perspective. While control over copyright and ownership was certainly changing, complete control was not lost (or gained) . . . yet.

## 1998: The Triumph of the Bills

Two significant pieces of legislation were passed in 1998 that significantly impact the discussion of copyright. Firstly, the Sonny Bono Copyright Extension Act was passed and changed the term of copyright protection from life of the author plus 50 years to life plus 70 years; for corporate owners, copyright protection was extended to 95 years, from 75. While this may seem fairly insignificant, numerous critics of the Extension Act point to the fact that the Disney Corporation, in particular, lobbied and contributed heavily to lawmakers to protect Mickey Mouse from falling into the public domain: "Facing the loss of their exclusive rights to Mickey Mouse, Donald Duck and other cartoon stars, Walt Disney Co. executives led a successful lobbying campaign to secure an extra 20 years of protection for their U.S. copyrights" (AP 1998). Standing with Disney in support of the Extension Act was the publishing industry, the music and motion picture industries, and the computer software industry. In response, Dennis Karjala, founder of the Opposing Copyright Extension Forum, states: "Like the Congress, President Clinton has sold out the interests of the American people to a few owners of valuable copyrights from the 1920's and 1930's" (Karjala 2003). And, while a 20-year extension may seem irrelevant, it is the continual expansion of protection, and the concurrent deprivation of materials from the public domain, that gives cause for concern. Disparate interests rallied around the opposition to the Extension Act: the Society of American Archivists, the Association of Research Libraries, the American Library Association, the Digital Futures Coalition, among others, filed an amicus brief with the Supreme Court, noting in particular the "irreparable harm done to historians and institutions that exploit the public domain when copyright term is excessive" (SAA 2002).

In terms of the impact on music in general, the Extension Act effectively prevented any sound recording from falling into the public domain as well, and it should not be surprising that the music industry stood hand in hand with Disney, contributing over $16 million to federal political campaigns (Karr 2003) in support of the Act. The PD Info Initiative analyzed "sound recordings" and their protection under the copyright law and found that no sound recording will fall into the public domain until 2067; they assert,

> If you choose to believe pre-1972 sound recordings are in the public domain and choose to use them publicly, you are subjecting yourself to a high probability of legal proceedings, financial liability, and major legal fees. We consider it absolutely imperative that you consult with an attorney before exposing yourself to this kind of risk. Don't even think about research in this area without major help from an attorney or rights clearance organization. (Haven Sound 2003)

These sorts of warnings, or worse, are becoming commonplace—whether they come from the RIAA, the MPIA, or the FBI directly. And, in addition to the terms of copyright protection, it is the Digital Millennium Copyright Act that provides the fuel to fire these warnings.

Also signed in 1998, the Digital Millennium Copyright Act (DMCA) has a significant impact on copyright in general, and on issues impacting online and offline music in particular. Among other concerns, Section 1201(a) of the DMCA criminalizes the use of—or any disseminated knowledge of how to enable—technologies that circumvent technological protection or encryption systems; in effect, both civil and criminal legal sanctions can be employed "by copyright owners to control access to their works." Ultimately, the copyright owner controls all access and use, thus, peer-to-peer file-sharing programs are under legal attack. Various technological measures such as encryption—in addition to legal measures—have been used to control such access and use.

Furthermore, the DMCA provision "permits copyright owners to force internet service providers to remove material from the internet and world wide web when the copyright owner believes the material is infringing" (Pallas Loren 2003). This provision is causing many universities, colleges, and schools that provide Internet access to their students to seriously reconsider what students are allowed to do on their networks. Such institutions, which used to be hotbeds of intellectual freedom and information sharing, are now in the business of censoring and surveilling their students' use for fear that they will be held liable.[1]

Others are simply in business—such as Penn State's business agreement with Napster, which allows students residing in the university's residence halls to use the Napster services. The students are not theoretically paying more in their tuition dollars for this service: "The IT fee will no doubt increase next academic year, but by no more than would ordinarily be necessary to support the University's IT infrastructure and other applications. There will be no additional increase because of our contract with Napster. This is possible because the cost to the University of providing Napster for students, although confidential, is very low as a result of Penn State being the pioneering school to launch an online music service" (Erickson 2003).

Not surprisingly, the DMCA debate garnered typical allies and opponents: For the Act, and contributing millions of dollars to political campaigns, were members of various "content industries," the music, motion pictures, and software industries, while researchers, librarians, and scientists saw the Act as a further encroachment on fair use, intellectual freedom, and the information commons (Buchanan and Campbell 2004). By turning control of access and use to the copyright owners, one must wonder how fair use will indeed fare.

The UCLA Online Institute for Cyberspace Law and Policy (2001) provides these highlights of the DMCA:

- Makes it a crime to circumvent anti-piracy measures built into most commercial software.
- Outlaws the manufacture, sale, or distribution of code-cracking devices used to illegally copy software.
- Permits the cracking of copyright protection devices, however, to conduct encryption research, assess product interoperability, and test computer security systems.
- Provides exemptions from anti-circumvention provisions for nonprofit libraries, archives, and educational institutions under certain circumstances.
- Limits Internet service providers, in general, from copyright infringement liability for simply transmitting information over the Internet.
- Expects service providers, however, to remove material from users' websites that appears to constitute copyright infringement.
- Limits liability of nonprofit institutions of higher education—when they serve as online service providers and under certain circumstances—for copyright infringement by faculty members or graduate students.
- Requires that "webcasters" pay licensing fees to record companies.
- Requires that the Register of Copyrights, after consultation with relevant parties, submit to Congress recommendations regarding how to promote distance education through digital technologies while "maintaining an appropriate balance between the rights of copyright owners and the needs of users."
- States explicitly that "[n]othing in this section shall affect rights, remedies, limitations, or defenses to copyright infringement, including fair use"

When considered in a larger picture, in a single act, the DMCA essentially negated the first sale doctrine and fair use principles, not through the process of revising those provisions of the copyright law, but simply by handing complete control of ownership and technology to copyright holders—private parties with no accountability to voters or to the common good. And more often than not, the copyright holders are not individuals but are media conglomerates or private interests, not the artists themselves. So, an individual artist who chooses to have his or her music online, *depending on who actually owns the copyright to that material,* may not have that choice. The individual artist, indeed, is facing fewer and fewer choices these days, undeniably a strange situation, given the "greater protections" afforded by laws such as the DMCA and the Extension Act. It is ultimately the commercial interests or the content industries, those who could afford to pay to be heard, who have apparently won this battle over what Karjala (2003) sees as our "cultural development." Once knowledge and information become bottled up, lost forever to the commons, cultural development suffers. And ultimately, with both the DMCA and the Copyright Extension Act, the Congress (and then the U.S. Supreme Court in the case of the latter) put the narrow interests of a few over the greater interests of the people. The legal climate has forever been changed, perhaps at the expense of an ethical climate that favors an information commons model.

## Don't Ask, Don't . . . Sample?

How have these new laws and the emerging legal climate impacted music, both online and off? Has this current climate changed the prospects for a "free-based" distribution system?[2] It has undoubtedly changed the prospects for the commons, and for those who rely on the commons for information and knowledge sharing, whether in the form of music or literature or art. These cultural artifacts will now be available to those who can afford them: The "new" mp3.com and Apple's iTunes appear to be paving the way for a completely fee-based system, controlled by the content industries, where all parties are happy. Or are they? While Napster brought considerable recognition to copyright laws, creating a negative legal discourse in which consumers operated, the DMCA also changed the creative climate for artists themselves. Chuck D. of Public Enemy considers the copyright situation as detrimental to the progress of art itself (and recall what the purpose of copyright was when the founding fathers imagined it):

> I take an outspoken role on everything I think is progressive for art. And I think this is progressive for the art because the industry and corporations have dominated and monopolized the outlets for the art whether it be radio, television or even the skewing of the price factor. Dominance of record companies dominating over retail and other outlets. (Rowell 1998)

As noted above, the principle of "fair use" is challenged under the DMCA. Traditionally, fair use principles allow for limited use of copyrighted works without permission of the owner in such situations as classroom purposes, research, criticism or commentary, news reporting, parody, transformative or productive uses, among others, given that the amount used is a small quantity of the work as a whole, and there is no significant negative effect on the market because of the use.[3]

John Perry Barlow, lyricist for the Grateful Dead and cyber philosopher, recognizes that there is no original music; that every song builds on one from before: Musicians from all genres rely in great part on fair use, some more explicitly than others. "Rock 'n' roll has always had a history of 'borrowing' previously existing musical ideas" (Carl Hampel 1992). For instance, folk and rap music depend heavily on the practice of sampling, where a riff, melody, or line is borrowed and reworked. In rap, such sampling is oftentimes a form of respect—paying one's dues to a predecessor or to the body of art that was the inspiration. Interestingly though, sampling and file sharing do not always meet cordially: Dr. Dre, an ardent opponent of file sharing, relied heavily on sampling from Parliament in his first album, *The Chronic,* and has gone on to speak out strongly against file-sharing practices. Too, Metallica has long crusaded against file sharing, delivering testimony to Congress on the practice, despite making available many songs for download on their website.

Moreover, current laws do not necessarily see sampling in such a positive, artistic light. Some consider this practice fair use under the realm of parody, as in the case of 2 Live Crew's version of "Pretty Woman" or De La Soul's use of four bars, amounting to 12 seconds of The Turtles' "You Showed Me." However, prominent attorney Alan Korn (no date) would suggest that the practice of sampling itself was shut down well before the DMCA—in 1991, a Federal District Court ruled that Biz Markie did infringe on Gilbert O'Sullivan's copyrighted material from his hit song "Alone Again, Naturally."

The real question becomes whether or not sampling can be considered fair use, but the emerging legal climate seems to be negating this possibility. If, for example, Public Enemy wanted to sample from someone's work, they would need to obtain copyright permission from the *owner* of that work, as well as obtain a license to sample. The Beastie Boys found this out, nine notes too late, when they failed to obtain a license to sample from jazz musician and professor James Newton on their 1992 *Check Your Head* album; the Beasties' *Pass the Mic* was supposedly ripped from Newton's song, *Choir,* even though Newton's record company was paid.

But the scenario and the implications are more complex: What if the Beastie Boys had asked for permission from Newton's record company (which they did), and had paid for the appropriate licensing (which they didn't)? Depending on how the copyright owner felt, he (or it, more likely, as in the case of corporate ownership), could deny the request, thereby restricting access to material previously considered under the fair use provision. Even more concerning is that by handing complete control of such decisions to copyright owners, thereby negating fair use, explicit censorship emerges. If Newton or his record company/copyright owner does not "like" or "agree with" the intended use, say, of the Beastie Boys' song, the request is denied, and no song using that sample is created. End of story. End of invention. End of progress of the arts and science. Moreover, these denials have been occurring, according to Pallas Loren

(2003), quite frequently in academic and research circles, not only in music. By denying the use of materials, whether art, literature, or music, or by negating the possibility that someone can write a review of some software, we have entered the realm of censorship, and we have moved many steps backward from the promotion of the arts and science; indeed, we have started negating the promotion of knowledge.

## Conclusion: The Day the Music Really Died?

It is difficult to predict how music will continue in the face of lawsuits and cumbersome laws such as the DMCA. The fate of online music seems more set, for better or worse, for consumers and for the content industries: it will be parceled out, at various costs, perhaps for one dollar, for a one-time fee, for the cost of a license to those who can afford to pay; others may take their chances, careful to avoid the magical 1,000—the number of downloaded songs by an individual that the RIAA has suggested is the target for their lawsuits. The free sharing of music online will be a distant memory, despite the millions of users still engaging in this "illegal" activity. Who has won this battle? This arms race?

> The battle over online song trading is over; the Internet has won. The music industry is grudgingly giving up on the idea that it can preserve the tightly controlled business practices that once made record companies and artists flush with cash. Instead, a transformation is underway. . . . On the legal front, the record companies have launched a high-profile campaign to sue people who distribute songs for free over the Internet in violation of copyright laws. At the same time they are working to plug the holes in existing laws. Earlier this month, Sens. John Cornyn (R-Tex.) and Dianne Feinstein (D-Calif.) introduced legislation to create the Artists' Rights and Theft Prevention Act, an amendment to existing copyright law that would make it illegal to use a camcorder to record a film in a movie theater for illegal distribution. For the music industry, however, the legislation aims to prevent exactly what happened to Jay-Z, making it illegal for anyone to distribute songs before their release date—a loophole not explicitly covered by copyright law. (Ahrens 2003)

In some ways, yes, the Internet has won: It has forced the entire entertainment industry to change its ways—its ways of access and use. It has changed the legal climate. It has changed the creative climate. Yet, it has not changed its morals, as Chuck D. had hoped:

> As an artist representing an 80-year period of black musicianship, I never felt that my copyrights were protected anyway. . . . I've been spending most of my career ducking lawyers, accountants and business executives who have basically

been more blasphemous than file sharers and P2P. I trust the consumer more than I trust the people who have been at the helm of these companies.

The record industry is hypocritical and the domination has to be shared. P2P to me means 'power to the people.' And let's get this to a balance, and that's what we're talking about. (Dean 2003)

Music in general will continue to be impacted by emerging laws and ever-expanding controls over access and use. Will the number of lawsuits for infringement explode? Will we see fewer and fewer individual artists at the expense of a "corporate artist"? Will individual artists be so overshadowed by the media giants that they stand no chance to be heard? Will we see more "Slave" à la Prince written across the faces of musicians, as they realize their creative control is no longer theirs, but in the hands of their industry owners and the laws that are bought by industry lobbyists?

Many other major factors play into this discussion about the future of music, both online and off. For instance, as media conglomeracy explodes, the owners of the music are increasingly the owners of the means of distribution. One can own the rights to the song, as well as the radio channels on which it *may or may not* be played, as well as the concert venues where a band *may or may not* perform; we are seeing this very reality play out with Clear Channel and their extensive powers (Sharlet 2003). If artists don't play by the rules, will they find themselves and their music blacklisted, silenced? Only time will reveal the repercussions of the FCC's 2003 loosening of media ownership on the future of music.

While this chapter has looked at the implications of the emerging legal climate on music in particular, so much more is at stake; Bollier (1999) argues,

At stake are the ability of public libraries to offer universal access to information; consumers to have competitive access to diverse sources of content, including non-commercial content; citizens to have free or cheap access to the government information that their tax dollars have financed; and students to perform research and collaborate online with each other. At stake are the ability of musicians and other artists to pioneer new forms of online creativity; creators in all media to freely quote and use a robust public domain of prior works; computer users to benefit from the innovations of competitive markets; and individuals to control how intimate personal information will be used.

The clash between an ethics of authorial/artistic control, intellectual freedom, and the ideals of an information commons with a legal climate that allows changes in copyright laws for the benefit of the "content industries" will continue, undoubtedly. These fundamentally democratic principles are indeed under attack, as a moral discourse surrounding them is replaced by legal and corporate control. There is an upside, as concerned consumers and artists speak out against this emerging climate. Such groups as the Future of Music Coalition, Media Reform, and others are springing to action. We can only hope that these voices are loud enough to replace the deafening silence that is becoming music in this day and climate.

## References to Chapter One

Ahrens, Frank. 2003. "Music Industry Reluctantly Yielding to Internet Reality." *Washington Post*, November 27, E-1.

Associated Press. 1998. "Disney Lobbying for Copyright Extension No Mickey Mouse Effort Congress OKs Bill Granting Creators 20 More Years." *Chicago Tribune*, October 17. Retrieved February 15, 2003, from http://homepages.law.asu.edu/~dkarjala/OpposingCopyrightExtension/commentary/ChiTrib10–17–98.html

Bollier, David. 1999. "Why We Must Talk About The Information Commons." Retrieved May 15, 2003, from http://www.newamerica.net/Download_Docs/pdfs/Doc_File_103_1.pdf

Bollier, David, and Tim Watts. 2002. *Saving the Information Commons: A Public Interest Agenda in Digital Media*. Washington, DC: New America Foundation and Public Knowledge.

Boucher, Rick. 2002. "Time to Rewrite the DMCA." *CNET*. Retrieved February 15, 2003, from http://news.com.com/2010–1071–825335.html

Buchanan, Elizabeth, and James Campbell. 2004. "New Threats to Intellectual Freedom: The Loss of the Information Commons through Law and Technology in the United States." In *Intellectual Property Rights in a Networked World: Theory and Practice*, edited by Herman Tavani and Richard Spinello, 225–42. Hershey, PA: Idea Group.

Carl Hampel, Sherri. 1992. "Are Samplers Getting a Bum Rap? Copyright Infringement or Technological Creativity." *University of Illinois Law Review* 559:583–84.

Dean. Katie. 2003. "Rappers in Disharmony." *Wired*. October 1. Retrieved February 15, 2004, from http://www.wired.com/news/mp3/0,1285,60650,00.html

Erickson, Rod. 2003. "A Message about Napster from the Provost." Retrieved from http://napster.psu.edu/provostmessage.html

Haven Sound. 2003. "Public Domain Music." Retrieved February 20, 2003, from http://www.pdinfo.com/record.htm

Karjala, Dennis. 2003. Opposing Copyright Extension. Retrieved November 2003 from http://homepages.law.asu.edu/~dkarjala/OpposingCopyrightExtension/

Karr, Rick. 2003. "Now With Bill Moyers." Retrieved October 8, 2004, from http://www.pbs.org/now/transcript/transcript203_full.html

Korn, Alan. (No date). "Digital Sampling." Retrieved from http://www.alankorn.com/articles/sampling.html

Masciola, Amy. 2002. "Timeline: A History of Copyright in the United States." *Association of Research Libraries*. Retrieved January 8, 2004, from http://www.arl.org/info/frn/copy/timeline.html

Pallas Loren, Lydia. 2003. "The Purpose of Copyright." *Open Spaces Quarterly* 2(1). Retrieved February 18, 2004, from http://www.open-spaces.com/article-v2n1-loren.php

Patry, William. 1995. *The Fair Use Privilege in Copyright Law.* Washington, DC: Bureau of National Affairs.

Rowell, Erica. 1998. "Rapping with Chuck D." *ABC News.* Retrieved February 15, 2003, from http://www.rapstation.com/files/news/archive/july2000ABCNEWS_com_rapping_with_chuckd.html

Sharlet, Jeff. 2003. "Big World: How Clear Channel Programs America." *Harper's Magazine* 307 (1843): 37–56.

Society of American Archivists. 2002. "Amicus Brief." Retrieved February 15, 2003, from http://cyber.law.harvard.edu/openlaw/eldredvashcroft/cert/library-amicus.pdf

Stahl, Leslie. 2003. "Pirates of the Internet." *60 Minutes.* Retrieved November 2003 from http://www.cbsnews.com/stories/2004/08/11/60minutes/printable635391.shtm 1%20%20%20%20%20?CMP=ILC-SearchStories

UCLA Online Institute for Cyberspace Law and Policy. 2001. "The Digital Millennium Copyright Act." Retrieved February 15, 2003, from http://www.gseis.ucla.edu/iclp/dmca1.htm

Vaidhyanathan, Siva. 2003. "After the Copyright Smackdown, What Next?" *Salon.* Retrieved October 8, 2004, from http://www.salon.com/tech/feature/2003/01/17/copyright/print.html

CHAPTER TWO

# Cybernetic Gift Giving and Social Drama: A Netnography of the Napster File-Sharing Community

## Markus Giesler

In consumer culture theory, little attention has been directed toward those forms of gift giving that can be achieved in electronic networks where a *polyadic*, rather than a dyadic or monadic constellation, marks the gifting situation. Grounded in the extensive netnographic analysis of the Napster music file-sharing community, this article explores the various structural and ideological dimensions of cybernetic gift giving—the polyadic giving and receiving of digitized information in peer-to-peer file-sharing communities on the Internet, in which multiple anonymous gifting agents share multiple gifts at the same time. My findings reveal that cybernetic gift giving differs markedly from traditional forms of gift giving in terms of the gift, gifting partners, process, reciprocity, and spirit. My findings also reveal that music consumers and producers form different ideological agendas surrounding Napster's cybernetic gift economy. On the macroscopic level of cultural dynamics, Napster's cybernetic gift economy sparks off a social drama between music consumers and producers that plays itself out in a sequence of processual acts across four phases that each brings dynamic shifts in scripts, characterizations, rhetoric, and symbolism. Implications for theories of gift giving and consumer resistance are discussed.

The view that gift giving integrates social relationships as *dyadic* interaction rituals between donor and recipient is ubiquitous in consumer research. This theme is implicit in literature on Christmas gifts (e.g., Fischer and Arnold 1990), Valentine gifts (e.g., Otnes 1993), and perfect gifts (e.g., Belk 1996), as well as in recent cross-cultural studies of gift-giving practices in Hong Kong (e.g., Joy 2001) or at Burning Man (e.g., Kozinets 2002). It is explicit in the *agapic* ("unselfish") love model of giving (Belk and Coon 1993), and the gift exchange model (Sherry 1983; Belk 1979). Recently, some scholars have therefore begun to explore self-gifts or *monadic* gift giving (e.g., Mick 1996; Mick and DeMoss 1990; Sherry, McGrath, and Levy 1995). However, and despite the rapidly growing significance of the Internet, little attention has been directed toward those forms of gift giving that can be achieved in electronic networks, in which a *polyadic*, rather than a dyadic or monadic constellation, marks the gifting situation. This article seeks to address this gap in knowledge.

I introduce the paradigm of cybernetic gift giving, the polyadic giving and receiving of digitized information in networked peer-to-peer file-sharing communities on the Internet, in which multiple anonymous gifting agents share multiple gifts at the same time. Through the extensive netnographic analysis of the Napster peer-to-peer music file-sharing community, I trace out and develop some of the structural and ideological particularities of cybernetic gift giving and the ways in which they enlighten our understanding of gift giving and consumer behavior as a whole.

Cybernetic gift giving is a postmodern consumption practice born between the dramatic technological networking of society (Castells 1996) and consumers' emancipatory desire to share information beyond the conventional market sphere. Researchers have been slow to see this relationship and slower still to take stock of its significance. Thus far, they have developed only the most rudimentary conceptual tools to study it systematically (e.g., Giesler and Pohlmann 2003a; Hemetsberger 2002). Consequently, they are unequipped to answer questions about the nature and extent of gift giving that can be achieved in cyberspace and the types of social practices that are involved in cybernetic gift giving. What are those practices? How does the paradigm of cybernetic gift giving foundationally challenge Sherry's (1983) and Belk and Coon's (1993) fundamental conceptualizations of the gift? What is the ideological context of cybernetic gift giving? And how does the fact that consumers can use cybernetic gift giving to challenge traditional market institutions precipitate new power relationships that are in turn contested by the market system? By exploring the cultural structuring and ideological dynamics of cybernetic gift giving, this article seeks to answer these questions. The insights gained will help researchers reformulate the ways in which they think about and theorize gift giving in an anthropological, sociological, and consumer literatures context.

To best reveal the paradigm of cybernetic gift giving, I begin with an overview of prior consumer studies on interpersonal gift giving, in particular Sherry's (1983) and Belk and Coon's (1993) foundational paradigms of dyadic gift giving, and discuss conceptual limitations of these and other existing theories of gift giving. The second section explores the microscopic structural particularities of cybernetic gift giving. The third section explicates how, at the macroscopic level of cultural dynamics, different ideological uses of cybernetic gift giving at Napster are formed and discursive tensions are developed in the course of Napster's history and beyond. I close by discussing implications and providing directions for future research.

## Gift Giving in a Consumer Context

Explorations of gift giving have a long tradition in the anthropology, social psychology, and sociology literatures. Each of these disciplines outside business schools has developed a particular perspective for studying the giving and receiving of gifts. Anthropologist Marcel Mauss (1925/1967), in his same-titled book, introduced *The Gift* as a total social fact. Gift giving, according to Mauss, must be understood as a phenomenon of social structure, involving economical, juridical, moral, religious, mythological, and esthetical properties (e.g., Levi-Strauss 1965; Weiner 1992). Sociologists have documented the social norms of gift giving, its relationship to social responsibility, and the role of reciprocity in characterizing social relationships (Cheal 1988; Bourdieu 1977; Sahlins 1972). In the discipline of social psychology, gift giving has been theorized as a complex movement in the management of meaning (Komter 2004; Schieffelin 1980). A merging of perspectives characterizes consumer researchers' attempts to develop interpersonal forms of gift giving in the consumer context (Belk 1979). Two contributions stand out as the most developed efforts: the gift exchange paradigm and the agapic love paradigm.

## The Gift Exchange Paradigm

Sherry (1983) has introduced a unifying typology of dyadic gift giving that sits at the core of consumer researchers' understanding of the topic and serves as the implicit conceptual springboard for most of the studies on gift giving in consumer research (e.g., Joy 2001; Kozinets 2002; Ruth, Otnes, and Brunel 1999; Otnes, Lowrey, and Kim 1993; Fischer and Arnold 1990). Sherry's exchange paradigm develops gift giving in the Maussian tradition as a continuous cycle of reciprocities and conceptualizes the gift exchange process as a dialectical chain of gift and token gift transactions. A gift exchange "spiral" unfolds that integrates social relationships informally as a dyadic interaction ritual. Three stages—gestation, prestation, and reformulation—specify the gift transaction through which donor and recipient progress. The gestation stage incorporates behavior antecedent to the actual gift exchange including, on the donor's side, the expression of motivation, and the internal and external search for and the purchase or even creation of a gift. The prestation stage marks the substance of the gift transaction and involves the recipient's (inferred) response and the donor's evaluation of that response. The reformulation stage finally concerns the disposition of the gift, its consumption, display, storage, or exchange, and maybe its rejection. Dependent on how the reformulation develops, the bond between donor and recipient may be strengthened, affirmed, attenuated, or severed. Reciprocation may accordingly take place resulting in the exchange partners' role reversal.

## Reciprocity

A reciprocity continuum offered by Sahlins (1972) is helpful in further understanding the roles of mutuality and time in Sherry's gift exchange paradigm. Three types of reciprocity can be distinguished. *Generalized* reciprocity is situated at one extreme on the reciprocity continuum and denotes informal *social gift exchange* situations for which no accounts are kept and no immediate or timely specific return is expected. What counts are the gift's expressive properties and its ability to reduce the existing social distance between donor and recipient. Situated in the middle of the reciprocity continuum, balanced reciprocity occurs in *economic gift exchange* situations that are characterized by a comparably high social distance between donor and recipient and the obligation to repay within a specific timeframe. Here, gifts are given "for something received previously or simultaneously, or in anticipation of future returns" (Belk and Coon 1993, 394). Negative reciprocity (e.g., Noonan 1984) is finally situated at the other end of the reciprocity continuum and stands for economic exchange situations such as stealing, theft, and bargaining. Here, the negative social relation between donor and recipient becomes a direct result of the material profit that the stronger part in the bargaining process makes. Negative gift transactions are therefore characterized by taking without giving and are also concluded as soon as one has received what one expected to receive.

## The Agapic Love Paradigm

"Do we give only to get something in return?" famously asked Belk and Coon (1993). In their inquiry of nonreciprocal forms of gift giving among daters, friends, or family members, these authors develop the idea of agapic or "unselfish" gift giving. This form of gift giving occurs in dyadic gifting constellations where only the altruistic desire to please the recipient motivates the giving of gifts. Agapic gift giving presents a nonbinding gesture of deep devotion. In contrast to Sherry's (1983) exchange paradigm, which is mostly instrumental and singularizes the object, the agapic love paradigm is strictly autotelic and singularizes the recipient. Echoing Malinowski's (1922/1961) concept of the "pure gift," the agapic love paradigm fundamentally brackets away any notion of immediate or staggered return. What counts is the unique expression of devotion, care, and love. Although some scholars have argued that agapic love is merely an extension of Sherry's (1983) gift exchange paradigm (e.g., Joy 2001), its nonreciprocal and noninstrumental character clearly position it as a distinct yet equally "niche" paradigm of gift giving (see also Vaughan 1997).

## The Challenge of File Sharing

The ongoing popularity of the Internet is a phenomenon that moves beyond technological development since it affects how consumers interact both socially and culturally (Shields 1996; Venkatesh 1998). In cyberspace, information is cheap, fast, and global, and "the economics of interaction, communication, and coordination are different than when people meet face-to-face" (Smith and Kollock 1998; Hemetsberger 2002). This concerns, in particular, the giving and receiving of *information as a gift*. A variety of semi-virtual or virtual gift transactions may be developed under the aegis of existing gift-giving paradigms. These are dyadic gifting situations that are situated in cyberspace, such as the birthday-related giving of an e-book from Amazon, a virtual greeting card at Christmas (cf. Sherry 1983), or a romantic poem via email (cf. Belk and Coon 1993).

Recently, however, we have seen the advent of so-called peer-to-peer file-sharing communities. A *polyadic,* rather than a dyadic, social constellation marks these electronically networked gift economies in cyberspace (in short, *cybernetic gift economies*) in which multiple anonymous gifting agents can share multiple gifts at the same time. Popular cybernetic gift economies like Napster, KaZaa, Lime Wire, or BearShare are attracting millions of consumers worldwide, enabling the free download of software, movies, songs, and much more. A matrix of cultural, institutional, and technological constellations engenders different ideological uses of the cybernetic gift by three powerful groups of stakeholders: Napster users celebrating alternative forms of music consumption through cybernetic gift giving, recording industry executives pointing to the existential threats cybernetic gift giving poses to their businesses, and artists diverging on the impact of Napster's cybernetic gift economy on the business, quality, and culture of music.

Premised upon gift giving in a dyadic social constellation, none of the above-reviewed gifting paradigms offers a suitable platform from which to analyze the complex dimensions of cybernetic gift giving. While Sherry's gift spiral concentrates on reciprocal gift giving and the obligation to give, receive, and repay, Belk and Coon's agapic love model centers the nonreciprocal form of gift giving among lovers. Both paradigms take a dyadic constellation between donor and recipient for granted and assume a social relationship between them. In addition, both existing paradigms have traditionally inspired primarily the study of material objects such as clothing, CDs, jewelry, or greeting cards. As a consequence, both existing paradigms are unqualified to frame the polyadic nature of cybernetic gift gifting. Through the extensive netnographic analysis of Napster's file-sharing community, I develop a theorization that addresses this gap of knowledge.

## Methodology

This article profits from seven years of personal involvement in the cultural politics of music file-sharing as a label owner and music producer and from four years of netnographic study of cybernetic gift-giving communities, including, among others, Napster, Hotline, KaZaa, and BearShare. My personal "revelatory event" (Belk, Wallendorf, and Sherry 1989) took place fairly early, in 1998, with the shocking rediscovery of significant portions of my copyrighted music catalogue on the Internet. Seventeen-year-old Jack,[1] a high-school student who was hired as a "studio hand" over the summer, had secretly uploaded my material to a public Internet website using the studio's Internet connection. Legal advisors concluded that Jack would have to expect prison should his case be taken to court. I decided to spare him this prospect but instead urged him to explain to me what had prompted him to do that. Jack's astonishing revelations about the recording industry, his role as a music consumer, and this unfamiliar notion of "music as a gift" as opposed to "music as a product" served as an impetus for this research project.

Only six months later, in May 1999, a new software application called Napster hit the spot, turning my horrifying one-time experience with Jack into an everyday reality. Aggregating more than 10 (!) million users in the first six-month period and attaining a growth rate of 200,000 new subscribers in a single day, Napster struck terror into the hearts of even the most sturdy of entertainment executives. Within a few weeks more than 4 million songs had made their way from consumers' CD shelves into the Napster network.

This article is based on a *hybrid* methodological design, including bidirectional field immersion and the prolonged engagement with Napster consumers in both online *and* offline context. Although Napster's cybernetic gift economy is situated in cyberspace, it still involves real people in real places. In fact, it presents what Fuchs (2001, 256) calls a "hybrid field of forces and relations." Only a netnographic design that is as hybrid as the phenomenon it investigates can help minimize methodological imbalance while maximizing the study's trustworthiness, representativeness, and informed consent (Giesler and Venkatesh 2005).

The online data used in this study stem from observations of Napster throughout May 1999 until August 2003. I installed a free version of the Napster software on my computer, which I had previously downloaded from http://www.napster.com. A primary data set including 20 cyber interviews was directly recorded through Napster's Instant Messaging System, a relay chat feature implemented in the software, documenting the normative expectations of behavior and the ideology attending the consumption of Napster. The cyber interviews were pasted into a text editor, resulting in an 89-page document of typed, double-spaced text. To solicit volunteers for the study, I used message board postings and an intrication website, http://www.napsterresearch.com.

Furthermore, I collected and reviewed observational data from 28 informant emails, several dozen threads of file-sharing–related Internet message boards, and connection data recorded off of Napster's logging function. An additional methodological component was historical information from numerous news stories, magazine articles, press releases, corporate websites, testimony protocols, and other communications.

The offline data used in this research stem from unobtrusive observations of Napster consumers and other file-sharing consumers (Hotline, KaZaa) while using their file-sharing software in their natural physical surroundings, throughout a period from August 2000 until December 2003. Through this channel, I conducted 13 in-depth interviews with users among the student population and staff of a North American university. To solicit potential offline informants, I used several posters stating my research interest in file-sharing communities on campus blackboards. Interviews were conducted in computer labs, fraternity houses, student rooms, and university offices. The length of these interviews ranged from 12 minutes to circa 1.5 hours. The offline interviews were recorded on tape and transcribed verbatim, resulting in a 78-page, typed, double-spaced text.

Data gathering and analysis were done in tandem utilizing reflexive field notes and a data analysis software to facilitate the data analysis. Interviews were commented upon, then comments and interviews were again read at a distance and analyzed. Several member checks were undertaken through the intrication page and email, and follow-up questions were posed to informants.

The goal of this article is to develop the paradigm of cybernetic gift giving, to trace out and define its most important theoretical features, and to situate these findings in the broader sociological, anthropological, and consumer literatures. I organize my netnographic findings in two major sections: (1) structural dimensions of cybernetic gift giving at Napster, and (2) related ideological uses of the cybernetic gift. In each section, insights are drawn from netnographic data.

## Structural Dimensions: How Does Napster Work?

### Cybergiftingscape

Napster constitutes a cybernetic gift economy that foundationally departs from and extends our understanding of gift giving and music consumption. It is situated within a radically different environment of bits and bytes rather than atoms. The setting is that of a computer network of digital information. Gifts are virtual rather than physical, and since they are digital they can be perfectly copied at infinite numbers and distributed in a polyadic constellation. Napster itself resembles what Howard Rheingold (1993) has referred to as *virtual community*, an *imagined* community "ersatz" (Anderson 1983) in cyberspace that provides meaningful social experience through the giving and receiving of mp3 music files. Napster cybernetic gifting rituals that contrast mainstream music consumption practices foster the "intrinsic connection to one another" and a sense of difference from others not in the Napster community (Muniz and O'Guinn 2001). Cybernetic gift giving thus marks the Napster community's prototypical distinction (Giesler and Venkatesh 2004) and leads to communal "we-ness" (Bender 1978). Venkatesh (1998) coined the term *cybermarketscape* to describe the dramatic profusion between consumers, the marketplace, and computer networks. I propose the term *cybergiftingscape* to signify Napster's hybrid social matrix that connects consumers through cybernetic gift giving. Napster's cybergiftingscape provides the sociotechnological grid that embeds the myriad of cybernetic gifts and organizes the social interaction between donors and recipients. In this section, I develop the most defining components of Napster's cybergiftingscape and introduce a structural framework for further, more systematic studies of cybernetic gift giving.

## Cybernetic Gifts

A cybernetic gift can be digitized information of any format, such as text, music, pictures, films, and software. At Napster the cybernetic gift is typically a digitized piece of music in the format of an mp3 file. An mp3 file is transformed into a cybernetic gift in the moment of its transaction from the donor to the recipient. The central feature of *networked divisibility* characterizes Napster's cybernetic gifts: they are identical pieces of cloned information that can be received from multiple donors in small portions and at the same time. It is important to note that the gift's "source element(s)" remain with the donors during and after the cybernetic gift transaction. In contrast to the material gift, which can only be received one at a time, the cybernetic gift can be received infinitely and by multiple recipients. After a cybernetic gift transaction, the original mp3 file is left with the donors and a clone is added to the recipient. The cybernetic gift is "kept-while-given" (Weiner 1992), and with each new gift transaction the number of clones of the corresponding gift in the cybergiftingscape increases.

This ongoing circulation of Napster's cybernetic gift evokes Mauss's (1925/1967) observation that the gift must always move (Hyde 1983). On its journey from one Napster consumer to the next, the cybernetic gift is in permanent motion. At Napster the cybernetic gift is *multiplied* through ongoing polyadic transactions rather than *exchanged* through one dyadic transaction (Sherry 1983). The cybernetic gift has social binding power (Hyde 1983) through polyadic multiplication rituals, providing the essential building block for Napster's cybergiftingscape and thus bringing the community to life.

## Donors and Recipients

Multiplication partners constitute another important aspect of Napster's cybernetic gift economy. In contrast to Sherry's (1983) exchange and Belk and

Coon's (1993) agapic gifting paradigms, Napster's file-sharing network is fully anonymous. Napster users employ name aliases to identify themselves in the cybergiftingscape. The gifting relationships between donor and recipient at Napster resemble those involved in organ or blood donation (e.g., Belk 1990), or in the Jewish tradition of charity (Twersky 1980) where donor and recipient do not know each other. Dyadic personal relationships between donor and recipient are entirely bracketed away in favor of spontaneously emerging polypolar gifting connections among anonymous Napster users. Opposing conventional forms of gift giving, which are donor driven, cybernetic gift giving at Napster is fully recipient driven. Gifting connections are established exclusively through the recipient's motivation to initiate a gift transaction and again terminated after the transaction is completed or, during the process, by any of the donors or the recipient.

Napster's gifting agents are *hybrids* in that their ability to give and receive cybernetic gifts is at every point driven, shaped, and constrained by technological considerations. Although Napster users are humans, their role as multiplication partners in the cybergiftingscape can only be understood through the technological matrix that they are so intimately connected to and that determines their existence as donors and recipients. In a recent epistemological discussion of intense consumer-technology interactions, Giesler and Venkatesh (2005) proposed the *cyborg* as "the prototypical posthumanist consumer, a cybernetic organism that signifies the symbiosis between animal and machine, but also reflects the transformative union between economic priority and insatiable desire, living being and observing system" (Haraway 1991). Empowered by high-technological products and networks, Napster's cyborg consumers "operate" as multidirectional gifting agents; they simultaneously perform the roles of donor and recipient, empowered to give and receive multiple cybernetic gifts at the same time.

## Gifting Rhizomes

Sherry (1983) notes that "it is the process—not the mere event—of gift giving that captures the anthropological imagination" (157). In the case of Napster, the process of gift giving is not dialectical but "root-like" or *rhizomorphous* (Deleuze and Guattari 1987). For instance, Recipient A can start downloading Song A from Donors B, C, D, and E, then decide to stop the transaction and restart it the next day, either from Donors B, C, D and E, or from Donors F, G, and H. All involved donors can also simultaneously be recipients of other cybernetic gift transactions that in turn involve again Recipient A, this time as a donor. This example illustrates that Napster can evoke multiple gifting relations in a single transaction and that multiple gifting transactions can occur at the same time. Cybernetic gift giving thus refuses the application of Sherry's (1983) dialectical gift exchange spiral. Instead, a *gifting rhizome* is forming around the wealth of

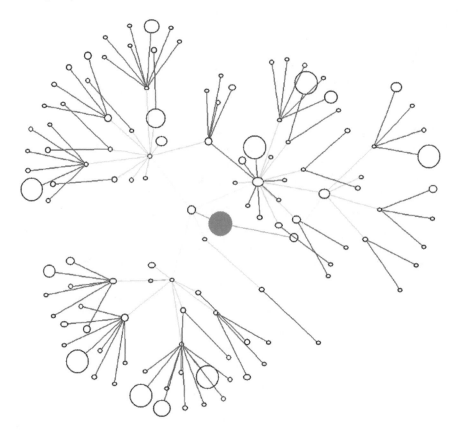

**Figure 2.1** A cybernetic gifting rhizome.

donors-recipient constellations. Like an evolving rootstock shown in time-lapse photography, the gifting rhizome connects the dynamic constellations between recipient and donors that emerge during a particular gift transaction.

Using the connection data provided by Napster's logging function, a gifting rhizome and its evolution over time can be illustrated (see Figure 2.1). Here, a modified version of the *GraphViz* network visualization tool was used to create an illustration of a gifting rhizome that unfolded during a cybernetic gift transaction at Napster on October 26, 2001. In this cybernetic gift transaction, the recipient (represented by the red dot) is receiving a cybernetic gift from multiple donors (represented by empty circles at the end of the lines). The size of the circles represents the digital bandwidth available to the multiplication partners while the lines illustrate the flow of the cybernetic gift from the donors to the recipient.

The design of the gifting rhizome determines the speed of the corresponding gift transaction. In particular, it concerns (1) the file size of the corresponding gift, (2) the degree to which it has already been disseminated in the cybergiftingscape, (3) traffic and bandwidth, and (4) the geographical distance between donor(s) and recipient. Observed gift transactions ranged from several days to only a few seconds. While some gifts were universally present, cultural preferences engender differences in regional availabilities in Napster's cybergiftingscape. For instance, it is virtually impossible to download a popular Swedish song in the U.S. while it takes only a few seconds to download the same song while in a location somewhere in Sweden. In sum, a cybernetic gift transaction moves from diachronic to synchronic the more efficient the gifting rhizome is designed.

## Metareciprocity

Perhaps the most fascinating and varied dimension of cybernetic gift giving involves the realm of reciprocity. My observations reveal that most consumers use Napster for the purpose of self-enrichment, seeking to maximize their personal music catalog, not actively considering reciprocation at all. However, since Napster's cybernetic gift multiplies with every transaction and the received file remains in the cybergiftingscape, reciprocation occurs quasi automatically. Even those Napster users who do not actively have reciprocation in mind therefore give back unconsciously what they have previously downloaded. With the installation of the Napster software, every user implicitly subscribes to a technologically determined balanced reciprocity contract: Every song one gets from the community one equally gives back to the community. In accordance, informants point to Napster's cybernetic ethos of sharing, describing music at Napster as a "communal property" that "makes the idea work" because everyone is "giving to and receiving from the community."

At Napster, consumers' altruism and self-interest seem to coexist and ensure that the cybernetic gift is in motion and that the cybernetic gift economy continues to flourish. A double paradox is underlying the consumption of Napster crossing Weiner's (1992) notion of "keeping-while-giving" with the unprecedented paradoxical notion of keeping-while-taking. To maintain and even extend the wealth of gifts in the cybergiftingscape, Napster users give from their own catalogue and at the same time take the mp3 files from other users. They can fulfill the split demands of self and other enrichment at the same time. The double paradox of keeping-while-giving and keeping-while-taking is also accompanied by consumers' ideologies of what is considered fair or unfair file-sharing behavior. However, reciprocity can occur only if Napster users leave their previously received gifts accessible on their computers so that other users are able to download them again. Of common concern to many users therefore is that some excessively receive gifts without making these gifts available again to other users. Consider, for instance, what Dawn had to say:

> What bugs me most about Napster is that there is a growing number of users that do not share what they've downloaded from others that download off me. If they're not into sharing, they should not be allowed to reap the benefits.

Why should they be allowed to take and not share? Just think about why Napster is so popular. If no one shared, what's the point?

Informants like Dawn referred to such behaviors as "stealing," "freeloading," "hoarding," or "leeching." Leeching, according to a definition from Wikipedia.com, "refers to the practice of joining a group for the explicit purpose of gaining rewards without contributing anything to the efforts necessary to acquire those rewards." At Napster it is generally considered unfair behavior to take without giving back and doing so prompted some donors to terminate the transaction ties. For instance, at the beginning of my fieldwork, when I attempted to download a song without having any material on my computer, I instantly received the following emphatic short note from Tom via Napster's instant messaging:

Hey, a***! Don't see a single file on your drive! No sharing, no Napster! Either you immediately add some or I kick you're a*** . . .

Contributing with the massive number of 639 files to Napster, Tom is an example of those Napster enthusiasts who are motivated to provide "as much music as possible to enrich the entire community." When asked about this incredible number of files (I successfully talked him into a conversation to learn more about his motivation after I had followed his request to make "at least a few files" available to others), Tom revealed not only that he is "keepin' an eye on how much people have on their hard drives when they download stuff from me" but also that he is competing with other Napster users over bringing massive amounts of new music into the Napster community. As he revealed:

I'm uploading my entire music collection step by step. I have about 400 CDs and 100 vinyl records. A bunch of other users and I are doing this. . . . it's for the community but it's also fun because we're all into music and we often look at what the others have aggregated. In the beginning it was just normal artists but now it's also the rare stuff. . . . I have put up a recording from that '96 Rage gig in CA (the band Rage Against the Machine played a concert in California in 1996). I figured that people usually have a hard time finding that stuff at the fairs so I'm pretty proud that I have a copy to offer them.

The case of Tom can be interpreted as agonistic and altruistic behavior. It demonstrates not only that some Napster users informally control the "communal contribution" of others and, if required, complain about and request additional contribution (altruistic). It also points to the existence of an (agonistic) ritualistic form of economic rivalry at Napster the anthropology literature has referred to as "tournaments of value" (Appadurai 1986; Harrison 1992). Like the Greek god Prometheus who steals the fire from the sun to enlighten the humans, some competitive heavy givers in the Napster community take away massive amounts of new music (i.e., the Promethean fire) from outside the cybergiftingscape to give it to the community. High social status is attached to those anonymous potlatch heroes and they constitute not only the functional backbone of Napster's cybernetic gift economy but also form the moral instance that helps control the flow of wealth in the cybergiftingscape.

Sherry (1983) has identified non-altruism as agonistic behavior in which the donor attempts to maximize personal satisfaction. At Napster the distinction between agonism and altruism has become fluid. Both altruistic and agonistic Napster users strengthen the Napster community as a whole since automatic reciprocity is a built in software feature. The only exception is the parasitic practice of leeching or freeloading where songs are downloaded and immediately taken out of the cybergiftingscape to exclude them from further multiplication. It is therefore difficult to relate my findings on Napster's reciprocity situation to one particular form of reciprocity within Sahlins's (1972) traditional reciprocity continuum. Napster automatically fosters balanced reciprocity on the technological level of analysis. Beyond that, however, generalized and negative reciprocities can apply in cases where Napster consumers give much more than they take or take much more than they give (generalized)—up to the point of excessive giving on the one end (generalized) or leeching on the other (negative). To describe this reciprocity situation, I propose the term metareciprocity. A technological consequence of cybernetic gift giving, metareciprocity is a formerly unprecedented postmodern reciprocity species that prevails in cybernetic gifting networks. It is defined as the informal multidimensional gifting relation of mutual action and reaction among agents within a gifting community or between an agent and the gifting community.

## Summary

In this section, I have analyzed the most important structural particularities of Napster's cybernetic gift economy on the microscopic level of interpersonal dynamics. In particular, I have developed the cybergiftingscape, a virtual community that socially embeds cybernetic gift giving and departs from the physical context in which gift giving is usually set. I have further shown that, in contrast to material gift giving, cybernetic gifts are multiplicatory and can be cloned in infinite numbers. Cybernetic gift-multiplication partners, my findings reveal, are fundamentally different from their counterparts in dyadic gifting constellations by dint of their ability to engage in polyadic gifting connections and simultaneous donor and recipient role splittings. My findings suggest that the anonymity of cybernetic giving strongly contrasts the intimacy reflected in Belk and Coon's (1993) agapic love paradigm and in Sherry's (1983) gift exchange paradigm. I have also illustrated that the rhizomorphous dynamics of the cybernetic gift multiplication process are fundamentally different from Sherry's (1983) dialectical gift exchange process. Finally, I have shown how cybernetic gift giving departs

TABLE 2.1

DIFFERENCES IN EXCHANGE, AGAPIC, AND CYBERNETIC
PARADIGMS OF INTERACTIVE GIFT GIVING

| Exchange | | Agapic | Cybernetic |
|---|---|---|---|
| Economic | Social | | |
| Economic utilitarian | Symbolic | Expressive | Economic utilitarian, symbolic, expressive |
| Balanced or negative reciprocity | Generalized reciprocity | Non-reciprocal | Metareciprocity |
| Dyadic | Dyadic | Dyadic | Polyadic |
| Bi-directional | Bi-directional | Uni-directional | Multi-directional |
| Dialectical | Dialectical | No process | Rhizomorphous |
| Simultaneous exchange | Staggered exchange | No exchange | Multiplication |
| Dependence feared | Bonding expected | Non-binding | Non-binding |
| High distance | Distance to be reduced through gift | Lowest distance | Highest distance |
| Market economy | Moral economy | Non-economy | Ecology |
| Gifts singularize objects | Gifts singularize objects | Gifts singularize recipient | Gifts singularize information |
| Instrumental | Instrumental | Autotelic | Instrumental |

from conventional forms of gift giving with respect to deconstructing previous reciprocity categories and instead foster metareciprocity. Once we move away from a dyadic to a polyadic gifting scenario, metareciprocity automatically emerges as the inevitable mode of cybernetic cooperation. In Table 2.1, the most important differences in exchange, agapic, and cybernetic paradigms of interactive gift giving are summarized.

## Ideological Dimensions: What Does Napster Mean?

Napster engenders different ideological uses of cybernetic gift giving by three powerful groups of stakeholders: Napster users celebrating alternative forms of music consumption through cybernetic gift giving, recording industry executives pointing to the existential threats cybernetic gift giving poses to their businesses, and artists diverging on the impacts of Napster's cybernetic gift economy on the business, quality, and culture of music. Napster opponents' disciplinary discourse centering file sharing as a form of theft and a deviance from societal norms is confronted with Napster proponents' resistant discourse bringing file sharing in ideological opposition to the music market system of corporations, commodification, and copyright. Ideological agendas are formed by and specific discursive tensions develop between these two groups in the process of what anthropologist Victor Turner (1986) has termed a *social drama*, "an eruption from the level surface of ongoing social life, with its interactions, transactions, reciprocities, its customs making for regular, orderly sequences of behavior" (196). According to Turner, whose theory can be developed both in the light of local face-to-face communities and larger anonymous social contexts, a social drama is "processually structured" and exhibits a regular course of events, which can be grouped in a successive phase of public action. These are: (1) a breach of regular norm-governed social relationships between consumers and producers; (2) a crisis or extension of the breach, during which there is a tendency for the breach to widen in public forums; (3) adjustive and redressive mechanisms brought into operation by leading members of the social group; and (4) reintegration of the disturbed social group, social recognition of an irreparable schism, or reversion to crisis. In this section, I examine the social drama staged by Napster's gifting rituals and develop how the various ideological uses of Napster's cybernetic gift economy have played themselves out in a sequence of dramatic acts and scenes across these four phases from the invention of Napster by college student Shawn Fanning in 1998 over Napster's shutdown due to bankruptcy in 2002 until today.

## Breach

According to Turner, the beginning of every social drama is marked by a breach of regular norm-governed social relationships between people in a social group. Napster's social drama began with the invention of the Napster software by Northeastern University college student Shawn Fanning in 1998. Fanning's recounting of the events back then exemplifies his motivation to depart from norm-governed forms of music consumption[2] and illustrates the emergence of the breach:

> I started my freshman year at Northeastern University in the fall of 1998 intending to major in computer science. Looking for a challenge beyond the entry-level courses, I decided to start writing a Windows-based program on my own. I spent a lot of time in Internet Relay Chat (IRC) rooms getting advice and information from the experienced developers and programmers who hang out there. IRC is a network of people organized into communities,

through real-time channels on various topics including programming and Internet security. "Napster" was my nickname, and I used it for my e-mail address and as my user name in IRC rooms. One of my college roommates loved listening to MP3s and used Internet sites such as MP3.1ycos.com to find them. He often complained about the unreliability of those sites, finding links to sites that were often dead ends, and indexes that were out of date because they were updated infrequently. I started thinking about ways to solve the reliability problems my roommate was experiencing. I began designing and programming a real-time system for locating MP3 files of other users on the Internet. I designed the Napster software to find MP3s because they are the most compressed format (in consideration of bandwidth) and they were very popular at the time. The system I had in mind was unlike ordinary search engines at that time. A traditional search engine sends out "robots" to roam the Internet periodically, updating itself every hour or more to remove sites that are down or unavailable. The database created is entirely driven by what the central computer finds by "crawling" the Internet. The indexes become outdated as sites go up or down, a significant problem when looking for MP3s because most of the files were housed on people's home computers. My idea was to have users list the files they were willing to share on a computer that they all could access. That list would then be updated each time a person logged on to and off of that computer. The index computer would at all times have an up-to-date list of the files people were willing to share, and the list would be voluntarily made by the users as they logged on and off the system. A user searching the index would see all the files shared by users on the network and available to others on the network at that moment. In contrast to traditional search engines, I envisioned a system that would be affirmatively powered by the users, who would select what information they wanted to list on the index. Then, when the user exited the application, their portion of the list (their files) would automatically drop from the index. The index was only one part of participating in the community. I also wanted users to be able to chat with each other and share information about their favorite music, so I added these functions to the application.

This passage highlights the norm-breaching event that prompted the emergence of Napster. Fanning introduced Napster as a community-oriented, more reliable alternative to traditional forms of online and offline music consumption. He drew a distinction between search-engine–based online music consumption or traditional CD-based music consumption and having "users list the files they were willing to share on a computer that they all could access." Instead of focusing on the traditional value chain that links music producer and consumer, he envisioned "a system that would be affirmatively powered by the users, who would select what information they wanted to list on the index." His vignette emphasizes a peculiar lack of possessive thinking replaced by a natural ethos of sharing music as a gift. Fanning describes Napster not only as a technologically superior form of music consumption. He also highlights Napster's ability to operate as a community and foster social cohesion.

Turner (1986) has characterized a breach as an infraction of binding rules governing the maintenance of power relationships between persons, statuses, or subgroups (43). In their award-winning analysis of brand community, Muniz and O'Guinn (2001) have urged consumer researchers to move attention from the traditional dyadic constellation between producer and consumer to the triangular producer-consumer-consumer constellation (427). Until Fanning's invention of Napster, a dyadic constellation between producer and consumer dominated the music marketplace, and an individual purchase and ownership of music as intellectual property was central: music, on- and offline, had to be purchased from and copyrights had to be granted by producers in order to be owned by individual consumers. The breach caused by Napster's cybernetic gift economy obliterated this traditional power relationship by adding to the norm-governed dyadic relation between producer and consumer a polyadic web of consumer-consumer relations, and thus initiating a shift from individuality to community, from purchase to sharing, and from ownership to access.

## Crisis

After developing the software prototype, Fanning started sending it to friends, who sent it to other friends. A few early adopters provided feedback and helped track down bugs in the software. The consistently supportive and enthusiastic responses he got convinced him to try to build out the system. Fanning and his uncle incorporated a company in May 1999 and raised some money from angel investors. An early beta version of the Napster software was released during the summer and spread quickly by word of mouth. In September 1999, Napster, Inc. obtained office space and Shawn Fanning moved to California. The free software portal Download.com featured Napster in its Download Spotlight in early fall 1999, and the user community grew significantly. In this crisis phase of Napster's social drama, the software attracted more and more public attention, the breach between music producers and consumers widened, and Napster became the noisy center of a new social reality that struck terror into even the most sturdy of music entertainment executives. Consider, for instance, the following board posting by Robert:

> I love downloading free music. I love burning that music into free CD's for my own personal usage. For decades the music industry has gotten away with highway robbery and now the consumer is getting some of it back. Before you bought an overhyped band, on an overhyped CD for maybe a few paltry songs. Now I can make whole CD's of every song I want to hear. As for the artist? They were getting hosed before by the music industry and now are getting doubly hosed.

However, now at least a hard working artist can put matters in their own hands. They can give the music away for free on the net, which would give them much needed exposure (I have discovered many a new band or artist I liked this way) and then still charge for live performances and all of the other crap that goes with it. The live experience is still sooo much better than anything else. The days of the lazy artist are over. Acts are going to have to get on the road more, tour more, and get out there with the fans. They can now keep this money and distribute their music over the net, without the help of any record labels. Furthermore, a slick artist can use this era of mass information to his or advantage and completely maintain creative control. As for Napster? Close it down if you must. But there are hundreds of other sites you can go to get free downloads. You can't kill the technology or the will of the people who want to get their hands on it. Furthermore making digital music and MP3's is getting easier all the time. I have digitized my entire 400 CD collection in one weekend on my Apple G-4 and can give anyone copies anywhere. Without Napster all you force one to do is get more resourceful. The new technologies being created are evolving too quickly for anyone to control. THANK GOD! So kill Napster but don't be fooled into thinking that the downloading of free music will be gone.

For Robert, Napster has the potential to compensate consumers for the music industry's ongoing "highway robbery." It liberates consumers from the economic and aesthetic tyranny of a music market system that has betrayed both artist and consumers. Robert's passage places considerable weight on the liberatory role of technology. He emphasizes how easily he digitalized his entire music collection over the weekend using his Apple computer. He also establishes an ideological link between technological innovation and the great gift of free music. Robert leaves no doubt that "the new technologies being created are evolving too quickly" to keep away the music from the consumers, no matter if these technologies were consumer or producer developed.

While Robert recognizes that artists are "getting doubly hosed" by the recording industry and by file-sharing consumers, he also argues that hardworking (as opposed to lazy) artists can now "put matters in their own hand" and emancipate themselves from their slave-driving recording labels. In Robert's narrative, the authentic encounter is prioritized over the artificial experience of the "overhyped." Accordingly, he urges artists to reconsider the live music experience as a great possibility to generate revenues. Through this ideological construction, Robert is able to mitigate consumers' co-responsibilities for the artists' perceived misery and to blame it mostly on the profane recording industry regime: the consumers and artists can "teamplay" on the authentic side of the game, bracketing out the recording industry on the artificial side. A similar interpretation is offered by pro-Napster artists. Consider, for instance, a statement from Prince (the Artist Formally Known as Prince):

What record companies don't really understand is that Napster is just one illustration of the growing frustration over how much the record companies control what music people get to hear, over how the air waves, record labels and record stores, which are now all part of this "system" that recording companies have pretty much succeeded in establishing, are becoming increasingly dominated by musical "products" to the detriment of real music. Why should the record company have such control over how he, the music lover, wants to experience the music? From the point of view of the real music lover, what's currently going on can only be viewed as an exciting new development in the history of music. And, fortunately for him, there does not seem to be anything the old record companies can do about preventing this evolution from happening.

This statement interprets the emergence of Napster as an opportunity for "real music lovers" who are looking for "real music" to emancipate themselves from a recording industry "system" and its musical "products" that terrorize and dupe the passive audience. *Taste* is the unwritten word in Prince's statement. In his Frankfurt School–flavored vignette, he criticizes the capitalist hegemony of musical tastes and expresses the technologically driven hope that an irreversible historical transformation is underway that fundamentally departs from the old structures that have long organized musical tastes. Not only does the Napster "evolution" provide freedom of choice for consumers. Implicitly for Prince, Napster also empowers artists to create and promote new musical genres and styles. Many popular artists including Dave Mathews, Courtney Love, Bono (U2), or Chuck D (Public Enemy) bestowed similar positions, celebrating the advent of Napster's file-sharing community as a victory of "real" art over the dreary plastic productions of the recording industry. Elsewhere (Giesler and Pohlmann 2003b), I have discussed Napster's potential to develop a paradox of consumer emancipation. Echoing Holt's (2002) theory that consumer emancipation must be understood as a paradoxical movement in the management of meanings, musicians favoring Napster were all members of the record industry that popularized their artistic works. Likewise, Napster users were downloading predominantly commercial songs whose existence they often demonized in ideologizing the cybernetic gift.

## Redressive Action

The egalitarian discourse of consumers and some artists is contrasted by the recording industry's disciplinary discourse. The Recording Industry Association of America (RIAA), which represents the four major record labels and a host of smaller labels, was annoyed at the sudden advent and rapid success of Napster. "We love the idea of using technology to build artist communities, but that's not what Napster is all about. Napster is about facilitating piracy, and trying to build a business on the backs of artists and copyright owners," complained Cary Sherman, then senior executive vice president and general counselor for the RIAA.[3] In December 1999, the RIAA therefore decided to sue Napster for copyright infringement. In the courtroom several artists appeared and spoke out against Napster. One of them was Lars Ulrich, drummer for the prominent rock band Metallica:

> We have many issues with Napster. First and foremost: Napster hijacked our music without asking. They never sought our permission—our catalog of music simply became available as free downloads on the Napster system. I don't have a problem with any artist voluntarily distributing his or her songs through any means the artist elects—at no cost to the consumer, if that's what the artist wants. But just like a carpenter who crafts a table gets to decide whether to keep it, sell it or give it away, shouldn't we have the same options? My band authored the music, which is Napster's lifeblood. We should decide what happens to it, not Napster—a company with no rights in our recordings, which never invested a penny in Metallica's music or had anything to do with its creation. The choice has been taken away from us. What about the users of Napster, the music consumers? It's like each of them won one of those contests where you get turned loose in a store for five minutes and get to keep everything you can load into your shopping cart. With Napster, though, there's no time limit and everyone's a winner—except the artist. Every song by every artist is available for download at no cost and, of course, with no payment to the artist, the songwriter or the copyright holder.

To clarify his concerns over Napster's gifting practices, Ulrich employs a pictographic capitalist market vernacular using words like authors, rights, investments, payments, copyright holders, or winners. For Ulrich, Napster is not a consumer community but "a company with no rights in our recordings." He makes clear that this company has taken away the decision of what artistic products should be online and what should not. Participation in the business-decision process, for Ulrich, is not a matter of cultural stakeholdership but exclusively relies on economic ownership. Those who have "never invested a penny in Metallica's music" are not allowed to participate. In Ulrich's vignette, consumers only play a very limited part. They implicitly exist as impudent pirates who are "hijacking" what is not theirs or as greedy value maximizers being turned loose in a store to grab everything they can because it is free. Uproar shook the music consumer community. Consider, for instance, the following informant quote:

> I feel for Lars and his multi-millionaire cronies. I know how he must feel. I feel abused every time I pay $17.99 for a $.50 cent (Manufacture cost) CD that has that one hit and 9 Lame-o's. Give me a break. It's OK to make a small profit on

CD's, not rape the consumer. If you want to rape your fans, do it in the TRUE arena. . . .the live show. There you can control everything from the price of admission to the cost of the T-shirts. And if you're good you'll rake it in. Most of the so-called mega bands are just RIAA-created hype monsters anyway. As soon as a band hits it big they look at the fans as one huge cash cow to be milked. Are you listening Lars? When will you be rich enough?!?? How much do you give to charity, eh? Pearl Jam had it figured out when they fought Ticketmaster. Metallica is pure crap and doesn't care about its fans at all. Only the ones with fat wallets are welcome.

In the phases of crisis and redressive action, according to Turner (1986, 34), "ancient rancours, rivalries, and unresolved vendettas are revived. Non-rational considerations prevail: temperamental dislikes, unconscious desires, and aggressions, reanimated infantile anxieties, as well as the conscious envies and jealousies which break loose when a major normative knot is cut." In the case of Napster, ideological positions revolved mainly around traditional tensions between authenticity versus artificiality, and cultural versus economic. Napster's cybernetic gift economy is viewed by consumers as authentic, often sacred, and liberatory. Employing cybernetic gift giving as an ideological vehicle, Napster users are able to re-enchant music consumption distanced from the market logic of the money driven, cold, and artificial. Napster users articulated this theme also in what Jenkins (1992) calls textual poaching, the cultural production of creative outlets such as fantasy stories, critical essays, or comic illustrations. For instance, Lars Ulrich and his fellow band mate James Hetfield were caricatured in the ironical "Napster Bad" cartoon series.[4] In these cartoons, Ulrich is portrayed as a notoriously complaining little manikin, nervously running back and forth in front of stacked money sacks, being frequently interrupted by his fellow band mate James Hetfield requesting "beeeer." Visual proof for the interest in the ironical sign game of combining the political matter of Napster with reanimated fragments of the Marxist capitalist critique is also found in old-looking socialistic poster and graffiti nostalgia like "Napster—la revolución," subtitling the portrait of Ché Guevara on the background of rebellious labor-class workers. "When you pirate MP3s you are downloading communism" is the message of a faked, retro-looking, ironical comic illustration subtitled "Reminder of the Recording Industry Association of America" (see Figure 2.2). It shows the diabolical accomplice Lenin encouraging an obviously American white Caucasian young male consumer who is sitting in front of his Apple iMac to download mp3s. The "Napster Manifesto," an anonymous call for "net communism," even made use of a modified version of Marx and Engel's (1848) *Communist Manifesto*, containing terms like "music industry" and "capitalism" instead of terms like "bourgeoisie," "bourgeois class," or "agriculture and manufacturing industry."

**Figure 2.2** Ironic Political Images

## Reintegration, Schism, and Reversion

In October 2000, the Napster community numbered over 32 million users. For the past four months, it had been growing at the rate of one million new users each week. There were consistently over 800,000 people using the system simultaneously. Napster users were in all corners of the world, and while mostly college students initially adopted it, a significant portion of Napster consumers were now over 30. Shawn Fanning and Napster had to deal with growing legal pressure and the ideological tensions between producers and consumers increased. Then, in late fall of 2000, German media giant Bertelsmann and Napster's Shawn Fanning formed a "strategic alliance" with the aim of turning Napster into a "secure commercial file-sharing application." Until then, Bertelsmann's subsidiary Bertelsmann Music Group (BMG) had been joining RIAA's efforts to bring Napster down. I quote the official press statement from Bertelsmann's international website as of October 31, 2000, in parts:

> Bertelsmann AG and Napster, Inc. today announced the formation of a strategic alliance to further develop the Napster person-to-person file sharing service.
>
> Bertelsmann AG's newly formed eCommerce Group, BeCG, and Napster have developed a new business model for a secure membership-based service that will provide Napster community members with high quality file sharing

that preserves the Napster experience while at the same time providing payments to rights holders, including recording artists, songwriters, recording companies and music publishers.

Napster and Bertelsmann will seek support from others in the music industry to establish Napster as a widely accepted membership based service and invite them to participate actively in this process. Under the terms of the agreement, once Napster successfully implements its new membership-based service, Bertelsmann's music division, BMG, will withdraw its lawsuit against Napster and make its music catalogue available. Bertelsmann eCommerce Group will provide a loan to Napster to enable development of the new service and will hold a warrant to acquire a portion of Napster's equity.

Terms like business model, payments, service, rights holders, warrant, or equity hearken back to Lars Ulrich's managerial critique of Napster and indicate that, henceforth, Napster's new administration expected the community to be the leading online music community "service." It is important to note that a "membership-based model" that combines "payments to rights holders" fundamentally violates Napster's prototypical contract of the cybernetic gift. For instance, whereas Napster's cybernetic gift economy is based on the premise of gift multiplication and a polyadic constellation, the institution of copyright assumes economic scarcity and a dyadic relationship between producer and consumer. Accordingly, shortly after this announcement, a new version of Napster's client software was published that contained links to Bertelsmann's subsidiary, the online CD distributor "CDNow." Links to Congress were also provided to let Napster users vouch for "free information exchange," under the control of Bertelsmann. "They want us to be the social dressing on their corporate salad," an informant gave to the testimony protocol. Napster's website also had a much higher quality in the graphical design as well as in written content. My field notes capture several situations in which informants complained about these changes and linked the "glossy and boring" look and feel of the "new Napster" to the non-emphatic appearance of commercial music websites and download services. Additionally, and as a result of the ongoing legal battle over copyright infringements between "Bertelsmann-Napster" and the RIAA, different filter systems were installed on Napster's central servers several times, aiming at limiting cybernetic gift multiplication to noncopyrighted material. Accompanied by massive worldwide consumer protests in July 2001, a federal judge ruled that Napster must block the sharing of all files infringing copyright, effectively forcing it to shut down. In September 2002, after a Delaware court had also blocked the Bertelsmann-Napster deal, Napster was finally forced to file bankruptcy and shut down.

Turner (1986) argues that "the fourth phase of the social drama consists either of reintegration of the disturbed social group or of the recognition and legitimation of irreparable schism between the contending parties" (35). In

Turner's (1957) study of the Ndembu, for instance, he revealed an irreparable schism that led an African village to split like cells, with one party abandoning its huts and moving out to found a new village. Turner also acknowledges a third case that, under conditions of major social change, in which a consensus over key values no longer exists and the redressive machinery based on such consensus loses its legitimacy, a reversal into the stage of crisis may also occur. My findings from Napster revise Turner's contention that a social drama ends either in restored harmony, irreparable schism, or reversion from redressive action to crisis.

Reintegration of Napster through corporate activities and redressive legal machinery was enforced and Napster had to shut down its central servers. In July 2003, the software company Roxio, which had purchased Napster's brand name from Bertelsmann, announced its plan to launch Napster 2.0, a subscription-based online music store. By October 2004, Napster 2.0 was the second largest commercial Internet music provider and sold music files on behalf of record companies.

However, reversion arose from the irreversible dissemination and further advancement of Napster's technological innovation. In early 2000, the software company Nullsoft had briefly released another file-sharing program called Gnutella. Gnutella was an advanced version of Napster, distinguished by its ability to operate independently from any central server. Although Nullsoft quickly withdrew support for the software, programmers started hacking it apart and published the code needed to adapt it and build new software based on it. In October 2004, the website www.gnutelliums.com listed 13 programs based on Napster and Gnutella, including BearShare, Morpheus, and KaZaa. The emergence of Napster marked the first systematic acts of consumer defiance from a music market that organizes music consumption around corporations, commodification, and copyright. Napster's cybernetic gifting economy and the related discourse were "antistructural" in character (Turner 1969), providing a persistent partisan protocol against the modern music industry's conviction to inclusion (Foucault 1984). Yet Napster's technology also marked the ideological starting point for a continuous music marketplace drama unfolding between music consumers and producers, enacted through an ongoing oscillation between crisis and redressive action. On October 1, 2004, for instance, the RIAA announced it would file a large number of lawsuits against music piracy.[5] As part of a legal salvo against 762 allegedly illegal file sharers, 32 individuals at 26 schools were to be sued by the major record companies for using their university networks to illegally distribute copyrighted sound recordings on unauthorized p2p services. "We want music fans to enjoy music online, but in a fashion that compensates everyone who worked to create that music," said Cary Sherman, now the RIAA president. In response to Sherman's statement, a consumer board posting replied, "You know, Cary, you may have been able to kill Napster, but you cannot kill the technology behind it."

## Summary

In this section, I have analyzed the most important ideological tensions invoked by Napster's cybernetic gift economy on the macroscopic level of cultural dynamics. I have shown that Napster opponents' disciplinary discourse centering cybernetic gift giving as a form of theft and a deviance from social norms is confronted with Napster proponents' resistant discourse bringing cybernetic gift giving in ideological opposition to the dominant music market regime. The emergence of Napster marks the starting point of a music marketplace drama that, employing Turner's (1986) theory of social drama, can be organized in a fourfold processual ritual model involving breach, crisis, redress, and reintegration and reversion. Before Napster, music, on- and offline, had to be purchased from and copyrights had to be granted by producers in order to be owned by individual consumers. A breach in this fundamental agreement that helps organize the relationship between music producers and consumers is created because Napster's cybernetic gifting rituals move from individuality to community, from purchase to sharing, and from ownership to access. In the stages of crisis and redressive action, this breach is amplified and the tensions between music producers and consumers are increased as both stakeholder groups promote different ideological interpretations of cybernetic gift giving. Employing a liberatory rhetoric, Napster proponents emphasize the role of cybernetic gift giving to release consumers from unethical corporate practices and greed, the bonds of copyright, and the hegemonic system of musical tastes. Paradoxically, my findings reveal, most advocates of this position predominantly share mainstream musical creations. Using a radical economic and legal vernacular, Napster opponents ideologically interpret cybernetic gift giving as lawbreaking. These stakeholders discursively position Napster in a criminal context and initiate a formal jural machinery. The fourth stage consists of Napster's shutdown and the publicly ritualized reintegration of the disturbed group of Napster consumers as well as a reversion and ongoing oscillation between crisis and redress based on the advancement of Napster's gifting technology and its implementation into other file-sharing communities.

## Implications for Research on Gift Giving

First, my research results significantly contribute to the study of gift giving. For the first time in social and consumer culture theory, I have developed the paradigm of cybernetic gift giving, the polyadic giving and receiving of digitized information in networked peer-to-peer file-sharing communities on the Internet. In particular, my analysis has significantly extended existing wisdom on the gift exchange process. The rhizomorphous structure of cybernetic gift giving differs fundamentally from the dyadic setup that dominates the conventional gifting process. The visualization of the cybernetic gifting rhizome undertaken herein offers a valuable inside perspective into the anatomy of the cybernetic gift-multiplication process. On the background of these insights, strategic questions could be asked such as: According to which pattern do certain cybernetic gifts become adopted in the cybergiftingscape? How can corrupt computer files infiltrated by corporations slow down or even stop cybernetic gift multiplications? Follow-up research, perhaps combining my rhizome visualization technique with a quantitative network analysis method (e.g., Iacobucci 1996), could examine these issues more deeply.

In addition, my analysis reopens the question of reciprocity and gift giving. The transition of the gift from the domain of atoms and materiality to that of bits and bytes, in combination with the establishment of polyadic gifting structures on the Internet, consequently entails a reciprocity species that not only echoes Marshall Sahlins's (1972) traditional reciprocity continuum but also extends it in important ways. The cybernetic gift moves away from Mauss's (1925) claim for the moral primacy of obligatory reciprocation and instead relies on an open system of continuous multiplicity. My study has laid out the technological and social circumstances under which this could happen. Nonetheless, further research is called for to examine in greater detail the various relationships among generalized, balanced, negative, and meta- reciprocity, and how different forms of polyadic gift giving engender different reciprocity constellations.

Future research on gift giving will benefit from the theoretical dimensions suggested herein. It is likely to expect that networked computer technologies like the Internet stimulate a plethora of new gift economies that still await sufficient interpretation by researchers. Recently, for instance, we have seen the advent of Wikipedia.com, another polyadic gift economy in which consumers co-create a publicly accessible Internet encyclopedia. While Wikipedia reflects some of the structural characteristics and ideological tensions described in this study on cybernetic gift giving, it probably diverges in many others respects. The paradigm of cybernetic gift giving developed herein will serve as the conceptual springboard for this and other future cases of polyadic gift giving.

## Is the Cybernetic Gift a Pure Gift?

The literature on gift giving is dominated by Marcel Mauss's fundamental assumption that the exchange of gifts must be understood as "an oppositional economy to that of the marketplace exchange" (Belk forthcoming). The gift belongs to the world of home and personal relationships whereas the commodity belongs to the world of commerce and impersonal relationships. As we move more and more into the market economy (Firat and Venkatesh 1995), Mauss argues, we have only vestigial remains of gift giving in contemporary Western societies. The majority of transactions today are commodity transactions that occur among strangers with a clean table left after the transaction is finished. Gift transactions in turn are far between and betwixt and occur among friends or family and reinforce emotional bonds (e.g., Sherry 1983; Belk and Coon 1993).

Derrida (1994) has violently rejected the Maussian tradition that distinguishes between the gift and regular market economics because both of them always come with the same reciprocal strings attached. This becomes especially clear in the Maussian conviction that the gift must always be understood as *voluntary yet obligatory* (Mauss 1950, 1925/1967; Titmuss 1992). Derrida argues that the gift that "puts the other in debt" appears to poison the relationship, so that "giving amounts to hurting, to doing harm" much in the same way economic exchange does (1994, 10). For Derrida, Mauss therefore more or less remains within the realms of the marketplace, his distinction between gift and market exchange just a dangerous myth.

But how does the "pure gift" look when what has been called the gift in anthropology does not seem to deserve its name? Derrida, following medieval Jewish philosopher Maimonides (1108), argues that the purest form of giving is achieved when donor and recipient do not know that they give or are being given to. The pure gift can only be realized when the gift is given with no expectation of a return at all; it must fall outside of the symbolic sphere to escape the vicious circle of social reciprocity. As Derrida (1994) argues, "For there to be a gift, there must be no reciprocity, return, exchange, countergift, or debt" (10). It must be an asocial and unconscious event and it must neither aggrandize the giver nor diminish the receiver; it is aneconomic, apolitical, and nonsacrificial (Kosky 1997; O'Neill 2001). In his powerful essay "The Double Inconceivability of the Pure Gift," Caillé (2001) has distilled the impossibility of Derrida's pure gift down to two hurdles that obstruct the path to its realization. First, there is the impossibility of deducting the gift entirely from egoistic interest. The pure gift has to be one that is liberated from any economic significance. Second, there is the impossibility of the gift not appearing as a gift. As Caillé points out, the pure gift "does not only have to carefully wash away all its stains of promiscuity in the face of interest, but also every threat of compromise with duty and morality" (32). Neither donor nor recipient must recognize the gift as a gift or themselves as donor or recipient. In the light of such difficult preconditions, for Derrida therefore the answer is clear. The only gift that qualifies as a pure gift is the nothingness of present time, in other words, the gift of death.

In consumer culture theory, Belk and Coon (1993) overcame at least the first hurdle in their agapic love paradigm: agapic love is strictly altruistic. A more drastic example would be organ donation where the donor passes away prior to giving away his or her organ (Belk 1990). However, both cases presuppose the recognition of the gift as a gift (of love or of life), which violates the second precondition necessary for the pure gift to exist.

However, my findings show that the cybernetic gift can be interpreted in the spirit of the pure gift. Not only does the cybernetic gift cut traditional economic strings, it also fundamentally brackets out social gifting relationships.

While some Napster users would recognize music from Napster as a "gift," most users are not actively aware that they are acting as donors or recipients. Effectively, Napster users can follow the logic of agonism and the logic of altruism at the same time, without even knowing each other. The cybernetic gift at Napster demands that it be unconstrained from scarcity, reciprocity, and the social. This is what awards it the status of the pure gift, and this is what makes it a viable alternative to Derrida's agnostic conclusions.

## Implications for Research on Consumer Resistance

In the consumer research literature, Thompson's (2004) recent investigation of marketplace mythologies provides the most suitable platform from which to evaluate my contributions to the study of consumer resistance. Contrasting previous theorizing from Firat and Venkatesh (1995), Holt (2002), and others, Thompson (2004) passionately encourages critical consumer researchers to take "a militantly agnostic perspective" (174) toward the question of consumer emancipation and to study consumer resistance *within* the marketplace rather than speculating if or how consumers can escape the marketplace at all:

> Rather than assessing whether the resulting transformation is genuinely emancipatory (Firat and Venkatesh) or paradoxically reproduces a dominant ideology (Holt), the critical objective is to understand the new configuration of power relationships that have emerged, the identity positions and identity practices they engender, the new array of ideological agendas that are formed, and the new opportunities for localized resistance that are produced in this matrix of overlapping discourses of power. (173)

My analysis of Napster's cybernetic gift economy and the ideological tensions it sparks off help extend Thompson's agnostic theorizing of consumer resistance in at least two important ways.

## The Role of Technological Innovation in Driving a Marketplace Conflict

First, my analysis shows an important linkage between the notion of marketplace conflict and the emergence of technological innovation. Of growing interest to consumer research is that entire categories of products, services, and consumption experiences are based on interactive consumer technology that had not been existent only a few years prior to their introduction (e.g., Kozinets 2002; Mick and Fournier 1998; Glazer 1995; Thompson 1994). It is widely accepted by now that technological products and networks all around us change not only the electronic infrastructure in the marketplace but also the social fabrics of consumers' lives (Sherry 2000; Venkatesh, Meamber, and Firat 1997; Firat and Venkatesh 1995). Although researchers have begun to explore the broader impacts of technological developments on the cultural structuring and political dynamics of consumer culture (Giesler and Venkatesh 2005; Kozinets forthcoming), none of the previous studies has investigated the important role of technological innovation in driving a marketplace conflict.

In the present study, I have shown that a technological innovation such as Napster's cybernetic gift technology fosters continuing contradictions between music consumers and producers. My empirical findings reveal an ongoing oscillation between crisis and redressive action because the consumer technology of cybernetic gift giving has spread out from Napster's dramaturgical site into every corner of cyberspace. Thompson (2004) has portrayed consumer emancipation as a "Sisyphean struggle" against "polymorphic power structures" (173). But even though Napster's cybernetic gifting technology does not release its users from the market's sign game (Napster users consume exactly the same music that the rest of the music market does, not to mention that their discourses aim at ideologically centering the music industry), it establishes an alternative exchange protocol that helps consumers contest prevailing power structures that have long organized the music marketplace and establish new patterns of power relations between music consumers and producers. Foucault (1984) has developed the urge to map out discursive fields, pieces of ideological territory with their own roles, procedures, and positions. Discourse, as the means through which the field speaks to itself, plays a major role in the operations of the field (Danaher, Schirato, and Webb 2000, 33 ). Technological innovations in turn help modify and extend fields; they help shape, drive, and constrain the ways in which different stakeholder groups play their games of truth (Foucault 1997). From a Foucauldian perspective, Napster is an antidisciplinary technology because it alters the ways in which the music industry can act upon the individual music consumer. Today's music consumers owe their ability to "take on" the recording industry to a consumer-created technology that has its roots in the invention of Napster. Since Napster, music consumers can effectively break the disciplinary bonds of copyright through cybernetic gift giving and the different ideological uses it engenders. Napster has rearranged the political economy of music by introducing an alternative technological protocol. The cybernetic gift today allows consumers to connect themselves in a different way and thus bypass certain market-institutional mechanisms. Napster's cybernetic gift economy has "rewired" what Giesler and Venkatesh (2005) refer to as the *marketplace matrix* not only on the ideological level of power discourse (Thompson 2004) as language in action (Foucault 1984) but also on the functional level of power practices with respect to technological networks in action (Fuchs 2001). Technological innovations of different kinds, this research has amply illustrated, foster the emergence of dramatic marketplace conflicts as they construct channels that empower consumers to collectively challenge societal mechanisms of discipline.

My findings concur with French sociologist Michel Serres (1980), who points out that "parasitism is the heart of relation" (52). Napster operates like an *endoparasitic consumer technology*, a parasitic technological system whose users discursively "relate to" and trouble its host, the music market system from within its own confines. Yet, rather than subverting the mainstream music market, Napster's endoparasitic gift economy functions as an insidious infection to it, nurturing itself from the recording industry's creative output, and thus fostering different ideological uses of Napster's cybernetic gift. The idea of endoparasitic consumer technology can also be expanded to incorporate other forms of technological innovations that modulate power dynamics in the marketplace. For instance, hackers frequently develop powerful technological mechanisms to challenge protection mechanisms in cable TV receivers, automobile computers, online bank accounts, or DVDs, and disseminate these antidotes to others as cybernetic gifts. And yet, endoparasitic consumer technologies do not always have to be the invention of consumers. Xerox machines, TiVo systems, or even the mp3 music file standard that preceded the invention of Napster illustrate how technological innovations from one consumer *industry* can become an endoparasitic innovation to another when consumers pick it up in formerly unprecedented ways.

## Marketplace Conflict as Disharmonic Process Performance

Second, my analysis extends Thompson's (2004) vision of marketplace conflict by interpreting music consumers' and producers' ideological accounts on Napster's cybernetic gift economy in the light of Turner's (1986) social drama theory. Different marketplace conflicts have been on the rise and of interest to researchers in consumer culture theory (Arnould and Thompson forthcoming). Yet although our literatures are rich in manifold theoretical angles on the nature and extent of consumer resistance (Thompson 2004; Firat and Venkatesh 1995; Holt 2002; Kozinets 2002; Murray and Ozanne 1991; Ozanne and Murray 1995), we know little about the actual *process*.

My research unpacks not only the discursive tensions and identity positions evolving around Napster's music marketplace conflict. Employing Turner's social drama theory, it also shows how the reordering of power relationships and status hierarchies that organize music consumers and producers plays itself out in a complex temporal rhythm of dramatic acts and scenes across four phases, each bringing dynamic shifts in scripts, characterizations, rhetoric, and symbolism. While researchers' field notes are charged with accounts of rich sequences of social interactions of conflictive, competitive, or agonistic types, our articles and books are too often limited to ontic abstractions of these processes, reduced to static concepts of social ordering at a particular point in time. This study reflects Norman Denzin's (2001) explanation that our accounts have to be dramaturgical (Goffman 1959; Lemert 1997; Branaman 1997) and performative (Turner 1986). My analysis helps initiate a shift in theoretical emphasis in the micro- and macroscopic study of marketplace conflicts and consumer behavior away from structure to process, from movement to motion, and from competence to performance. Researchers can now articulate and trace out different power resistance dynamics not only from the viewpoint of different identity positions but also in the context of historically developing dramatic technological, social, and political shifts in the course of time.

Ultimately, at the level of praxis, examining file sharing in an anthropological perspective, my analysis helps to demystify and even out the public discourse on the topic. Thus far, this discourse has focused predominantly on the economic and legal consequences of an otherwise little understood social phenomenon. In order for public policymakers to make informed decisions with regard to future technological developments, however, the cultural and political dimensions of technological innovation have to be taken into consideration. The process of technological innovation must be examined in the ideological context in which it is set. With the anthropological reading offered in my study, policy decision makers and the general public will be better informed in their strategic decision to govern the development and consumption of the discussed and other consumer technologies in the future.

## References to Chapter Two

Anderson, Benedict. 1983. *Imagined Communities: Reflection on the Origins of Nationalism*. London: Verso.

Appadurai, Arjun. 1986. *The Social Life of Things: Commodities in Cultural Perspective*. Cambridge: University of Cambridge Press.

Arnould, Eric J., and Craig J. Thompson. Forthcoming. "Consumer Culture Theory (CCT): Twenty Years of Research." *Journal of Consumer Research*.

Belk, Russell W. 1979. "Gift-Giving Behavior." *Research in Marketing* 2:95–126.

———. 1990. "How Perceptions of the Body Influence Organ Donation and Transplantation: Me and Thee versus Mine and Thine." In *Psychological Research on Organ Donation*, edited by James Shanteau and Richard J. Harris, 139–49. Washington, DC: American Psychological Association.

———. 1996. "The Perfect Gift." In *Gift Giving: A Research Anthology*, edited by Cele Otnes and Richard F. Beltramini, 59–84. Bowling Green, OH: Bowling Green State University Popular Press.

———. Forthcoming. "Exchange Taboos from an Interpretive Perspective." *Journal of Consumer Psychology*.

Belk, Russell W., and Gregory Coon. 1993. "Gift Giving as Agapic Love: An Alternative to the Exchange Paradigm Based on Dating Experiences." *Journal of Consumer Research* 20 (December): 393–417.

Belk, Russell W., Melanie Wallendorf, and John F. Sherry Jr. 1989. "The Sacred and the Profane: Theodicy on the Odyssey." *Journal of Consumer Research* 16 (June): 1–38.

Bender, Thomas. 1978. *Community and Social Change in America*. New Brunswick, NJ: Rutgers University Press.

Bourdieu, Pierre. 1977. *Outline of a Theory of Practice*. Cambridge: Cambridge University Press.

Branaman, Ann. 1997. "Goffman's Social Theory." In *The Goffman Reader*, edited by Charles Lemert and Ann Branaman. Malden, MA: Blackwell.

Caillé, Alain. 2001. "The Double Inconceivability of the Pure Gift." *Angelaki, Journal of Theoretical Humanities* 6 (August 2): 23–39.

Castells, Manuel. 1996. *The Information Age: Economy, Society and Culture*. Vol. 1: *The Rise of the Network Society*. Oxford: Blackwell.

Cheal, David. 1988. *The Gift Economy*. New York: Routledge.

Danaher, Geoff, Tony Schirato and Jennifer Webb. 2000. *Understanding Foucault*. Thousand Oaks, CA: Sage.

Denzin, Norman. 2001. "The Seventh Moment: A Qualitative Inquiry and the Practice of a More Radical Consumer Research." *Journal of Consumer Research* 28:324–30.

———. 2003. *Performance Ethnography: Critical Pedagogy and the Politics of Culture*. Thousand Oaks, CA: Sage.

Deleuze, Gilles, and Felix Guattari. 1987. *A Thousand Plateaus: Capitalism and Schizophrenia*. Minneapolis: University of Minnesota Press.

Derrida, Jacques. 1994. *Given Time 1: Counterfeit Money*. Chicago: University of Chicago Press.

Firat, A. Fuat, and Alladi Venkatesh. 1995. "Liberatory Postmodernism and the Reenchantment of Consumption." *Journal of Consumer Research* 22 (December).

Fischer, Eileen, and Stephen J. Arnold. 1990. "More Than a Labor of Love: Gender Roles and Christmas Gift Shopping." *Journal of Consumer Research* 17, no. 3 (December): 333–45.

Foucault, Michel. 1984. *Power/Knowledge: Selected Interviews and Other Writings: 1972–1977*. Edited by Colin Gordon. New York: Pantheon University Press.

———. 1997. "The Abnormals." In *Michel Foucault Ethics: Subjectivity and Truth, Vol. 1*, edited by Paul Rabinow, 51–58. London: Penguin Press.

Fuchs, Stephan. 2001. *Against Essentialism: A Theory of Society and Culture*. Cambridge, MA: Harvard University Press.

Giesler, Markus, and Mali Pohlmann. 2003a. "The Anthropology of File Sharing: Consuming Napster as a Gift." In *Advances in Consumer Research*, edited by Punam Anand Keller and Dennis W. Rook, 30. Valdosta, GA: Association for Consumer Research.

———. 2003b. "The Social Form of Napster: Cultivating the Paradox of Consumer Emancipation." In *Advances in Consumer Research*, edited by Punam Anand Keller and Dennis W. Rook, 30. Valdosta, GA: Association for Consumer Research.

Giesler, Markus, and Alladi Venkatesh. 2004. "Consuming Cyborgs: Researching Posthuman Consumer Culture." Special Session Summary, in *Advances in*

*Consumer Research,* edited by Barbara Kahn and Mary Frances Luce, 31. Valdosta, GA: Association for Consumer Research.

———. 2005. "Reframing the Embodied Consumer as Cyborg: A Posthumanist Epistemology of Consumption." In *Advances in Consumer Research,* edited by Geeta Menon and Akshay R. Rao, 32. Provo, UT: Association for Consumer Research.

Glazer, Rashi. 1995. "Consumer Behavior in High Technology Markets." In *Advances in Consumer Research,* edited by Frank Kardes and Mita Sujan, 22. Valdosta, GA: Association for Consumer Research.

Goffman, Erving. 1959. *The Presentation of Self in Everyday Life.* New York: Doubleday.

Gouldner, Alvin W. 1960. "The Norm of Reciprocity: A Preliminary Statement." *American Sociological Review* 25:176–77.

Haraway, Donna. 1991. "A Cyborg Manifesto: Science, Technology, and Socialist-Feminism in the Late Twentieth Century." In *Simians, Cyborgs and Women: The Reinvention of Nature,* 149–81. New York: Routledge.

Harrison, Simon. 1992. "Ritual as Intellectual Property." *Man* (New Series): 225–44.

Hemetsberger, Andrea. 2002. "Fostering Cooperation on the Internet: Social Exchange Processes in Innovative Virtual Communities." *Advances of Consumer Research* 29:354–56.

Holt, Douglas B. 2002. "Why Do Brands Cause Trouble: A Dialectical Theory of Consumer Culture and Branding." *Journal of Consumer Research* 29 (June): 70–90.

Hyde, Lewis. 1983. *The Gift: Imagination and the Erotic Life of Property.* New York: Vintage.

Iacobucci, D., ed. 1996. *Networks in Marketing.* Thousand Oaks, CA: Sage.

Jenkins, Henry. 1992. *Textual Poachers: Television Fans and Participatory Culture.* New York: Routledge.

Joy, Annamma. 2001. "Gift Giving in Hong Kong and the Continuum of Social Ties." *Journal of Consumer Research* 28 (September): 239–56.

Komter, A. 1996. *The Gift: An Interdisciplinary Perspective.* Amsterdam, Netherlands: Amsterdam University Press.

———. 2004. "Gratitude and Gift Exchange." In *The Psychology of Gratitude,* edited by R. A. Emmons and M. E. McCullough, 195–213. New York: Oxford University Press.

Kosky, Jeffrey L. 1997. "The Disqualification of Intentionality: The Gift in Derrida." Emmanuel Levinas, and Michael Henry, *Philosophy Today* 41 (Supplement): 186–97.

Kozinets, Robert V. 2002. "Can Consumers Escape the Market? Emancipatory Illuminations from Burning Man." *Journal of Consumer Research* 29 (June): 20–38.

Lemert, Charles. 1997. "Goffman." In *The Goffman Reader,* edited by Charles Lemert and Ann Branaman. Malden, MA: Blackwell.

Levi-Strauss, Claude. 1965. "The Principle of Reciprocity." In *Sociological Theory*, edited by L. A. Coser and B. Rosenberg. New York: Macmillan.

Marx, Karl. 1867/1946. *Capital*. New York: Everyman's Library.

Marx, Karl, and Friedrich Engels. 1848/1999. *The Communist Manifesto*. New York: St. Martin's Press.

Malinowski, Bronislaw. 1922/1961. *Argonauts of the Western Pacific*. New York: E. P. Dutton.

Mauss, Marcel. 1925/1967. *The Gift: Forms and Functions of Exchange in Archaic Societies*, edited by Ian Cunnison. New York: Norton.

————. 1950. *Sociologie et Anthropologie*. Paris: Presses Universitaires de France.

Mick, David Glen. 1996. "Self-Gifts" In *Gift Giving*, edited by Cele Otnes and Richard F. Beltramini, 99–122. Bowling Green, OH: Bowling Green State University Popular Press.

Mick, David Glen, and Michelle DeMoss. 1990. "Self-Gifts: Phenomenological Insights from Four Contexts." *Journal of Consumer Research* 17 (December): 322–32.

Mick, David Glen, and Susan Fournier. 1998. "Paradoxes of Technology: Consumer Cognizance, Emotions, and Coping Strategies." *Journal of Consumer Research* 25 (September): 123–43.

Muniz, Albert M., and Thomas C. O'Guinn. 2001. "Brand Community." *Journal of Consumer Research* 27 (March): 412–32.

Murray, Jeff B., and Julie L. Ozanne. 1991. "The Critical Imagination: Emancipatory Interests in Consumer Research." *Journal of Consumer Research* 18 (September): 129–44.

Noonan, John T. 1984. *Bribes*. Berkeley: University of California Press.

O'Neill, John. 2001. "The Time(s) of the Gift." *Angelaki: Journal of the Theoretical Humanities* 6, 2 (September) 41—48.

Otnes, Cele, Tina M. Lowrey, and Young Chan Kim. 1993. "Gift Selection for Easy and Difficult Recipients: A Social Roles Interpretation." *Journal of Consumer Research* 20 (September): 229–44.

Ozanne, Julie, and Jeff Murray. 1995. "Uniting Critical Theory and Public Policy to Create the Reflexively Defiant Consumer." *American Behavioral Scientist* 38 (February): 516–25.

Rheingold, Howard. 1993. *The Virtual Community: Homesteading on the Electronic Frontier*. Reading, MA: Addison-Wesley.

Ruth, Julie A., Cele C. Otnes, and Frederic F. Brunel. 1999. "Gift Receipt and the Reformulation of Interpersonal Relationships." *Journal of Consumer Research* 25:385–402.

Sahlins, Marshall. 1972. *Stone Age Economics*. New York: Aldien de Gruyter.

Schieffelin, Edward. 1980. "Reciprocity and the Construction of Reality" *Man* 15, no. 3: 502–17.

Serres, Michel. 1980. *La Parasite*. Paris: Grasset.

Sherry, John F., Jr. 1983. "Gift Giving in Anthropological Perspective." *Journal of Consumer Research* 10 (September): 157–68.

———. 2000. "Place, Technology, and Representation." *Journal of Consumer Research* 27, no. 2: 273–78.

Sherry, John F., Jr., Mary Ann McGrath, and Sidney J. Levy. 1995. "Monadic Giving: Anatomy of Gifts Given to the Self." In *Contemporary Marketing and Consumer Behavior: An Anthropological Sourcebook,* edited by John F. Sherry Jr., 399–432. Thousand Oaks, CA: Sage.

Shields, Rob. 1996. *Cultures of Internet.* Thousand Oaks, CA: Sage.

Smith, Marc, and Peter Kollock. 1998. *Communities in Cyberspace.* London: Routledge.

Thompson, Craig J. 1994. "Unfulfilled Promises and Personal Confessions: A Postpositivist Inquiry into the Idealized and Experienced Meanings of Consumer Technology." In *Advances in Consumer Research,* edited by C. Allen and D. R. John, 104–8. Provo, UT: Association for Consumer Research.

———. 2004. "Marketplace Mythology and Discourses of Power." *Journal of Consumer Research* 31 (June): 162–80.

Titmuss, Richard M. 1992. *The Gift Relationship: From Human Blood to Social Policy.* London: Allen & Unwin.

Turner, Victor. 1957. *Schism and Continuity in an African Society: A Study of Ndembu Village Life.* Manchester, UK: Manchester University Press.

———. 1969. *The Ritual Process: Structure and Anti-Structure.* Chicago: Aldine de Gruyter.

———. 1986. *The Anthropology of Performance.* New York: PAJ.

Twersky, Isadore. 1980. *Introduction to the Code of Maimonides (Mishneh Torah).* New Haven, CT: Yale University Press.

Vaughan, Geneviève. 1997. *For-Giving: A Feminist Criticism of Exchange.* Austin, TX: Plain View Press.

Venkatesh, Alladi. 1998. "Cyberculture: Consumers and Cybermarketscapes." In *Servicescapes: The Concept of Place in Contemporary Markets,* edited by John F. Sherry Jr., 343–75. Chicago: NTC Business Books.

Venkatesh, Alladi, Laurie Meamber, and A. Fuat Firat. 1997. "Cyberspace as the Next Marketing Frontier(?)." In *Consumer Research: Postcards from the Edge,* edited by Stephen Brown and Darach Turley, 300–21. London: Routledge.

Weiner, Annette. 1992. *Inalienable Possessions: The Paradox of Keeping while Giving.* Berkeley: University of California Press.

CHAPTER THREE

# Do U Produce?: Subcultural Capital and Amateur Musicianship in Peer-to-Peer Networks

## Andrew Whelan

This chapter offers a modest ethnographic account of interaction in musical communities online. The focus is on the consequences of CMC (computer mediated communication) becoming integrated into the traditional "career," in Becker's (1963) sense, of the "amateur" electronic musician. Specifically, it explores the use of peer-to-peer (p2p) distribution networks by "bedroom" electronic producers for the purposes of musical learning, exchange, and "professional" advancement in terms of distribution and the like. Through analyzing "real-time" interaction online in a number of "communities of sound" associated with a p2p network, I hope to show how p2p is experienced and utilized by musicians. In particular, I hope to sketch out some of the implications of such interactions for our conceptions of "subcultures," musical learning, and the uses of p2p itself.

## Situating the Research: P2p and "IDM"

P2p is a form of decentralized, distributed networking, as opposed to hierarchical, "client/server" networking, allowing users who have the appropriate software installed to duplicate files directly across the network. Effectively, p2p devolves responsibility and control onto users themselves, in the following ways: firstly, direct connections between users and file duplication across the network eliminate "server fatigue," the tendency for central servers to crash when subject to multiple requests for the same file. Secondly, with regard to the law, "the time-consuming process of seeking permission from copyright holders on a song-by-song basis [is] avoided by having users post songs themselves and, more importantly, holding users responsible for adhering to copyright law" (Woodworth 2004, 163).

Thus, p2p users themselves constantly update a potentially limitless catalogue, which is, because decentralized, easily accessible—unlike the cumbersome centralized distribution models advocated by the industry. The combination of these features makes it clear why p2p became a source of concern for the industry oligopoly of the "Big Four" (Universal, Sony-BMG, EMI, and Warner Brothers), who account for some 80% of music sales globally. The recording industry reaction was, notoriously, forceful; as one industry insider put it, "we are going to strangle this baby at birth" (Kretschmer, Klimis, and Wallis 2001, 426). The strategy for doing so was fourfold: lobbying (successfully) for extended intellectual property rights; litigating against p2p platforms and users in a strategy dubbed "fear and awe" (Parker 2003); developing technological restrictions to digital reproduction; and mounting a PR campaign against the "epidemic" of "piracy" which, as Seagram (Universal's parent company) CEO Edgar Bronfman put it, is threatening our "principles of law, justice and civilization" (Kretschmer et al. 2001, 434). The rhetoric of this campaign conflates the language of moral degeneracy ("thieving" and "piracy") with that of (sexual) hygiene; p2p is depicted as a "viral" disease, leading to rampant reproduction of illegitimate files, which are, moreover, rife with contagious computer viruses (Woodworth 2004, 179–80).

From the perspective of fans, the threat was that p2p would "kill" music. The industry's lobbying body, the RIAA (Recording Industry Association of America), argued that p2p use was directly implicated in falling CD sales (Caney 2002). However, even by the RIAA's own figures, whether or not this was the case remains uncertain. Recent research suggests that the effect of file sharing on CD sales is "statistically indistinguishable from zero" (Oberholzer and Strumpf 2004, 4). The debate, and the industry's conservative response to the new technology, is a replay of previous clashes between consumers and elements of the global entertainment industry, most notably, the "home-taping" controversy over audiocassettes in the 1970s. In that instance, the RIAA succeeded in getting a levy implemented on sales of blank cassettes—the implication being, as "plunderphonic" musician John Oswald pointed out—that even if the cassette is used to record "baby's first words," the "Big 4" are still entitled to recompense for lost revenue (Jones 1995).

Despite the widely publicized legal clampdown, p2p now dominates Internet traffic. It is estimated that for every legally downloaded song, 250 "pirated" files are exchanged (MacDonald 2004). Over a billion music files are downloaded every week from p2p networks (Oberholzer and Strumpf 2004, 2). The Electronic Frontier Foundation estimates that over 60 million Americans use p2p programs (Sherman 2003). With 84% of users unwilling to pay to download music, the onus of proof as to why they *should* still lies with the industry (Buquet 2003). Regardless of the unfolding moral and legal issues (see chapter 1, this volume), from the perspective of music *fans*, p2p provides a revolutionary resource for the exchange of music and information about music. For the recording industry, artists, and fans alike, p2p has become a fact of the "audioscape" (Lovering 1998, 46).

Whilst much ink has been spilt on the possible repercussions of p2p for the recording industry, less is known about how the technology of p2p, now naturalized as an everyday part of many people's lives, has been adopted by particular musical "subcultures." In what follows, I hope to illustrate some of the ways in which p2p is being used by "bedroom producers,"[1] drawing on ethnographic fieldwork carried out from May 2003 to February 2004. The focus of this research is on how technologies of music production and distribution are being incorporated into the practices of "ordinary" fans, and particularly, how such fans begin making music.

In the course of this research, I sought to immerse myself in what Kendall (2002) describes as a "partly compatible setting" (244–45). Broadly speaking, I am from a similar demographic background as many of those "native" to the field (albeit a few years older). I also have a long-standing interest in music, particularly electronic music. Consequently, I was relatively familiar with the bodies of work, and more importantly, the subcultural discourses around them, specific to the communities in question. Being there to learn, my interaction was initially limited and purposive, and for the most part the focus here is on observed interaction. I sometimes came across language and discourse I found objectionable, but I do not see my role there as being, as Bell (2001) puts it, "to intervene in the lives of participants to enhance their well-being" (199). Rather, it is to investigate the micro-social, seemingly mundane activity of fans and "amateur" musicians and the discourses surrounding this activity, and to attempt an assessment of how such activity and discourse might best be understood.

On the p2p network under discussion, out of around 250 chatrooms, the most populous was a hip-hop room with an average of just over 600 users.[2] The material cited below, though, originates in the "ragga jungle" and "Breakcore" rooms, both of which had approximately 50 occupants at any given time. For the uninitiated, one way to conceptualize the social groupings around these relatively obscure subgenres is as intersecting "regimes of value" (Appadurai 1986, 4; Hollows and Milestone 1998, 89). What they share is a prioritization of rhythmic and percussive intensity and complexity. Ragga jungle initially came to mass attention in the U.K. in the early '90s at the height of "rave," fusing "hardcore" breakbeats with bass-lines and vocal samples derived from dub and reggae. Breakcore (the name is a contraction of "breakbeat" and "hardcore") emerged in the late '90s, bringing "together elements of drum and bass, hardcore techno, rhythmic noise, illbient and 'IDM,' into a breakbeat-oriented sound that encourages speed, complexity, and maximum sonic density."[3] What is worth bearing in mind about these related styles is that they both eschew the looped, 4/4 "basic disco rhythm" of house and techno (Toynbee 2000).

My interest in these genres is twofold: firstly, the emphasis on speed and complexity entails a high degree of investment in terms of time and concentration to produce. Learning to successfully sequence such music can be difficult; therefore, how "competent members" become such warrants scrutiny. Moreover, at the risk of falling into the trap of the "mainstream"/"underground" binary, these genres are not widely commercially successful; hence, the discourses of oppositional "authenticity" around them display many of the characteristics traditionally of interest to subcultural theorists. Secondly, having been (somewhat peripherally) involved in the English free-party movement of the early and mid-1990s, witnessing its politicization and ultimate retreat as an effect of the 1994 Criminal Justice and Public Order Act, I am interested in how the "intense, frenetically percussive soundscape" to this movement has been disseminated in the intervening years (Gilbert and Pearson 1999, 79).[4] As we shall see, jungle, originating in the ethnically mixed inner cities and suburbs of London, Bristol, and Birmingham, has been taken up and developed by musicians from all over the industrialized world.

## Subcultural Theory and Subcultural Capital

In order to contextualize how this came about, it is worth elaborating on some of the theoretical perspectives that have been deployed to account for subcultural activity. The pioneering texts of British subcultural theory (Hebdige 1979; Hall and Jefferson 1976) originated in the Birmingham Center for Contemporary Cultural Studies (CCCS) in the mid-1970s. Following Gramsci, the CCCS describes "dominant culture" as hegemonic: having the capacity to ideologically subsume those in a subordinate social position. From this perspective, subcultural stylistic features (such as skinhead apparel) are semiotic "messages" articulating symbolic (and for the CCCS, class-based) resistance. Such "homological" arguments are a common explanatory device. Gilbert and Pearson (1999), for instance, deliver a homological account in describing the "loose, asexual clothing typical of acid house dancers" as "an active refusal of the highly sexualized discourses of style culture, with all of their perceived closeness to Thatcherism" (166). Similar homological arguments have been made about aural aesthetics, for instance, "lo-fi" (Grajeda 2002), and "the decline of figure and rise of ground" in dance musics (Tagg 1994). According to the CCCS, stylistic signifiers (be they oversize jeans, Rizla cigarette papers, or what have you) are "consumed" by the masses, but "appropriated," in an inherently oppositional way, by subcultures.

The account furnished by the CCCS, though, is problematic insofar as it gestures towards an "authentic" moment of subcultural/stylistic creativity, of "semiotic guerrilla warfare," supposed to occur prior to "commercial diffusion/defusion" (Brown 2003, 213). This subversive innovation is conceptualized as occurring before the style has been, in Gramscian terms, "incorporated," thus rendering inexplicable how and why the style gained momentum. An "authentic" subcultural "truth," antecedent to the market—and more pertinently, the media—is surely a naïve political fiction. Such an account elides the existence of subcultural markets and media, in part because it tends to valorize subculture as subversive and resistant, operating through symbolically radical "signifying practices." As Larry Grossberg justifiably wonders, "if everyone's going around resisting all the time, why are we losing?" (Wilson-Brown and McCarthy 1999, 346). A further limitation of the CCCS approach is the danger of overdetermination, of depicting aesthetic practice as "cloaking a social game of which the actors are not aware" (Hennion 2001, 5). "Taste" is not merely an index of social position; rather, subjectivity and aesthetic practice are mutually constitutive.

In stark contrast, Sarah Thornton does not see subcultures as being in opposition to a dominant hegemonic ideology. Rather, social groups use subcultural ideologies to differentiate themselves from other groups. The "mainstream," Thornton suggests, "would seem to be yet another niche culture—one positioned as the norm" (1995, 108). Thornton's *subcultural capital* perspective, derived from Bourdieu (1984), abandons the fallacy that subcultures are inherently politically radical. Bourdieu departs from classical "reductionist" Marxism in distinguishing social, cultural, and economic capital, with subcategories of capital that operate within particular fields, such as "political," "intellectual," and so on. These distinct forms of capital function according to their own distributive logics; the "overarching field, of which these narrower fields are subsets, is the field of power" (Stahl 2003, 32). Social capital, according to Thornton (1995), is "*who* you know (and who knows you)," while cultural capital is knowledge "accumulated through upbringing and education which confers social status" (10). The "cultivated disposition" that indicates cultural capital is "revealed in the nature of the cultural goods consumed" (Bourdieu 1984, 13). Like cultural capital, subcultural capital can "be *objectified* or *embodied*"; instantiated in slang, physical mannerisms, clothing, possessions, and so on (Thornton 1995, 11).

Bourdieu's work goes some way towards rendering multidimensional forms of social differentiation theoretically intelligible. Cultural capital is an "ideological resource" mobilized in the struggle for social status (Weinzierl and Muggleton 2003, 9). Thornton's conception of subcultural capital, however, advances Bourdieu insofar as subcultural capital is no longer necessarily mapped back onto sociocultural variables (specifically, class). Subcultural social distinctions, Thornton (1995) argues, willfully obscure class differentiation: "subcultural capital is the linchpin of an alternative hierarchy in which the axes of age, gender, sexuality and race are all employed in order to keep the determinations of class, income and occupation at bay. Interestingly, the social logic of subcultural capital reveals itself most clearly by what it dislikes and by what it emphatically isn't" (105). Which is to say, subcultural capital is often articulated oppositionally with reference to the "phony" or "sellout." For example, ragga jungle or breakcore "authenticity" is in part defined by its relationship to "commercial" drum and bass, to other (sub-)cultural formations, and beyond this, to a vague, indefinite abstraction of "the mainstream."

From within, subcultural ideology serves to reinterpret the existent social order, repositioning those who are usually socially subordinate (in particular, young men). Subcultural capital is a discursive means of "distinction," articulated through specialized knowledge. Those in possession of subcultural capital are conversant with, and able to an extent to define, the parameters of "cool," thereby accruing subcultural status. How subcultural capital is elaborated varies contextually, but possessing it implies knowing what is (and *being*) "hip," and displaying this ineffable knowledge in ways that render the possession of it seemingly intuitive; it is well expressed in the comment attributed to Louis Armstrong: "Man, if you gotta ask, you'll never know."

Thornton's development of Bourdieu is a significant advance in subcultural theory, insofar as it opens up the possibility of investigating intra-cultural conflict and competition. It does so, however, at the risk of overemphasizing the hierarchical nature of subculture by foregrounding the internal struggle for "cool" status (Weinzierl and Muggleton 2003, 12–13). Unlike the CCCS, Thornton (1995) problematizes subcultural difference and distinction: "If one considers the function of difference within an ever more finely graded social structure, its political tendencies become more ambiguous" (166). The risk of this interrogation, though, is that subcultures become reduced to competitive hierarchies, as "however 'radical' a group may consider their particular practice to be, in truth they are merely trying to accumulate subcultural capital at the expense of the unhip" (Gilbert and Pearson 1999, 159–60). Despite these possible shortcomings, the concept of subcultural capital is something I hope to develop with reference to p2p; it provides the "subculturalist" ethnographer with a useful conceptual framework for the analysis of aesthetically aligned social groups.

## Subcultural Capital on P2p

Chatroom participants on p2p are mostly young men—male p2p users outnumber females by around two to one (Jones and Lenhart 2004, 190). There is also, as Kendall (2002) suggests, a "default assumption of whiteness online" (210). This assumption incorporates normative heterosexism and the subtle elaboration of a regulatory class position: "IDM is a community heavily composed of young guys who have internet connections in their bedrooms—totally scary in other words."[5] Chatroom interaction itself possesses a number of idiosyncrasies consequent on the nature of the medium itself: abrupt conversational pauses and "lags" are commonplace, as are overlapping sets of responses as two or more participants type simultaneously. Also, the communicative style of chatroom interaction tends to appear more confrontational than that which occurs offline, with higher levels of profanity and apparent aggression. This is often attributed to the limited social "bandwidth" of CMC—the absence of audiovisual cues such as intonation, gesture, and so forth (Shaw 1997, 135). Such disinhibited interaction has been described in terms of a "reduced social cues" model of CMC (Sproull and Kiesler 1991). What is more interesting for current purposes, as will be shown shortly, is the ritualized form that these exchanges take, and the norms that govern them.

Individuals using p2p can be said to display subcultural capital through two principal means: the music in their "share" (that is, their mp3 collection) and their textual interaction. In relation to the latter, subcultural capital is articulated idiomatically and linguistically through displays of easy familiarity with the musical "canon" of the chatroom in question, the use of diverse subcultural argots, and an enthusiasm for transgressing the bounds of acceptable bourgeois conversational decorum. In relation to the former—the music collection— Straw (1997) has argued that such collections "are seen as both public displays of power/knowledge and private refuges from the sexual or social world; as either structures of control or the by-products of irrational and fetishistic obsession; as material evidence of the homosocial information-mongering which is one underpinning of male power and compensatory undertakings by those unable to wield that power" (4). Thus, a comprehensive, well-ordered mp3 archive, a primary means of displaying subcultural capital, can be read as simultaneously a "cool" form of subcultural mastery and, in another sense, as an indicator of a certain (specifically masculine) form of social incompetence.[6] At best, the downloader is seen as a cool scavenger, trawling through the niche oddities of commodity culture, at worst, an obsessional, potentially deviant misfit.

This ambiguity or double nature of subcultural capital is reproduced in chatroom interaction, and also compounded by collision or amalgamation of frames of reference or "repertoires" (Gilbert and Mulkay 1984, 90). A measure of social success for chatroom occupants is the extent to which they successfully negotiate and articulate specific forms of subcultural capital *and* high degrees of technological competence. These two forms of knowledge mastery and the discursive repertoires through which they are elucidated (socially coded as "cool" and "nerdy" respectively) are, in fact, in dialectical relation to each other.[7] Both are based on the cultivation of knowledge, on "the mastery of a symbolic field" (Straw 1997, 9); be that encyclopedic knowledge of the body of work that constitutes a genre, or accomplished technological literacy. However, the social status ascribed in one case is the opposite of that in the other; certain forms of intellectual or technological competence are often seen to result in a devaluation of social status. Yet to produce music effectively (and thereby accrue subcultural capital) requires a high level of technological competence. Subcultural capital and technological competence are thus inextricably linked. "Nerd-dom" is the underside of subcultural capital, the "square" within.[8]

The repertoire of technological competence, which runs in uneasy parallel or conjunction with that of subcultural "cool," is elaborated through sophisticated knowledge of aspects of music production, the use of unelaborated technical shorthands and acronyms, and so on. It is possible and permissible to jump from one repertoire to the other, or indeed, for those merely "passing through" rooms, to refrain from either. However, deliberately highlighting the ambiguous disjunction between the two (generally achieved with the accusation "nerd") is invariably received poorly. Group members carefully maintain the attitudes and norms of collective self-presentation underlying specific subcultural repertoires. Consider the following two extracts from the Breakcore room, which are illustrative of a well-established routine in which a newcomer inquires as to what, exactly, breakcore is:

Extract 1: Breakcore room 10/08/03[9]
[dfksdiholsdoih] is breakcore hardcore breaks?
[[Ci@iCo]] yes
[[Ci@iCo]] with piano
[r4t4t4c] it's a bit of granny snares and safary kick
[[Ci@iCo]] yes
[Fas3r3d] is it ment to be 32 seconds long
[[Ci@iCo]] those are foundamental and mainly instruments in break core
[[Ci@iCo]] for sure
[r4t4t4c] what about breakcore attitude
[r4t4t4c] have to spit on fluff core :)
[MonkSinSpace] leather jackets with pink socks and a tie with flowers
[r4t4t4c] oh
[r4t4t4c] i mistook
[r4t4t4c] :)
[MonkSinSpace] its written in the breakcore code
[MonkSinSpace] how to be breakcore

The routine closes with the joke "MonkSinSpace" offers, which is a joke precisely because it draws attention to the ineffability of subcultural capital: "insiders" (which is to say, those possessing subcultural capital) all "know" what "breakcore attitude" is, it is so self-evident that we merely have to follow the mythical "breakcore code" (again, "if you gotta ask, you'll never know").

Extract 2: Breakcore room 11/02/03
[Nomorph] what kind of music is break core?
[Nomorph] can you gimme an example artist?
[touchtoi] no
[Nomorph] great

[touchtoi] yes maybe
[touchtoi] that is breakcore

Note that "touchtoi" defines the refusal of an illustrative definition as itself a definition, rendering the refusal an indirect speech act about "breakcore attitude": "the message itself is interactionally produced in the very course of the exchange" (Hutchby 2001, 75). Here, group membership, by definition, implies knowing what breakcore is, knowing "how to be breakcore." Conversely, those who don't know, and reveal their ignorance in attempting to find out, are excluded. Hence Thornton's findings are borne out: subcultural capital is used by those in possession of it to, among other things, establish and negotiate social hierarchy. These features of the specialized knowledge that constitutes subcultural capital are so commonplace that they are regularly parodied:

Extract 3: Breakcore room 07/27/03
[Torasaburo_Kobayashi] don't be silly, everyone knows you can't possibly make "breakcore" without really obscure tracker software that only runs on modified Polish Macintoshes.

"Being breakcore" is a cohesive, well-formed conversational repertoire, and such repertoires are ways of both ordering and representing the world and its contents, and performing and presenting identity. Different subcultural repertoires dominate in different rooms, as evidenced by the preponderance of Jamaican patois in the ragga jungle room, or the attitude of studied indifference in the Breakcore room. Other rooms similarly have their own expressive mannerisms and idiosyncrasies of deportment. Deploying the "wrong" repertoire in a chatroom is an embarrassing faux pas, as evidenced by the following:

Extract 4: Breakcore room 07/30/03
[dystop] you heard ne john. me and my two pals listened to the amenloop (you know the one in no remorse) for 12 hours straight.[10]
[dystop] and now it's fucking 0900. gnight.
[DeathBreathing] HAHAHA
[b-bOy_MASTA-fLy] hi all
[b-bOy_MASTA-fLy] :)
[b-bOy_MASTA-fLy] whats up
[b-bOy_MASTA-fLy] ?
[DeathBreathing] yo
[b-bOy_MASTA-fLy] :)
[b-bOy_MASTA-fLy] som1 wanna trade BREAK VIDEOS
[b-bOy_MASTA-fLy] ?
[DeathBreathing] i dont have any

[b-bOy_MASTA-fLy] whats is this chanel
[b-bOy_MASTA-fLy] ?
[b-bOy_MASTA-fLy] for what?
[DeathBreathing] breakcore
[b-bOy_MASTA-fLy] whats is this
[b-bOy_MASTA-fLy] BREAK CORE?
[A9010] hahaha
[DeathBreathing] uh oh
[b-bOy_MASTA-fLy] . . . BREAKDANCING CORE?
[DeathBreathing] no
[b-bOy_MASTA-fLy] :PPpPPp
[A9010] are you drunk ?
[A9010] i think yes . . .
[DeathBreathing] hes gone

Here, "b-bOy_MASTA-fLy" has mistakenly wandered into the Breakcore room. His name alone is sufficient to give away his subcultural allegiance. Few room occupants were willing to become entangled in this confusion; "Death-Breathing" expresses his mortified incredulity that breakcore could be confused with anything—which, for breakcore dilettantes, would be as hopelessly déclassé as break-dancing. Discrete subcultural styles are invariably in "cooler-than-thou" competition: "subcultural affiliation and hostility to those who do not adhere to your homological inclinations is a badge of commitment; a means of signifying a degree of passion and involvement" (Gilbert and Pearson 1999, 26). P2p chat-rooms are bounded social spaces, and those boundaries are policed.

## The Careers of "Bedroom" Producers

One way of elaborating upon this policing is through analyzing how amateur musicians utilize p2p. One regularly sees such musicians approaching rooms in an effort to gain listeners. For instance:

Extract 5: Breakcore room 11/23/03
[Fas3r3d][11] i just finished my newest track brutha
[Fas3r3d] wana chek it?
[oldman] yeah hook it up

Extract 6: ragga jungle room 09/09/03
[Preecha] hello
[Preecha] I just put a new 25 tune mix for you guys in my folder
[Preecha] the tracklisting is in my personal info
[cvao] WENAS
[cvao] PREECHA

Extract 7: ragga jungle room, 11/23/03
[bumbaclot selektah] check out the choon called gem sound 2003
[scottfrohawk] grabbn it
[bumbaclot selektah] lemme know what ya think
[scottfrohawk] ok
[scottfrohawk] what are you using to produce
[bumbaclot selektah] its not finished yet, but id say its my best work so far
[scottfrohawk] cool
[bumbaclot selektah] for that i used soundforge and fruity loops[12]
[Babylon_Demolitionist] mind if I nab it?
[scottfrohawk] how many tracks do you haev done
[bumbaclot selektah] go for it bro
[bumbaclot selektah] i want some feedback!!!
[bumbaclot selektah] ive got like 8 to 10 complete tracks of my own
[Babylon_Demolitionist] alright zen!!!
[scottfrohawk] nice

However, there is a fine line between asking for feedback and "spamming," and this is often pointed out to those who are considered to be too enthusiastically plugging their own work:

Extract 8: Breakcore room 09/27/03
[Fas3r3d] wuzup homies
[Fas3r3d] anyone from MIAMI, FLORIDA, USA???
[NoizHed] dude your spamming every room im in
[Fas3r3d] lol
[Fas3r3d] im not spamming dude
[Fas3r3d] imjust bored
[Fas3r3d] =]

It is evident from this exchange that "NoizHed" has just seen "Fas3r3d" in another room, perhaps "advertising" his music. NoizHed's interjection is designed to preempt the guerrilla marketing he suspects is imminent. P2p users, in fact, seem quite sensitive to self-promotion of this form, where the sensitivity is more or less inversely proportional to the amount of time the user spends online; "veteran" chatroom occupants will tend to be those who react most sharply to unsolicited promotion.

Extract 9: Breakcore room 07/28/03
[beatfreak13709] hi, I write this since you might be interested, on www.orbo.ws you can find freejazz/metal from Germany, it goes in the directions of Meshuggah, Dillinger Escape Plan or Neck.
[dystop] why would we be interested in stuff thats not even remotly connected to breakcore?

[beatfreak13709] mmh I think it is, cause the stuff is completely instumental and based on fast odd time signatures
[dystop] you suck
[beatfreak13709] sorry man and fuck you

In Extract 9 above, interaction rapidly breaks down, leading to the departure of "beatfreak13709" immediately after the exchange cited. The objection "dystop" raises is framed in terms of beatfreak13709's offer being "off-topic" and therefore situationally inappropriate. However, this is not the entire reason such propositions are so routinely rejected.

There is a right way and a wrong way to garner support within rooms: unsolicited requests from strangers are poorly received because participatory "dues" must be "paid"; users are reluctant to download something about which they know nothing, from a producer who is simply, as one musician put it to me, "trying to whore" their music to anyone they think might listen.[13] In order to gain listeners, one must be conversant with the set of aesthetic priorities that constitute the genre with which the room is affiliated—which is to say, one must spend some time in the room. This is why unsolicited requests for listeners so often receive negative reactions. Just as in the offline world, it is necessary to spend some time participating to receive the benefits of group membership. We can see this if we return to the case of Fas3r3d, in a conversation that occurred at a time between the two already cited (Extracts 5 and 8)

Extract 10: Fas3r3d, 10/20/03
[AW] but when i get it i'll let you know what i reckon. has anyone else heard it?
[Fas3r3d] yea a couple of people have heard it, oldman blaerg and rtd edge and some other peeps
. . .
[AW] what did they reckon?
[Fas3r3d] they liked it told me to make more and send to their label
[AW] cool
[Fas3r3d] :]

If we put these extracts featuring Fas3r3d in sequential order, we can trace his admission into the Breakcore room community. On the 27th of September (Extract 8), he is admonished before even entering into dialogue: NoizHed tells him, "dude your spamming every room im in." A month later, on the 20th of October, he is able to tell me that he successfully got feedback from "blaerg," "oldman," and "rTD_EdgE" (three regular and active participants in the room at that time). We can be sure that the time Fas3r3d invested in participating in the room and getting to know its occupants resulted in a reciprocal return on their part, because a month after that, on the 23rd of November (Extract 5), when Fas3r3d informed the room he had produced "fresh" material, the immediate response from oldman was "yeah hook it up." Through becoming a member of the group, Fas3r3d establishes direct personal contact with other musicians who are in a position to actually release his material as a commodity.

I want to illustrate this further by going upstream, as it were, looking at the outset of a musician's "career" as it is facilitated by p2p. The musician in question, a 17-year-old named "kaffiend," is a ragga jungle room regular.

> Extract 11: ragga jungle room, 10/03/03
> [kaffiend] can somebody help me realquick?
> [kaffiend] im having trouble with reason liscence number

Kaffiend has downloaded a "pirated" version of Reason, a music software package (which retails for $499). Dave Smith, the inventor of the Midi interface, estimates that between 80 and 90% of all such software in use is similarly "pirated" (Mackintosh 2003). What kaffiend is looking for in Extract 11 is a "keygen," a piece of software that will generate a registration key with which to authenticate Reason on his computer. The software is designed so as to be inoperable unless so authenticated, but enterprising ("hacking") electronic musicians are able to "crack" the software, devising key generators that will "con" the software into "thinking" it has been legitimated. It is actually unusual that the copy of Reason kaffiend downloaded came without such authentication. It does not take kaffiend long to find a "keygen" though; two days later, we see that he is looking for the Reason "pdf"—the "help" document that will teach him how to use Reason:

> Extract 12: ragga jungle room, 10/05/03
> [kaffiend] man i feel so behind
> [kaffiend] i just started using reason, i mean just installed it yesterday
> [kaffiend] all you silly bastards have records out and stuff
> [el_cabron_loco] not me
> [el_cabron_loco] i dotn produce . . .
> [el_cabron_loco] i soo wnat too but it just confuses the fuck out of me
> [kaffiend] yeah but alot of people in here do
> [kaffiend] reason is fucking confusing
> [el_cabron_loco] yup
> [kaffiend] anyone have the reason pdf?

Nine days later, kaffiend is looking for samples:

> Extract 13: ragga jungle room, 10/14/03
> [kaffiend] any of you have any good bass samples?
> [illacrew] you there milk?
> [illacrew] add Breakmasteruk

[illacrew] and browes him
[illacrew] he haz everything a junglist could want
. . .
[illacrew] well anyway he has wikkid samples
[illacrew] you should leave him a thank you note, if you get crazy
[kaffiend] where can i find these at?
[illacrew] downloading
[illacrew] Breakmasteruk
[illacrew] in his shared directory
[illacrew] ill find it 1 sec
[kaffiend] k
[illacrew] breakmasteruk
[kaffiend] trying to load his file list
[kaffiend] takeing a long time
[illacrew] dhe has 300 gigs of samples

"Illacrew" refers kaffiend to another user, "breakmasteruk," who has 300 gigabytes of samples available for download (we will return to the issue of samples shortly). Just two days later, kaffiend is requesting feedback:

Extract 14: ragga jungle room, 10/16/03
[kaffiend] you wanna here a track im workin on?
[Junkie_Drunk] yeah
[kaffiend] its in new folder. my tracks
[Junkie_Drunk] i've got some tracks i've been working on as well
[kaffiend] its very ruff and distorted kinda like pisstank, amboss etc
[Junkie_Drunk] cool
[Junkie_Drunk] i'll check it
[kaffiend] ok. im looking for critisism
[nikk0806] see ya
[kaffiend] keep in mind that i was going for the fucked up distortion
[kaffiend] and this is my first attempt at a track

Five days after this, kaffiend has produced another track, and is again getting advice and support concerning what he has achieved thus far from another room occupant:

Extract 15: ragga jungle room, 10/21/03
[Jungle_Bastard] kaffiend the vocals sound off
[Jungle_Bastard] need to turn them up as well
. . .
[Jungle_Bastard] there needs more in it
[Jungle_Bastard] and more for an intro

[kaffiend] yeah, im working with one speaker at the moment so balance is off

[Jungle_Bastard] change the bass n drums up more

[Jungle_Bastard] not bad now

[Jungle_Bastard] got more drum work going

[kaffiend] yeah i really need to work on the structure of my tracks

[kaffiend] as far as when what should come in

[Jungle_Bastard] but your new to it

[Jungle_Bastard] and its not bad at all for being new to production on jungle

[kaffiend] yeah, these are my first tracks

[Jungle_Bastard] i dread the first song i ever made

Through the experiences of Fas3r3d and kaffiend, I am attempting to show how amateur musicians, at the outset of their musical learning, are using p2p. When one witnesses the scale of such activity, it becomes clear that such experiences are not isolated. Space precludes me from including further examples to advance this claim, but such examples are readily forthcoming. I am not suggesting that *all* electronic musicians utilize p2p, but rather that for those young musicians with access to it, p2p can constitute the basis of musical community: "dispelling the alienation that followed the industrialization of pop music; highlighting the consumption of music as an active, incorporative practice" (Kibby 2000, 100). It can play a vital role in facilitating young people who are *learning* how to compose music. Not only does p2p provide Fas3r3d and kaffiend with everything they need to make music, it also furnishes them with their first supportive audiences. This can prove particularly important where budding musicians are geographically isolated from those with similar musical interests. As one user put it, "none of my friends listen to it, small small dnb[14] scene in my town. had to figure out shit for myself."[15]

Green (2001) argues that: "some post-1970s popular music involving the purely or mainly electronic production of sound (sampling, synthesizing) tends to be developed by a solitary musician, in various locations from the teenager's bedroom to the professional studio, and involves fewer or no peer-directed or group-learning activities in bands" (77). It is not that such activities do not take place, but rather that they are for the most part undocumented. The explosion in Internet access gives us an unprecedented insight into how exactly "peer-directed or group-learning activities" are engaged in by the "solitary musician, in . . . the teenager's bedroom." Conversations of the sort cited above are commonplace, as indeed are discussions of a much more technical nature. Moreover, for the average beginner or fan, exposure to such interaction establishes music making as a normal, accessible activity, for which technical and social support is readily available.

## The Search for Samples

P2p chatrooms and online "places" like them are among the few locations outside of formal courses in music technology where an electronic composer can get a real-time answer to a technical query, and p2p networks can provide the raw materials out of which music is made, particularly for those otherwise unable to afford or source these materials. This returns us to the search for samples,[16] as evinced by the following extracts:

Extract 16: ragga jungle room, 10/02/03
[St1D] GOt ne good D&B samples to produce in Fruityloops?
[Annias] ya
[Annias] you can have the hoover packs and amens i have shared to start
[Annias] B)
[St1D] Whats the hoover packs?
[Annias] old school leads you can pitch down into wierd basses
[St1D] k00
[Annias] we have a fast connect
[freezergeezer] hey dude they sound useful
[freezergeezer] am i ok to grab?

Extract 17: ragga jungle room, 10/14/03
[scottfrohawk] anyone got some good samples of a up strum on a guitar
[scottfrohawk] like a reggea guitar sound

Extract 18: Breakcore room, 10/25/03
[fcide001] where can i d/l[17] good drumkit samples?
. . .
[fcide001] i need 1000s of cymbals, rides, especially (heavy) chinas
[SHATTERBREAK] hmmmmmm
[rTD_EdgE] fcide
[rTD_EdgE] check my samples folder
[rTD_EdgE] grab what ya like

Extract 19: ragga jungle room, 11/13/03
[Line 47] looking for some ragga samples /hits?
[Line 47] if you have some drop me a line

Extract 20: Breakcore room, 01/16/04
[hidgekill] hey. . you happen to know where I could get drumkit from hell?

Sample searches tend to be genre specific; hence such queries in the Breakcore room are generally oriented towards finding percussion sounds. Similarly, the reliance of ragga jungle on the vocals of Jamaican MCs or rappers means that exchanging "acapellas" (the vocal line of a particular song, isolated from the instrumental or "riddim") is a constant in the ragga jungle room:

Extract 21: ragga jungle room, 11/11/03
[Asterisk] anyone have acapella of sizzla-grab on, lexxus-bigup bigup, anthony
b-forward,
[Asterisk] sizzla-empty the clip
[Asterisk] capleton-push wood,
[Asterisk] or "pum pum mix" elephant, capleton, sizzla, lexxus?
[Asterisk] remixing grabon riddim, need acapellas . . .

Extract 22: ragga jungle room, 02/02/04
[DJ-DS] any1 here got any reggae acapellas?

The search for samples is highly instructive insofar as it reveals how over
time, young producers' attitudes to making music develop. In electronic
music composition, apprenticeship tends to rely solely on sequencing and
perhaps manipulating "loopable" drum patterns, effects or bass sounds (such
as those kaffiend was looking for in Extract 13). In much the same way, guitarists familiarize themselves with their instrument by learning to play, for
instance, Led Zeppelin's "Stairway to Heaven" (for which they increasingly
view the "tabs" online). Without formal instruction, the learning curve with
music software can be steep; developing the skills for original production is
time consuming. As electronic musicians progress, though, they learn to
master software synthesizers and take an interest in sequencing their own
drum patterns, just as guitarists learn to craft their own compositions. Perhaps more importantly, a musical ethic of professionalism and originality
comes into play:

Extract 23: blærg 10/27/03
[blaerg] yea i never share my samples
[AW] its like blaergs eleven secret herbs and spices ;)
[blaerg] hah
[blaerg] ;yea it is a bit like recipes

Extract 24: Breakcore room, 12/16/03
[GabbaNoize Terrorist] i don't like to sample nothing
[GabbaNoize Terrorist] just do it all myself
[/dev/null] but, if trapped, WILL resort to an mp3 ripped sample : (
[UndaCova] the better you know how to make your own samples, the better
your compositions will be . . . sample sites are a bad habit except maybe if
you're looking for a specific recognisable sample
[/dev/null] always nice to at least grab breaks from the original context of the
tune though, gives you a real different feeling when dl'ing the beats isolated en-
masse from phatdrumloops or something

[UndaCova] plus if you make your own samples your breaks won't sound the same like all the other cliche breakcore

[d_sc_mb_b_1_t_r] i've used mp3 breaks (from the old funk / soul tunes) in the past—i'm not sure on the quality (even high rate VBR[18]ect) i seem to lose "punchiness"

[GabbaNoize Terrorist] yes, i agree with undacova

[sheen] yeah, or you can use your editing / modifying capabilites to give it edge

[[{-_-}]vek[{-_-}]] i have a question. . . .

[d_sc_mb_b_1_t_r] all these differing methods!

[GabbaNoize Terrorist] own samples = own breaks = original

    This is not to say that sampling per se becomes frowned upon; different musical styles (and indeed different musicians) have different aesthetics of sampling, and prerecorded sounds (for instance, drum hits) form the basis of much electronic music. Rather, simply *looping* found sounds comes to be seen as insufficient and dissatisfying in creative terms—as legendary hip-hop producer Dr. Dre puts it, "I don't really dig working with samples because you're so limited when you sample. . . . I've tried to stay away from it as much as possible throughout my career from day one" (Torres 2004, 76). Samples become a means rather than an end. In particular, they become a means of referring to shared knowledge with the listener, establishing subcultural capital, and embedding one's own work in a cultural tradition. This is what "UndaCova" is referring to in Extract 24 above, when he mentions "looking for a specific recognisable sample." Samples thus become a channel for relaying and displaying *specialized knowledge,* for communicating in terms of the musical language of a subcultural discourse and articulating one's position through reference to that subculture's "canon." As the bedroom producer progresses, subcultural capital comes to be displayed not by possessing or knowing the whereabouts of samples, but by abstaining from such discussion and thereby indicating one's creative maturity.

    The sample and its circulation play a fundamental role in the bedroom producer "scene," arguably more so even than the released material that binds a chatroom as an aesthetically aligned subcultural site. The sample can be viewed as a particular type of signifying "raw material," the location and exchange of which become crucial at a certain stage in any given bedroom producer's career. The search for samples can be depicted as, in one sense, rather Baudrillardian: "there are no commodities left, just signs, the logical conclusion of a move away from use-value (authentic-modern) to exchange-value (manufactured-modern) and finally to the apotheosis of sign-value (post-modern). . . . If there is no originality there is no authenticity" (Stahl 2003, 29). This kind of relativist cultural-pessimism, however, is unable to account for how such signs/samples become invested with meaning, let alone how "authenticity" is itself a construction.

    Samples could be better said to possess, with a startling degree of fit, some or all of the following attributes: (1) restriction, either by price or by law, to elites; (2) complexity of acquisition, which may or may not be a function of real "scarcity"; (3) semiotic virtuosity, that is, the capacity to signal fairly complex social messages (as do pepper in cuisine, silk in dress, jewels in adornment, and relics in worship); (4) specialized knowledge as a prerequisite for their "appropriate" consumption, that is, regulation by fashion; and (5) a high degree of linkage of their consumption to body, person, and personality. (Appadurai 1986, 38)

The status of samples in this register is processual, and this process is determined largely by the perceived aesthetic status of the sound. The accomplished producer is able to manipulate familiar sounds in a novel way; technical ability and sample-literacy sediment into subcultural capital.

One implication of this is that it calls for a more subtle reading of subcultural capital with reference to musicians and musical genres, for negotiating what is and is not "cool" is a constant, iterative process of assessment and reflection. Aesthetic hierarchies do not appear as stable as all that; such stability would be stagnant, whereas genres tend, in fact, to evolve, mutate, and hybridize quite rapidly. The struggle for subcultural status (rather like the struggle for "intellectual" status) involves, among other things, legitimating one's claim that a conceptual or stylistic novelty is simultaneously innovative and within the bounds of the "canon," that it *advances* that canon. "Cheesy sounds are cool, and great sounds become cheesy."[19] Successfully navigating or steering the trajectory of such sounds confers subcultural capital upon musicians. It is for this reason that I described the ragga jungle and Breakcore rooms as "regimes of value": sonic artifacts of little or no monetary worth, which are often inaccessible via the commercial market, are widely circulated, much sought after, and serve as indicators of subcultural capital. Rooms are niche, noncommercial proto-markets. It is not just new music and information pertaining to it that are circulated. In this sense, p2p constitutes a cultural economy in the broadest sense of the term. "Consumption is part of a process that includes production and exchange, all three being distinct only as phases of the cyclical process of social reproduction, in which consumption is never terminal" (Gell 1986, 112–13). As drum and bass producer Goldie puts it, advancing his own homological argument, "I was using fourth or fifth generation samples, just trash sounds, but they had a grittiness and a roughness which identified with the feel of the street" (Barr 1996, 148). The circulation of "commodities" such as drum hits and acapellas is unending, and the "diversion of commodities from specified paths is always a sign of creativity or crisis, whether aesthetic or economic" (Appadurai 1986, 26).

## Distribution

The search for listeners with which we began finds its fullest expression in the struggle to become an "established" musician with an "official" release. Thus, where to send demos is a common topic of conversation among amateur producers. Many choose to bypass this route altogether though, starting their own labels and organizing independent distribution.

Extract 25: Breakcore room, 01/16/04
[mic_mainstream] k5k i gotta an email from enduser
[mic_mainstream] sonicterror
[true_k5k] yay
[mic_mainstream] they loveM$ & Bloodyfist
[true_k5k] naturally
[mic_mainstream] you should go there
[mic_mainstream] post a message send your shit
[true_k5k] sonicterror?
[mic_mainstream] southern Hemi demi[20]
[true_k5k] soon enough
[mic_mainstream] hang on i get it
[true_k5k] endusers doin a trak fr a comp I'm helpin do
[true_k5k] I know the site n stuff
[mic_mainstream] yeh
[true_k5k] talked wit him about trading distro etc
[mic_mainstream] I am on his last release
[mic_mainstream] BRS01
[true_k5k] I'm down dude!
[mic_mainstream] yeh they are keen
[mic_mainstream] even a link is cool

In Extract 25, "true_k5k" and "mic_mainstream," who reside in New Zealand and Australia respectively, discuss the possibility of "trading" distribution ("distro") with "enduser," a musician who runs an independent label in the U.S. What renders such conversations particularly fascinating is that musicians who are in a unique position to understand the distributive potential of p2p nonetheless want their music released as a commodity. Putting out an independent release is a risky, costly venture, but many are willing to embark upon it—despite the fact that in all likelihood that release will *then* go on to find its greatest audience through p2p. They see no contradiction in investing in putting a product on the market that will then be freely circulated with no remuneration to them. In fact, many successful "signed" artists within the genres or communities under consideration still share both their released and unreleased material on p2p; such behavior, in anthropological terms, is characterized as "in-group reciprocity" and "out-group exchange" (Polanyi, Arensberg, and Pearson 1971). In the long run, an official release has greater credibility on p2p (though only a fraction of users ever actually *bought* it).

Also, an official release will (hopefully) reach an audience beyond the p2p community, and for dance musicians, a vinyl release is important—so that it can be played by DJs. This is clear in Extract 26:

Extract 26: Breakcore room, 08/01/03
[blaerg] cutups did you ever make your way around to my demo man ?
[blaerg] i bet you didn't
[oldman] you have your own label!!!
[blaerg] cmon mr pittsburgh scene creator—i'm worth your time :)
[oldman] lol
[oldman] your worth my time blaerg
[blaerg] see that ? . . testimonials
[oldman] hahaha
[blaerg] join the dark forces inherent in toledo
[blaerg] lol -
[cutups] no, i downloaded the trax. i liked em for sure.
* blaerg joking around just for lucas
[cutups] i'm by far not the scene creator, just somebody trying to do some shit just like everybody else
[oldman] woohoo
[blaerg] well van3eck and xano say contrary cutups : )
. . .
[cutups] although i am accepting demos because i'm looking at starting a label.
[blaerg] yea thats it
[blaerg] its hard to piece together abstractly
[cutups] something good that is coming out soon: society cleaners LP on isolate. his stuff is real good.
[blaerg] i will put that under my hat
[blaerg] will you be carrying that on compact disc ?
[cutups] not sure what the cd status is. the lp is coming out next week.
[blaerg] damn turntables
[blaerg] i was into metal before . . no need for wax
[cutups] one thing i've been thinking about with considering starting a label is whats the best format to put stuff out in. because i'm a big vinyl fan. but i don't want to ignore new technology and realities. such as people who are mostly into digital formats, but also allowing for something tangible that will make it desirable for people to pick up the release, so the artist is going to get something out of it.
[blaerg] have to go both ways
[blaerg] i don't own a turntable, but i am about to plunk down over $1000 to press vinyl—Of an artist besides myself
[blaerg] mp3's and wax can easily co-exist i feel

[blaerg] mp3's should be free, but wax is different, you have to pay for that
[cutups] yeah. for sure. i think it makes sense to help both camps get what they
want/need. just the best configuration of releases.

Whilst the unreleased music of genuinely talented and committed musicians can, and does, circulate on p2p merely via word of mouth, most bedroom
producers still want the formal recognition an official release implies. Moreover, if they are sufficiently talented and spend enough time socializing online,
their work will eventually come to the attention of those in a position to distribute it as product:

Extract 27: ragga jungle room, 01/14/04
[Tykal] nah i'm for real though we got a label goin & i was thinkin bout you if
you're willing
[deportee] yes indeedio
. . .
[Tykal] not like now or anything we got the first couple releases filled but a lil down
the line . . . from what i've heard of yours it blows most producers out tha water

## Conclusions

I have sought to furnish an account of how p2p facilitates the careers of amateur
musicians, and in particular, the role p2p communities play in musical development, subcultural exchange, and the use of p2p as a sort of proto-market.
Clearly, where p2p plays a crucial role in the development of musicians' talents
and careers, it does so where they are able to interact with, and integrate into,
collectives of like-minded individuals. How best to conceptualize these collectives has been a subject for exhaustive debate in the "virtual community" literature. As Watson (1997) points out, debates about "community" status ascription
are political: insofar as such status has social value, applying the term has implications for the treatment of that group offline (121). The debate, and the high
hopes invested in the possibility of online community, reflects contemporary
anxiety about the perceived disintegration of offline community and the degra-
dation of public discourse more generally. Thus, p2p chatrooms are branded
communities or "pseudocommunities" respectively by each pole in the dispute.
As Putnam (2000) argues in a telling passage,

Face-to-face networks tend to be dense and bounded, whereas computer-
mediated communication networks tend to be sparse and unbounded. Anonymity
and fluidity in the virtual world encourage "easy in, easy out," "drive-by" relationships. That very casualness is the appeal of computer-mediated communication

for some denizens of cyberspace, but it discourages the creation of social capital. If entry and exit are too easy, commitment, trustworthiness and reciprocity will not develop. (177)

Yet, arguing over whether online interaction parallels what does (or *should*) constitute "real" community distracts us from what is happening online regardless (Hine 2001, 19). Where musical learning occurs on p2p, it does so "at a distance," but remains an inherently social experience, and musical learning, for those who occupy the social spaces of p2p, often comes to be naturalized as a norm. Of course, not everyone can get an official release: p2p distribution, and ultimately distribution beyond p2p, is effectively meritocratic for the musicians we have been considering. Those who work hard enough, for long enough, and are good enough (and lucky enough), stand a good chance of succeeding.

Hence, how we evaluate p2p and its role for amateur musicians depends on what we think music *is*, and this gets us to the heart of the debates about copyright infraction: is music primarily a creative form of individual and collective expression, or a commodity? The material I have presented here appears to suggest that consumers and producers of music consider the former to be the case. It is these contesting conceptions that define the terms of the legal struggle over p2p, and both of these perspectives rely on antecedent political and aesthetic commitments, concerning how music *ought* to sound, how it *ought* to be made, and how it *ought* to be distributed. If we consider music primarily as a cultural commodity, we might be alarmed at the disruption p2p is said to cause to traditional music distribution channels. If we consider music as primarily a form of expression, we can be glad that amateur musicians and fans are availing themselves of the creative opportunities inherent in new technologies.

## Acknowledgments

This research was partially funded by the Irish Research Council for the Humanities and Social Sciences. I am indebted to Michael Ayers and Barbara Bradby for their comments on earlier versions of the text, and to Rachel Grimwood and Cian O'Donoghue for their ongoing support and guidance.

## References to Chapter Three

Appadurai, Arjun. 1986. "Introduction: Commodities and the Politics of Value." In *The Social Life of Things*, edited by Arjun Appadurai, 3–65. Cambridge: Cambridge University Press.

Barr, Tim. 1996. "Concrete Jungle." In *History of House*, edited by Chris Kempster, 145–52. London: Sanctuary.

Becker, Howard. 1963. *Outsiders*. New York: Free Press.

Bell, David. 2001. *An Introduction to Cybercultures*. London: Routledge.

Bourdieu, Pierre. 1984. *Distinction: A Social Critique of the Judgement of Taste*. London: Routledge and Kegan Paul.

Brown, Andy R. 2003. "Heavy Metal and Subcultural Theory." In *The Post-Subcultures Reader*, edited by David Muggleton and Rupert Weinzierl, 209–22. Oxford: Berg.

Buquet, Gustavo. 2003. "Las Multinacionales Desbordadas: Luchan por el Control del Mercado Online de la Música." Paper presented at the IASPM Spain conference *Global y Digital*, November 8, 2003, University of Valladolid, Spain.

Caney, Derek. 2002. *CD Sales Down*. Reuters, August 26. Retrieved August 2, 2004, from http://news.dmusic.com/article/5340

Gell, Alfred. 1986. "Newcomers to the World of Goods: Consumption among the Muria Gonds." In *The Social Life of Things*, edited by Arjun Appadurai, 110–38. Cambridge: Cambridge University Press.

Gilbert, Jeremy, and Ewan Pearson. 1999. *Discographies*. London: Routledge.

Gilbert, Nigel G., and Michael Mulkay. 1984. *Opening Pandora's Box*. Cambridge: Cambridge University Press.

Grajeda, Tony. 2002. "The Sound of Disaffection." In *Hop on Pop*, edited by Henry Jenkins, Tara McPherson, and Jane Shattuc, 357–75. London: Duke University Press.

Green, Lucy. 2001. *How Popular Musicians Learn*. Aldershot: Ashgate.

Hall, Stuart, and Tony Jefferson. 1976. *Resistance Through Rituals*. London: Routledge.

Hebdige, Dick. 1979. *Subculture: The Meaning of Style*. London: Routledge.

Hennion, Antoine. 2001. "Music Lovers: Taste as Performance." *Theory, Culture and Society* 18, no. 5: 1–22.

Hine, Christine. 2001. *Virtual Ethnography*. London: Sage.

Hollows, Joanne, and Katie Milestone. 1998. "Welcome to Dreamsville." In *The Place of Music*, edited by Andrew Leyshon, David Matless, and George Revill, 83–103. London: Guildford Press.

Hutchby, Ian. 2001. *Conversation and Technology*. Oxford: Polity Press.

Jones, Andrew. 1995. *Plunderphonics, 'Pataphysics & Pop Mechanics*. London: SAF.

Jones, Steve, and Amanda Lenhart. 2004. "Music Downloading and Listening: Findings from the Pew Internet and American Life Project." *Popular Music and Society* 27, no. 2: 185–99.

Kendall, Lori. 2002. *Hanging Out in the Virtual Pub*. London: University of California Press.

Kibby, Marjorie. 2000. "Home on the Page." *Popular Music* 19: 91–100.

Kretschmer, Martin, George Michael Klimis, and Roger Wallis. 2001. "Music in Electronic Markets." *New Media and Society* 3, no. 4: 417–41.

Lovering, John. 1998. "The Global Music Industry: Contradictions in the Commodification of the Sublime." In *The Place of Music*, edited by Andrew Leyshon, David Matless, and George Revill, 31–56. London: Guildford Press.

MacDonald, Fraser. 2004. "Downloader's Guide to MP3." *Stuff* (June): 48–59.

Mackintosh, Hamish. 2003. "Talk Time: Dave Smith." *Guardian* (November 20): 21.

Oberholzer, Felix, and Koleman Strumpf. 2004. "The Effect of File Sharing on Record Sales: An Empirical Analysis." University of North Carolina at Chapel

Hill, March. Retrieved August 3, 2004, from http://www.unc.edu/~cigar/papers/FileSharing_March2004.pdf

Parker, Nick. 2003. "Quiet Riot." *Daily Tar Heel,* October 2. Retrieved August 4, 2004, from http://www.dailytarheel.com/vnews/display.v/ART/2003/10/02/3f7c23669a0fa

Polanyi, Karl, Conrad M. Arensberg, and Harry W. Pearson, eds. 1971. *Trade and Market in the Early Empires.* New York: Gateway/Free Press.

Putnam, Robert D. 2000. *Bowling Alone: The Collapse and Revival of American Community.* New York: Touchstone.

Shaw, David. 1997. "Gay Men and Computer Interaction." In *Virtual Culture,* edited by Steven Jones, 133–45. London: Sage.

Sherman, Chris. 2003. "Are You Wanted by the Recording Industry?" *Search Engine Watch,* November 8. Retrieved November 16, 2003, from http://searchenginewatch.com/searchday/article.php/2241591

Sproull, Lee, and Sara Kiesler. 1991. *Connections: New Ways of Working in the Networked Organisation.* Cambridge, MA: MIT.

Stahl, Geoff. 2003. "Tastefully Renovating Subcultural Theory." In *The Post-Subcultures Reader,* edited by David Muggleton and Rupert Weinzierl, 27–40. Oxford: Berg.

Straw, Will. 1997. "Sizing Up Record Collections." In *Sexing the Groove,* edited by Sheila Whiteley, 3–17. London: Routledge.

Tagg, Philip. 1994. "From Refrain to Rave." *Popular Music* 13, no.2: 209–222.

Thornton, Sarah. 1995. *Club Cultures.* Cambridge: Polity Press.

Torres, Andre. 2004 "The Architect." *Scratch* 1, no. 1 (Summer): 72–80.

Toynbee, Jason. 2000. *Making Popular Music: Musicians, Creativity and Institutions.* London: Arnold.

Watson, Nessim. 1997. "Why We Argue about Virtual Community." In *Virtual Culture,* edited by Steven Jones, 102–32. London: Sage.

Weinzierl, Rupert, and David Muggleton. 2003. "What Is 'Post-subcultural Studies' Anyway?" In *The Post-Subcultures Reader,* edited by David Muggleton and Rupert Weinzierl, 3–23. Oxford: Berg.

Wikipedia. (n.d.). *Breakcore.* Retrieved July 8, 2004, from http://en.wikipedia.org/wiki/Breakcore

Wilson-Brown, Carrie, and Cameron McCarthy. 1999. "The Organization of Affect: Popular Music, Youth, and Intellectual and Political Life (An Interview with Larry Grossberg)." In *Sound Identities,* edited by Cameron McCarthy, Glenn Hudak, Shawn Miklaucic, and Paula Saukko, 343–59. New York: Peter Lang.

Woodworth, Griffin Mead. 2004. "Hackers, Users and Suits: Napster and Representations of Identity." *Popular Music and Society* 27, no. 2: 161–84.

CHAPTER FOUR

# Building a Virtual Diaspora:
# Hip-Hop in Cyberspace

## Andre Pinard and Sean Jacobs

How can all these people, who probably never seen each other face to face
make such a tight connection on the 'net? (Anonymous 2004)[1]

## Introduction

From its inception in the 1970s, hip-hop culture has been concerned with creative modes of expression and resistance, forming and building alternative communities and identities, the appropriation of space, and of course, having a little
fun. Until quite recently these entities existed solely within the domain of the
offline world. Initially most hip-hop sites resembled and functioned as shop
fronts and it took a while for hip-hop to catch up to the creative possibilities of
the Internet. Since at least the late 1990s, some hip-hoppers began to realize
the creative possibilities of the Internet to actively undermine existing cultural
flows, restructure identities, and impact political power. We are concerned with
that subgenre of hip-hop loosely identified by fans, and sometimes by the artists
themselves, music executives, and the media, as "alternative hip-hop." This
chapter explores how "alternative" hip-hop sites and the social actors who ani-
mate them create communities that straddle on- and offline. We also examine
whether these websites have any impact on cultural flows, how they cement or
undermine and/or reshape identities and, finally, what implications they have
for strategies for political organization and participation.

## "Alternative," Diaspora, Community, and Publics

It has been suggested that cybercommunities coalesce around "shared interests and backgrounds" (McLaine 2003, 233). Race and ethnicity, in particular, are seen as the primary "ties that bind an [online] community together" (239). Through a study of two seemingly different music-based web portals—www.Okayplayer.com and www.Africanhiphop.com—we question these assumptions. The first is aimed primarily at a U.S. audience, while the second is produced and aimed at the African continent and the African diaspora in Western Europe (and to some extent, North America). Drawing on insights from, among others, Anderson's (1991) and Ikegami's work on offline communities (2000) and through a brief discussion of what we term the "virtual diaspora," we argue that both sites offer new strategies for exploring the construction of both off- and online communities.

Traditionally, a "diaspora" is defined as "the dispersal of an ethnic population from an original homeland into foreign areas, often in a forced manner or under traumatic circumstances" (Giddens et al. 2002). Updating this definition, we suggest that virtual diasporic communities are constructed according to their (symbolic) marginalization as a result of their cultural, ethnic, and most importantly, musical orientations within the broader hip-hop genre. The virtual diaspora is also to be understood as a metaphor for a terrain in which, due to experiential and historical dynamics, social agents (i.e., musicians, web designers, students, journalists, teachers, office workers, and others who make up these distinct communities) position themselves oppositionally as well as opportunistically to the status quo or the dominant ideology. In doing so, the virtual diaspora establishes its own sociopolitical space or field (Bourdieu 1993; Bourdieu and Wacquant 1993).

We conceptualize virtual diasporic communities as spaces or fields in which social agents struggle for more autonomy over their cultural production. According to Bourdieu, these "fields" are domains of social life such as the arts, within which actors struggle for power, status, and autonomy. A field is a "network, or configuration, of objective relations between positions" (e.g., among social agents and institutions). As "spaces of potential and active forces, the field is also a field of struggles aimed at preserving or transforming these forces" (Bourdieu 1993).

Our understanding of the "diaspora" is coupled with Anderson's notion of the "imagined community." Anderson's conceptualization of the nation as an "imagined community" is comprised of four major elements: imagined, limited, sovereign, and community. What we found was that all of these elements—some more than others—manifest themselves within the cybercommunities that we investigated.

Members of the virtual diasporas under discussion are consciously aware of their "imagined" nature. For example, in response to a questionnaire for this research, a member of the Okayplayer message boards posted the following statement on one of the portal's message boards: "How can all these people, who probably never seen each other face to face make such a tight connection on the 'net?" For us, this speaks to and expands Anderson's notion of "imagined communities." For Anderson, the nation is imagined because "members . . . will never know most of their fellow members . . . yet in the minds of each, lives the image of their communion" (1991, 6). Expanding Anderson's notion of imagined communities as it applies to nations is a helpful point of departure to understand the potential and challenges of cybercommunities.

In Anderson's analysis, the possession of citizenship in a nation allows and prompts the individual to imagine the boundaries of a nation, even though such boundaries may not physically exist. Substituting nation for cybercommunity, we note that the (symbolic and real) boundaries erected by members of these cybercommunities serve a similar purpose as those within the real world; demarcation of an "us" in relation to "them." Alternatively, due to an online and offline dimension, which we will explore later, there seems to be a space for the "communion" which Anderson thought would solely and most likely exist in the minds of citizens. For us, cybercommunities break with Anderson's understanding of how nations have limits or borders. Due to their existence on the Internet and, more importantly, to social agents' shared interest in alternative hip-hop, these spaces are conceptualized by their members as terrains that (a) are much less grounded than nations and (b) as spaces that enable the transcending of traditional boundaries such as ethnicity, race, and gender.

The sense of a strong allegiance to a specific virtual musical community pervaded the cyberspaces we explored. Throughout our research, the notion of community as "a deep, horizontal comradeship" (Anderson 1991, 7) in large part shaped the conceptualization and conversations about, for example, Okayplayer.com. As one of our key informants put it, the spaces or boards were designed with the intention of "opening a pathway between cultural creator and consumer by erasing the line dividing the artist from the fan" (Poetix 2004).

Our third guidepost is the notion of "online publics" that we adapted from earlier offline constructs (Habermas 1989; Ikegami 2000). By "online publics" we mean spaces (artistic, discursive, and ideational) created by the interplay between online and offline alternative hip-hop communities. These virtual and real spaces allow social agents to build independent cultural worlds (or "interpretive communities") in the midst of what are effectively repressive social, economic, and cultural forces. Within these (alternative) publics, social agents redefine themselves, voice calls for self-determination, and they form relationships (horizontal associations) that would not normally occur in a solely offline environment. Historically speaking, the U.S. case is very instructive. Within the American sociohistorical context, due to a lack of freedom in the sociopolitical sphere, African Americans oftentimes transformed the cultural sphere into a multifaceted agentic space from which calls for self-improvement, opposition, critique, subversion, and political action emanated. What makes the virtual diaspora dynamic is the presumption that the actors within these "alternative enclaves" have the capacity to build their own internal logics and aesthetic sensibilities independent of or relationally to the "dominant" public. In addition, it challenges the dominant public head on.

## Okayplayer.com

By 1999, the hip-hop band The Roots—established in 1987 in Philadelphia—had released two critically acclaimed albums[2] and had developed a widespread and diverse fan base. Later that year, the band was preparing to release its third album, *Things Fall Apart*. Despite the fact that The Roots were signed to a major label, from the time of their debut, the music industry had difficulty in placing or categorizing the band's music. Much of the reason rested in The Roots' decision to use live instruments when most hip-hop groups consisted of an MC and a DJ with a set of turntables. Second, despite their lackluster record sales, The Roots continuously played to sold-out crowds and had developed a reputation for a stellar stage act. Third, while The Roots had a wide following among blacks in their hometown, Philadelphia, and among African American college students and young professionals, they attracted an equally significant white fan base. This both allowed and caused them to break through simple demarcations of traditional (and heavily racialized) marketing in the record industry, how genres are classified, and how concerts are promoted. But it proved to be a hindrance in a record industry not known for innovation with genre bending. Finally, the group appeared to assail market and popular pressures by persisting in bringing out "conscious" music with a high political content.[3]

As result, despite earning the moniker of "hip-hop's most celebrated band," The Roots understood that they could only rely so much on the traditional distribution and marketing channels to promote and distribute their album as well as help them in expanding their fan base.

Of all the members of The Roots, it was drummer/producer Ahmir ("?uest-love") Thompson who was especially attuned to the developments around the Internet and its potential in not only promoting the group's music but also creating a sense of community for its fans and occasional collaborators.[4] Thompson felt The Roots had a "special audience" and reasoned, "In the age of information and the Internet, it would be ignorant not to make steps closer to them (our audience), especially when others in hip-hop and black music aren't really making moves towards that" (Katiebree 2003).

In late 1999, Thompson teamed up with Angela Nissel, his former classmate at the Philadelphia School for Creative and Performing Arts, who had extensive knowledge of and familiarity with the usages of the Internet. They launched the website www.Okayplayer.com. Initially Nissel (who later became the portal's web mistress) and Thompson set out to design a space where The Roots would be able to actually interact with their audience and loyal fan base and keep them updated on the band's whereabouts.

According to the FAQ (Frequently Asked Questions) section on the portal, an "okayplayer" is:

> the shorthand name for Okayplayer.com. Okayplayer is not a record label. Okayplayer.com is an online community. This community is made up of like-minded recording artists (who keep their official Internet homes here) and visitors to the site. "Okayplayer" is also, simply, the name of a person who enjoys this site. All of the artists and staff are Okayplayers. Hopefully, most people who visit this site are Okayplayers as well. I guess we're a light version of Trekkies or Deadheads. (Okayplayer.com, accessed October 15, 2004)

It ends by suggesting tongue-in-cheek that:

> Okay, if this wasn't supposed to be a dictionary entry, we'd be biased and say "Okayplayers are the smartest, best-looking people on the Internet. They also have an uncanny ability to gather offline in peace. Oh, and they also listen to really good music." (Okayplayer.com, accessed October 15, 2004)

By 2000, The Roots had a cultlike following; Thompson estimated that they had a worldwide fan base of approximately one million by then (Katiebree 2003). This fact forced a rethinking of the uses and potentials of the website. Thompson and Nissel now wanted to create a virtual "artist collective, forum, fanclub, meeting-place and mess hall" for The Roots, their affiliates, and their respective audiences (Wiltz 2000).

Thompson and Nissel appeared to have had perfect timing. As hip-hop moved from the margins to command the center of American popular culture and became increasingly hypercommercialized, Okayplayer.com soon became a "music home for artists sometimes existing, because of choice or otherwise, beyond the reach of the so-called mainstream" (aoxomoxoa 2004). Left-field artists such as Common, Talib Kweli, Dilated Peoples, Meshell Ndegechello, and D'Angelo—who had all won critical acclaim among both critics and fans but experienced difficulty with the marketing and promotion of their music—soon commissioned Okayplayer.com's web designers to build them customized and interactive websites (Louie 2002).

The website also had a number of other unique features. Okayplayer.com did not simply cater to musicians. Fans, who were considered as "e-family," were not left out. Interactive message boards became an integral component to the sites; participation between artists and fans is a prerequisite for Okayplayer.com-crafted sites. Loyal fans and regular message board participants were rewarded with the insider status of "Okayplayer."

Identification as an Okayplayer enables members into a community that is first, virtual, but also real in that members form social networks, date, carpool, and to some extent use their in-group status to initiate wider political action. What adds to the site's uniqueness is the involvement or close participation of the artists themselves. Thompson (aka "?uestlove") contributes a weekly "tour journal" (with photographs and audio clips). Other artists like D'Angelo and Talib Kweli often join in spirited discussions with Okayplayers on the site's boards. Other features include links to the "affiliates" websites (that is, the artists they've build websites for), links to concert schedules, downloads (music and videos that sometimes debut "exclusively" on the site), extensive message boards,[5] and an online store where fans and visitors can order music or Okay-player apparel.

## Africanhiphop.com

Elsewhere there was a similar process taking place in terms of a turn to the Internet by hip-hop artists and enthusiasts, but for different reasons and with different consequences. Unlike in the U.S. context, hip-hop on the African continent struggled to establish a significant presence and even a commercial niche beyond a few artists as it faced a number of structural and technical obstacles. These included the reluctance of record companies to sign or promote hip-hop artists and groups. This reluctance was informed by a notion of hip-hop's "non-indigenous" nature. Coupled with this was the fact that radio and television stations were averse to supporting the genre (Neate 2004). The situation was not helped by the fact that early African hip-hop, with few exceptions, was a virtual carbon copy of commercial U.S. rap in terms of lyrics and language (English) and resembled "old school" hip-hop with the use of sparse beats. When hip-hop came of age on the continent (in the mid to late 1990s), any hip artists or groups with hopes of using the Internet to overcome some of these obstacles had to face challenges of cost, connectivity, and access. The fact that most Africans access the Internet through dial-ups is a challenge for a continent where access to communication technology and phone density compares unfavorably with the rest of the globe (Bahi 2004; Brown and Licker 2003; Chivhanga 2000; Jensen 2000). The first hip-hop groups on the African continent emerged in the mid to late 1980s. Young people, particularly in the urban ghettoes of Senegal (particularly the capital Dakar), Nigeria (especially the commercial capital Lagos), and South Africa (Cape Town and Johannesburg), were the most receptive to the music and culture. Not long thereafter, hip-hop rapidly spread to other African countries, particularly its major cities like Nairobi (in Kenya), Dar es Salaam (in Tanzania), Algiers, Cairo (Egypt), and Harare (Zimbabwe).

By the mid-1990s African hip-hop began to embrace its local context; artists began to incorporate indigenous discourses, sounds, and local languages into the music. Only a few managed to secure record contracts or "distribution deals" with major labels and most artists continued to struggle to make a living, find a space to produce and practice their music, develop an audience, or even link up with their counterparts in other African countries. By the end of the decade, however, a number of artists had secured record contracts, and radio and television stations began to play hip-hop more regularly. In some countries—most notably South Africa, Senegal, and Tanzania—artists make a fairly comfortable living as commercial hip-hop artists (Neate 2004).

Most observers of African hip-hop agree that the website that can actually claim the honor of "first" African hip-hop website was a personal web page by a South Africa–based hip-hop DJ, Shamiel X, which he posted for the first time in 1995. The web page provided information on African-based groups. However, Shamiel X's website was overwhelmingly focused on South African hip-hop; it reflected the early uneasiness with the potentials of the web and as a result did not reach the potential that he had envisioned.

Africanhiphop.com would be up within the next two years. In 1996, a Dutch student and African hip-hop enthusiast, Thomas Gesthuizen (aka Juma4), traveled to Tanzania where he encountered the beginnings of that country's hip-hop scene. Gesthuizen soon became exposed, through his hosts, to the music of the groundbreaking South African hip-hop group, Prophets of the City, and members of the Senegalese group Positive Black Soul.[6] According to Gesthuizen "since there was little communication among hip-hop artists from various countries, for example between Senegal and South Africa," he decided to create a website www.rumba-kali.com (Gesthuizen 2004).[7] Utilizing open-source software, in early 1997, Gesthuizen expanded www.rumba-kali.com into www.Africanhiphop.com. There are specific reasons, central to our argument later, as to why Gesthuizen had the ability to access resources to start the web portal as well as travel widely in West and East Africa, and we discuss that later in the chapter.

By 2004, Africanhiphop.com had information on hip-hop groups from more than 30 countries. The front page features regular news updates of album releases by members. It also actively promotes new music by members on its front page. It posts features on groups and opinion pieces on the state of the genre. Africanhiphop.com contains lively boards despite the technical and other obstacles to access to the Internet on the continent. It has become clear that while a number of other hip-hop websites have since sprung up claiming to cover hip-hop on the continent, none of these has been as widespread and as consistent in its coverage and support of African hip-hop groups and the culture.

Mustafa Maluka, a South African artist who, while based in the Netherlands, was a crucial part of Africanhiphop.com's editorial team, asserts:

> The website [Africanhiphop.com] forums have different rooms in which you could discuss topics ranging from music production, history, politics, and general discussions, as well as online battles forums, . . . where users come to challenge

other users to lyrical battles [and an] active membership of characters with elaborate online personalities. (Maluka 2003)

Members can download music and video images. Another key development is the addition of a radio station, Radio Rumba-kali, that webcasts through the portal. The site's creators are involved in producing music, filming music videos of artists (mainly from Tanzania), concert promotions both on the continent and in Western Europe, and have become the arbiters of continental hip-hop outside Africa. According to Maluka, "There is indeed a lively online presence in African hip-hop virtual communities and judging by the amount of daily traffic these sites generate, these communities are growing daily." He also points to the different benefits the site presents to its varied audience: "They are becoming a place where young people come to discuss various topics and also ask for advice on anything from dj and music production equipment to sexual relationships."

## What Is "Alternative"?

Although rigid categorization is regarded as anathema within hip-hop culture, it would not be farfetched to characterize the artists and creators of Okayplayer.com and Africanhiphop.com as part of what is widely now referred to as "alternative hip-hop." We have been reluctant to set up a mainstream/alternative dichotomy. However, artists and members of the boards of both portals point to such a divide.

For example, Jonker, a DJ and researcher based in Cape Town who has closely followed the hip-hop movement there, is skeptical of applying the word *alternative* to any aspect of Africanhiphop.com:

I'm not convinced that the mainstream/underground paradigm works very well in African hip-hop. There needs to be a commercial mainstream before an aesthetic "underground" develops. There is a lot of talk about underground-ness in lyrics, but that's often just rhetoric, claims made on the social capital of "realness" and underground-ness that are not based on aesthetic or political difference from an existing mainstream. (Jonker 2004)

However, Jonker insists that there is definitely an "alternative" element to Africanhiphop.com:

[Africanhiphop.com] could very well be seen as alternative though, as one should not compare it with other African hip-hop websites but rather with American websites and others in the North. From that perspective, it's perhaps alternative in the sense that any appropriation of culture by the South becomes alternative to its original in the North. (Jonker 2004)

The creators of the websites have a more imaginative way of relating to it, often expressing contradictory stances in the same statement. For example, Thomas Gesthuizen of Africanhiphop.com responded to a question about the site's musical stance as follows:

> The term "alternative hip-hop site" doesn't mean much to me, . . . though the idea behind [the site] is maybe a bit different from many sites. Hip-hop is a bit different now from [what it was] ten years ago, in that right now hip-hop is no longer the world's alternative, revolutionary music, but the world's pop music. So in a way its core business has come a bit closer to what the established industry is interested in. Though [in our case] we still tend to focus more on non-commercial and conscious artists. (Gesthuizen 2004)

While attempting to avoid the categorization that could be understood as constraining, the creators indeed acknowledge that their portals' musical orientation is oppositional to "mainstream" culture. Tim Adkins, a filmmaker who has been documenting the real and virtual words of Okayplayers for over four years, echoes this stance:

> Left-of-center music . . . that is what they [Okayplayer] are trying to present. I noticed in your project [Pinard and Jacobs] you guys are talking about alternative hip-hop in quotes. I think you could use alternative hip-hop and left-of-center music to mean the same thing. Left-of-center on the musical and political spectrum . . . I guess the left-of-center taste in music seems to naturally incur a great sense of liberalism. If you spend enough time on the activist board you'll definitely see that. (Atkins 2004)

In effect, the term *alternative* persists and is used by both artists and music critics to characterize a group of artists as well as their audiences. The distinction arose mainly due to the conflation of hip-hop and rap genres within the culture industry (Solomon 2002, 129). Alternative hip-hoppers have sought to position themselves as "hip-hop artists" as opposed to simply commercial rappers, as social activists, and cultural ambassadors (see El-Muhajir 2003).

Alternative hip-hop has come to define itself as a diverse genre that often defies mainstream radio formats and intentionally pushes its content beyond the popular themes of materialism, drug use, sex, and violence that inundate mainstream rap music, favored by the record companies and culture industries. Alternative hip-hop artists keenly incorporate this awareness into their lyrics. On "Big Ole Words," the Atlanta-based MC Cee-Lo (a one-time member of the Goodie Mob), vocalizes his frustration with the constricting formulas that the rap industry prescribes, when he raps: "I gotta play your game of gimmick and gun firin." Even mainstream artists recognize the pressure of the market on their cultural production and express their affinity to alternative artists and their ethos. The very successful commercial and mainstream artist Jay Z raps on "Moment on Clarity" (*The Black Album*, 2004):

> I dumb down for my audience
> And double my dollars
> They criticize me for it
> Yet they all yell "Holla"
> If skills sold
> Truth be told
> I'd probably be
> Lyricly
> Talib Kweli
> Truthfully
> I wanna rhyme like Common Sense
> (But i did five Mil)
> I ain't been rhymin like Common Sense.

Both the artists and audiences who fall within the Okayplayer.com or Africanhiphop.com communities are conscious of the cultural and economic exploitation that the record and culture industries represent. As a result, these artists are incorporating this awareness into their lyrics and, most importantly, into the imagined communities which they have fostered in cyberspace.

## Cultural Flows and Cyber Hip-hop

"Cultural flows" relates to the ways in which music is produced, distributed, and consumed. We also understand that the production of culture—in this case, hip-hop—impacts the production of ideas and values. This being the case, Okay-player.com and arguably Africanhiphop.com, its creators, artists, as well as the members of the cybercommunity, appear to actively seek to make true the idea that hip-hop music has the potential to influence, educate, and transform society.

At its outset, hip-hop was pioneered by independent (mainly black) entrepreneurs and labels, while the mainstream record industry and radio stations were generally uninterested. However, once some commercial viability was established by the mid to late 1980s, the major labels began their quest to dominate production and distribution. This coincided with the consolidation of the music industry under essentially six major record companies—CBS, Polygram, Warner, BMG, Capitol-EMI, and MCA. This process of consolidation was more or less complete by 1990 (Rose 1994, 6). By the end of the decade, it was widely agreed that hip-hop had more or less become standardized and diluted, largely driven by profit margins.

Independent labels like Tommy Boy, Profile, and Def Jam continued to flourish, surpassing the profits of the major labels because of their "much greater understanding of the cultural logic of hip-hop and rap music" and the business. Rose argues that the major labels soon developed a new strategy: "buy the independent labels, allow them to function relatively autonomously, and provide them with production resources and access to major retail distribution" (Rose 1994, 7). In mid-2004, four major groups had consolidated the business: Universal Music Group, Warner Music, BMG/Sony, and EMI. For example, Universal Music Group includes the labels Geffen (which has Okayplayer.com artists Common, Talib Kweli, and The Roots on its roster), as well as Bad Boy, Interscope, Aftermath, Motown (Okayplayer artist Erykah Badu), Island Def Jam, and Def Jam South.

This development benefited the majors' own pockets given that they did not have to invest large upfront capital. Rap artists now had access to the large record and CD chains stories that would never have considered carrying their work before. They also had access to the more lucrative white teenage market.

At the same, a number of strategies continued to be employed by artists, fans, and promoters to make money or to counteract what many saw as exploitive and stifling influences of the dominant record industry. For example, hip-hop has always relied on an underground economy for the illegal dubbing of music—"bootlegs"—through the sale of mixtapes for audiences who could not afford retail CD prices. Rose points out that by the early 1990s "technological advances in electronics brought significantly expanded access to mixing, dubbing, and copying equipment for consumers and black-market retailers" (Rose 1994, 7). But even strategies like these have not allowed the escape from the major labels. Nevertheless, they came in handy as strategies to be emulated on the Internet.

The artists featured on Okayplayer.com have generally been signed to independent labels and their music has been marketed and distributed by one of the four major companies. This means they have access to production resources and major retail distribution. The crucial difference between most of them and other commercially orientated artists who are also signed to independent labels is that they are reflexive and critical of the cultural and economic exploitation that the record and cultural industries represent. Thompson of The Roots states, "There is an audience that isn't into the bling-bling lifestyle, that isn't into music that was created on a Casio. So I take the Internet and use it as a strainer" (Wiltz 2000, C1).

Okayplayer.com stands out as a space that actively seeks to bridge the gap between creativity and commerce. The more time we spent on the boards and received responses to our questions, we found that an odd amalgamation of mainstream and alternative values and ideologies informed the space and its members. When asked what type of relationship the portal had to the mainstream, Poetix, a member of the portal from its early days, stated:

> By and large, folks want their artists to eat and have all the resources available to mega-selling performers, yet still have the same ethos as an up and coming crew trying to put out shit from the heart for themselves, history, and a few dozen of their closest peoples. (Poetix 2004)

Spurred on by the artists featured on its websites, members celebrate a kind of politics that attempts to move away from hedonistic capitalism towards a more conscious or communal capitalistic model. Tim Adkins, an active Okayplayer, described this sensibility as "being like Kanye West" (Atkins 2004). West, a Chicago producer-turned-hip-hop artist is very critical of the materialism, nihilism, and misogyny that pervades mainstream hip-hop. Yet at the same time, West is signed to a label, Rocafella on Def Jam, that actively promotes such images and lyrics. According to Adkins, "we [like Kanye West] understand capitalism as foisted upon us, but at the same time we know we can manipulate it."

Okayplayer.com has become an important part of the marketing as well as determining consumer demand for its roster of artists. Because of the community it has created, Okayplayer.com has a captured audience. In effect, it is continually and constantly in contact with its virtually created market. However, it should be noted that although perceived as a "market," Okayplayer is more a dynamic space, where the site and its creators actively engage their "e-family" to not only sell music to them but also have direct communication with fans. In this way, they not only establish a sense of community but also serve to offer an opportunity for marketing feedback that not only complements traditional marketing techniques but also gives it the extra edge.

This can be illustrated by looking at the career of the "Nu-Soul" artist Jill Scott. In early 2000, The Roots released a live album called *Come Alive* on which they featured a relatively unknown vocalist from Philadelphia, Jill Scott. That same year, Scott released her debut album, *Who Is Jill Scott? Words and Sounds Vol. I.* Despite being released on a small label, and not commanding the same marketing budget as a marquee artist, the album surpassed expectations; it stormed the charts. For Scott's record company, Okayplayer.com played a central part in the album's sales:

> We've developed an army of interns who's [sic] been a big part of spreading the word about Jill [Scott]. Before the album was released, we started distributing "Who Is Jill Scott?" promotional items such as T-shirts and stickers. Okayplayer.com embraced Jill early on. (Hall 2000, 60)

The record companies that are home to the artists on the website have also seen the benefits that the site offers. More and more they refer to the "Okayplayer market." According to Tim Reid, the marketing director of MCA, the Okayplayer.com message boards have become a crucial factor in securing exceptional record sales:

You instantly see the feedback from your target audience, and there is a nice cross-section of hip-hop community. The board also offers an opportunity for instant marketing feedback. MCA is trying to corner the Okayplayer market with the Roots, Common, and the Jazzyfatnastees. I use the site a lot because [its visitors] are the people I want to sell to. (Hall 2000, 60)

Despite sentiments like the above, both the creators, "Okayartists" as well as Okayplayers, insist on a more creative tension with the record companies. Poetix suggests:

?uestlove an 'nem have a love-hate relationship with mainstream hip-hop and its politics. There are necessary evils and politics of participation that govern what they can say and do. That said, I think they are very progressive, and have long been advocates for the advancement of hip-hop (qualitatively and substantively). (Poetix 2004)

While Okayplayer features the work of mainly U.S. artists who have contracts with either major or (leading) independent labels, the same cannot be said for their African counterparts. As a result, Africanhiphop.com has a very different relationship with production processes, starting from a lower base. Gesthuizen, founder of Africanhiphop.com, suggests that first and foremost the portal is:

an online platform site which aims to be a place where people can learn about hip-hop on the African continent. All the information on African rap was very scattered. Our site has played an important role in creating awareness internationally that there's hip-hop in Africa, and it was also among the first to talk about "African hip-hop" where most people would talk about rap from a specific country, e.g. Senegal. (Gesthuizen 2004)

Gesthuizen works for a Dutch nongovernmental organization, Madunia. According to its website, Madunia was founded to "promote African music and support local initiatives of African musicians" (Kwaku 2001). The organization funds recording sessions and provides education about African music and musicians through its websites. This means the server, as well as the key creators, is located in the Netherlands. As a result, the creators of Africanhiphop.com, especially Gesthuizen, have not been immune to questions about motives and the geographical location of their server. However, it is clear that Africans still retain major control over the direction, content, and key parts of the production process. Apart from Gesthuizen, the core "staff" consists mainly of transplanted Africans (students, artists) as well as a number of correspondents actively involved in various African hip-hop scenes. The criticism has led to the creators of the site posting the following message on its "About" section: "The Africanhiphop.com website is 100% independent, uncensored, and receives no financial or material support from any organization" (African-hiphop.com, accessed on October 31, 2004). And as we will later point out, the site's creators cite the dispersed and multinational backgrounds of its creative core as one of its strengths.

It is also clear that the location of the server has probably more to do with technological issues (i.e., the lack of technical infrastructure on the African continent as opposed to Western Europe). And as one observer notes, "If it's necessary [to locate the server in the Netherlands], then it's not unusual. And, going with the distributed nature of the net, isn't it more important where the writers are located than the server?" (Jonker 2004). In addition Gesthuizen's motives are not questioned: "[Gesthuizen] has won the trust of respected hip-hop heads, whose judgment I trust" (Anonymous 2004). However, Gesthuizen and his team are pessimistic about the potential to restructure the record indus-try. He has no illusions about the expected interest of major labels in the music and artists circulating on their website. At best, Africanhiphop.com has devel-oped cultural capital in which less commercial, but equally mainstream, outlets consult with or use Africanhiphop.com as a resource or as a sounding board when accessing African hip-hop. Gesthuizen points out that:

> I never trusted that the mainstream music industry would ever pick up on hip-hop from Africa, so the site has always been a site on its own where people could exchange and learn about the music without having to worry about for-eign label policies. And throughout the years the site became a gathering point for information and contacts on African rap, and now the major labels are finding their way there and take what they can. (Gesthuizen 2004)

Probably the most significant impact offline on cultural and musical flows has been the impact on content of mainly European radio stations. The British public broadcaster through its BBC3 Radio recently launched a series of digital music radio programs (also available on the Internet) dedicated to African music, called "Africa on Your Street," which relied extensively on the informa-tion collected by Africanhiphop.com. According to Gesthuizen, "They [the BBC] mine the tunes we dug up." It should be noted, however, that BBC3 acknowledges due credit to Africanhiphop.com on its (BBC3) website. In addi-tion, the popular Rough Guide compilation produced a "Rough Guide to African Rap"—which, in the context of hard-to-get African hip-hop recordings in the West, is an achievement—for which Gesthuizen and his colleagues advised the producers and compiled (and provided) a significant number of the songs and bands featured. According to Gesthuizen, Africanhiphop.com has plans to release its own compilation "some time" (Gesthuizen 2004).

More significantly, through Madunia, Africanhiphop.com has not only connected artists from various parts of the continent but also exposed their work to audiences outside Africa:

It has brought a number of people together and has linked local hip-hop heads with the rest of the continent in important ways. Ask [the South African group] Black Noise about their interaction with heads from further north on the continent, for example. It has also helped to link European heads with people from the South. (Haupt 2004)

Apart from influencing the listening patterns of consumers in the West, Africanhiphop.com plays a central role in aiding the building of a viable, independent recording industry for hip-hop on the continent. In Tanzania, it has helped to build a recording studio, shot and produced videos for hip-hop groups, and improved access to local media.

As a result, Gesthuizen is adamant about the site's future outlook:

The site is non-commercial and intended to stay that way. We'd like to make it a platform which isn't much biased and not linked too closely to the recording industry. Because in Africa, many of the biggest talents haven't managed to secure recording deals while these days they may be able to hook up a computer and a soundcard so that they can record their own tracks and release them on the web. So the function of the site supporting an alternative network of music exchanging is more important than its potential to support commercial releases. However, in order to promote African hip-hop in the West, these releases are sometimes highlighted.

Despite the obstacles presented by an increasingly stifled record industry that more than ever privileges profits over artistry, what we find is that efforts such as Okayplayer.com and Africanhiphop.com—the former perhaps more than the latter—develop a greater autonomy over their cultural output; that is, the Internet seems to give them an edge and a greater sense of agency over the production, marketing, or distribution of their music.

## Identity

Okayplayer.com, while very much a site started by and catering to a largely black audience, has understood that within musical communities, categories such as race, class, and ethnicity can be malleable. Within the virtual diaspora, cross-cultural and multiethnic identities align themselves under the banner of alternative hip-hop. In fact, most of the Okayartists have attracted racially diverse audiences. The message boards of Okayplayer.com reflect this.

Here is a sample of how Okayplayers perceive their participation on the site and the ways in which its message boards have contributed to changes in Okayplayers' identity. Poetix, the "charter member" with over 12,000 posts on the various message boards, expressed what the site means to him:

This is a site that was created by members of a black group working in what is predominantly and historically a black musical idiom, and there is necessarily a cultural baseline here that is steeped in the black community. That said, we have every race and ethnicity fabricated by humankind represented on the boards, and we largely get along very well. But (and I'm Black, by the way), it's a place where "we" can and should feel comfortable. (Poetix 2004)

Adkins, the filmmaker, says:

If you're doing a demographic breakdown you're looking at 60 to 70% black, probably a good 15% white and then after that a mix of Asian and Latino. There's definitely a minority of Asians and Latinos and the next group would be whites . . . and black folks make up the majority of Okayplayers. . . . You recognize this is a black art-form. These are primarily black folk here . . . [however] whatever your background is . . . you can come in and be accepted. There is . . . a healthy black nationalism. (Atkins 2000)

Finally, Firebrand, another prolific participant on the message boards, weighs in:

Well, this is America. Race matters. There is a mix of class, sex, race, and ethnicity here that makes for interesting exchanges. More often than not there is a respect level that makes most of these exchanges positive, and educational. Some are not. Most of the social groupings seem to be idea based, and not ethnicity or racially based. (Firebrand 2004)

What these responses point to is an acknowledgement of the material and political importance as well as socially constructed nature of seemingly ossified racialized and class-based identities. At the same time, they point to the tensions and possibilities of changing ascribed identities on and through the Internet.

In late 1990s, Africanhiphop.com was the only website whose objective was to build a pan-African website—that is, attempting to survey and provide access to local and national hip-hop cultures from all over the continent. It could be argued that the site retains that premier position in 2004—it now provides extensive and up-to-date information on hip-hop in at least 30 African countries (from minimal information on 10 countries in the beginning). According to Gesthuizen, the site has between 800 and 1,200 unique visitors daily (as opposed to "hits" which is really a count of the number of files—including separate pages—transferred).

The profiles of the average forum members active on the message boards are generally English-speaking young males (90% according to Gesthuizen) who live either in large African cities or in immigrant communities in the U.S. or Western Europe. Jonker identifies two main purposes for the site:

It does a very good job of showcasing African music, and reflecting how Africa is. . . . On the other hand, it also seems to be working towards re-creating hip-hop as an African thing. They're doing a positive job of "continentalising" the African hip-hop movement. That seems to be the site's aim, a kind of pan-Africa consciousness through a shared musical form, and that sounds like a good start to me. (Jonker 2004)

That quest, however, is not at the expense of inclusive identity. As Gesthuizen (2004) explains:

People visiting the site and especially the forum are usually aware that they are visiting a site which is constructed around an identity and a topographical definition (in the word "Africanhiphop.com") so they have a certain expectation when visiting. For the editorial part we try to answer the demand by focusing on artists from all over the continent, even though it's easier to get info from countries where we have someone writing stories such as Nigeria or South Africa.

From the FAQ and the site intro page, it is obvious that the creators of Africanhiphop.com are not about limiting the site and forums' use to "African" or black people only. They are intent on seeing "African hip-hop" as the body of work produced on the African continent, which can be consumed by anyone interested. Gesthuizen and the site's other creators felt the need to respond directly to some questions regarding race and identity of the site's producers, pointing to the contextual politics of race:

Some people asked us if the people doing this site are all Africans/blacks (interestingly, it's only Americans that have asked this). The people that maintain this site are from different origins and backgrounds, both African and European. Currently most contributions are written by people from Tanzania, Senegal, Holland and South Africa—black, white and anything in between. Our philosophy is that it is not important where you are from, it's where you at . . . and hip-hop is our tool to reach our shared goals, and [to] build on the revolutionary power of rap. The site was started out to promote the work, views and achievements of hip-hop artists from urban Africa, and it will always support the developments at street level. We will not allow other interests to take over. (Africanhiphop.com, accessed on October 31, 2004)

Probably the best example of how Africanhiphop.com goes about identity can be gauged from Gesthuizen's own biography, which not only reflects the global appeal of hip-hop but also the philosophy of the site's creators. Born in 1973 in a village in the eastern part of the Netherlands (the province of East Holland), Gesthuizen (a white male) has "been listening a lot to hip-hop since about 1987." As he pointed out in answer to questions, "I was very deeply into the music and also learning about hip-hop history." Gesthuizen's cousin was a hip-hop DJ and producer and "he taught me a lot about the records and the original samples used for hip-hop beats." In 1992, he enrolled at the University of Leiden, which has probably the biggest and most influential African Studies program in the Netherlands:

> I learnt about African pop music during my studies and became a DJ playing African pop in 1994. But at the time it was still unusual to mix African music and hip-hop in one DJ set as those were 2 different audiences. From about 1995 on there were a handful of African rap acts visiting Holland and I interviewed Positive Black Soul (Senegal) that year. Their work, and a few releases by groups like POC (South Africa) and Da Multy Krew (Ghana/Holland) pro-vided the first content for [the website] Rumba-Kali. (Gesthuizen 2004)

Gesthuizen's subsequent studies took him to Tanzania: "The first two times, I found little presence of a local hip-hop scene but when I bought a tape and read some newspaper stories I became fascinated and tried to get in touch with these artists. In 1996 I did meet with a rapper who had the same interests in hip-hop as I did and from trying to promote his crew, I started the site" (Gesthuizen 2004).

Rose (1994) argued that "identity in hip-hop is deeply rooted in the spe-cific, the local experience, and one's attachment to and status in a local group or alternative family." As a result, these crews are "new kinds of family forged with intercultural bonds that . . . provide insulation and support in a complex and unyielding environment and may serve as the basis for new social move-ments" (34). Rose may not have foreseen the potential of the Internet, but a decade later we are confronted with an almost identical configuration in cyber-space. What Rose described as "the local experience" has become a global expe-rience through the music aided by the Internet.

## Representational Politics

To what degree do cybercommunities translate their virtual capital into *real*, offline political power?

It is now common for organizations openly competing for political power in industrial societies to utilize the Internet (Rheingold 1993; Negroponte 1995; Dertouzos 1997; Swartz 1996; Norris 2003). The website Moveon.org in the United States represents such an organization. It has emerged as a key portal assisting Democratic Party activists organizing since the disputed 2000 election of George W. Bush as U.S. president. In the initial phases of the 2004 Democra-tic primaries for the 2004 presidential campaign, the campaign of Howard Dean was boosted considerably by grassroots organizations utilizing the Internet—

both in raising money and coalitions and in signing volunteers (Justice 2003; Trippi 2004). Conservatives have also tuned into the potential of the Internet. At a global level, groups extolling the virtues of globalization as well as those opposing it—whether on uneven trade regimes, odious government debt, or the activities of multinational corporations—also see the virtue of the Internet. Examples outside the U.S. include Jubilee 2000, the World Social Forum, ATTAC, and the various indymedia websites that have sprung up since 1999.

While both Okayplayer.com and Africanhiphop.com are primarily con-cerned with music, they also actively engage in politics, in some cases by facili-tating debates on message boards (the "Okay-activist" board specifically) or by actively taking on political issues. For example, Okayplayer.com has organized city cleanups in over four cities and coordinated voter registration drives. In June 2004, Okayplayer.com acted as a major discursive catalyst and promoter of the National Hip-Hop Political Convention.[8] The convention's goals as pro-moted on the portal were to harness the power of hip-hop generation and develop a national political agenda. At the end of the four-day convention, which was discussed daily on Okayplayer message boards, members of the Okay-player virtual diaspora agreed, both on- and offline, on a political platform set-ting out a series of demands and an action to engage local and national legislative institutions and government agencies.

On Okayplayer.com's message boards, artists and fans can regularly engage in and provoke conversations (on- and offline) centered around a worldview that seeks to challenge the status quo while simultaneously fostering alternative means of addressing (and attempting to resolve) pressing societal ills. As one longtime Okayplayer puts it:

> Sometimes when I become discouraged with the current state of the country, the thing that raises my hopes is the intelligence and concern for issues dis-played here. That does not mean that all posters are smart or show their intelli-gence, or that all posts are political in nature. But it gives me hope nonetheless? (Janey 2004)

The way Okayplayers understand and form opinions about foreign policy have been impacted by the presence of non-U.S. citizens on the message boards. Poetix highlights this impact:

> It's a place where people can interact within a wildly diverse demographic within a loosely binding theme of hip-hop. We politick on the daily with cats from all over the globe. Talk beats with producers in Belgium. Argue politics with Israelis, Palestinians, and Nigerians. Shit is very global. (Poetix 2004)

The Okayactivist message board is a space in which Okayplayers debate about how to move beyond talking about social change and start creating change. We found that the overall effectiveness of the discussions that take place on the boards is a topic of debate.

Discussion topics on the message boards range from headings such as "should rumsfeld be forced to resign," "confronting the realities of forced migration," and "black banks unite" to "why are black folk so materialistic?" to "men of color: would you marry a white woman?"

We encountered perspectives that the layperson might not generally ascribe to members of the hip-hop community. Informed perspectives were common and usually aligned themselves with those on the left of the sociopolitical spectrum.

Throughout our exploration of the site and its offline initiatives, we encountered a number of instances of offline action emanating from online discussions. One of the first initiatives coming out of these debates—exemplifying the concrete links between online and offline communities—was a city-to-city cleanup drive that reportedly involved over 1,000 participants in four major cities. The next initiative brought about a voter registration drive in which Okayplayers registered thousands of voters in ten cities.

However, it would be amiss to overstate the political potential of the website. In our research, we discovered that it was more than that: The cybercommunity is a safe haven for some who are "socially awkward" and who are seeking out significant relationships online that are lacking in the real world, but want to retain their anonymity. As one Okayplayer told us:

> They [members of Okayplayer] sought the internet out as a means to gain control over their identity and express themselves in a way that is comfortable for them. . . . They wanna use it because they don't have to worry about . . . they weigh too much . . . or they don't have the right social skills . . . and maybe they are self-conscious about some little personal thing . . . whatever the case . . . they wanna be online so they can feel normal, so they can have some control. (Atkins 2004)

A second function of online music communities is to extend these friendships and camaraderie around music to other spheres offline. Okayplayer members have organized interstate carpools, accommodations, concerts, reunions, promoted each other's art, and formed political action communities.

From its outset, Africanhiphop.com has attempted a very specific mandate: to promote greater access to music technologies and production for African artists. However, at the same time, the site's creators were very aware of its political potential: "This was an idea that hip-hop can be a platform for people to express themselves and bring about change, a change which can extend to other areas than the cultural," according to Gesthuizen.

Right from the start, the site was very explicit in its political stance when the following message was posted on the first version of Africanhiphop.com:

Remember the words of Fela Kuti: "In 2000 Africa must be one." We will not wait for the politicians to bring unity to us—instead we will come together to fulfill the promise. On these pages you can read about the revolution of the mind that is taking place among the urban African youth. (Africanhiphop.com, accessed October 15, 2004)

The JavaScript message that scrolled across the page quoted another musician with explicitly political views, Gill Scott-Heron: "The revolution will not be televized." The site's creators have had to trim down their political ambitions though:

With the current budget and available time restrictions, it's not really possible to maintain an active involvement in offline discussions on politics etc. Most of the opinions will be expressed on the website and maybe through mailing lists or in interviews with magazines doing a special about the website. (Africanhiphop.com, accessed October 14, 2004)

There are times, though, when they break through these limitations. Recently, a petition against the ban of hip-hop in Congo brought a lot of new visitors to the site and 300 people signed the petition, which was forwarded to the Congolese cultural ministry. In the end, it became "a very interesting example of the power of online communities since this petition was sent to the secretary of one government member and apparently the message has reached them, and they are considering undoing the ban" (Gesthuizen 2004).

## Conclusion

In this chapter, we have found through the study of two online hip-hop communities that the Internet has some, if not significant, impact on cultural flows, identity, and political struggles. The evidence suggests that by adopting an explicit and active political stance on the music and culture industries, Africanhiphop.com and Okayplayer.com seek to undermine, redirect, and reshape cultural flows. Significantly, both portals actively strive to create a commercially viable environment, both alongside and separate from the mainstream, in which to produce, distribute, and sell their art. While doing this, the artists and activists behind the portals do not reject commercial success, but seek to redefine the terms upon which their music is made, received, marketed, and distributed. As a result, we argue that these cybercommunities provide a space within which to restructure or renegotiate the terms of cultural production, however limited and improbable that may appear at first sight. However, a number of questions remain: What factors might cause the uniting of the virtual and the real? What are the potentialities of the virtual diaspora? For us, while more research is needed on these questions, our research shows that the portals impact cultural flows in the sense that they create spaces in which the artists and audiences who are not necessarily orientated and inclined toward the sounds and politics of the dominant culture industries can speak to dominant cultural flows or create alternative flows. Africanhiphop.com and Okayplayer.com enable people worldwide to negotiate new conceptions of identity. The actors within these virtual diasporas interact across ethnic and racial boundaries in a way that we posit offers dynamic possibilities, presented by technology, to overcome some of the more considerable and traditional obstacles to effective and progressive political action.

## References to Chapter Four

Anderson, Benedict. 1991. *Imagined Communities: Reflections on the Origin and Spread of Nationalism*. London: Verso.

Bahi, Aghi. 2004. Internet Use and Logics of Social Adaptation of Youth in Abidjan Cybercafes. *CODESRIA Bulletin* 1–2:67–71.

Bourdieu, Pierre. 1993. *The Field of Cultural Production*. New York: Columbia University Press.

Bourdieu, Pierre, and Loic Wacquant. 1993. *Invitation to Reflexive Sociology*. Chicago: University of Chicago Press.

Brown, Irvin, and Paul Licker. 2003. Exploring Differences in Internet Adoption and Usage between Historically Advantaged and Disadvantaged Groups in South Africa. *Journal of Global Information Technology Management* 6, no. 4: 6–26.

Chivhanga, B. M. 2000. An Evaluation of the Impact of the Internet in Africa. *Aslib Proceedings* 52, no. 10: 373–83.

Dertouzos, Michael. 1997. *What Will Be: How the New Information Marketplace Will Change Our Lives*. San Francisco, CA: Harper.

El-Muhajir, Muhammeda. 2003. *Hip-hop: The New World Order*. SunLeo Productions.

Gesthuizen, Thomas (Juma4). 2004. Interview with the authors, via email. July 4, 2004.

Giddens, Anthony, et al. 2002. *Introduction to Sociology*. London: Norton.

Habermas, Jurgen. 1989. *The Structural Transformation of the Public Sphere: An Inquiry into a Category of Bourgeois Society*. Cambridge, MA: MIT Press.

Hall, Rashaun. 2000. "The Roots Boost Artist, Fan Interaction with Okayplayer Tour." *Billboard Magazine* (October 7): 60.

Ikegami, Eiko. 2000. "A Sociological Theory of Publics: Identity and Culture as Emergent Properties in Networks." *Social Research* 67, no. 4 (Winter): 989–1030.

Jensen, Mike. 2000. "Making the Connection: Africa and the Internet." *Current History* 99, no. 637 (May): 215–20.

Jonker, Julian. 2004. Email communication with the authors. June 16.

Justice, Glenn. 2003. "Howard Dean's Internet Push: Where Will It Lead?" *New York Times*, November 2, p. 4–5

Katiebree. 2003. "Taking the Right Root." *Club Vibes Magazine*. Online.

Kwaku. 2001. "Words and Deeds." *Billboard* (October 27).

Louie, Rebecca. 2002. "Roots: True to the Name." *USA Weekend.com*. Retrieved December 1, 2002, from http://www.usaweekend.com/02_issues/021201/021201 roots.html

Maluka, Mustafa. 2003. "The Search for Ira Goldstein: A Cultural Analysis of African Hip-hop Virtual Communities." Unpublished paper, Amsterdam.

McLaine, Steve. 2003. "Ethnic Online Communities: Between Profit and Purpose." In *Cyberactivism: Online Activism in Theory and Practice*, edited by Martha McCaughey and Michael D. Ayers, 233–54. New York: Routledge.

Neate, Patrick. 2004. *Where You're At: Notes from the Frontline of a Hip-Hop Planet*. New York: Riverhead Books.

Negroponte, Nicolas. 1995. *Being Digital*. New York: Knopf.

Norris, Pippa. 2003. "Preaching to the Converted? Pluralism, Participation and Party Websites." *Party Politics* 9, no. 1: 21–45.

Rheingold, Howard. 1993. *The Virtual Community: Homesteading on the Electronic Frontier*. Reading, MA: Addison-Wesley.

Rose, Tricia. 1994. *Black Noise: Rap Music and Black Culture in Contemporary America*. Middletown, CT: Wesleyan University Press.

Solomon, Akiba. 2002. "Who You Callin a Backpacker?" *Source* (July): 129–30.

Swartz, Edward. 1996. *Netactivism: How Citizens Use the Internet*. Sebastapol, CA: Songline Studios.

Trippi, Joe. 2004. *The Revolution Will Not Be Televized: Democracy, the Internet, and the Overthrow of Everything*. New York: Harper Collins.

Williams, Christine, Bruce Weinberg, and Jesse Gordon. 2004. "When Online and Offline Politics 'Meetup': An Examination of the Phenomenon, Presidential Campaign and Its Citizen Activists." Paper presented at the annual meeting of the American Political Science Association, Hilton Chicago and the Palmer House Hilton, Chicago, IL, September 2.

Wiltz, Teresa (2000), "Taking the Rap Online and Off; with a 44-City Tour, Okayplayer Links Its Website to a New Generation of Fans." *Washington Post*, October 9, C1.

### Interviews and email communication

Atkins, Tim. May 24, 2004.

Gesthuizen, Thomas. June 13, July 4 and 5, 2004.

Haupt, Adam. June 17, 2004.

Jonker, Julian. June 16, 2004.

Respondents at Okayplayer message boards.

Anonymous. May 14, 2004.

Aoxomoxoa, July 24, 2004.

Firebrand. August 15, 2004.

Janey. July 1, 2004.

Poetix. May 5 and July 22, 2004.

CHAPTER FIVE

# The Technology of Subversion: From Digital Sampling in Hip-Hop to the MP3 Revolution

## Adam Haupt

This chapter explores ways in which technology has been used to frustrate corporate interests. Specifically, I examine the ways in which digital sampling in hip-hop and mp3 technology have effectively issued challenges to the major record labels' near-absolute control over music production and distribution. This exploration speaks to my ongoing interest in instances where agency becomes possible in Empire. By "Empire," I am referring to Michael Hardt and Antonio Negri's (2000) concept of Empire as "a global concert under the direction of a single conductor, a unitary power that maintains the social peace and produces its ethical truths" (9). At the very outset, though, these authors warn that they are not offering a "conspiracy theory of globalization" (2000, 3). Instead, they are attempting to describe the complex ways in which power is manifested within the context of global capitalism, a context that is both postimperialist and postcolonial:

> [W]e think it is important to note that what used to be conflict or competition among several imperial powers has in important respects been replaced by the idea of a single power that overdetermines them all, structures them in a unitary way, and treats them under one common notion of right that is decidedly postcolonial and postimperialist. This is really the point of departure for our study of Empire: a new notion of right, or rather, a design of the production of norms and legal instruments of coercion that guarantee contracts and resolve conflicts. (Hardt and Negri 2000, 9)

Hardt and Negri contend that "the juridical concept of Empire" took shape in the "ambiguous experiences of the United Nations" (2000, 6). However, they also contend that "there is no need to limit our analysis to or even focus it on the established supranational regulatory institutions" (2000, 31) due to the influence that transnational corporations exert on a global scale:

> The great industrial and financial powers thus produce not only commodities but also subjectivities. They produce agentic subjectivities within the biopolitical context: they produce needs, social relations, bodies, and minds—which is to say, they produce producers. (Hardt and Negri 2000, 31–32)

This chapter taps into these authors' conception of the notion of Empire in order to discuss some of the ways in which these "agentic subjects"/"producers" engage with corporate attempts to maximize revenue streams and consolidate control over the field of music production and distribution. I argue that hip-hop, much like reggae and punk, once offered an example of a counterculture that presented a challenge to hegemonic representations of marginalized subjects. I shall take this a step further by suggesting that one key element of the production of hip-hop music texts in the '80s and early '90s—digital sampling—challenged conventional assumptions about authorship and copyright and thus compromised corporate interests. I also suggest that the practice of digital sampling in hip-hop in a sense prefigured some of the events that transpired during the mp3 and Napster legal battles. Ultimately, I argue that it is the very technology that has helped Empire—signified by the impressive market share of the major record labels in this context—to prosper, yet is used to supposedly subvert its interests. However, I must point out from the outset that I am aware that websites such as mp3.com and Napster.com—as well as Napster clones such as Gnutella, KaZaa, and Morpheus—were also driven by profit motives. These sites were not necessarily developed as part of a counter-hegemonic agenda to the near-absolute control that the "Big Four" record labels (i.e., Empire—Universal Vivendi, Sony-BMG, AOL Time Warner, and EMI) have over the production and distribution of music across the globe. What is worth noting here is that audio file swapping on the Internet became the pastime of millions of people in a large number of countries. I suggest that the significant uptake of mp3 technology among end users marks a return to some key fears that the Big Four labels faced when they challenged hip-hop artists' use of digital sampling technology in earlier legal battles.

## Life before MP3: The Politics of Digital Sampling in Hip-hop

One key difference between the rise of the mp3 revolution and the use of digital sampling in hip-hop is that hip-hop artists make informed artistic/political choices when using samples during the construction of new music texts, whereas audio piracy on the Internet offers consumers a new means of consuming commodities (although this very alternative is transgressive). The latter centers around new modes of consumption and the former focuses upon creative composition. Napster supporters typically bypassed conventional retail avenues and engaged with online communities of music fans on a peer-to-peer level. No cash changed hands and no royalties were paid during these exchanges. This type of interaction is not to be confused with the cash sale of bootleg or pirated CDs. Online music swapping differs from digital sampling because the technology was initially restricted to music producers, who used snatches from other songs or instrumental music in order to produce new music. Hip-hop producers in the '80s and early '90s often did not secure copyright clearance from the relevant publishers when they used samples from other musical or other media sources; this formed the basis of major record labels' objections to sampling (see Buchanan, this volume). Legal objections aside, Tricia Rose (1994) contends that "[s]ampling in rap is a process of cultural literacy and intertextual reference" that celebrates black artistic achievement and challenges audiences to "know these sounds, to make connections between the lyrical and music texts [songs and instrumental music]," thereby affirming "black musical history" (89). Rose's comments apply to black consciousness-inspired hip-hop of the '80s and early '90s, particularly. Rose taps into Dick Hebdige's work on punk subculture in order to suggest that hip-hop speaks through commodities:

> As Hebdige's study on punk subculture illustrates, style can be used as a gesture of refusal or as a form of oblique challenge to structures of domination. Hip hop artists use style as a form of identity formation that plays on class distinctions and hierarchies by using commodities to claim the cultural terrain. (Rose 1994, 36)

Here, Rose is referring to clothing and consumption rituals specifically, but these comments can be applied to reflection on music texts as well. A hip-hop artist from the '80s and early '90s might typically sample a familiar drumbeat or chorus line from a James Brown song in order to produce a new hip-hop song. In short, an existing music text—a commodity item from the music marketplace—is sampled in order to produce a new music text that will itself become a commodity in the music marketplace. It is in this sense that hip-hop speaks through commodities in order to redefine the "constitution of narrative originality, composition, and collective memory" and thereby "challenge institutional apparatuses that define property, technological innovation, and authorship" (Rose 1994, 85). Hebdige suggests that subcultures speak through commodities "even if the meaning attached to those commodities [is] purposefully distorted or overthrown" (1979, 95). This distortion is crucial to our understanding of sampling. Hebdige suggests that subcultures represent "noise," as its use of commodities causes "interference in the orderly sequence which leads from real events and phenomena to their representation in the media" (1979, 90). This interference therefore draws our attention to the very constructed nature of media/music texts. Rap songs that use key elements of familiar soul and R&B songs draw our attention to what Rose calls "black cultural priorities" (1994, 91). Such intertextual references create new layers of meaning and draw our attention to the very process of production of the hip-hop songs themselves; it is these aspects of hip-hop's self-referential and intertextual practices that often make hip-hop texts postmodern. As Nelson George suggests, sampling has always formed a key part of the hip-hop sound:

> Before hip hop, producers would use sampling to disguise the absence of a live instrument. If a horn was needed or a particular keyboard line was missing, a pop producer might sample it from another record, trying to camouflage its artificiality in the process. However, a hip hop producer, whose sonic aesthetic was molded by the use of break beats from old records pulled away from dirty crates, wasn't embarrassed to be using somebody else's sounds. Recontextualizing someone else's sounds was, after all, how hip hop started. (George 1998, 92)

Hip-hop producers, unlike pop producers, have therefore chosen not to mask the means of production and have often chosen to draw our attention to the fact that they have recontextualized elements from another artist's song. These acts of recontextualization may, at times, as Rose suggests, prioritize black cultural priorities, or they may also amount to what Linda Hutcheon (1989) calls "postmodern parody" (93–98). She argues that postmodern parody involves a double process of inscription and subversion in an attempt to deconstruct its subject. In an earlier work I argue that Prophets of da City (POC)[1] employ postmodern parody (Haupt 1996a, 29–40) when they challenge the master-narrative of apartheid in a 54-second track titled "Blast from da Past." The track comprises no lyrics and is essentially a mix by founder members Ready D and Shaheen Ariefdien. Here, POC do more than sample music texts—they also sample media snippets, government propaganda, and spoken word poetry by Mzwakhe Mbuli.[2] Much of the government propaganda is made to appear ridiculous within the context of the piece, which is decidedly anticolonial and derisive of the discourse of apartheid. It is in this way that hip-hop artists' use of sampling is "both deconstructively critical and constructively creative, paradoxically making us aware of both the limits and the powers of representation—in any medium" (Hutcheon 1989, 98). Sampling in hip-hop thus has a significant amount of subversive potential and resonates with Dick Hebdige's discussion of subcultural style as a "signifying practice." Here, I am not referring to the discursive and historical relevance of Henry-Louis Gates's work in *Figures in Black* and *The Signifying Monkey* to contemporary rap music, which I discuss elsewhere (Haupt 1996a, 41–51). Instead, I am referring to Hebdige's discussion of the Tel Quel group's theoretical approach toward the "construction and deconstruction of meaning":

> This approach sees language as an active, transitive force which shapes and positions the "subject" (as speaker, writer, reader) while always itself remaining

"in process" capable of infinite adaptation. This emphasis on signifying practice is accompanied by a polemical insistence that art represents the triumph of process over fixity, disruption over unity, "collision" over "linkage"—the triumph, that is, of the signifier over the signified. (Hebdige 1979, 119)

This perspective, in turn, resonates with Gates's discussion "Signifyin(g)" and "Signification." According to Gates, signification occupies the syntagmatic axis, whereas Signification occupies the paradigmatic axis and "concerns itself with that which is suspended, vertically" (1988, 49). With the linear/horizontal/ordered construction of meaning finding itself suspended, "Signification luxuriates in the inclusion of the free play of these associative rhetorical and semantic relations" (Gates 1988, 49). This, in essence, is what sampling in '80s and early '90s hip-hop represents: the triumph of the signifier over the signified or significant measure of free play in the construction of meaning. Ultimately, sampling offered its audiences and artists alike a certain measure of agency in their attempts to challenge hegemonic/fixed representations and definitions of blackness, ownership, and authorship. It is in this way that sampling allows hip-hop DJs to emphasize "black cultural priorities" (Rose 1994, 91) as they are able to offer alternative narratives to oppressive master-narratives. However, as I will suggest in the next section, this kind of agency and subversive cultural practice would soon be curtailed via legal and bureaucratic processes as well as strategies of recuperation. These action and strategies would ultimately benefit corporate entities, as opposed to artists or marginal communities.

## And the Hype Fizzles Out: Sampling, Ownership, and Recuperation

As Thomas Schumacher's work on digital sampling and the law suggests, sampling in hip-hop also offers challenges to legal definitions of ownership as well as the author function. The practice also offers a challenge to the conventional understanding of the "ownership of sound and 'Rockist' aesthetics which remain tied to the romantic ideals of the individual performer" (Schumacher 1995, 266). Schumacher contends that the concept of "copyright is still influenced by the ideological construct of the 'author' as a singular origin of artistic works" (1995, 259). Hip-hop problematizes this construct as the performer/artist is no longer the key focus of attention; a number of subjects (DJs, engineers, and producers) are also inserted into the creative process, thereby changing "the notion of origin (the basis of copyright) to one of origins" (Schumacher 1995, 262–66). The integrity of the "original" music text as a coherently branded commodity item is also "violated" during the process of recontextualization/(re)composition. Ironically, since the U.S. case *Bleistein v. Donaldson Lithographic Co.*, authorship "can now be assigned to corporate entities" and Schumacher observes that contradictions have often been resolved "in the interests of copyright holders," who may very well be corporate entities as opposed to individual artists (1995, 259). Siva Vaidhyanathan, author of *Copyrights and Copywrongs: The Rise of Intellectual Property and How It Threatens Creativity*, concurs with this contention when he says that "the copyright holder is very rarely the artist herself" (McLaren 2004). Therefore, the popular belief that copyright is really meant to protect the interests of the artists becomes questionable. One key exception is the U.S. Supreme Court decision in *Campbell v. Acuff-Rose Music, Inc.* in which the court ruled that parody "may be protected as a fair use exception under the Copyright Law" (Girasa 2002, 180). However, it is interesting to note that by the time Rose wrote *Black Noise*, she predicted that sampling would slow down:

> Maybe rap music represents the real "big payback." . . . The very laws that justified and aided in the theft from and denigration of an older generation of black artists have created a profitable, legal loophole and a relatively free-play zone for today's black artists. This creative cul de sac is rapidly evaporating. The record companies are increasingly likely to hold albums until samples are cleared, until publishers and other record companies negotiate their profits. (Rose 1994, 93)

Rose suggests that sampling as a counter-hegemonic/subversive practice is bound to become delegitimated due to corporate and legal bureaucracy. By the time Nelson George wrote *Hip Hop America* in 1998, it appears that her predictions had largely become true. George contends that "the level of ambition" in the use of samples has declined:

> Obviously, sampling hasn't disappeared from hip hop, but the level of ambition in using samples has fallen. The high-intensity sound tapestries of [Public Enemy] have given way to often simpleminded loops of beats and vocal hooks from familiar songs—a formula that grossed Hammer, Coolio, and Puff Daddy millions in sales and made old R&B song catalogs potential gold mines. (George 1998, 95)

Within what has now become "mainstream" rap music, sampling is by and large no longer a subversive practice that threatens corporate interests or offers direct/parodic political challenges to hegemonic representations. One might also argue that the very idea that millions are potentially made from the sale of old R&B catalogues further reinforces this perspective if one accepts Rose's claim that most record labels cheated earlier generations of black musicians (1994, 92). These musicians, in all likelihood, are not the copyright holders of the songs in these old catalogues and are probably not the key beneficiaries in the payment of any royalties. This impression is strengthened by Schumacher's observation that, under American case law, corporate entities are now legally recognized as authors and, thus, are recognized as copyright holders (1995,

259). In essence, the law and corporate priorities have ensured that sampling's subversive/counter-hegemonic potential to create legal and political "noise" has been resolved in the interests of record labels. Rap group Public Enemy's Hank Shocklee confirms Schumacher and George's reading of these developments in his discussion of how the law affected hip-hop producers' aesthetic approaches in the recording studio:

> We were forced to start using different organic instruments, but you can't really get the right kind of compression that way. A guitar sampled off a record is going to hit differently than a guitar sampled in the studio. The guitar that's sampled off a record is going to have all the compression that they put on the recording, the equalization. It's going to hit the tape harder. Something that's organic is almost going to have a powder effect. . . . So those things change your mood, the feeling you can get off a record. If you notice that by the early 1990s, the sound has gotten softer. (McLeod 2004)

Public Enemy's Chuck D suggests that copyright laws "led people like Dr. Dre to replay the sounds that were on records, then sample musicians imitating those records" (McLeod 2004). In this way, Dr. Dre managed to sidestep having to pay for the rights to the master recordings of songs and only paid for the publishing rights. Ultimately, Chuck D confirms Nelson George's claims about sampling in the late '90s becoming less ambitious: "It's easier to sample a groove than it is to create a whole new collage. That entire collage element is out the window" (McLeod 2004). One could make sense of these shifts by tapping into Dick Hebdige's discussion on the recuperation of subculture in mod and punk subculture. He suggests that the process of recuperation takes place in the following ways:

> the conversion of subcultural signs (dress, music, etc.) into mass-produced objects (i.e., the commodity form); the "labeling" and redefinition of deviant behavior by dominant groups—the police, the media, the judiciary (i.e., the ideological form). (Hebdige 1979, 94)

In his discussion of the commodity form, Hebdige reminds us that subcultures speak through commodities (1979, 95). This certainly is true of hip-hop with regard to dress, graffiti art as well as music. As I suggested earlier, sampling in hip-hop relies on the use of elements of music texts that are already in existence in the marketplace. These texts are thus already commodity items and are used to produce new music texts that will become new commodities. A significant amount of tension thus exists in the creative process of producing counter-discursive music texts, as the process of music production is already quite complicit in commercial processes. In this regard, Hebdige (1979) contends that "the creation of new styles is inextricably bound up with the process of production, publicity and packaging which must inevitably lead to the defusion of the subculture's subversive power" (95). This certainly seems to be true when one considers the ascendance of gangsta rap on the pop music scene. Gangsta rappers, such as Tupac Shakur, Dr. Dre, Coolio, P Diddy, and Eminem, have overshadowed politically conscious hip-hop artists such as Public Enemy, KRS One, Afrika Bambaata, and Dead Prez. Here, I make the distinction between gangsta rap and hip-hop because hip-hop is considered to be politically conscious and is driven by the concept of "knowledge of self" (Haupt 2001, 182), whereas gangsta rap celebrates what is often called "thug life," a celebration made popular globally by MTV and locally by Channel O and many radio stations. It is this form of rap that has been appropriated by gangsters on the Cape Flats (Haupt 2001, 177). In a recent interview with ex-POC member Shaheen Ariefdien, he suggests that, just as classical strings in a Britney Spears song does not make her music classical music, rap in mainstream/gangsta rap does not make this music hip-hop (Ariefdien 2002, 4). Whether one believes that gangsta rap is hip-hop or not, what is true is that one key element of hip-hop, rap, has been co-opted/recuperated by key record labels to be repackaged—devoid of counter-hegemonic content—as a highly saleable commodity.

Hebdige's discussion of the ideological form resonates with mainstream media responses to hip-hop as well as the legal response to sampling in rap. Over the years we have seen a large number of (mostly gangsta) rappers receive negative press coverage over their brushes with the law and rap's gender discourse has also been a key focus of attention, even when it has been considered to be politically conscious (Haupt 2001, 183–88). It is in this way that rap music has come to be characterized as deviant in the sense that Hebdige uses the term. The corporate challenge to sampling in hip-hop via court battles— such as *Acuff-Rose Music Inc. v. Campbell, Boyd Jarvis v. A&M Records et al.*, and *Grand Upright Music v. Warner Bros Records*—comes to characterize hip-hop in this way as well. The recuperation of hip-hop via the ideological and commodity forms ultimately delegitimate hip-hop's subversive potential to a certain degree, thereby making it a more marketable commodity. Hebdige's ideological form of recuperation resonates with Hardt and Negri's (2000) concept of the "just war" in Empire (10). The authors argue that Empire "deploys a powerful police function against the new barbarians and the rebellious slaves who threaten its order" (Hardt and Negri, 2000, 20). Here, the rebellious agents within Empire's borders are '80s and early '90s hip-hop samplers as well as subversive MCs who speak through commodities (Hebdige 1979, 95) and thus operate within the field of capitalism and Western cultural production. It is from this perspective that subculture's subversive potential lies in a measure of complicity with commercial processes (Hebdige 1979, 95). This notion of using the means at hand resonates with Hardt and Negri's claim that the potentials for liberation "exists within Empire" (2000, 46). However, this perilous position places it in danger of recuperation and this seems to have happened with one aspect of hip-hop. As I will suggest later on, this pattern of recuperation repeats itself during the rise of mp3 technology and the growth of music file sharing on the Internet. Again, we see tension between the will of the major record labels, the law, technology and the will of the subjects of Empire.

## The Digital Continuum: The Threat Mutates and Multiplies

Although it appeared that this particular battle had been won by the major record labels, they would later find themselves fighting a similar battle on a much larger scale. Whereas the war against digital sampling in hip-hop was restricted to artists who produced a very particular genre of music, the war against mp3 technology—as well as the kind of peer-to-peer platform offered by Napster—potentially broadened the battle to every consumer of music on a global scale. By the late '90s, the mp3 format was becoming incredibly popular amongst surfers on the Internet. As Cooper and Harrison (2001) reveal, mp3 files are "tremendously more dense than raw audio data" and that these files can thus be transferred via telephone and cable modem connections at relatively great speeds (73). By November 1997, Michael Robertson had recognized that the mp3 format's popularity was a potential goldmine and launched mp3.com (Alderman 2001, 46–47). At this stage, it is important to note that mp3.com was not meant to be an initiative that would challenge the near-absolute control that the major labels had over the music industry. In fact, Alderman characterizes Robertson as a "natural-born capitalist" who wanted to acquire music legally so as to build a legitimate business (2001, 46). Alderman points out that Robertson's attempts to woo the major labels and the Recording Industry Association of America (RIAA) at an mp3 summit in 1997 was met with skepticism (48–54). By contrast, the "hacker developers of the mp3 revolution displayed a remarkable amount of respect and empathy for the record industry" and "seemed to bend over backwards to suggest ways for record labels to make money" (49–50). These early developments were by no means revolutionary in the sense that digital sampling has proved to be mp3.com's success depended on whether the major labels would be willing to give Robertson permission to make its songs available on the website and, without the names of well-known artists on the site, mp3.com would probably not become a big contender in the field. In a sense, one might say that if the Big Four were not ready to acquire market share in this new medium, no one else would either.

The launch of Napster[3] in June 1999 was met with far more than skepticism and, by December 1999, the RIAA launched legal action against Napster on behalf of its members, the Big Four (Alderman 2001, 104). Shawn Fanning's initial version of Napster was a platform that allowed its users to swap music files on a peer-to-peer basis—in other words, end users could communicate directly with other Internet surfers in their attempts to acquire or share music files. Surfers would typically meet in Internet Relay Chats (IRC), which serve "as the focal point for the audio piracy subculture," and have become "one of the oldest institutions of the internet" (Cooper and Harrison 2001, 74). IRC allows surfers to communicate with multiple partners at the same time. This is where Shawn Fanning spent a great deal of time before developing Napster. Alderman claims that all "Fanning really wanted was to make music easier to trade online" but, under the guidance of his uncle, Napster became a money-spinner (2001, 103). The RIAA responded swiftly to Napster's launch because it soon realized that the news of a platform that allows users to acquire popular songs for free was spreading rapidly and that its members stood to lose substantial revenue. Napster offered a similar kind of challenge to the major labels that digital sampling in hip-hop had in earlier years. Audio file sharing on the Internet is counter-hegemonic for the following reasons: the integrity of the music text is violated because individual songs from albums can be downloaded, traditional notions of authorship are challenged/violated due to the fact that digital technology makes it easier for individuals to sample music in the production of new music, and brand integrity is violated. Music texts are packaged as complete albums/CDs that are branded and marketed as saleable products through marketing and retail processes. Napster's true subversive potential lies in the fact that it offered consumers more agency than the conventional model offered by the major labels, notwithstanding the fact that copyright was violated. Consumers were now able to bypass conventional retail outlets and access only those songs on specific albums that they preferred, as opposed to buying the entire album. It also allowed consumers to access rare music tracks that may not have been readily available in stores. In this regard, the mp3 revolution also offered unsigned artists a possible means of bypassing major record labels—entities that perform a very influential gatekeeper function in the music industry—in their attempts to reach audiences and thereby establish their music careers. Websites such as the United Kingdom's Peoplesound.com and the now-defunct South African pay-for-play website friedjam.com and free music service Digitalcupboard.com are examples of these sorts of possibilities.

## Empire Rears Its Head ... As if It Ever Left the Building

Here, my earlier reference to Schumacher's discussion of *Bleistein v. Donaldson Lithographic Co.* finds some resonance. He contends that, since this case, authorship could be assigned to corporate entities and contradictions have often been resolved "in the interests of copyright holders" (Schumacher 1995, 259). Again, the question that is raised is whether the RIAA's response to this kind of copyright violation is really in the interests of musicians as opposed to that of the Big Four. Alderman's observations are quite interesting in this regard. He comments on remarks made by the RIAA's Hilary Rosen at a press conference after a legal victory over Napster:

Hilary Rosen repeated the company line that Napster's business model was "built on infringement" and was not only morally and legally wrong, but was also "a threat to the development of the legitimate online music market." . . ."The choices available to consumers of legitimately licensed music are now much greater than just a year ago. Music based on the subscription model is around the corner," she said, ignoring that MP3.com and Emusic were already offering just that, largely out of desperate competition with Napster. It was also strange that she would pull out an appeal to nationalism, pointing out that 30 percent of Napster users were not Americans when 80 percent of the big five labels weren't American either. Regardless, Rosen painted the victory as one for nationalism: "American intellectual property is our nation's greatest asset. We cannot stand idly by as our rights and our nation's economic assets are in jeopardy or dismissed by those who would negate its value for their own enrichment." (Alderman, 2001, 173–74)

Firstly, one should note that this victory was somewhat hollow at the time, as Napster's technology makes it possible for users to operate independently. Users do not need to connect to Napster itself in order to swap files, as they need only frequent an IRC to find trading partners. A number of Napster clones, such as Morpheus, Gnutella, and KaZaa, had also been launched. In this speech, Rosen seems to tap into a moral and nationalist discourse that is meant to legitimate the RIAA's position. One can make sense of Rosen's claims by returning to my initial reference to Hardt and Negri's concept of Empire. Earlier I referred to their claim that "the juridical concept of Empire" took shape in the "ambiguous experiences of the United Nations" (Hardt and Negri 2000, 6). However, they contend that transnational corporations also exert a comparable amount of influence on a global scale. One might say that the RIAA protects the corporate interests of the major record labels in much the same way as the United Nations protects the interest of imperial powers, such as the United States, via "the production of norms and legal instruments of coercion that guarantee contracts and resolve conflicts" (Hardt and Negri 2000, 9). Rosen's choice of language recalls Hardt and Negri's discussion of the concept of "just wars" within Empire:

> The concept of Empire is presented as a global concert under the direction of a single unitary power that maintains the social peace and produces its ethical truths. And in order to achieve these ends, the single unitary power is given the necessary force to conduct, when necessary, "just wars" at the borders against the barbarians and internally against the rebellious. (2000, 10)

Rosen's speech suggests that a "just war" is being conducted against audio pirates who act "immorally" and place the American "nation's greatest asset" in jeopardy (Alderman 2001, 173). The "just war" is not merely conducted "internally against the rebellious" but also against the 30% of non-American pirates—the barbarians at the country's borders (Hardt and Negri 2001, 10). Alderman's observation that 80% of the Big Four labels are not American is also worth noting. Labels such as Vivendi Universal are French, for example. It is in this way that Empire's notion of right "envelops the entire space of what it considers civilization . . . and . . . encompasses all time within its ethical foundation" (Hardt and Negri 2000, 11). Rosen's speech also affirms Hardt and Negri's claims that "communication production and the construction of imperial legitimation march hand in hand and can no longer be separated" (2000, 33). Specifically, Rosen's use of patriotic/nationalist discourse makes sense in relation to these authors' claims that Empire "actually produces and reproduces [master narratives] in order to validate and celebrate its own power" (Hardt and Negri 2000, 33).

Although Napster is a business, much like mp3.com or Emusic, its subversive potential lay in the fact that the convenience that its technology offered consumers essentially fuelled what Cooper and Harrison call the mp3 subculture. They contend that audio "pirates operate in a complex and highly structured social and economic environment that has its own particular matrix of roles, norms and mores" (Cooper and Harrison 2001, 71–72). Furthermore, their research suggests that audio pirates largely ignore or disregard copyright law, while other "pirates take an active stance against the very concept of copyright law, believing that 'information wants to be free'" (Cooper and Harrison 2001, 87). It is in this way that their actions are counter-hegemonic. The corporate response to audio piracy on the Internet could be likened to record labels' response to hip-hop. Dick Hebdige's discussion of recuperation could be applied here as well (1979, 94). One might argue that the commodity form comes into play via corporate attempts to co-opt the online music market through attempts to launch pay-for-play sites and through the development of subscription models (Pressplay, for example). A key example of attempts at co-optation is Vivendi Universal's acquisition of mp3.com. None of these attempts has really seen any significant returns as yet. The ideological form comes into play via the RIAA's attempts to label/redefine audio pirates as deviants through the media as well as the judiciary. Rosen's press statement comments and the music industry's legal action against Napster, mp3.com, and Diamond Multimedia Systems (Girasa 2002, 173–213) confirm this view. Two years ago, for example, the RIAA engaged in legal action to "force internet service provider Verizon to reveal the identity of a subscriber who allegedly uses its services to trade copyrighted songs" (BBC New World Edition 2002). This sort of action paved the way for the RIAA to approach the subscriber directly without having to take lengthy and costly legal action. At the time of writing, the "music industry has already sued 2,947 people in the United States and has announced more than 230 suits in Denmark, Germany, Italy and Canada" (Warner 2004). In one instance, the International Federation of the Phonographic Industry (IFPI) won 8,000 Euros in compensation from a 23-year-old German man for the possession of 6,000 mp3 files on his PC's hard drive as well as on 70 CDs (Warner 2004).

It appears that key U.S. legislation actually does make it possible for corporate action of this nature to be pursued. In an article titled, "From Private to Public: Reexamining the Technological Basis for Copyright," Matt Jackson argues that the Digital Millennium Copyright Act of 1998 (DMCA) "was a significant step toward the reprivatization of copyright" (2002, 418). Jackson contends that a 1995 influential white paper by the Information Infrastructure Task Force—and, subsequently, the DMCA—works from the assumption that the first copyright legislation, the Statute of Ann, was a reaction to technological advances in 15th-century England (2002, 417–18). Instead, the legislation was actually passed to break London's publishing monopolies, thereby replacing "the private law of printing privileges and Stationers' copyrights with a public law of statutory copyright" (Jackson 2002, 427). Legislators' technologically determinist view has thus led to copyright being privatized once again:

> The DMCA thus signals a paradigm shift from copyright as a legal concept to copyright as a technological concept. This shift has enormous implications for society. First, technological control, contractual control, and increased liability all effectively reprivatise copyright, making it more difficult for courts to enforce important free speech interests. Second, this shift and the changing legal landscape promote the use of communication networks for one-way distribution rather than two-way dialogue. As new communication technologies are introduced, laws are adapted to make commercial content distribution their primary use. (Jackson 2002, 431)

This legal shift therefore compromises the interests of civil society by placing the corporate need to consolidate revenue streams first and, in effect, frustrate agentic subjects' abilities to utilize communication networks in the public sphere. In short, the law effectively places corporate interest above that of civil society. Vaidhyanathan (2001) concurs with this contention in his discussion of the DMCA as well as the preceding white paper. He contends that the DMCA "essentially nullified the role of deliberation and legislation in determining copyright" (159). Vaidhyanathan outlines "four surrenders of important safeguards in the copyright system" (159–60). These include the "surrender of balance to control"; the "surrender of public interest to private interest"; the "surrender of republican deliberation within the nation-state to unelected multilateral organizations"; and the "surrender of culture to technology" (159–60). Essentially, we see the declining role of civil society and the nation-state in favor of corporate entities. This, in effect, amounts to the encroachment of Empire/corporate entities upon the public domain and compromises the functioning of democracy.

A similar dynamic seems to operate in the international arena. James Boyle suggests that the U.S. has been using the General Agreement on Tariffs and Trade (GATT) as an enforcement mechanism in multilateral trade agreements

(1996, 122–23). The U.S. has been able to exert this kind of control in its trade negotiations with other nation-states by "recharacterizing failure to respect even the most expansive Western notions of intellectual property as a 'significant barrier to trade' or a 'subsidy' conferred upon domestic industries" (Boyle 1996, 122–23). It is in this way that U.S. government is able to protect U.S. corporate interests on a global scale, thereby compromising individual nation-states' abilities to protect their constituents' corporate and community interests. In this regard, Michael Parenti discusses how GATT and the North American Free Trade Agreement (NAFTA) allow U.S. transnational corporations to circumvent the sovereignty of nation-states. He contends that these trade agreements are presented as benign and natural historical developments that take us "from regional to national and now to international market relations" (1995, 31). However, GATT's body of non-elected World Trade Organization (WTO) panelists have "financial stakes in the very issues they adjudicate," do not operate transparently, and are not accountable to the communities whose lives their decisions impact upon (1995, 32). Ultimately, Parenti's claims resonate with Boyle's discussion of GATT when he explains just how Empire triumphs over democracy and how international finance triumphs over democracy (1995, 35):

> Signatory governments must lower tariffs, end farm subsidies, treat foreign companies the same as domestic ones, honor all corporate patent claims, and obey the rulings of a permanent elite bureaucracy, the WTO. Should a country refuse to change its laws when a WTO panel so dictates, GATT can impose international sanctions, depriving the resistant country of needed markets and materials. GATT will benefit strong nations at the expense of weaker ones, and rich interests at the expense of the rest of us. (Parenti 1995, 32)

Parenti offers an example in the field of agriculture in which GATT makes it possible for "multinationals to impose compulsory licensing and monopoly property rights on indigenous and communal agriculture" under the guise of intellectual property rights (1995, 33). This is how globalization becomes a "logical extension of imperialism" (35) and, ultimately, how democracy and the sovereignty of nation-states are eroded. It is from this perspective that globalization, or Empire, can be viewed as anything but a natural and inevitable process that benefits all.

## The Battle Is Lost and Won?

The concept of the "just war" is taken to a new level so that "rebellious" individuals within Empire may be singled out. The industry has thus initiated a process of recuperation of audio piracy on the Internet via a duel process of co-optation and force. This process echoes the approach that was taken with sampling by hip-hop artists, which had proven to be largely successful. In both instances, particular kinds of technology were used to frustrate corporate interests. In the case of hip-hop, samplers (for example, the E-mu SP-1200 or the Akai MPC-60) were used in ways that their manufacturers had not intended. Ironically, these manufacturers benefited financially from their products' popularity amongst hip-hop producers. The same could be said for software such as Acid, Sonic Foundry Sound Forge, and Reason, except that software piracy has become as much of a problem to manufacturers as audio piracy in the music industry. In hip-hop, music texts were also being "violated" in the process of producing new music texts. In the case of audio piracy on the Internet, the integrity of the music text as a branded and marketable package is violated. However, this violation itself does not amount to parody in the way that sampling in hip-hop does. This is why the court rejected Napster's fair use defense in *A&M Records, Inc. v. Napster, Inc.* (Girasa 2002, 180). But the very idea that this relatively new medium is being employed by large numbers of consumers to subvert/compromise corporate interests presents a serious challenge to the major record labels and Empire. An examination of sampling and the mp3 revolution reveals that corporate attempts to bring "deviants" to book has been frustrated by new developments in technology. It appears that new shifts in technology and distribution techniques make new possibilities for subversion possible. At the same time, software developers, hackers, artists, and consumers who are hell-bent on challenging hegemony are likely to pioneer new ways to circumvent obstacles presented by the corporate world or by technology itself.

## Acknowledgments

Previous drafts of this paper were read at the University of Cape Town's (UCT) Sociology Seminar Series (2002) and the Centre for Higher Education Development Seminar Series (2003). Many thanks for comments from Prof. Dan Moshenberg (George Washington University), Julian Jonker (UCT), Dr. Ermien van Pletzen (UCT), Dr. Jane Stadler (UCT), Rochelle Kapp (UCT), and Gary Stewart (UCT).

## References

Alderman, John. 2001. *Sonic Boom: Napster, P2P and the Future of Music*. London: Fourth Estate.

Ariefdien, Shaheen. 2002. Interview conducted and transcribed by Adam Haupt, October 25, 2002. Unpublished.

Associated Press. 2001. "Record Industry Says Napster Hurt Singles Sales." *CNN*, February 26, 2001. Retrieved from http://www.cnn.com/2001/SHOWBIZ/Music/02/26/napster.cdsales.ap/index.html

Ballantine, Christopher. 2002. "Rethinking 'White' Identity? Some Issues in Popular Music in Post-Apartheid South Africa." Proceedings of the eleventh biannual IASPM Conference, Turku, Finland, July 6–10, 559–64.

BBC News World Edition. 2002. "Judge Brands Song Swap Laws 'Unclear.'" October 4. Retrieved from http://news.bbc.co.uk/2/hi/business/2300113.stm

Berne Convention for the Protection of Literary and Artistic Works. Paris Act of July 24, 1971, as amended on September 28, 1979.

Boyle, James. 1996. *Shamans, Software, and Spleens: Law and the Construction of the Information Society*. Cambridge, MA: Harvard University Press.

Caney, Derek. 2001a. "Labels Brace for Post-Napster Music World." February 27. Retrieved from http://dailynews.yahoo.com/h/nm/20010227/en/music-napster future_1.html

———. 2001b. "Vivendi CEO Balks at Bertelsmann-Napster Deal." February 27. Retrieved from http://biz.yahoo.com/rf/010227/n27231088_2.html

Convention for the Protection of Producers of Phonograms against Unauthorized Duplication of Their Phonograms. October 29, 1971.

Cooper, Jon, and Daniel M. Harrison. 2001. "The Social Organisation of Audio Piracy on the Internet." *Media, Culture & Society* 23, no. 1: 71–89.

Feltes, N. N. 1994. "International Copyright: Structuring 'The Condition of Modernity' in British Publishing." In *The Construction of Authorship: Textual Appropriation in Law and Literature*, edited by Martha Woodmansee and Peter Jaszi, 271–80. Durham, NC: Duke University Press.

Foucault, Michel. 1979. "What Is an Author?" In *Textual Strategies: Perspectives in Post-Structuralist Criticism*, edited by Josué V. Harari, 141–60. Ithaca, NY: Cornell University Press.

Gates, Henry Louis. 1988. *The Signifying Monkey: A Theory of Afro-American Literary Criticism*. New York: Oxford University Press.

George, Nelson. 1998. *Hip Hop America*. New York: Penguin.

Ghosh, Shubha. 2002. "MP3 v. the Law: How the Internet Could (but Won't) Become Your Personal Jukebox." *GigaLaw.com* (July). Retrieved from http://www.gigalaw.com/articles/ghosh-2000-07-p2.html

Girasa, Roy J. 2002. *Cyberlaw: National and International Perspectives*. Upper Saddle River, NJ: Prentice Hall.

Goodin, Dan. 2001. "The Billion-Dollar Gambit." February 28. Retrieved from http://biz.yahoo.com/st/010228/22442.html

Graham, Gordon. 1999. *The Internet: A Philosophical Inquiry*. London: Routledge.

Gröndahl, Boris. 2001. "Bertelsmann Testing Secret Napster Clone." *CNN*, February 27. Retrieved from http://www.cnn.com/2001/TECH/internet/02/27/napster.clone.idg/index.html

Grossman, Mark, and Allison Hift. 2002. "Behind the Music Files: The MP3 Legal Controversy." *GigaLaw.com* (April). Retrieved from http://www.gigalaw.com/articles/grossman-2000–04c-p1.html

Gurnsey, John. 1995. *Copyright Theft*. Hampshire: Aslib Gower.

Habermas, Jurgen. 1989. *The Structural Transformation of the Public Sphere: An Introduction into a Category of Bourgeois Society*, trans. by Thomas Burger and Frederick Lawrence. Cambridge: Polity Press.

Hardt, Michael, and Antonio Negri. 2002. *Empire*. London: Harvard University Press.

Haupt, Adam. 1996a. *Rap and the Articulation of Resistance: An Exploration of Subversive Cultural Production during the Early 90's, with particular reference to Prophets of da City.* M.A. mini-thesis. Unpublished. Bellville: University of the Western Cape.

———. 1996b. "Stifled Noise in the South African Music Box: Prophets of da City and the Struggle for Public Space." *South African Theatre Journal* 10, no. 2: 51–61.

———. 2001. "Black Thing: Hip-Hop Nationalism, 'Race' and Gender in Prophets of da City and Brasse vannie Kaap." In *Coloured by History, Shaped by Place: New Perspectives on Coloured Identities in Cape Town*, edited by Zimitri Erasmus, 173–91. Cape Town: Kwela Books and SA History Online.

Hebdige, Dick. 1979. *Subculture: The Meaning of Style.* London: Routledge.

Hopper, D. Ian. 2002. "Music Industry Targets Net Swapper." *Yahoo! News.* October 4. Retrieved from http://story.news.yahoo.com/news?tmpl=story2&cid=56 . . . /internet_swapping_20

Hutcheon, Linda. 1989. *Politics of Postmodernism.* New York: Routledge.

Isenberg, Doug. 2000. "What Napster Teaches Us about Copyright Law." *GigaLaw.com* (September). Retrieved from http://www.gigalaw.com.articles/isenberg-2000–09-p2.html

Jackson, Matt. 2002. "From Private to Public: Reexamining the Technological Basis for Copyright." *Journal of Communication* 52, no. 2: 416–33.

Jameson, Frederic. 1991. *Postmodernism, or, The Cultural Logic of Late Capitalism.* Durham, NC: Duke University Press.

Jaszi, Peter. 1994. "On the Author Effect: Contemporary Copyright and Collective Creativity." In *The Construction of Authorship: Textual Appropriation in Law and Literature*, edited by Martha Woodmansee and Peter Jaszi, 29–56. Durham, NC: Duke University Press.

Kirkpatrick, David D., and Matt Richtell. 2001. "Napster Near Accord on Music Sales." *New York Times*, June 5. Retrieved from http://www.nytimes.com/2001/06/05/technology/05MUSI.html?pagewanted=print

Kirkpatrick, David D., and Andrew Ross Sorkin. 2001. "Bertelsmann in Deal to Buy Music Start-Up." *New York Times*, May 30. Retrieved from http://www.nytimes.com/2001/05/30/technology/30MUSI.html

Landau, Michael. 2001. "Questions and Answers about the Napster Case." *GigaLaw.com* (May). Retrieved from http://www.gigalaw.com/articles/ 2001/landau-2001–05-p2.html

McLaren, Carrie. 2004. "Copyrights and Copywrongs: Interview with Siva Vaidhyanathan." *Stay Free!* Retrieved from http://www.stayfreemagazine.org/archives/20/siva_vaidhyanathan.html

McLeod, Kembrew. 2004. "How Copyright Law Changed Hip Hop: An Interview with Public Enemy's Chuck D and Hank Shocklee." *Stay Free!* Retrieved from http://www.stayfreemagazine.org/archives/20/ public_enemy.html

mp3.com. No date. "Important Announcement for mp3.com Customers." Retrieved from http://www.mp3.com/corporate/vivendimp3.html

Negri, Antonio. 1999. *Insurgencies: Constituent Power and the Modern State*. Minneapolis: University of Minnesota Press.

———. 2003. *A Time for Revolution*. New York: Continuum.

Parenti, Michael. 1995. *Against Empire*. San Francisco: City Lights Books.

Reuters. "BMG to Share MP3.com Settlement More Widely." May 29. Retrieved from http://www.emarketer.com/estatnews . . . /05_29_2001.rwntz-story-bcnet-musicbmgdc.html?ref=d

Richtel, Matt. 2001a. "New Suit to Bar Trading Music on Net." *New York Times*, May 25. Retrieved from http://www.nytimes.com/2001/05/25/technology/25MUSI.html?pagewanted=print

———. 2001b. "The Recording Industry vs. Aimster." *New York Times*, June 2. Retrieved from http://nytimes.com/2001/06/01/technology/01MUSI.html?pagewanted=print

Rome Convention. 1961. International Convention for the Protection of Performers, Producers of Phonograms and Broadcasting Organizations. October 26, 1961.

Rose, Mark. 1993. *Authors and Owners: The Invention of Copyright*. Cambridge, MA: Harvard University Press.

Rose, Tricia. 1994. *Black Noise: Rap Music and Black Culture in Contemporary America*. Hanover: Wesleyan University Press.

Sanjek, David. 1994. "'Don't Have No to DJ No More': Sampling and the 'Autonomous' Creator." In *The Construction of Authorship: Textual Appropriation in Law and Literature*, edited by Martha Woodmansee and Peter Jaszi, 343–60. Durham, NC: Duke University Press.

Sausner, Rebecca. 2001a. "Aimster Tries Legal End Run around Record Industry." May 3. Retrieved from http://www.ecommercetimes.com/perl/story/9461.html

———. 2001b. "MusicNet Warbles in Washington." May 18. Retrieved from http://www.ecommercetimes.com/perl/story/9847.html

Schumacher, Thomas G. 1995. "'This Is a Sampling Sport': Digital Sampling, Rap Music and the Law in Cultural Production." *Media, Culture and Society* 17, no. 2: 253–73.

Shade, Leslie Regan. 1996. "Is There Free Speech on the Net? Censorship in the Global Information Infrastructure." In *Cultures of Internet: Virtual Spaces, Real Histories, Living Bodies*, 11–32. London: Sage.

Stille, Alexander. 2001. "Adding Up the Costs of Cyberdemocracy." *New York Times*, June 2. Retrieved from http://www.nytimes.com/2001/06/02/technology/02INTE.html?pagewanted=print

Sullivan, Jennifer. 1999. "Napster: Music Is for Sharing." *Wired*, November 1. Retrieved from http://www.wired.com/news/print/0,1294,32151,00.html

Tedeschi, Bob. 2001. "E-commerce Report: Record Labels Struggle with Napster Alternatives." *New York Times*, April 23. Retrieved from http://www.nytimes.com/2001/04/23/technology/23ECOMMERCE.html?searchpv=site01

U.S. Copyright Office. 1998. *Digital Millennium Copyright Act of 1998*. Washington, DC: GPO.

Vaidhyanathan, Siva. 2001. *Copyrights and Copywrongs: The Rise of Intellectual Property and How It Threatens Creativity*. New York: New York University Press.

Vaughan-Nichols, Steven J. 2001. "The RIAA's Billion Dollar Blunder." *Yahoo! News*. February 28. Retrieved from http://dailynews.yahoo.com/h/zd/20010228/tc/the_riaa_s_billion_dollar_blunder_1.html

Vivendi Universal. 2001. "Vivendi Universal Acquires MP3.com in Move to Strengthen Digital Distribution and Web Audience." May 20. Retrieved from http://pr.mp3.com/pr/337.html

Warner, Bernhard. 2004. "Music Industry Readies Fresh Wave of Net Lawsuits." *Yahoo! News*. June 8. Retrieved from http://news.yahoo.com/news?tmpl=story&u=/nm/20040608/wr_nm/media_music_lawsuits_dc_8

Weil Gall, Barbara. 2000. "What Is 'Fair Use' in Copyright Law?" *GigaLaw.com* (December). Retrieved from http://www.gigalaw.com/articles/gall-2000-12-p1.html

Wipo Performances and Phonograms Treaty. Adopted by the Diplomatic Conference on December 20, 1996.

Woodmansee, Martha. 1994. "On the Author Effect: Recovering Collectivity." In *The Construction of Authorship: Textual Appropriation in Law and Literature*, edited by Martha Woodmansee and Peter Jaszi, 15–28. Durham: Duke University Press.

Zeidler, Sue. 2001a. "Napster Out to Woo Music Publishers." *IOL* (May 30). Retrieved from http://www.iol.co.za/general/newsprint.php3?art_id=qw99117474183B232

———. 2001b. "Napster Starts Limited Blocking, Users Unfazed." March 6. Retrieved from http://www.mg.co.za/mg/art/music/0103/010306-napster.html

CHAPTER SIX

# The Cyberactivism of a Dangermouse

## Michael D. Ayers

Tuesday, February 24, 2004, was a typical winter day in Manhattan. The city awoke to dark grey skies, pouring rain, and the unfortunate realization that one would be battling the elements if one ventured outside. The real world in New York was bleak and dreary, just another 24 hours in a seemingly endless parade of unfortunate weather patterns that once again conjured up Manhattan's alter-ego "Gotham City" of the Batman comics. Cyberspace was also grey this day as well. Not from weather, obviously, but from several hundred activists all rally-ing around an unknown DJ named Dangermouse.

Grey Tuesday, as it was dubbed, was a day where symbolic, cultural, and political protest converged in the virtual. The activists were rallying around several causes, but most apparent was the actions EMI Group were taking against Dangermouse. Briefly, Dangermouse blended the vocal tracks from hip-hop artist Jay-Z's *The Black Album* with the Beatles' *The White Album*, hence calling it *The Grey Album*. He only pressed, or burned, 3,000 copies and pro-vided them to friends and independent record stores for sales. Once the artistic endeavor was heard by the select few, word spread in underground networks of the album's "brilliance," which eventually led to reviews by *Rolling Stone* and *The New Yorker*, dubbing it a "masterpiece." As what is underground rises to the mainstream, eventually EMI, the holders of the Beatles' copyrights, were not pleased with their "work" being appropriated in this way without permission. Thus, they sent a cease and desist order to Dangermouse, demanding that he remove his album from the Internet and to not distribute it any further. This, in turn, spawned a budding activist organization, Downhill Battle, to get involved; they provided the outlet and creative activism behind Grey Tuesday and their site greytuesday.org. Their call for action was simple: on Tuesday, February 24, Grey Tuesday—and anyone else that wanted to join in—would make Danger-mouse's work available for free download. And the response was phenomenal. Hundreds of sites participated in hosting the work, and hundreds of others who were skeptical about the legal ramifications in turn "greyed" their site, meaning, they changed their original interface to all grey, in support of this protest. The sites were not organizational in the traditional sense of "organized" but were primarily individuals' weblogs. And this disruptive tactic of civil disobedience all occurred in six days. This chapter addresses the Grey Tuesday case in terms of new forms of online protest, new forms of music activism, and finally, new ways of constructing resistance. I look at this case not as an isolated event but as an ongoing dialogue between cyberactivists, one that fuses cultural and political movements through decentralized networks.

Since the rise of the culture industries, music and activism have never been mutually exclusive social processes. To say that music could be a reactionary art form would be a fair assessment. Of note is that in the pre-cyber society, artists who were seen as activists all had outlets for their creativity. In other words, they had record deals that would distribute their art/product to the mass public. But the times, they have changed: the 1990s witnessed a sharp decrease in personal computer prices and an increase in networked computers via the proliferation of private firms such as America Online and Earthlink.[1] The cost of software dropped too. Programs that were once reserved for professional studios could now transform a home computer into a place of production. CD burners were bundled with every new PC, making the process even easier to "mix and burn." Thus, what has recently occurred has been the birth of the *new* amateur: an amateur where the use of computer technologies solidifies him or her within a larger artistic matrix, even if he or she is not part of the "industry."

This notion of musical amateur—where the blending and blurring of listener, musician, and activist—has been realized by the case of Grey Tuesday, which I explain below. In other words, the social mash-up of "bedroom activists" is occurring where politics, artistic creativity, and Internet technologies created a highly visible grassroots campaign.

## Rip, Mash, and Burn

As mentioned briefly above, the rallying cry was centered on a "mash-up" album, one in which the creator takes two or more songs and blends them together. Readily available sound-editing programs that are cheap and user friendly let anyone with the time and motivation try and become a producer. To recast Lawrence Lessig's (2001, 2004) phrase "rip, mix, and burn," amateurs now also have the ability to rip, mash, and burn. Add a clever title to your creation and you are done.[2] Mash-ups can be thought of as a logical derivation of hip-hop. Essentially, the mash-up artists are taking the sampling element of hip-hop, but instead of sampling one or two beats as a backdrop for lyrical or musical expression, mash-ups take samples and throw them all together, creating a unique blend of artists, words, lyrics, and music that had never existed prior to that time. Queen and David Bowie never recorded music with Michael Jackson, yet Go Home Productions' mash-up entitled "Jacko under Pressure" blends the Queen/Bowie classic "Under Pressure" with Jackson's "Rock with You." This song was released a few days after Michael Jackson was taken into custody for alleged child molestation; we might see its release as a political and cultural response to current events—cultural because of the responsive artistic creativity, and political because of the use of copyrighted material with no copyright clearance.

Through word of mouth and p2p Internet networks, *The Grey Album* slowly made the rounds among music lovers through the months of December 2003 and January 2004. In what follows, I examine how this one act of bedroom creativity sparked an enormous online campaign that yielded a new generation of hundreds of bedroom activists as well as the birth and organization of a legitimate social movement. It is my intention to demonstrate that through the mash-up principle of blurring past cultural creativity, the bedroom activist, within the musical context at least, has blurred activism and politics with musical fandom and creativity. And this was activism carried out not in the streets; these were cyberactivists, utilizing the weblog as the primary method of protest.

What sparked the outrage was EMI Records' cease-and-desist order issued to Dangermouse alone. He had provided the album for free download on his website, but once the letter arrived, he immediately took it down and put a text version of the letter up for explanation. Because of the power of word of mouth, especially through the Internet, the news eventually reached Downhillbattle.org, an online social movement organization that seeks to reform the way music is distributed and how artists are paid for their work.

Founded in August 2003, Downhill Battle got its start helping to raise money for legal defense funds when the RIAA announced they would be suing individuals for file sharing. But it wasn't until *The Grey Album* that they really garnered the attention they needed to create a fullscale cyberprotest. A press release on February 11, 2004, framed their position around two key issues: (1) the stifling of creativity and (2) copyright law. They noted that mainstream media outlets such as *Rolling Stone* and *The New Yorker* had reviewed Dangermouse's work, yet had to obtain it through an illegal method (either a burned CD or file-sharing network). Three days later, *Wired News* picked up the story and ran with it, and several other news outlets soon followed suit.

Over the course of the next two weeks, the Internet community was sparked into heated debate over the cultural values of artistic merit and who had the "ownership" or rights to the music in Dangermouse's album. The foundation for the activism was in place: a cause to rally around, a "site of resistance" (cyberspace), and a few days to plan a tactical demonstration.

Also within this press release was a date and the action that would take place: Tuesday, February 24. A coalition of sites would either host *The Grey Album* for free download and/or change the color of their site to grey, creating a drab, visual aesthetic that symbolized the host sites identification with this "grey" matter.

There are several questions that this case provides for social activism as well as music in an online environment. What was the central method of protest and how has this differed from previous cyberactivist techniques? Why did this one act of creativity spark a slew of bedroom activists, when questions of copyright and file-sharing ethics had been raging for years at this point? In terms of symbolic action, what was the significance of Grey Tuesday? And lastly, how successful was Grey Tuesday? Throughout this chapter I hope to answer these questions, or at least provide a foundation for understanding how the music and the Internet have fused together to become the primary medium through which information is disseminated. In other words, the protest music might be a dying genre, but protesting about how to consume music is a relatively recent phenomenon.

## Cyberactivism and a New Method of Disruption

To begin examining this case, it is important to map out how earlier individuals and organizations have utilized Internet technologies, and the theories they have inspired have driven social causes. Social movements have historically appropriated technology and mass media for their own causes—the printing press, radio, and television (Habermas 1989; Meikle 2002; Morris 1984).

Online activism is typically contextualized in how the information is disseminated. Email, websites, online sit-ins, virtual protests, chatrooms, and discussion boards—these are all different ways of communicating via cyberspace, and also different ways in how the information is received by another party. Email calls to action are typically forwarded to people within one's social life; websites are visual hosts to an organization or a person in which interactivity (web chatrooms) could or could not be utilized; graphics and other pertinent information are typically arranged in an easy-to-digest format. All forms of web interactivity allow for the user to navigate his or her own path, taking in information that could or would be relevant to his or her own life and leaving behind the information that is not needed.

For cyberactivists, the past has yielded varying results. Gurak and Logie (2003) show that the web was critical in calling to action a massive online protest against Yahoo! in which protesters "haunted" their own (free) websites with alternate graphics to make a political statement regarding Yahoo!'s new policies. Indymedia.org has successfully utilized the Internet to create alternative media where ordinary citizens can easily contribute to "making" history on a day-to-day basis (Kidd 2003). At the same time, McLaine (2003) argues that certain websites manufacture community, where the sites themselves are thinly veiled disguises for niche advertisers.

What has not been researched or theorized is the role of the weblog within cyberactivism. Weblogs (or just simply "blogs") are deviations of personal homepages. The mass media definition labels blogs as "personal, online diaries" but oftentimes they are much more than that, or something different all together. Bloggers aspire for a fan base, or readership, and they often update their blogs daily. Updates include the everyday mundane writings about anything to very specific thematic writings. In other words, some blogs solely focus on certain music scenes as their daily topics, and rarely do they deviate from this. The "blogosphere" can be characterized as an informal collection of blogs that are bound together in a decentralized, seemingly endless string of other blogs in which the hyperlink is the key element in connecting other readers to the blogger's interests or agenda.

Blogs as a cyberactivist tool, or platform, are unique in a few different ways. First, they are passive in how they present their information and rely on an audience to seek them out. Second, the creator or owner of the blog must use hyperlinking as the primary source of information—by this, I mean that via their writing, their arguments are backed up by hyperlinking to another portion of the web that in turn should validate what they are discussing. Third, because blogs are updated frequently, they occur in "real time" as opposed to newspaper sites, which have to go through editorial processes, or sites that are only updated in a less than frequent manner.

The sites of protest for the Dangermouse case were in fact primarily blogs. Downhill Battle, while not a blog, provided the foundation for how the protest would take place and what bloggers should do to demonstrate their collective identity, or solidarity, for *The Grey Album*. The protesters either "hosted" the entire album for free download, they simply turned their blog grey for a day. The protest became an act of civil disobedience if one was to host the album and although the exact number is unknown, according to Greytuesday.org (2004), around 170 sites around the globe hosted *The Grey Album* for a one-day-only download. Hundreds more followed suit with the day-only grey interface.

EMI vigorously confronted the bloggers with cease-and-desist emails that scared some into removing the mp3s, but still others quietly remained defiant. Many of the bloggers who received the emails, in turn, posted verbatim the letters they received so that online audiences could hopefully lend a sympathetic ear in regards EMI's "bully" tactics.

What the protest blogs also did was create awareness through a decentralized forum of participation. None of the participants actually "belonged" to Downhill Battle, because there was nothing to "join." Participation was therefore gauged on the bloggers' relationships to another entity: music. Copyright activism has been on the rise over the years, primarily because the rise of p2p platforms has challenged issues of the "public domain" (Vaidhyanathan 2001;

Howard-Spink 2004). Nevertheless, the likelihood that so many bloggeres would risk prosecution over mere issues of copyright is slim. While the issue of "who owns what" is at the heart of why this started in the first place, the actual music, or art, was the spark that got this movement up and running.

## The Activism Surrounding the Music or the Music Surrounding the Activism

If *The Grey Album* had not been so good then EMI or Downhill Battle might not have batted an eye. But that was not the case, as the work of this mash-up resounded in critic circles from the high-end tastes of *The New Yorker* to the pop-culture topics of *The Rolling Stone* as well as making the top ten albums of 2004 in *The Village Voice*. Dangermouse's creation was not ostensibly political.

Taking two iconic artists in their respective genres and combining them into something accessible was political in this case. In this sense, the subtle political "grey area" was what made this music more than just a flavor of the month. Grey not only is a shade of black and white but it is also a descriptive term that signifies "fuzzy" or "unclear." The significance of calling the work "grey" is an example of how this musical work makes a statement about the state of music in general. Genres are not cut-and-dried spaces, nor have they been historically. Often, music consumers pick and choose different genres to listen to, depending on one's tastes.

"Grey" in this case points to two genres coming together to create something altogether new, but different from previous "rock-rap" hybrids. "Walk this Way," which was a collaboration between Aerosmith and Run-DMC, was just one song, and thought by some as just a culture industry attempt at ushering in a new type of rap fan. The now defunct Rage Against the Machine used elements of rap in their vocal stylings, and who were widely known for being political, were just a band; the turntable—which is such a vital element within hip-hop—never was an integral part of their sound.

What Dangermouse did was create an album, not just one song, that was made for long-term, repeated listens. What ended up being "grey" or "fuzzy" was the response from the artists who were mashed-up: there was *no* response. This is what ended up legitimizing the cyberactivists' claims that art was being sacrificed. It also spawned a myriad of new mash-up albums, all taking artists from different genres and blending them together, utilizing home computer applications. *The Double Black Album* mashed Metallica's *The Black Album* with Jay-Z's; *The Slack Album* mashed Jay-Z with indie-rock pioneers Pavement and their 1992 release, *Slanted and Enchanted*; and *The Black and Blue Album* saw Jay-Z meet alternative rockers Weezer and their self-titled debut (which had a blue cover). All of these creations were "released" via the Internet and were met with varying success. None of the aforementioned creations, which were now mashed into Jay-Z's and Dangermouse's cultural grey area, received any scrutiny from lawyers or record labels. The RIAA did send a cease-and-desist letter to the author of *The Double Black Album*, but it did not seem to cause much commotion.

## A New Breed of Activists

Not only does this case point to a new method of cyberactivism as well as music activism, but it also points to a new type of activist. The term "bedroom DJ" has come to mean an amateur producer who has the know-how, the technology, and the will to create music via computer programs and sampling within the confines of his or her own room. With a connection to the net, the recluse now can distribute his or her work with, of course, varying degrees of success (see Whelan, this volume).

The rise of the bedroom DJ is part of a much larger phenomenon of bedroom activists. The bedroom activist is a cyberactivist who is not necessarily participating in collective resistance, but instead acting in singular resistance. As this case shows, it was hundreds of single (yet similar) acts of resistance that made up the bulk of the protest; not a collective resistance, such as a sit-in at a lunch counter. The singularity of the bedroom activist has distinct characteristics that this case has made apparent.

First, bedroom activists have a platform that they own at their disposal. Prior cyberactivists often used public space that was subject to gatekeeping or regulations (Ayers 2003) or they used email. Email is thought of as being "personal" or private. Blogs, on the other hand, are very much a part of the public domain and the public sphere. And while I pointed out that one feature of the blog is its "connectivity" or hyperlinks, blogs stand alone as their own entity.

Second, bedroom activists in this instance are articulating their identity via their blog, but the identity of the activist is not solely dependent on this activism. Whereas "collective identities" within online worlds are sometimes called into question (Ayers 2003; Gamson 2003), the identity of the bedroom activist is embedded within the blog as a whole. And the blogs in this case were not solely blogs about *The Grey Album*, or blogs about copyright activism. They were blogs representing the bedroom activist and everything about his or her life. The blogger became active for a short period of time, and then the daily entry about Grey Tuesday and the reason for hosting or turning the site grey became archived into the blog's history. Therefore, the bedroom activist is not necessarily a committed political activist, but possibly a temporary activist who fades in and out when an issue catches his or her interest, and is not necessarily taking part in a larger, sustained project.

Third, because bedroom activists are not tied into a social movement organization per se, they are acting as free agents in their own self interest. Although the activism was a form of collective resistance, what each person was fighting for was the right to consume, at an individual level. In other words, the social issues were framed around copyright law and "art for art's sake" but underlying this notion is the idea that these participants felt that each one of them had a right to hear this music, and in turn, do whatever he or she wanted with it. This is different from previous actions because it removes the "we" in "we believe" and solely puts on the face of "I should do be able to do this, and I will let you know via my blog."

## Success or Failure?

Grey Tuesday was successful in the sense that EMI dropped its proposed cases. No lawsuits were filed against DJ Dangermouse, Downhill Battle, or any of the civil-disobedient blogs. *The Grey Album* was downloaded over 100,000 times in a single day, making it the most "consumed" album that day (Greytuesday.org 2004). Major media outlets picked up the story, and aided Downhill Battle's cause by lending a sympathetic spin to the issue. Dangermouse himself went from relatively obscure DJ to cult hero, selling out midsized clubs around the nation.

Significantly, for a few weeks, the public was pressed into considering the state of copyright law. Downhill Battle themselves branched their operations further by creating a spin-off site called Bannedmusic.org, where illegal music would be hosted. They continued their quest against Apple's iTunes Music Service by culture jamming a fake Apple website, detailing how the iTunes Music Service pays the artists. So in this respect, we can say that Grey Tuesday was indeed successful.

It is too early to give a definitive answer as to whether or not the actual *movement* could be called successful. Whereas the focus of this debate was directed towards the owners of production, or the record labels, they do not really have any control over copyright legislation. Powerful lobbying efforts exist to keep copyright in their favor, so to create the change that this online protest called for, the energies not only would have to be directed at the labels but more so at the policymakers, aka the government. As radical and disruptive as the act might have been, ultimately, nothing about copyright law was changed. But we do know that social change is a slow, complicated process at times.

One of the core issues impacting the relationship between individual blog protestors and the larger copyright reform movement, is the ethereal nature of blog content. Historically, participants who are consistently dedicated to a social cause have led to social and political changes. Therefore, it would only make sense to say that in order for copyright reform to actually happen, the participants themselves would have to be active. And the primary way that they chose to be active—their blogs—became dormant a day later. By dormant, I mean a majority of them returned to their "regularly scheduled programming." The protesters' blogs reverted back to what their original function was—a simple, unregulated outlet for thought. How effective can blogs be if they are not used by bloggers consistently?

This points to an inherent problem with this medium, the blog, as a tool for social protest and reform: There is no consistency, no ways of utilizing the medium, to frame the issues to the broader public—unless, of course, the blog itself morphs into a "blog of resistance" where the sole purpose is to articulate the movement's causes.

To say this day of protest was successful might be premature at this point. The activists did raise awareness and did defy the corporate demands without legal repercussions. But the next major artistic achievement within music will undoubtedly face the same exact challenges that Dangermouse and his newfound fan base did. That is not to say that the protest was devoid of meaning. Grey Tuesday was loaded with symbolic and cultural resistance, and for the actors involved, it appeared to them as if they made a difference, as told by Greytuesday.org after the fact: "The Grey Tuesday protest was simply amazing. . . . Everyone who participated in the Grey Tuesday protest has sent a strong message in support of common-sense changes to copyright law" (Greytuesday.org 2004).

## Grey Discussion

I have argued that this case serves as an example in which music, social activism, and the Internet have fused in a way that was new and unique. Cultural and technological factors made this possible, and the sheer number of participants seemingly pointed to success. But for scholars, musicians, and activists alike, questions still remain.

Throughout this chapter I have pointed to a new type of activist—the bedroom activist. These activists "felt" as if they were making a difference, standing up for what they believe in, but how long did that actually last, and to what degree were they "transformed"? My argument here is that they utilized their own medium, their blogs, for one-day action, but a majority returned to blogging about the everyday. So if blogs in this instance were utilized to host illegal music, make a political stand, or simply to raise awareness (by turning grey) but only did so for one day, how could blogs be used in a fashion that lends itself to continued activism? In part, it probably depends on the activist and his or her choices. Then why did so few blogs change in this case?

Fans of music will continue to appropriate Internet technologies for their own uses, but will artists continue to release illegal music if they know a situation like Grey Tuesday could happen? The amount of exposure that an innovative artist could receive might be massive, or it could bring about legal woes that very few could afford to tackle. The artists' willingness to use the Internet for distribution of illegal work might be discouraged, for fear of litigation.

This case, however, did raise the bar in terms of coordinated (note: not necessarily collective) action online. Music and creativity were the catalyst, but would other issues elicit the same response? What would it take to ensure the participation of hundreds of websites, each with a distinct audience? And when it comes down to it, will this case be seen as a model of how cyberactivists should broach issues within the cyber domain? Or as time progresses, will this case fade into a cyber landscape as just another day of downloading music?

## References to Chapter Six

Ayers, Michael D. 2003. "Comparing Collective Identity in Online and Offline Feminist Activists." In *Cyberactivism: Online Activism in Theory and Practice*, edited by Martha McCaughey and Michael D. Ayers, 145–64. New York: Routledge.

Downhillbattle.org. 2004. Available at www.downhillbattle.org

Friedman, Debra, and Doug McAdam. 1992. "Collective Identity and Activism: Networks, Choices, and the Life of a Social Movement." In *Frontiers in Social Movement Theory*, edited by Aldon D. Morris and Carol McLurg Mueller, 156–73. New Haven, CT: Yale University Press.

Gamson, Joshua. 2003. "Gay Media, Inc.: Media Structures, the New Gay Conglomerates, and Collective Sexual Identities." In *Cyberactivism: Online Activism in Theory and Practice*, edited by Martha McCaughey and Michael D. Ayers, 255–78. New York: Routledge.

Greytuesday.org. 2004. Available at www.greytuesday.org

Gurak, Laura J., and John Logie. 2003. "Internet Protests, from Text to Web." In *Cyberactivism: Online Activism in Theory and Practice*, edited by Martha McCaughey and Michael D. Ayers, 25–46. New York: Routledge.

Habermas, Jurgen. 1989. *The Structural Transformation of the Public Sphere: An Inquiry into a Category of Bourgeois Society*. Cambridge, MA: MIT Press.

Howard-Spink, Sam. 2004. "Grey Tuesday, Online Cultural Activism and the Mash-up of Music and Politics." *First Monday* 9:10. Retrieved October 2004, from http://www.firstmonday.org/issues/issue9_10/howard/

Kidd, Dorothy. 2003. "Indymedia.org: A New Communications Commons." In *Cyberactivism: Online Activism in Theory and Practice*, edited by Martha McCaughey and Michael D. Ayers, 47–70. New York: Routledge.

Lessig, Lawrence. 2002. *The Future of Ideas: The Fate of the Commons in a Connected World*. New York: Vintage.

———. 2004. *Free Culture: How Big Media Uses Technology and the Law to Lock Down Culture and Control Creativity*. New York: Penguin.

McChesney, Robert. 1999. *Rich Media, Poor Democracy: Communications Politics in Dubious Times*. New York: New Press.

McLaine, Steven. 2003. "Ethnic Online Communities: Between Profit and Purpose." In *Cyberactivism: Online Activism in Theory and Practice*, edited by Martha McCaughey and Michael D. Ayers, 233–54. New York: Routledge.

Meikle, Graham. 2002. *Future Active: Media Activism and the Internet*. New York: Routledge Press.

Morris, Aldon D. 1984. *Origins of the Civil Rights Movement*. New York: Free Press.

Vaidhyanathan, Siva. 2001. *Copyrights and Copywrongs: The Rise of Intellectual Property and How It Threatens Creativity*. New York: NYU Press.

# CHAPTER SEVEN

# Music B(r)ands Online and Constructing Community: The Case of New Model Army

## Daragh O'Reilly and Kathy Doherty

Give me some place that I can go
Where I don't have to justify myself
Swimming out alone against this tide
Looking for family looking for tribe

—from "Family" (Sullivan/Heaton 1987)

### Introduction

In this chapter, we examine the case of a long-established U.K. rock band, New Model Army (NMA), and its online interaction with its fans. Specifically, we examine this case as an instance of an online popular music brand community, in which the "b(r)and" offers a metaphorical frame to facilitate fans' sense-making about their involvement with the band, and fans negotiate the use of the NMA brand as a symbolic resource with which to construct identities for self and others. Discursive-psychological discourse analysis is used to examine band and fan postings on the NMA website Noticeboard. The analysis focuses on the discursive construction and function of the categorization "family," proffered online by NMA to conceptualize the relationships between band and fans. On the band's side, the Family is imagined as an emotional sanctuary and a symbol of integrity and acceptance, a place to experience solidarity, protection, and comfort in contrast to the cynical consumerism of mainstream music. The fans differ in their uptake of this interpretative resource. For some, the Family is an apt characterization of their understanding of the NMA-fan relationship, whereas others question the appropriateness of this image of family as a way of framing their experience with the NMA. Some argue that the concept of family is dangerous because it carries with it expectations of unquestioning solidarity and conformity to group norms. "Family" is reformulated in negative terms as potentially oppressive and as a threat to the values of individuality and freedom of speech. The fans also dispute how inclusive membership of the "NMA Family" really is, arguing that in practice, subgroups of fans may attempt to regulate entry to the family, setting criteria for who is or isn't an authentic fan. We argue that the "family as sanctuary" repertoire helps to ease the tension between the band's need to survive economically and its creative project. The family construct can be seen as an imaginative attempt to articulate the production and consumption of the NMA brand in a way that foregrounds social relationships, offering a social identity that is congruent with NMA's values.

## New Model Army

NMA played its first live performance at Scamps disco in Bradford, England, in 1980. The band's name was inspired by the parliamentary, antimonarchist New Model Army formed in 1645 by Oliver Cromwell and led by Sir Thomas Fairfax during the English civil wars (Downing and Millman 1998)—and, as such, evokes and celebrates an antiestablishment ethos. According to Justin Sullivan, NMA founder and lead singer, the English civil war was, "the nearest thing we had to a revolution" (Sullivan, interview with Russell, retrieved April 14, 2000, www.rock-city.co.uk). Sullivan, the writer or cowriter of most of the band's lyrics, is the only remaining member of the original band. The band tends to avoid categorization of its music. When asked during an interview in 1999 where it fits into the current music scene, Sullivan replied:

> It doesn't. Never has. Probably never will. . . . I can't think of any other band that . . . tries for the same range of musical and emotional experience that we do at the same time as remaining entirely themselves. We've been labelled as punks, post-punks, Goths, metal, folk—the lot, but we've always been beyond those kind of style confines. (interview with Ned Ludd, NMA website)

In general, NMA philosophy (as communicated through their lyrics and in interviews) counsels wariness about conventional, "establishment" values and attitudes, and in the music business, NMA positions itself against the "fat golden goose of mainstream rock n' roll" (Denby 2004), publicly rejecting the cynical commercialism of "hyped" pop music outfits. When the band plays at a benefit or charity gig, for example, it will do so "without any fanfare or self-promotion" and with no "hidden expenses or backhanders" (Denby 2004).

The current lineup is Justin Sullivan (lead vocals, guitar), Dave Blomberg (lead guitar), Nelson (bass), Dean White (keyboards), and Michael Dean (drums). The band has released fifteen albums to date, debuting with *Vengeance* in 1984, and including four albums with EMI and one with Sony/Epic. Their experience with major labels was somewhat mixed, and the band now operates its own label (Attack Attack) and works out of its own recording studio in Bradford, U.K. NMA had twelve U.K. chart singles between 1985 and 1991 (Berelian 1999, 683). The band still records and tours, and when not working with NMA, Sullivan tours regularly with NMA associates under a number of banners, such as Justin Sullivan and Friends, Big Guitars in Little Europe, or Red Sky Coven. The band has a particularly strong following in the U.K., the Netherlands, and Germany but its tours take in much of Western and Eastern Europe as well as three times to the United States and Canada in 2004–2005.

## The NMA Website

The key components of the official NMA website are a home page (http://www.newmodelarmy.org/fhome.htm), a series of monthly newsletters regarding the band's activities, samples of the band's music for downloading, the entire corpus of NMA lyrics, a tribute to Robert Heaton (longtime NMA drummer and co-songwriter who died in November 2004), a news archive, record and tour news, selected interviews with the band, album cover artwork by Joolz Denby, links to other websites (including some well-developed NMA fan sites), a shop selling NMA and other products and merchandise, and the Noticeboard, to which any visitors to the site may post content and communicate with each other. Communication via the Noticeboard is mostly, though not exclusively, between fans. Tommy Tee, the band's manager, occasionally posts to explain or clarify band decisions, and the Boardmaster sometimes comments about board-related technicalities. Sullivan almost never contributes to the Noticeboard; the most frequent band-side poster is Joolz Denby. While she is very clear to say she does not speak on behalf of the band, she does function (as we will see) as a kind of band advocate, interacting with fans on certain topics and clarifying the band's position on a wide range of issues.

## The Significance of the Website for NMA and Their Fans

For a band like NMA, which enjoys very little media coverage, the website provides a vital means of communication with its fans (Joachimsthaler and Aaker 1997) and a vehicle for promoting the band. Ultimately, the website contributes significantly to the ongoing viability of the NMA project. The site is used to post information about the band and its activities, and also operates as an online store. In addition to these practical functions (and the focus of this chapter), the site also enables the band to construct, differentiate, explain, and elaborate its brand identity within the pop music industry, via the publication of band texts (in the wider sense), in posts about the band and in its interactions with fans.

The fans use the discussion area of the site to keep in touch with each other between gigs and use the Noticeboard to solve practical problems such as arranging pre-gig meet-ups, checking directions to venues, and arranging accommodation. However, the thread content of Noticeboard postings is not purely of a practical nature. Of central interest to the analysis in the present chapter is the sense in which the Noticeboard also works as an online site for the fans to "do being a NMA fan" (see, for example, Sacks 1984), that is, to construct, maintain, and evaluate their identity as an NMA fan in interaction with other contributors to the site. For example, posters to the site sometimes relate how they first encountered the band, and narrate passionate conversion stories extolling the significance of the band in their lives. There are detailed discussions about the meanings of band lyrics, favorite NMA gigs, songs, artwork, and popular music industry issues (e.g., copyright, bootlegging, trading, and levels of media attention). The characteristics and behavior of different band members are interrogated, as is fan behavior at gigs, including circle forming, moshing, drinking, and talking while the band is playing. Through this discursive interaction, the fans negotiate what the band means to them and what it means to be an NMA fan and a member of the wider community of NMA fans.

## Popular Music Brand Communities Online

In this chapter, we characterize the NMA as a brand and adopt the shorthand "b(r)and" to denote the status of the band as a popular music brand. Several different types of brands can be identified in the popular music business, including performer or talent brands (like NMA), media brands (e.g., record labels, radio and TV stations), cultural intermediary brands (e.g., record producers), or event and venue brands (e.g., Glastonbury Festival or the Brixton Academy) (O'Reilly 2004). Popular music brands can be conceptualized in symbolic terms as a web of cultural texts (see, for example, Shuker 2001), the aggregate of their communicative power constructing the brand identity. Texts that a brand may weave for consumption include publicity texts, where the b(r)and sets out its stall in terms of musical and commercial identity (where distinctions between authenticity and "selling out" may be crucial), lyrics, artwork, live performance, and of particular interest here, web postings (O'Reilly 2004).

The NMA website Noticeboard offers a way of establishing and maintaining an online community of fans. As Anderson (1983) asserts, contemporary communities or "neo-tribes" are typically fluid and dispersed, experiencing only occasional physical gatherings and depending to a large extent on the idea of imagined others. The Internet offers a material infrastructure that can support online social exchanges between members of a neo-tribe such as the NMA collective. Such online groups are also very much woven into the fabric of offline life (Baym 1995; Kozinets 1998) and online interaction displays all the typical social dynamics of community life (Baym 1995). As we will see, participants develop forms of expression that are unique to the group, form and actively explore group identities and relationships, and create group norms and sanctions.

Recent marketing literature has been concerned to define and explore how some online communities of interest might be conceptualized as "brand communities." Muniz and O'Guinn (2001) define a "brand community" as a specialized, nongeographically bound community, based on a structured set of social relations among admirers of a brand. McAlexander, Schouten, and Koening (2002) see a brand community as a fabric of relationships in which the customer is situated. They identify key relationships as including those between customer and brand, between customer and firm, between customer and the product in use, and amongst the customers themselves. Kozinets (1999) characterizes an online brand community as an electronic tribe, or "E-Tribe," united by a common consumer interest. He notes that many virtual communities are based on consumption and marketing interests and, as such, a sophisticated understanding of the different categories of Internet user and their patterns of interaction and the social functions and purposes of E-tribe membership is of substantial importance to marketing and business strategies. The marketing literature has begun to explore the possibilities of building stronger brands by establishing, facilitating, or contributing to online brand communities (e.g., McWilliam 2000; Williams and Cothrel 2000) in order to enhance brand loyalty (Armstrong and Hagel 1996; McAlexander, Schouten, and Koening 2002). Brand loyalty is understood by Kozinets as tied to the consumer's passion for the consumption object. He argues:

> Members of these virtual communities have implicated their own identities deeply and lastingly with the consumption object and its symbolism. . . . The more marketers can provide members with the meaning, connection, inspiration, aspiration even mystery and shared sense of purpose that is related to their shared consumption identities, the more those consumers will become and remain loyal. (Kozinets 1999, 261)

McWilliam (2000) notes that it is not only the desire to engage with the content that draws consumers back to an interest-based website on a frequent basis but also the attraction of forming relationships with like-minded people. The combination of brand interest coupled with the desire and competence to satisfy social needs and experience a sense of belonging is construed in the marketing literature as a powerful marketing tool.

This chapter focuses on how the symbolic dimension of the NMA b(r)and comes into play in an online community of fans and on the brand development work engaged in by members of the NMA as they construct and promote their b(r)and identity. There is a potential tension here between the activities of producers on the band side and consumers on the fan side, which is nicely articulated by Venkatesh (1998) in his identification of two recurring narratives in discussions about consumers in cyberspace. One refers to marketing's drive to annex cyberspace to make profits where consumers are regarded as "fair game" in this profit seeking enterprise. The second narrative views consumers as agentic, self-actualizing individuals who have the freedom to express and establish identities, using brands as resources through their activities online. This tension may be particularly acute in the management of a rock b(r)and such as NMA, whose brand image is associated with left-wing politics, antiglobalization, and a rejection of consumerism, and we will return to this theme in the discussion. In the next section we further explore the relationship between brand identity, social identity, and subjectivity.

## Brands as Resources for Identity Construction

The culturalist approach to popular music identified by Middleton (1990) constructs the consumption of popular music brand texts as an active rather than passive process. Consumption is conceived as a process of meaning making, and the notion of "active" or "creative" consumption recognizes that consumers are reflexive about their consumption activities, actively interpreting or judging, appropriating or resisting, the texts offered for consumption. De Certeau, Giard, and Mayol (2002) argue that meaning is produced by consumers as they use and experience consumption offerings in the context of their everyday lives. Beck (1992), Rose (1996), Giddens (1991, 1998), and Fairclough (2000) argue that there has been a fundamental shift in Western society toward neoliberal rationalities that encourage people to fulfill themselves as free individuals and be linked to society through their consumer choices. Musical preferences offer rich opportunities for individuals to forge social identities and experience the solidarity, security, and sense of belonging attached to identification with like-minded peers (see, for example, Larson 1995). In these writings, identity is conceived as a kind of "project" that "the individual must actively construct out of the available symbolic materials, materials which the individual weaves into a coherent account of who he or she is, a narrative of self-identity" (Thompson [1997] cited in Elliott and Wattanasuwan 1998, 132).

Elliott & Wattanasuwan use the term "discursive elaboration" to label the social process by which the individual's interpretations of brand meanings are worked out in interaction with others and "described, discussed, argued about and laughed at" (137). The focus of this chapter is the online discursive elaboration of NMA brand texts where participants reveal themselves to be "not merely passive recipients of consumption information, but active creators deeply involved in articulating and rearticulating their consumption activities" (Kozinets 1999, 257), as they do "being an NMA fan."

The postmodern understanding of identity adopted here then rejects the underlying assumption in mainstream social science that identity is something stable, consistent, and internally owned, and replaces it with a conceptualization of identity as dynamic and fragmented. Identity is understood as a flexible accomplishment, the sense of which is actively renewed by self and others in the context of consumption activities and offline and online social interaction. Identity is not something that you "are," something tangible; it is a process, something that you "do" (Sacks 1984). This orientation points to an analysis of the ways in which different identities are made visible within an interaction and the consequences of categorizing self and others in one way rather than another.

To summarize, in this chapter, we conceptualize identity as provisional, to be constructed and negotiated in the context of social interaction online. The band-side communications about the b(r)and are treated as interpretative resources, frameworks of meaning that the fans can appropriate, resist, reconfigure, or subvert as they make sense of their experiences with the band and other fans as they do "being an NMA fan."

## Methodology

"Netnography" is a term coined by Kozinets (1998, 2002) to describe an ethnographic research approach adapted to online fieldwork. This approach involves the collection of a range of raw data sources (which can include downloaded files of postings, email exchanges, sound/picture files, interviews with key informants, and field notes taken as a participant observer or "lurker" in online or related offline contexts) in order to study the distinctive meanings, customs, practices, and artifacts of the social groupings and connections between their online and offline life.

In line with netnographic methodology, the data presented here consist of an online essay written by Joolz Denby (2004) and fan postings to the NMA Noticeboard, offered in asynchronous interaction between posters to the site. This online talk and text lends itself well to analysis using the principles and techniques of discourse analysis. The interpretation of the data is also guided by insights gleaned during an extended period of ethnographic fieldwork, including observation of live gigs and the Noticeboard, interviews with key informants from the band and with fans, and an analysis of band artifacts.

## Data and Sampling

From an examination of the site and from observation of the Noticeboard, a range of postings was selected for analysis that bears on the notion of "family." Site "traffic" was tracked over a number of years as part of a wider study of the band-fan interaction. During this period, a number of themes were observed to recur, among them the nature of the NMA collective. The band-fan discourse on the question of what one might call their joint project is an ongoing negotiation. Then in May 2004, a band-side posting by Joolz Denby (2004) crystallized the band's thinking on this issue for the first time. The posting is an essay entitled "Some Thoughts on the Idea of the NMA Family." This piece is published online, but not in any other medium, and runs to about 1,500 words. It can be found by clicking on the side menu item entitled "Talk" and then clicking on "What is the 'NMA Family'? Some Thoughts by Joolz Denby— 15/02/04." Joolz, the band's artist, has been closely acquainted with the band since its origins, and is in regular contact with the fans on the Noticeboard, in the merchandise booth at gigs, and at other venues where she performs in her own right (see www.joolz.net). This piece is particularly interesting, because it was deemed of sufficient importance by the band to be posted alongside the relatively few other items in the "Talk" part of the site, and because it is a text through which a respected band associate can be seen to be actively working to "provide members with the meaning, connection, inspiration, aspiration even mystery and shared sense of purpose that is related to their shared consumption identities" (Kozinets 1999, 261). The piece is in part a fierce polemic, partly a retrospective essay, and partly a manifesto, communicating core b(r)and values.

We also selected fan postings that touch on the notion of the NMA collective as family. Some were in immediate response to this "family" document whereas others were drawn from the period before and after its appearance. In order to preserve the anonymity of fan posters, thread titles, contributor handles, dates, IP addresses, and any other data that could reveal the identity of the poster have been removed. Misspellings have not been corrected.

## Discursive Psychology: Analytic Principles

A discursive psychological (DP) approach to discourse analysis was utilized (Wetherell 1998; Potter and Wetherell 1995, 1987) in the analysis of texts. This approach to analysis is influenced by social constructionist theory, which argues that descriptions of events, people, groups, institutions, and psychological phenomena are only ever one version of reality and should be treated as open ended and flexible. Analysis thus involves a search for actual or potential variability in constructions and asks, why this formulation at this point in the strip of text? This constructive work is linked to the accomplishment of social actions. As Parker (1997) argues, "When we seem to be merely describing a state of affairs, our commentary always has other effects; it plays a part in legitimizing or challenging, supporting or ironizing, endorsing or subverting what it describes" (290). Analytically, a focus on social action involves interpreting the interactional pragmatics and the ideological work that is accomplished by constructing one particular version rather than another. Discourse analysts are also sensitive to the rhetorical organization of arguments, opinions, and the discursive strategies used to make an argument seem factual or persuasive, including attention to the speaker's construction of their credentials as a "qualified," "neutral," or "sympathetic" observer.

DP discourse analysis also examines the interpretative resources that are mobilized in the text (Potter and Wetherell 1995; Wetherell 1998). In the DP literature, systems of content, coherent ways of talking about objects, subjects, and events in the world are referred to as "interpretative repertoires" (Potter and Wetherell 1987; Wetherell and Potter 1988; Edley 2000). These are conceived as the "building blocks" of sense making, the range of interpretative resources (cultural themes, arguments, and assumptions) that can be utilized in the course of social interaction and that form the "commonsense" basis for shared understanding. An interpretative repertoire is constituted from a limited range of lexical items, stylistic constructions, and the use of a range of metaphors (Potter and Reicher 1987). Selections can be made from available repertoires to suit the occasion and function to which the discourse is put (Potter, Wetherell, Gill, and Edwards 1990) and are in use when constructing descriptions of people, groups, objects, institutions, and events and when offering opinions, evaluations, and explanations. Analysis involves clarifying and discussing the interpretative resources that members draw on and the development of a critical commentary on the cultural significance of the discursive patterns and resources in play.

## Analysis

In this section, we will show how the band shapes the culture of offline and online interaction by characterizing the community in which band-fan and fan-fan interactions take place. It does so by mobilizing a repertoire of concepts, arguments, and metaphors that construct the notion of "family as sanctuary." The analysis starts by examining Joolz's account for the emergence of the NMA family and then moves on to examine how the interpretative repertoire of "family as sanctuary" is deployed to describe and positively evaluate involvement in the NMA project, to outline the band-fan and fan-fan relationships and responsibilities that might be expected, and ultimately as a way of invigorating and sustaining the NMA b(r)and within the online community of fans.

### The Band-Side Account for the Emergence of the NMA Family

Seeing and feeling the persecution of a creative force that intelligently addressed and examined the ideas and beliefs they held dear, that never patronised them, that spoke the secrets of their hearts and was not afraid to stand up and be counted, fans became more loyal, more devoted and identified even more strongly with NMA than ever before. It was as if the band in some way became a genuine part of their lives, became, in fact, part of the fans' families [not a] formal, contrived organisation, but a spontaneous sense of fellowship that has developed over the years. (Denby 2004)

The emergence of the family is presented in this text as a spontaneous, organic reaction (not formal or contrived) to the sustained "persecution of a creative force" and, by implication, the ideas, beliefs, and values of their fans. In response, the fans are constructed as strong-minded and independent in their refusal to be influenced by negative evaluations of the NMA and the dismissal of the band. They are characterized as possessing a strong psychological and emotional connection with the band that transcends any attempt to sabotage the NMA project and that engenders a desire to defend and protect it as if it were a family member. This is couched in terms of loyalty, devotion, and the notion of shared hurt. A spatial metaphor is used to describe the division between "the family," characterized here as a "fellowship," standing together and closing ranks against the NMA detractors outside of the NMA family. This version of family also contains a moral dimension, implicitly invoked here, that it is the responsibility of those bound by family ties to be loyal to each other and thus defend and protect each other, sometimes unquestionably. Potentially then, there are beneficial consequences for the band in constructing the NMA as joined by family ties to the community of fans. By implication, the fans are asked to remain loyal, even in the face of public criticism.

## Imagining the Family

In this section we examine how the criteria for NMA Family membership and the boundaries and spatial location of the Family are constructed. The Family is not defined as a fixed social grouping but as

it's a feeling; some would say, an instinctive emotional response to the intensely emotional music created by the band. (Denby 2004)

This construction of what the Family is here takes the emphasis completely away from "outer" signs of identity and moves it into the "inner" sphere of feelings and "instinctive"—genuine and true—emotional response.

NMA and the Family has simply become a place of emotional sanctuary where they don't have be anything but themselves and where they can be proud, not ashamed, of their deepest feelings in an atmosphere of comradeship, love and support. (Denby 2004)

Family here is constructed as a "sanctuary" where members can "be themselves" and display, without fear of judgment, the worth of their own deepest emotions, because the Family is imagined here as a place of solidarity, "comradeship," and love. The categorization "sanctuary" mobilizes a religious metaphor to characterize the experience of being with the Family and evokes strong images of protection, safety, and comfort against one's enemies on the outside.

The NMA song "Family" also describes how it might feel to be dislocated or misunderstood and to be searching for a place of acceptance. In the song this experience is vividly imagined as like swimming alone in the ocean, struggling against the tide of one's detractors (in a society where there is pressure to be accountable to values that are not shared) to find a somewhere to be oneself. In this metaphor, the Family (or tribe) as sanctuary is constructed as a "harbor" of support and acceptance:

> Give me some place that I can go
> Where I don't have to justify myself
> Swimming out alone against this tide
> Looking for family looking for tribe
> (from "Family," Sullivan/Heaton 1987)

In NMA texts, Family is therefore configured as a sanctuary, a place of comfort and relief from feelings of dislocation and alienation, a place where one can find a sense of belonging and tribal solidarity or an emotional "consciousness of kin" (see Muniz and O'Guinn 2001)—an intrinsic connection that members of a neo-tribe feel towards each other based on shared attitudes, perceived similarity, and importantly, a collective sense of difference from those not in the community.

The NMA Family is explicitly linked to the idea of a "new kind of consciousness" in the following extract from "Some Thoughts":

> There are those who say NMA is now much more than just a rock band, that it has slowly metamorphosed into a kind of Movement: not resembling accepted forms of conventional religious or political movements, but rather a new kind of consciousness derived from archaic tribal roots and the most basic human need for a sense of belonging, transplanted into the fragmenting twenty-first century to create stability and a sense of collective power via NMA's music, ideas and creative endeavours. (Denby 2004)

The collective sense of difference in the above extract is once again formulated in terms of a rejection of convention, this time in terms of a refusal to identify the NMA Family with "conventional religious or political movements." The emergence of NMA consciousness is constructed as something much more essential, naturalized as derived from "the most basic human need for a sense of belonging" (more urgent in the "fragmenting twenty-first century") and connected to ancient tribal forms. This extract is also interesting for the way in which the focus of shared attitudes and sense of similarity is detached from specific players on the band side or from a core grouping of primarily music fans. The Family is categorized as a "Movement" that has "metamorphosed" into "much more than just a rock band," keeping the boundaries free-floating and membership inclusive rather than exclusive. This "inclusivity" is more likely to sustain and renew the NMA Family, enabling the NMA to retain and develop its position in the cultural industry. Throughout this extract, organic metaphors (e.g., metamorphose, transplant, essential, and basic) are mobilized, constructing the emergence of the NMA family as natural rather than strategic or manufactured. This theme is echoed in the following extract where the relationship between the band and fans is configured in terms of mutual pride and respect and an honest unmediated love of the music. The assertion that the NMA may strategically manipulate their fans (like so many others in the music industry) and be, at the end of the day, "only in it for the money," is mobilized and vehemently rejected:

> The band, unlike so many others in the music industry, have never manipulated or lied to the fans for financial gain and in return, generation after generation of fans come to the music and love it honestly. (Denby 2004)

## NMA B(r)and Values

NMA's preferred construction of the band-fan collective as a *family* is an important part of its brand identity work. As discussed above, in a range of band texts the NMA explicitly positions itself against the "fat golden goose of mainstream rock n' roll"; where certain music fans are seen as "enmeshed in the illusion of consumerism and what they sadly consider 'normal society' and where the media celebrate fake celebrity and plastic superficiality" (Denby 2004). Deploying the "Family as sanctuary" repertoire to give meaning to being part of the NMA collective helps to create and maintain this brand identity. It promises fans the opportunity to experience a sense of solidarity, acceptance, and emotional honesty. The band's positioning of themselves as bound by family ties to their fans also breaks down any perceived divisions between the band and the fans and backgrounds the commercial stake of the band in the longevity of the NMA project.

### The Fans: Interrogating the Concept of the NMA Family

The "Family as sanctuary" repertoire is a cultural resource that fans are invited to use to frame their experience of participation in the NMA collective. In this section we shall see how they discursively elaborate (Elliott and Wattanasuwan 1998) this resource and as they do "being an NMA fan." We start by examining posts where the family construct as formulated in the web posting is enthusiastically embraced by some fans as a way of making sense of their encounters with the b(r)and and each other. We then move on to look at instances where fans question the appropriateness of the "Family as sanctuary" repertoire as a way of framing their experience with the NMA. This discursive work centers on charges that the concept of "family" is dangerous because it carries with it expectations of unquestioning solidarity and conformity to group norms. An alternative "Family as constraining" repertoire is deployed to reimagine the collective in negative terms as potentially oppressive and a threat to the values of individuality and freedom of speech. The fans dispute how inclusive membership of the NMA Family really is, arguing that, in practice, individual or subgroups of fans may attempt to regulate entry to the Family, setting criteria for who is or isn't an authentic fan. Specifically, we look at the way this is played out to defend or criticize "moshing" at gigs.

## "The Family Feeling Is What Keeps Us Coming Back"

Joolz's piece and her construction of the NMA collective using the "Family as sanctuary" repertoire was hailed enthusiastically on the Noticeboard by a number of posters. This selection of extracts provides a flavor of this kind of posting:

Joolz as ever sums it up perfectly, the family feeling is EXACTLY what keeps us all comming back

Top read! Almost brings a lump to your throat when it reminds you of all those happy times, all those fellow fans you love so much!

Thanks Joolz for finding a way of saying what we can't find the words to! But then, that's your job innit? ;)

The following post is interesting as an example of those that endorse the appropriateness of the "Family as sanctuary" repertoire as a way of making sense of their experience in the NMA collective but in so doing, invoke a more complex version of "family life" than is offered in the band-side postings:

NMA fans I've encountered, many of whom I'm familiar with through this board, haven't been the easiest bunch for me to associate with (hell, I even once bitched out Justin here), and quite honestly, many times I've felt alienated by the "Family." But it doesn't really matter. I've been listening to NMA since 1986, and anything you do for that long will have a profound effect on who you are as a person. No petty differences or faux pas can change that. NMA is a significant part of my life, and I willingly respect that they are so in the lives of any NMA fan here, even if they wouldn't be so generous to me in return. And I can honestly say that I love anyone for whom NMA plays a similar role in their lives, because that shared experience means more to me than anything they may say or do that might otherwise piss me off. . . . We're an incredibly passionate bunch and we're very human in some very real ways; we are also very blessed and we probably need each other more than fans usually do, if only to remind each other of just how blessed we are. I think that need to remind each other of our own blessings [is] the most convincing evidence that this is a "family."

This poster raises the possibility of sometimes feeling alienated from the Family and foregrounds the idea that sometimes Family members may not be the easiest people to be around. However, this tension is resolved by minimizing the significance of the differences between Family members ("petty differences or faux pas") and by reaffirming the primary significance of the glue that holds them together as a Family: their shared love and respect for each other, their mutual experience as fans and their passion for the NMA project. In this eloquent posting, a religious metaphor is invoked to describe the connection with the music and association with the band as a "blessing."

## "It's a Bit Sheepish"

However, the family idea is not always unquestioningly adopted. For some, being in a family, and the NMA Family is no exception, means feeling pressure to do things they don't like doing. For example, for a time it was common practice for some NMA fans at a gig to make certain arm and hand movements synchronized with song lyrics. The poster in the following extract considers this kind of group behavior "completely ridiculous" and too big a price to pay if this sort of behavior is the criterion for admittance to the NMA Family.

so to be part of the family you need to be a huge fan and do the same as everybody else does? so i agree i am not and will never be part of the family . . . but i know people who are big fans and still find all this hand business completely ridiculous

For some fans, ritualistic behavior at gigs may well be experienced positively as a signifier of solidarity and belonging to the NMA collective. However, others reject these practices. This therefore marks a potential difference between the fans, which can then be constructed as, on the one hand, a marker of authentic fanhood (where people who don't do the gestures are excluded or may feel excluded) or, on the other hand, as a "ridiculous" example of conformity. "Doing the same as everybody else in the family does" can thus be characterized positively or (as above) negatively as the fans actively make sense of their identity as an NMA fan.

Offline, in interview, some fans are also clear that they do not buy into the family idea if this means being a "sheep" or a "lemming"—powerfully pejorative cultural identity labels used to categorize those who are unable to think for themselves:

> Everybody thinks that—every fan thinks they are part of New Model Army for some reason. They belong together, that's why they're called a tribe, a family. Which I don't necessarily agree with too much. I think that's a bit sheepish, a bit following each other, like lemmings. (fan interview with author)

## "It's More Like a Club Than a Family"

Discussions about the differences between "club" and "family" and the appropriateness of these terms as descriptions of the NMA collective come up frequently in postings to the Noticeboard. This dispute is of some significance, as clubs can be construed quite negatively as elitist and divisive whereas the family construct in band-side texts banishes notions of elitism and embraces inclusiveness.

In this extract the poster considers what counts as a club and what counts as a family and concludes that, although the collective does have the capacity to behave like a club, it does, for him, remain a place of sanctuary and solidarity. This is accomplished by arguing (in a similar move to the post examined above) that members of the family are bound together on a very deep level through love that is bred from "being together and shared circumstance and shared experiences." Family members are allowed to be controversial and critical within a general context of love and acceptance. The tension between "club" and "family" membership is resolved by this fan in a way that ultimately protects the investment in his social identity as an NMA fan:

> I once got on my soapbox a few years back about how NMA fans here tend to act more like a club than a family. I'd like to return to that, for a moment: a club has rules and regulations that you have to follow in order to be a member. Clubs therefore have a natural expectation for its members to behave and conduct themselves in a pre-ordained manner. A family is an entirely different scenario—there are no "rules" to being a family. GK Chesterton once said that the family was the only truly anarchist institution in human society because its members cannot be governed by rules, but only by love that is bred from being together through shared circumstances and shared experiences. Nothing is pre-ordained for a family—Behavior and conduct is determined by love. At times, fans here have acted like members of a select club, even viciously, yet over the years this board has never entirely been converted into a members-only clubhouse, thankfully. I think that's because, even during our most hostile, prideful, stubborn moments, like any family, we know deep down we really can't get along without each other.

The distinction between club and family also arose in another online interaction, when one fan posted bemoaning the lack of interesting content on the Noticeboard:

> It seems to be "dominated" by about 5 people who keep writing childish (non NMA related obviously!!) things to each other

A second fan posts in response:

> Yes, sometimes I get tired of finding nothing of interest on the NB for me too . . . but you know what? Such is life. If it doesnt look like a thread that interests me, I pass it by & dont let it bother me. There are so many more important things in life . . . why worry fret over the content of some posts on the NMA NoticeBoard? [name] . . . take a deep breathe in . . . breathe out . . . take it all in stride. We are all family here . . . yes?

And this triggers a reply from a third poster setting out the difference in his or her mind between a club and a family:

> I do not think that simply listening to a band makes people "family." Sharing a common interest, at best, makes a club. To be family requires a certain degree of hospitality, generosity and etiquette by which members actively seek to include the other members. A true family is willing to change, grow and sacrifice in order to bring others into it or to bring back those cut off, alienated, or disenfranchised. An attitude like "This is how it is—just accept it" is really more appropriate for a club than a family . . . Confusing what is more of a club for a family only makes your response sound patronizing, which only adds salt to the wound.

In this extract, the second fan is castigated for her "patronizing" attitude to the first posting. A particular definition of family is offered in order to draw a contrast between "true family" behavior and the alleged behavior of regular posters to the Noticeboard. They are indirectly challenged for a perceived lack of hospitality and generosity and deep-seated conservatism. They are categorized as more like a "club," an elite, with hurtful "take it or leave it" rules or attitudes, who don't actually care about those who may be disenfranchised from the group and who fiercely protect a nonnegotiable set of core values. This alternative picture of experience in the NMA collective is, of course, potentially troubling to the broader integrity of the NMA project and its brand identity as discussed above. In the final section of analysis we look further at how individuals or subgroups of fans regulate entry to the NMA collective by setting criteria for who is or isn't an authentic fan. Specifically, we examine the way this is played out to defend or criticize moshing at gigs.

## Family Membership and Moshing

A mosh-pit has the potential to be experienced in a number of ways and may be perceived by some as a violent place. Debates about "what's going on" in mosh-pits frequently engage posters to the Noticeboard. Accusations of violence may be particularly significant in this community not least because issues of violence or violent feelings are problematized in NMA lyrics. Fans often discount levels of violence at NMA gigs by saying that if you fall down at an NMA gig there will be friendly hands to pull you up. This tends to be true, from observation. Whereas, at other bands' gigs, the implication is that one can suffer injury from deliberate violence or the uncontrolled aggression of other "fans."

One NMA fan is able to resolve the controversial nature of moshing by drawing on positively evaluated elements of the "Family as sanctuary" repertoire as follows:

> I go down the front for the feeling of family you get, looking out for everyone not just your friends seeing new people and getting to know them after the gig NOT to try and hurt as many people as possible.

The mosh-pit here is characterized as a safe place and moshing is reconfigured as a necessary part of the rough and tumble of family life where "everyone looks out for everyone." Notions of "tough love" and "not being wrapped in cotton wool" are also hinted at and positively evaluated.

In contrast, a considered opponent of moshing posts:

> mosh is mosh, and it hurts people, both physically and emotionally. Not moshing doesn't hurt anyone in any way.

This poster positions himself as a long-time student of music, and argues that moshing is intrinsically violent. His assertion is challenged strongly by another fan in the next post and in the extended interaction following:

> and my question to u is have u ever even been to nma concerts? or [name] that started the whole topic has she seen nma more then once? at first i thought that those that were complaining were frequent followers, or u are u talking from the outside[?]. i'm not english myself but i can say that nma followers are very friendly and respectful (at least for most parts) of each other, very [rare] our days. i'm glad to have know great people with big hearts and a musician with great view, while following the army. do u have any positive input into all this or all u have to do is bitch about the following which u [might] not even know at all?

The objections to moshing are reformulated in the above post as "bitchings about the following" and the poster's move is to try and discredit the anti-moshers by making relevant the frequency of gig attendance as an important difference marker between real fans and those on the outside. The anti-moshers are argued to have no speaking rights on the subject of moshing because they are accused of only superficial involvement with NMA. In addition, the notion of respect is invoked as a necessary quality in a family member, one that is argued to be lacking in the anti-moshers:

> well like most families (not all) respect of . . . it's culture and it's people is a must and u have very little of both.

Mobilizing another category of identity, nationality, he labels the anti-mosher pejoratively as

> u talk like american that thinks as if tv teaches u how to think

So far then we have seen that a critique of moshing on the Noticeboard is treated in practice by another fan as evidence that the poster must be someone who stands outside of the community of fans and who has no respect for the NMA family culture. A pro-moshing stance is constructed and defended as a marker of authentic fanhood, and the pro-mosher attempts to exclude the anti-mosher from the NMA family using this criterion and further accuses the poster of possessing undesirable "American" values. The opponent's response is to recategorize himself as non-American, an outsider in his own country, in a move that seeks to restore his credentials as an NMA fan:

> Your observations about Americans are, sadly, mostly true. I've always been an outsider in my own country. A Polish guy I used to work with, a physicist who had lived in France, England and Israel, told me that I was the first American he had met who had a European mind. Whatever that means. Just my way of saying that you've pegged me wrong. I'm not one of these Land of Opportunity androids.

Note that the authority invoked here is European, quite well traveled, and an educated scientist. On this person's authority, not only has the anti-moshing poster a "European mind," he is to be treated as a human being, not an android. He places himself outside the category of those who believe in the "land of opportunity"—a term synonymous with capitalistic exploitation in this context. Laying claim to the categories of being human and non-American (or perhaps even un-American?) is to lay claim to categories or values that are important parts of NMA discourse, and helps to reestablish the right to be part of the NMA Family.

The pro-moshing contributor then moves to explicitly exclude his opponent from the NMA collective:

> u are not part of the nma family and never will be

Others challenge this eternal exclusion of the anti-mosher from the NMA Family, invoking notions of childishness to sideline the pro-mosher and to reformulate the dispute as a playground squabble:

> all this reminds me of being in the junior school.
> "do you want to be in my gang? Well you can't!"
> "don't want to be anyway"
> "good"
> etc etc . . .
> Aren't we a bit old for this?

And the pro-moshing poster comes in for other criticism, both indirect:

> He'll kick you out of the family too if you can't pass the test.
> Too friggin' ridiculous,

and direct:

> I think if you keep going you may end up with a family all of your very own with just you in it!

The "anti-mosher," perhaps playing to the audience, positions him/herself as a reasoned debater, a strong character and impervious to harm:

> Maybe you think I've been harsh, but the discerning reader will see that I have not taken the many opportunities that you have given me to attack. You, on the other hand, turned the debate into a personal attack on me. Don't sweat it, though, I'm a big boy. No harm done. The only other comment I want to make is that you should try not to let your prejudices color any further issues you choose to debate. Although the USA may be culturally repulsive in many ways, my nationality had nothing to do with what we were discussing, and falling to the level of bigotry is not an effective or productive way to debate any issue. The effect of expressing bigotry is to discredit oneself. I'm sure you don't think of yourself as a bigot, and probably don't deserve to be called one, but you did slip this time. Anyway, having said my final piece, I want to add: No hard feelings. No bitterness. Go in peace, please feel free to have the last word if you wish.

This post represents an accomplished example of NMA fan- and Family-work, performing as it does, some "core values" of the NMA ethos, namely tolerance and forgiveness.

## Discussion

In this chapter we have argued that a website empowers a band in many ways. Of particular interest has been the way in which it offers a band the chance to control and project its brand identity to a potentially global community of consumers. NMA does so partly through offering the construct Family, as a way for fans to make sense of their experiences with the NMA collective. This construct offers fans some "added value" to their involvement with NMA—it's not just about the music; participation also offers the promise of the experience of belonging, a sanctuary from an alienating society and a space in which fans can be themselves. A consistent b(r)and identity is offered not just through online experiences but also through lyrics, gigs, and even artwork and merchandise.

The fan-posting analysis examined how consumers appropriate the "Family as sanctuary" repertoire as they do "being an NMA fan." Some fans enthusiastically accept the band-side framing of their experience as a member of the NMA collective. However, not all contributors to the Noticeboard straightforwardly accept this consumption information. An alternative "Family as constraining" repertoire is deployed to reimagine the collective in negative terms as potentially oppressive and a threat to the values of individuality and freedom of speech. Also the NMA collective is argued by some to be an exclusive "club," and we saw how authenticity of NMA fanhood may be actively disputed in the context of a dispute over the validity of fan practices such as moshing at gigs.

There are other metaphors that the band could have used to frame the NMA collective. One metaphor for collective identity often applied to underground bands is that of a "cult." Underground bands are seen as occluded from mainstream public view, their lead singers imagined as objects of worship by a minority who are somehow "in the know," positioned as countercultural and subversive. NMA has been labeled a cult band in the past. However, this metaphor has not been adopted in band texts. Nor does it retain much purchase amongst the fan base. There are two potential reasons for this. Firstly, the term "cult" carries connotations of organized religion and of a hierarchy between object of worship and devotees. NMA band members would be very uncomfortable about the notion that anyone would literally worship them and as we have seen, prefer to promote a much more organic version of the emergence of the NMA collective. Secondly, connected to the notion of cult is the vexing question of celebrity. Being pop idols or celebrities would also be anathema to NMA band members. They (and their fans) are more likely to mobilize utterances about NMA as "musicians doing a job of work," "professionals," and being unlike stars in their behavior. The notion of "tribe" has enjoyed a lot of popularity among NMA fans, aided by the visual culture, created by Joolz Denby, involving album covers, body modification, and tattoos (tattooing lending itself helpfully to the notion of NMA people as disenfranchised outsiders). Tribe, like family, also carries the notion of blood kinship, though perhaps in an attenuated form. "Tribe" is more promising than "cult," but a potential problem with this categorization is that it can become associated with visual markers of membership, and lead to clannishness and therefore a sense of exclusiveness. NMA's use of the family construct, on the other hand, is all-encompassing, inclusive, and open to any who have an emotional connection with the music.

Earlier in NMA's life, some fans were known as "The Following" and this term is occasionally used still to mean the fan base in general or a smaller section of it who literally "follows" the band from one tour venue to another. Finally, an earlier collective noun used to describe fans was "The Militia." This appellation had the advantage of tying in with the military connotations in NMA's name. However, both The Militia and to some extent The Following became associated, rightly or wrongly, with behavior that was categorized as "elitist." As we argued above, the family construct in the band texts examined is articulated against notions of elitism and cliques, and functions to keep the boundaries of the NMA fan base as broad as possible.

The Family construct can also be read as a means of displacing the producer/consumer dichotomy, which a more commercialized model of band-fan relationship would endorse. We would not wish to suggest that this is the primary motivation for the construction of the NMA collective as a family, nor that this band text was in some way deliberately conceived as a marketing tool. However, it is consistent with the branding of NMA, and as we have shown has the potential to positively reaffirm involvement with the project and to attract new members into the Family. In the case studied here, the fans are invited to endorse a noncommercial, affective version of the NMA collective and are also, it must be said, afforded the opportunity via the Noticeboard to debate and negotiate the wider meanings and implications of this framework of meaning and the broader musical project. The notion of Family can, finally, be seen as an imaginative attempt to deal with the producer/consumer and performer/audience divides in a manner which foregrounds human, social relationships, offering a positively evaluated social identity for existing and potential members of the NMA collective which is congruent with NMA's values.

## Acknowledgment

The authors gratefully acknowledge the help of New Model Army and their fans.

## References to Chapter Seven

Anderson, Benedict. 1983. *Imagined Community*. New York: Verso.

Armstrong, Arthur, and John Hagel. 1996. "The Real Value of Online Communities." *Harvard Business Review* 74, no. 3: 134–40.

Baym, Nancy K. 1995. "The Emergence of Community in Computer-Mediated Communication." In *Cybersociety: Computer-Mediated Communication and Community*, edited by S. Jones. London: Sage.

Beck, Ulrich. 1992. *Risk Society: Toward a New Modernity*. London: Sage.

Berelian, Essi. 1999. "New Model Army." In *Rock: The Rough Guide*, edited by J. Buckley, O. Duane, M. Ellingham, and A. Spicer, 683. London: Rough Guides.

De Certeau, Michel, Luce Giard, and Pierre Mayol. 2002. *The Practice of Everyday Life*. Berkeley: University of California Press.

De Chernatony, Leslie, and Gil McWilliam. 1989. "The Varying Nature of Brands as Assets: Theory and Practice Compared." *International Journal of Advertising* 8, no. 4: 339–49.

Denby, Joolz. 2004. "What Is the 'NMA Family'? Some Thoughts by Joolz Denby. Bradford, UK: New Model Army. Retrieved 1 October, 2004, from http://www.newmodelarmy.org

Downing, Taylor, and Maggie Millman. 1998. *Civil War*. London: Parkgate Books.

Edley, Nigel. 2000. "Analysing Masculinity: Interpretative Repertoires, Ideological Dilemmas and Subject Positions." In *Discourse as Data: A Guide for Analysis*, edited by M. Wetherell, S. Taylor, and S. J. Yates. Milton Keynes, U.K.: Open University Press.

Elliott, Richard, and Kritsadarat Wattanasuwan. 1998. "Brands as Symbolic Resources for the Construction of Identity." *International Journal of Advertising* 17, no. 2: 131–44.

Fairclough, Norman. 2000. "Language and Neo-liberalism." *Discourse & Society* 11, no. 2: 147–48.

Giddens, Anthony. 1991. *Modernity and Self-Identity: Self and Society in the Late Modern Age*. Cambridge: Polity Press.

———. 1998. *The Third Way: The Renewal of Social Democracy*. Cambridge: Polity Press.

Joachimsthaler, Erich, and David A. Aaker. 1997. "Building Brands without Mass Media." *Harvard Business Review* 75, no. 1: 39–50.

Joolz Denby website: www.joolz.net.

Kozinets, Robert V. 1998. "On Netnography: Initial Reflections on Consumer Research Investigations of Cyberculture." *Advances in Consumer Research* 25:366–71.

———. 1999. "E-Tribalized Marketing? The Strategic Implications of Virtual Communities of Consumption." *European Management Journal* 17, no. 3: 252–64.

———. 2002. "The Field behind the Screen: Using Netnography for Marketing Research in Online Communities." *Journal of Marketing Research* 39, no. 1: 61–72.

Larson, R. 1995. "Secrets in the Bedroom: Adolescents' Private Use of Media." *Journal of Youth and Adolescence* 24:535–50.

McAlexander, James H., John W. Schouten, and Harold F. Koening. 2002. "Building Brand Community." *Journal of Marketing* 66, no. 1: 38–54.

McWilliam, Gil. 2000. "Building Stronger Brand through Online Communities." *Sloan Management Review* 41, no. 3: 43–54.

Middleton, Richard, ed. 1990. *Reading Pop: Approaches to Textual Analysis in Popular Music*. Oxford: Oxford University Press.

Muniz, Albert M., and Thomas C. O'Guinn. 2001. "Brand Community." *Journal of Consumer Research* 27, no. 4: 412–32.

New Model Army website. 2004. http://www.newmodelarmy.org/fhome.htm

O'Reilly, Daragh T. 2004. "The Marketing of Popular Music." In *Arts Marketing*, edited by F. Kerrigan, P. Fraser, and M. Ozbilgin, 6–25. Oxford: Elsevier.

Parker, Ian. 1997. "Discursive Psychology." In *Critical Psychology: An Introduction*, edited by D. Fox and I. Prilleltensky. London: Sage

Potter, Jonathan, and Stephen Reicher. 1987. "Discourses of Community and Conflict: The Organization of Social Categories in Accounts of a 'Riot.'" *British Journal of Social Psychology* 26:25–40.

Potter, Jonathan, and Margaret Wetherell. 1987. *Discourse and Social Psychology: Beyond Attitudes and Behaviour.* London: Sage.

———. 1995. "Discourse Analysis." In *Rethinking Methods in Psychology*, edited by J. Smith, R. Harre, and L. Van Langenhove. London: Sage

Potter, Jonathan, Margaret Wetherell, Ros Gill, and Derek Edwards. 1990. "Discourse: Noun, Verb or Social Practice?" *Philosophical Psychology* 3:205–17.

Rock City website. http://www.rockcity.co.uk.

Rose, Nikolas. 1996. *Inventing Our Selves: Psychology, Power and Personhood.* Cambridge: Cambridge University Press.

Sacks, Harvey. 1984. "On Doing 'Being Ordinary.'" In *Structure of Social Action: Studies in Conversation Analysis*, edited by J. M. Atkinson and J. Heritage. Cambridge: Cambridge University Press.

Shuker, Roy. 2001. *Understanding Popular Music.* London: Routledge.

Thompson, Craig. 1997. "Interpreting Consumers: A Hermeneutical Framework for Deriving Marketing Insights from the Texts of Consumers' Consumption Stories." *Journal of Marketing Research* 34:438–55.

Venkatesh, Alladi. 1998. "Cybermarketscapes and Consumer Freedoms and Identities." *European Journal of Marketing* 32, no. 7–8: 664–70.

Wetherell, Margaret. 1998. "Positioning and Interpretative Repertoires: Conversation Analysis and Post-structuralism in Dialogue." *Discourse and Society* 9, no. 3: 387–412.

Wetherell, Margaret, and Jonathan Potter. 1988. "Discourse Analysis and the Identification of Interpretative Repertoires." In *Analysing Everyday Explanation. A Casebook of Methods*, edited by C. Antaki. London: Sage.

Williams, Ruth, and Joseph Cothrel. 2000. "Four Smart Ways to Run Online Communities." *Sloan Management Review* 41, no. 4: 81–91.

CHAPTER EIGHT

# Beating the Bootleggers: Fan Creativity, "Lossless" Audio Trading, and Commercial Opportunities

## Chris Anderton

The popular recording industry has traditionally followed a mass-market productivist model that has treated music fans as passive, rather than active, consumers. As a result, there has been a failure to understand or meet the demands of fans for live and archive (unreleased studio) material, or an inability or unwillingness to satisfy them. As Neumann and Simpson (1997) have stated:

> Faced with the steady output of a commercial recording industry that sets the terms for manufacturing and marketing popular music to various demographic audiences, the practices of bootleg producers and collectors suggest the music industry does not account for all aspects of popular taste or the meanings popular music carries in people's lives. (321)

In the past, this shortfall of live concert recordings and archive material has been filled by a combination of commercial bootlegging and noncommercial trading. Commercial bootlegging is the profit-seeking reproduction and sale of unauthorized recordings of live performances, or of broadcasts made on radio, television, and the Internet; they may also include archive studio recordings.[1] Commercial bootlegs are generally a physical product such as a cassette, CD, or CDR. In contrast, noncommercial trading is the not-for-profit reproduction and distribution of recordings from those same sources through physical media or Internet connections. Trade associations such as the Recording Industry Association of America (RIAA) and the British Phonographic Industry (BPI) regard all such activities as forms of audio piracy, seeing them as a challenge to the commodification of popular music, and to the exploitation of copyrights (see Marshall 2001; Leyshon 2003; Leyshon et al. 2005; Graham et al. 2004). Such organizations demonize all forms of trading activity and the music fans who engage in them—even though some artists actually authorize not-for-profit trading. The trade associations' attitude may be interpreted as an attempt to discipline music consumers in general, to continue to position them as passive rather than as active. However, I argue that this is a dangerous position to take, as it fails to take into account recent technological and social developments that are changing the ways in which artists and fans interact with each other. These developments are discussed in this chapter to show how more fans than ever before are seeking to satisfy their need for live/archive music recordings through not-for-profit trading networks organized via the Internet. These networks have developed from the audiocassette trading groups of the 1970s, creating and adapting new storage technologies and distribution methods over time. They are increasingly shifting towards "lossless" compression standards for digital music storage that can be readily and rapidly transferred through Internet connections (the various standards are discussed in section 2 of this chapter). Individual traders and trading networks take a strong moral stance with regard to the rights of the artist, hence the activity should be repositioned as a complementary shadow economy, rather than an oppositional one, as has been suggested in the past (see Heylin 1995; Neumann and Simpson 1997; Cooper and Harrison 2001; Marshall 2001). The industry has also failed to consider the possible benefits that these networks may have, even though, as we shall see, many smaller-scale and independent artists have now started to recognize and use their potential. This can range from becoming trade-friendly to creating alternative income streams such as Internet-only fan club releases. In addition, anecdotal evidence from fans suggests that the commercial bootleg market has suffered due to trading activities. Therefore, rather than continue with a blanket demonization of all forms of trading, the recording industry should attempt to understand the motivations of its consumers, and adopt a more service-oriented approach. By doing so, and by working both with and through music fans, there are substantial benefits to be gained.

The research for this chapter was conducted in three main ways. Firstly, I have been an active participant in a number of not-for-profit trading networks since 1999, gaining an insight into their workings and the changes that have affected their practice over the last six years. Secondly, I used the contacts built up to arrange informal semi-structured interviews with traders from a wide variety of genre backgrounds in order to gain an insight into their motivations and demands. I also studied a number of individual and collective trading sites, and placed interview requests on the emailing listservs of trading groups in which I had not been an active participant. I directed my initial requests to the list owners and asked that they post the requests on my behalf—thereby increasing response rates, as list members are far more likely to read an email sent by the list owner. The interviews were carried out for a research project in 2002 and the pseudonyms provided by the interviewees at that time have been used here. Lastly, I examined the websites and business practices of a wide variety of artists who are using trading for their own benefit or providing alternatives to meet the demands of fans.

The chapter is structured in four sections. The first evaluates ideas of the passive/active audience and ways in which notions of music fandom have impacted upon the business practices of the mainstream music industry. The second presents the "how" of trading, providing a history of not-for-profit practices and an explanation of the various ways in which trading is carried out today. The next examines the "what" and "why" of trading, delineating the various sources of traded recordings and investigating the motivations and moralities of traders. The final section explores the various promotional and commercial opportunities that meeting the needs of music fans can provide, demonstrating how the shift towards a more service-oriented approach has been facilitated by recent technological developments.

## Fans and Fandom

"Fans are, in fact, the most visible and identifiable of audiences. How is it, then, that they have been overlooked or not taken seriously as research subjects by critics and scholars?" (Lewis 1992, 1). This question could also be directed at many record companies and artists, for music fans are all too often regarded as merely passive consumers, rather than as active, imaginative people who actively participate in the process of creating meanings for popular music (Negus 1996, 26). Jensen (1992) argues that popular portrayals of fans tend to follow two paths: that of the "obsessed individual" and that of the "hysterical crowd" (9), and that each of these constructs fandom as a deviant response to the star system (10). Such constructions have their roots in the work of the Frankfurt School theorists of the 1940s. Authors such as Theodor Adorno depicted popular music fans as a manipulated mass, passively accepting the products of a monolithic culture industry that sought to control them for the benefit of the capitalist classes (Adorno 1990; Adorno and Horkheimer 1993). For Adorno, the exchange value of popular music had eclipsed its use value: objectified in terms of money, it was meaningless in itself (Adorno and Horkheimer 1993, 29). Its structures were characterized as standardized and "pre-digested," formulaic, and mechanical: "The composition hears for the listener . . ." (Adorno 1990, 306). Following from this, the veneer of choice offered by the music industry can be regarded as one simply of "pseudo-individualization," of making the homogenous appear different. The outcome of these processes is, for Adorno, the satisfaction of false needs: "the people clamor for what they are going to get anyhow" (310).

Adorno's thesis can be criticized in a number of ways. His treatment of the music industry and popular music audiences as homogenous entities reduces their complexities and ignores the many internal differences of, for example, race, gender, age, genre, and corporate strategy (Docker 1994; Negus 1996, 1999). His notions of predigestion and pseudoindividualization are unable to account for changes in public tastes or for the volatility of the popular music market (as shown in studies by Rothenbuhler and Dimmick 1982; Peterson and Berger 1990; Lopes 1992; Christianen 1995). His work focuses very narrowly on the highly commercialized genre of 1940s Tin Pan Alley, but ignores other popular music styles of the time, such as jazz. In doing so, he predetermines the outcome of his critique and fails to recognize that music can provide the capacity for freedom of choice for, as Attali (1985) notes, "with music is born power and its opposite: subversion" (6).

Adorno's neo-Marxist critique of music consumption has been an abiding and influential theme (e.g., Hirsch 1990; Peterson and Berger 1990), and continues to have some resonance today. For example, his "hypodermic" model of the media (Morley 1980, 1) has strong parallels in the beliefs of the People's Music Resource Center (see Walser 1993). It can also be argued that the idea of the passive consumer continues to hold sway among the recording companies. For instance, their globalization strategies require the homogenization of tastes across different territories in order that global stars can be established capable of being "communicated across multiple media" (Negus 1992, 1). It can also be identified in their portfolio management approach which, while recognizing that different genres can be linked to particular markets, continues to function on the basis of "consumer strategies" that construct an ideal consumer—one that may be only tentatively connected to reality (Negus 1999, 173–74). However, Adorno's thesis has largely fallen from favor in academic circles and has been increasingly challenged by an active audience thesis that places popular music consumers at the center of the creation, mediation, and transformation of popular music meanings (e.g., Hebdige 1979; Chambers 1985; Lewis 1992; Valentine 1995).

In the 1970s, researchers at the Centre for Contemporary Cultural Studies (CCCS) at the University of Birmingham, and the Centre for Mass Communications Research at Leicester University, began to draw on the ideas of Walter Benjamin—a contemporary of Adorno who wrote on film and cinema (Morley 1980; Docker 1994). Writing in 1944, he argued that popular audiences were neither passive nor uncritical in their response to films, suggesting that they exercised conscious choice and discrimination (Benjamin 1968). The British Cultural Studies academics expanded this argument to include other popular cultural forms, arguing that audiences are capable of decoding dominant discourses in a counter-hegemonic way: a "uses and gratifications" model in which audiences use music and other media to gratify individual and collective needs or wants (Morley 1980; Meyrowitz 1985; Longhurst 1995). However, the assignment of complete agency to popular music consumers allows for too much freedom of choice and ignores the ways in which society in general, and cultural producers in particular, can restrict usage through the structuring of texts and meaning. For instance, Morley (1980) suggested that television audiences are given "preferred readings" by program makers, which may be unquestioningly accepted, strictly opposed, or negotiated and adapted. Similarly, the social situations in which audiences are involved will affect the ways in which they use and interpret cultural artifacts. Hence, while production can provide a framework within which consumption operates, it does not determine the meanings that the consumer takes.

A focus on agency indicates the manner in which individual and collective identities need to be actively produced and maintained: they are "a process rather than an outcome" (Keith and Pile 1993, 28). In a discussion of fandom, John Fiske (1992) suggests that popular culture is created by audiences through their usage of the products of the cultural industries and that they take part in three forms of creative productivity: the semiotic, the enunciative, and the textual. Semiotic productivity relates to the ways in which people make sense of the world around them and incorporate their experiences internally: "the making of meanings of social identity and of social experience from the semiotic [symbolic] resources of the cultural commodity" (Fiske 1992, 37). These meanings take on a public form through immediate face-to-face interactions: enunciative productivity. Factors such as fan talk, or hair and clothing styles, are included within this form of production, which exists only in the "moment of speaking" (39). With the advent of the Internet, such enunciative productivity may be extended to include interactions on mailing lists, message boards, and chat rooms. Fans also create unofficial products for circulation within their "communities": textual productivity that differs from official culture in that it is generally neither mass-marketed or for commercial gain (39). "Products" include websites (Watson 1997), fanzines (Duncombe 1997) and the unofficial concert recordings and trading sites that are the subject of this chapter. Fan productivity can be linked to the notion of "cultural capital" (Bourdieu 1977, 1986), as textual production by fans often only begins when they have collected all the officially available products related to the object of their fandom (Heylin 1995; Marshall 2001). This is referred to as "secondary involvement" (Shuker 1998, 4): the seeking of rare releases, mispressed recordings, bootlegs, tour programs, and merchandise. Fans have a high degree of cultural capital in that they demonstrate a broad knowledge of their favorite music artist. This allows for social distinction and power within a group (Fiske 1992, 43) and is enhanced by knowledge of, and participation in, noncommercial trading networks. The mobilization of cultural capital in the trading context will be examined in detail in section 2. However, there is a need to take Fiske's ideas further, as his analysis suggests that fan creativity is limited to the use of the products of the official culture, whereas trading in concert recordings actually helps to create that culture. For example, whereas the music industry has traditionally downplayed the importance of live music recordings (which often do not count towards the fulfillment of an artist's recording contract), fans "rescue" these otherwise ephemeral performances and circulate material that creates new meanings and associations within the fan community. Hence, the materials circulating within trading communities are co-constructions, a joint product of the creativity of artists and fans, which is then incorporated into fans' semiotic productivity. This leads on to further enunciative and textual productivity, creating a spiral effect that binds fans and artists together, maintaining their interest and increasing their loyalty. At a time where music production and distribution is rapidly proliferating and supplying an almost bewildering amount of choice to consumers, it is vitally important for artists to undertake any activities which help support that loyalty.

## Not-for-Profit Trading

Noncommercial trading began in the late 1960s and for many years ran in parallel to commercial bootlegging (see Heylin 1995 and Marshall 2001 for good reviews). While the latter moved from vinyl to cassette and then to CD and CDR, the noncommercial trade underwent even more changes, adopting and creating a variety of new storage and distribution systems and technologies over time. This demonstrates the creativity of fans in meeting their own demands rather than relying on official or illicit sources to do it for them. As we shall see, the introduction of domestic personal computers, the Internet and consumer broadband connections has allowed fans to gain far greater control than ever before. However, fans continue to use offline trading and storage formats, even though these are often organized through Internet mailing lists and email.

The Grateful Dead and its fans are generally acknowledged as the forerunners in the field of noncommercial trading, as they were among the first artists to freely allow audience members to tape their concerts for personal use and not-for-profit trade. Paper mailing lists emerged in the 1970s (as they did for commercial bootlegs) with the introduction of compact audiocassettes. Fans would subscribe to these lists at concerts or through friends, then organize trades on a personal basis. These trades were often one for one, so equal numbers of cassettes would be swapped. If a fan had nothing to swap, then a "Blanks and Postage" (often referred to as a B&P trade) exchange could be organized, whereby an appropriate number of blank cassettes plus a self-addressed and stamped envelope would be sent in return for the dubbed (copied) cassettes. The highest quality concert recordings of the time were made using reel-to-reel tapes. When dubbed to compact cassette, they lose some audio fidelity, with repeated dubbing from cassette to cassette reducing quality still further. This is referred to as "generational loss" and meant that the concert tapes circulating among fans could often be of very poor audio quality. For this reason, *tape trees* were established. Here, the *seed* (the original taper with the master copy of the reel-to-reel recording) would dub multiple copies of the concert directly from his master recording. These would then be sent to a number of *branches* (first generation) in return for other concert recordings or blank media. The branches similarly organized trades with *leaves* (second generation). This method of distribution ensured that those participating in the tape tree would get high-generation (i.e., high-quality) copies of the concert. In the 1980s, Digital Audio Tape (DAT) was introduced to the personal hi-fi market, allowing perfect copies of a master recording to be traded. DATs were often distributed in the form of *digital tape trees,* aping the method already in use for compact cassette traders. However, DAT never really caught on as a mass-market product, although concert tapers continue to use portable DAT recorders on account of their audio fidelity and the ease with which the resulting recordings can be transferred to recordable compact discs and other digital formats. The quality of a seed recording remains vitally important to many traders and its provenance is often advertised when making it available to trading communities.

Recordable compact discs (CDR) became available to the consumer market in the 1990s and CDR recorders are now routinely included in home personal computer (PC) packages, including budget and laptop models. The latest generation of PCs now has the memory capacity, processing speeds, and software to make CDR recording a very quick and easy process (Tang 1997, 192–93). As CDR is a digital format, the problem of generational loss is, as with DAT, bypassed, and CDRs have the advantage of being playable on standard hi-fi CD players. Blank media are now also readily available from stores at cheap prices. New computer graphics software packages and printers allow for the creation of amateur album art, while PC-based remixing and remastering programs are now also available. Thus, the technology exists today for fans to create their own CDRs with as high (if not higher) quality standards as those of commercial bootleg CDs, hence undermining the market for the latter. It should be noted that commercial bootlegs (whether on tape, vinyl, or CD) have often been transferred to CDR by traders; indeed, some will buy a single commercial bootleg, then distribute it noncommercially on CDR throughout their trading network, further cutting the market for commercial bootleggers. As with compact cassettes and DATs before them, CDR traders use B&P trades, direct reciprocal swaps, and tree-format distribution networks, although these are now often organized through Internet discussion groups, email listservs, chat rooms, and portals.[2] Traders also create their own web pages to list their concert recordings, want lists, terms of trade, and contact details.

As noted above, the processing power and storage capacity of PCs has expanded rapidly since the 1980s, as has the ability to transfer computer files along telephone communication networks. However, the music files used by computers (.wav) are very large, making their transfer and manipulation time-consuming. Software formats that can reduce the size of these .wav files are therefore of great interest to music traders seeking to distribute music through the Internet. One of the earliest formats was mp3 (created in 1996),[3] which allows the compression of .wav files to around a tenth of their original size. Their distribution was originally accomplished through Internet Relay Chat (IRC) networks (see Cooper and Harrison 2001; Leyshon 2003). A trader would upload a music file to his or her site on the network, and allow others to download it according to a set of exchange rules and ratios that were carefully established and guarded (see Slater 2000; Cooper and Harrison 2001). The use of IRC networks involved a high degree of technical expertise, which served to make them exclusionary and reduced their potential as a broad-based distribution model. Alternatives were soon to develop—for example, the use of an FTP protocol (File Transfer Protocol) that utilizes a server/client relationship. Here, a central server hosts the music files and allows clients (personal computers connected to the server through the Internet) to download those files. The SugarMegs.org website, founded by Peter Hedeman in 1996,[4] was one of the first to set up such a distribution system. He uploaded his collection of Grateful Dead concerts in two formats: mp3 and Real Audio. The former could be downloaded and saved to any computer connected to the server, while the latter allowed concerts to be listened to in the manner of a narrowcast radio station. A mailing list was added to make announcements about recently uploaded concerts, and non–Grateful Dead material began to be made available through the same server. While stylistically diverse, these artists bore a similarity to the Grateful Dead in that they incorporated a large amount of improvisation into their concerts: they are now referred to collectively as "jambands." SugarMegs.org continues to trade concerts in mp3 format, but other trading sites using a client-server model have shifted to the newer compression standards discussed below.

The advantage of using an online distribution method is that there is no need to rely on or pay for postal services and blank media, hence making global trades or very large trades much easier to undertake and less risk-prone (as CDRs can be damaged or lost in the postal system). However, there are two main disadvantages to the mp3 codec (compression-decompression algorithm software). Firstly, it is proprietary and patented software, hence protected by intellectual copyrights and subject to the payment of mechanical royalties (Leyshon 2003, 540). Secondly, the mp3 codec is "lossy"; in compressing .wav files to a tenth of their original size, the software discards some of the audio data (White and White 2001, 15–16). This is unacceptable for traders who have long sought to obtain, archive, and trade only the highest quality copies of original master recordings. These shortcomings have led to the creation of at least three further codecs. The first to be discussed here is Ogg Vorbis, which has been "designed to completely replace all proprietary, patented audio formats" (www.vorbis.com, accessed 5/24/04). Like mp3, it is a "lossy" format, but is seen as a way for artists/labels to encode music digitally without having to make a payment to a patented format provider. The other two codecs considered here are "lossless" and as such are the preferred formats among numerous trading groups and traders: SHN (aka "Shorten") and

FLAC (Free Lossless Audio Codec).[5] While these only compress .wav files by around 50%, they do not discard any of the audio data; hence, a perfect clone of the original .wav file is reproduced upon decompression, allowing the music to be burned to CDR. One of the most prominent trading communities, etree.org,[6] supports SHN as its primary format, but it is likely that FLAC will become more popular in the near future. This is because it has a slightly better compression rate than SHN, and improvements are continuing to be made within an active development community. It is important to note that music encoded into these formats is not only traded through Internet connections, but also on CDR in offline trading networks. This is because compressed files require fewer discs, and because these formats come with a data integrity check program.[7]

There is one final online distribution system to consider: peer-to-peer networks. These act as an alternative to the client-server models discussed above, and tend to be slightly quicker. In this model of distribution, there is no central server storing music files; instead, individual traders connect directly to each other to facilitate the file transfer. This removes the necessity to connect to a server, but still requires that the entire file be downloaded from one peer (PC) directly to another. However, if the connection between them is severed (for example, when a peer disconnects from the Internet), the transfer is halted and the file can only continue to be downloaded when the source peer reconnects. Some more recent peer-to-peer programs, such as BitTorrent and FurthurNet,[8] seek to circumvent this problem by allowing peers to download files from multiple sources. Thus, if a transfer is halted by one peer going offline, the partially downloaded file can be completed by transferring to any other peer that also hosts that file. It is therefore vitally important that each copy of the file is a perfect clone: an additional reason to adopt lossless compression standards. If a large number of peers are collectively connected (sometimes known as a "swarm") around a particular file, then the speed at which peers will receive it is rapidly increased. The system functions best when all peers are simultaneously uploading and downloading tracks, and so it is deemed good etiquette to remain online even after collecting all the pieces of a concert in order to allow others to continue downloading.

This section has traced the history and development of not-for-profit trading from its roots in reel-to-reel and compact cassette technology to the trading of "lossless" music files on CDR and through Internet connections. It has suggested that there has been an abiding interest among traders of live concert recordings in achieving the highest quality recordings and distribution methods possible. I show how this interest has been translated into textual productivity, in Fiske's (1992) terms, through the creation of new software formats and Internet-based distribution systems. Moreover, the collecting and trading of recordings can be seen as a form of "secondary involvement" (Shuker 1998, 4), which increases the cultural capital (Bourdieu 1977, 1986) of the traders. The following section investigates the motivations and moralities of the traders themselves, rather than simply their technical/material productivity.

## Motivations and Moralities of Traders

The motivations behind not-for-profit trading are similar to those for bootleg collectors, and the people involved are often the same. However, traders are generally both producers (in as much as they provide CDRs or downloads to others) and consumers of unofficial recordings at the same time, whereas in the bootlegging economy these two functions are more often discrete. Several authors (e.g., Heylin 1995; Marshall 2001) have noted how bootleg collecting often only begins when a fan has already purchased an artist's entire available back catalogue. However, in trading networks, this can be reversed, for traders may only start to buy official recordings after they have traded or downloaded a concert by a previously unheard artist. This is because there is a lower opportunity cost involved in downloading a sample track or concert, rather than risking a prospective purchase—trading can therefore be a source of new fans for an artist. The moral stance taken by bootleg collectors and not-for-profit traders also differs in various ways. This section will tease out the similarities and differences in the motivations and moralities of bootleg collectors and not-for-profit traders by referring to prior studies of bootleg collectors (Heylin 1995; Neumann and Simpson 1997; Marshall 2001) and examine the ways in which the traders view themselves and talk about their activities. However, it is perhaps best to initially clarify the different sources from which bootlegged and traded recordings come, since attitudes towards the different kinds of source are variable and contested. Seven categories are identified here:

1. *UNL/Audience recording:* made during a concert by an audience member with a portable recording device and microphone.
2. *Soundboard recording:* made by connecting a recording device to an audio output of a concert-mixing desk.
3. *FM/AM radio broadcast:* home taping of a live concert or in-house studio session.
4. *TV/Video soundtracks:* recording the audio element of a television or movie soundtrack (whether taken from a broadcast, a cable or satellite narrowcast, or a videocassette/DVD).
5. *Internet webcast:* although webcasts utilize audio streaming formats, the music can be recorded directly to a computer's hard drive if the relevant software is installed; alternatively, it can be recorded to DAT/CDR via a connection to the sound card/audio output of a receiving computer.
6. *Studio tape:* includes studio rehearsals, demo tapes, and test pressings.
7. *Rare officially released material:* includes music only available on highly limited releases, promotional-only releases and long-deleted releases; also, those recordings currently unavailable for purchase due to copyright problems.

Commercial bootleggers recognize no legal distinctions between these seven categories and are happy to release music from any of these sources; however, not-for-profit traders have rather more variable attitudes. Music that has not seen any form of official release is regarded as being "legal" if the artist concerned has given specific or implied permission for taping and trading to occur. We have already seen above that the Grateful Dead were the first rock band to give such permission, and their legacy to the trading community will be discussed further in section 4. Audience and soundboard recordings of such "trade-friendly" artists therefore form the bulk of not-for-profit trading activities. This is also due to the far greater availability of live concert recordings; for example, each date on a concert tour is often made available by tapers for trading. In contrast, there are far fewer recordings from the other sources.

Recordings that have been officially released—including studio tapes, rare material, and videocassettes/DVDs—are not for trade, and many trading sites state explicitly that trading in such recordings will lead to the offending trader being banned from their sites.[9] For example, the Yes Fans website forum states:

"There are a few things not tradable. Those are demo songs, studio out-takes, and especially those items that are commercially available . . . Granted Yesfans.com, or anyone else for that matter, cannot stop this from happening, but if you insist on doing it, keep away from here, if found out you will be banned from this site" (Nightliner 2001).

Studio recordings that have not received any official release or are out-of-print, plus radio broadcasts and Internet webcasts, are similarly anathema. However, some traders are willing to swap such material, feeling that it is not morally wrong to do so because the recordings have either not received an official release or are no longer commercially available:

> I won't trade studio material unless it's out of print, and not available to the public anymore. The studio works are the artist's bread and butter, selling/trading stuff that is currently available for purchase is like stealing food off of their plate. (Interview with JWDQ 2002)
>
> I think if an album can be bought in a store or online on an artist's website, it should not be traded. These artists make money based on sales, and we would be decreasing their sales by trading. It also infringes copyright laws. (Interview with Jen 2002)

It is interesting to note that the latter interviewee implies that trading an out-of-print studio recording does not infringe copyright laws, whereas this is most definitely not the case legally. It is an attitude that is quite pervasive, with many of the traders I have talked to having little accurate knowledge of the copyright implications of their activities, even considering live concerts to incur no copyright. In fact, trade-friendly artists are in essence providing tapers and traders with a limited, revocable license that prescribes the uses to which recordings may be put.[10]

The motivations and aesthetic justifications of bootleg collectors and not-for-profit traders are similar; Marshall's (2001) work on commercial bootlegging is a useful comparison. He suggests that, as live performances are a snapshot of an artist's ongoing creativity, bootlegs can capture the numerous variations of an artist's work "that cannot be adequately covered by the record industry" (184–85). This is particularly the case for the jamband and jazz genres, as they regularly incorporate a high degree of improvisation into their concerts, but it is also the case for many other artists. For example, they might play tracks with different tempos, arrangements, or lyrics, perform unreleased songs and cover versions, or vary their onstage banter/stories. As DW testifies: "I like hearing the evolution of songs, and different arrangements. Also unreleased material, and even some new songs being performed before release." However, in some cases, the traders are simply evidencing an obsessive completism, seeking to track down and own every recording made available both officially and unofficially:

> I'd like to own every [Mike] Keneally show there has ever been. That's priority number one. Then I'd like to own the best available recording of each show, that's priority number two. I haven't even listened to some [of the ones of I have got]—I just don't have the time. . . . Honestly I get more of a fanboy thrill out of looking at the rows of show CDs on my shelf. (Interview with Ron S. 2002)
>
> I am looking for completion. While I like a really good recording, I just want everything no matter how bad it sounds. (Interview with King 2002)

Fiske (1992, 45) describes this as an urge to accumulate quantity rather than quality, demonstrating parallels with Frith's (1987, 143) notions of fan possession/ownership and Bourdieu's (1977, 1986) notion of cultural capital: fans with larger collections accrue the greater respect, being seen as more committed and knowledgeable, and able to supply requests for less commonly traded concerts. Other traders seek only the highest quality concerts, defined in terms of both performance and audio fidelity. For example:

> I try to get high quality recordings, and I wanted to have at least one live version of each of my favorite songs by my favorite bands, so I sought out first the best concerts by those bands, and then searched for concerts with the less-often-played songs that I liked. (Interview with Melusine 2002)

There are also many fan-led projects in existence that actively seek master copies of their favorite artist's concerts so that they can remaster them and create definitive versions for the fan/trading community. In nearly all cases the focus for these projects is on obtaining the highest quality, most complete and unedited version of a concert, without any overdubs, fixes, or edits. Examples of such projects are the Tangerine Tree and Tangerine Leaves, which by mid-2005 consisted of over 100 volumes (with more to come) of not-for-profit CDRs produced by members of the Tangerine Dream discussion group Tadream. The Tangerine Tree volumes present recordings of the highest obtainable audio quality, while the Tangerine Leaves volumes are aimed at the die-hard fans, as they consist of slightly poorer quality recordings or concerts with little or no improvisation.[11] Each volume of the Tangerine Tree and Leaves has been digitally remastered from a source tape, two or more generations higher than the versions previously available on bootleg or in general circulation, and come with full cover artwork designed by various Tadream members and friends. The remastered work is of such a high standard that the band has taken ten concerts from the Tangerine Tree and successfully released them as *The Bootleg Box Volume 1* and *Volume 2* via a licensing agreement with Sanctuary Records.[12]

Marshall (2002) suggests that commercial bootleggers have in the past sought to release only the best available recordings in good quality packaging as, due to their small-scale economic base, they need to achieve a reputation for producing high-quality products. Although this came under threat in the early 1990s when entrepreneurs exploited legal loopholes in European law (see Heylin 1995; Marshall 2001), Marshall sees the biggest threat to bootleg quality as the introduction of CDR, suggesting that reduced production costs will lead to a reduction in quality control. While this is a valid point, it neglects the increasing role of informal noncommercial releases such as those produced by the Tangerine Dream traders. Marshall also suggests that the use of CDR will lead to a less certain fan knowledge, because numerous CDR sources will exist of varying quality. However, the Internet now allows for a much greater interaction of fans than ever before, allowing them to gain the information they need to make an informed choice. The most dedicated fans assist them in this, for they have in many cases created homepages that provide advice about the various versions available. Furthermore, remastering projects such as the Tangerine Tree maintain high aesthetic levels and act as a trademark of quality in much the same way as the trade names of classic bootleg manufacturers did in the 1970s (see Heylin 1995).

Traders may also seek recordings where there is a personal memory attached, such as a souvenir of a concert attended, or where the recording includes or represents some rare or landmark event:

> It's always great to have a copy of a show that you were in actual attendance at. Brings back memories of a great time. (Interview with Aurora 2002)
> Isn't it great to pull out a show where members of Aerosmith and Led Zeppelin are performing live together? . . . You can't find moments like this on any commercial release, but they are precious moments indeed. (Interview with Digital Dan 2002)

Not only do traders look for souvenirs of concerts that they actually attended, but they also search out concerts that they could not attend, because of geographical distance, personal commitments, or because the concerts took place before they became fans (or before they were born):

It allows me to get an early view of a band I might have been too young to see in concert, and to hear special performances I was not able to attend because of geographical concerns. (Interview with Brian 2002)

I can't afford to travel around following bands on tour, so trading allows me to hear performances that I would normally miss. (Interview with AT 2002)

Marshall (2001) notes that live recordings allow fans to recreate the experience of a concert in their own home, to recapture a moment of intimacy between the performer and audience (186), yet this was not seen as a primary motivator among the traders interviewed in the research discussed here. Instead, and as noted above, many collected live recordings in order to hear different set lists, new songs, unusual cover versions, onstage banter between the band or with the audience, and the evolution of song arrangements. However, I concur with Marshall's suggestion that these factors can allow traders to actively engage with an artist's career (185), and feel that they have a greater understanding of an artist's creativity and personality. This relates to Neumann and Simpson's (1997) notion of distanciation in which fans are seen as attempting, through live recordings, to bridge the artificial gap between musician and audience that the marketing and promotional aspects of the recording industry create. It also relates to the concept of authenticity, through the prioritization of the "real," "authentic" live experience captured by fans over the "artificial" versions officially released by record companies:

[Unofficial live CDRs are] normally the only way to hear an artist live honestly. Too often, official live releases are doctored in the studio because the artist wasn't happy with a note or phrase. When I buy a live album, I'm buying it because I want to hear that raw energy that only a live performance offers. (Interview with AT 2002)

[They give] you more insight as to what kind of performer the musician really is. You get a real "feel" for their work, since there are no overdubs or corrections made in the recording studio. (Interview with Weaver 2002)

Traders regard live performances as unique moments in time. Recordings therefore offer snapshots of a band's history and development, the preservation of events that might otherwise be lost, and the piecing together of a personal history of the artist. This archivist motivation has also been identified among bootleg collectors (Neumann and Simpson 1997; Shuker 1998; Marshall 2001), and is most strongly articulated in the Live Music Archive (LMA), a massive collection of concerts freely available for download from the Internet Archive.[13]

The urge to document the excitement of live performances can also be linked to the work of Roland Barthes, who assigned an active participatory role for audiences in the creation of musical experiences (1977a); this followed from his well-known literary argument on the "death of the author" in which the meaning of a book's text is held not by its author or the text itself, but in the creative act of reading (1977b). This can be taken further, for the audience of a concert is not simply experientially consuming it, but experientially producing it: the artist does not simply "give" a performance, but participates with the audience in a joint creation that "mediates a relationship between the player and the listener" (Fripp 1979). Arguably, it is the effect of this relationship on the resultant performance that is being captured and celebrated by tapers and traders. This helps to explain why some traders are keen to get several concerts from tours in which the set list did not vary.

However, for many traders it is not just the collecting of recordings that is central to their involvement. Instead, there are often strong social motivations for distributing recordings among fellow fans: for example, the making of contacts with traders of similar interests, the discussions that can follow, and the recommendations of people who become trusted online friends. In many cases these friendships will spill over into offline contacts; for example, many meet at concerts or at fan conventions. Several traders felt that their most important role was in helping to hold fans' interest between official releases, and in the promotion of lesser-known acts to others. The fostering of a community spirit among traders is an important motivational aspect of the activity itself, and parallels similar findings among bootleg collectors (Marshall 2001, 191). An additional point may be made here: if an artist supports (or at least tolerates) fan trading, the creation of a community spirit can only lead to increased loyalty, and thus have great implications for maintaining the fan base and utilizing it for grassroots promotions. Indeed, many traders felt that their activities were of indirect benefit to artists, deeming it a form of free advertising and arguing that trading only begins when all officially available material has already been bought:

> Frankly, I don't see any ethical problems with "bootleg" trading as long as no one's making money off the recordings. It doesn't hurt the bands (because no one's making a profit that should belong to the bands) and may in fact help them by increasing fan interest and devotion. I didn't know anyone who was in trading without at least owning all or most of the band's official albums. (Interview with Melusine 2002)

The noncommercial nature of trading is key to the moral stance of traders, for the sale of recordings is regarded as anathema (whether or not those recordings were made with the authorization of the artist). This was true for all of the traders in the study, and is replicated across a variety of trading pages and communities. Their opposition extends to the sale of CDR copies of officially released products, as well as to the sale of commercial bootlegs, and any forms of profit making by traders. For example, most traders regarded requests for additional blank media as exploitative: if asked for three concerts recorded over six CDRs in a B&P trade, the supplier should not request any more than six blank disks.

Traders' knowledge of copyright was sketchy, but they agreed that the system was necessary in order for artists to continue to make a living. Their not-for-profit ethic and opposition to both commercial bootlegging and the trading of copies of officially released recordings suggests that the activity is not in competition with the official music industry, but complementary to it. Indeed, if an artist makes a concert available to the public as a commercial release, traders will usually remove that concert from their trading lists altogether. Such attitudes and actions are contradictory to the findings of Heylin (1995), Neumann and Simpson (1997), and Marshall (2001). Their studies of mp3 traders and commercial boot-leggers/purchasers stressed the illicit appeal of these activities, portraying the people involved as anticommercial and antiestablishment, and their deviant quality as an "essential component" (Neumann and Simpson 1997, 339). As Flanagan (1994) similarly noted: "the illegality of bootlegs is, of course, part of their appeal. It's music someone doesn't want you to hear or didn't want you to take away from the concert, thus making you covet it all the more" (38). Little evidence for this attitude was found among the traders I interviewed or encountered, with most strongly disagreeing with the suggestion. This might be expected from those traders whose activities are condoned by the artists concerned, but it was also found to be the case among most other music traders too. For them, obtaining live and rare recordings is primarily about hearing and sharing the music:

> I don't feel like I'm getting one over "Big Brother" when I make a trade with someone. I'm simply trading with somebody who enjoys the live experience of an artist they enjoy. (Interview with Aurora 2002)
> For me it's the thrill of being able to hear a concert that I wasn't able to attend and also to hear songs that may not normally be performed by the artist. . . . The day after George Harrison died Tori [Amos] performed in Mannheim, Germany and one of her encores was "Something." How else would I have been able to hear that if it wasn't for a [traded] bootleg? Those are the moments we are trying to capture. (Interview with King 2002)
> [Record companies] are but one element in an industry I happen to love. It may have its faults and could certainly improve, but as a mechanism for creating, supporting, promoting and distributing music it works and thus should be important to every music fan. I trade because I love music. (Interview with Hopwood 2002)

## Promotional and Commercial Opportunities

The previous sections suggest that there are advantages to be gained by under-standing the motivations that drive traders and by utilizing the new business opportunities that continuing developments in computer and communications technology are opening up. These include supporting not-for-profit trading for promotional purposes; producing archive and live albums for mainstream retail release; and making concerts and other material available for digital download or audio streaming. These opportunities will be considered in turn, together with examples and a discussion of their benefits and limitations. Yet, in order for any of these opportunities to be successful, the artists must actually be willing to endorse not-for-profit trading or release their own untouched archive and live recordings. This is not always the case; for example, Nick Cave alludes to his moral rights to control any recordings of his music or performances:

> If I find people bootlegging my stuff, I do my best to confiscate it. I'm very precious about what I release, and certainly very precious about what gets released in a live concert [recording]. (Nick Cave, cited in Marshall 2001, 211)

Robert Fripp has a different take on the matter, as explained in an email to a King Crimson fan message board:

> The financial aspect is not the key issue for me. . . . If we try to capture the moment [of live performance], the moment escapes us. . . . If we deliberately put our attention outside the moment of the show . . . intensity escapes. (Fripp 1997)

Here, he refers to the intimacy of the concert experience and the rapport that exists between audience and artist. For Fripp, activities such as taping, filming, and photography disrupt that intimacy and rapport, hence ruin the concert; this is his main objection, and one that has resonance with Roland Barthes' (1977a) notion of the co-construction of the musical event discussed earlier. It was also commented upon by ex-tapers who found that they failed to enjoy the concert experience because they were worried about getting a good recording of it. Other artists accept taping and trading as a legitimate interest of their fans, but do not support it in any way. In essence, they "turn a blind eye" to the practice so long as no one is making any money from it. For example, Tangerine Dream's manager Martin Kasprzak (who regularly posts messages to the Tadream discussion group) encourages fans to let him know if they find someone trading for commercial gain or selling copyright infringing items through Internet auction sites such as eBay.com.

Ever since the Grateful Dead first allowed free taping and noncommercial trading of concerts in the 1960s, there has been a host of artists (often jambands) who have been supportive of the practice. This has increased markedly with the introduction of the Internet. One of the first comprehensive trading policies to tackle the legal position of the activity was that of Phish.com, who set up a temporary, revocable license. Under such a license, the artist retains the primary copyright in the live performance, but assigns a right to copy to the taping/trading fan. A number of limitations are common: (1) that no officially released recordings be traded; (2) that no money ever be exchanged as part of a trade; (3) that trading websites and other media not be commercialized; (4) that if an official version of a particular performance is released, amateur versions of it should no longer be traded; and (5) that CDRs and other media should "not be displayed or distributed at or around concert venues" (Phish.com 2002). In some cases, particularly in the jamband genre, artists will demarcate a dedicated taping area at their concerts to facilitate the production of unofficial recordings. These artists often also use their official websites to publish taping/trading policies, list their tour dates, and provide hypertext links to fan-run trading websites. The term *jamband* has therefore come to denote not merely a musical style but a pro-taping/trading attitude, for these artists seek to meet the needs of fans, promote themselves amongst a community of interested traders, and distribute material that they could not afford to make available themselves:

> We want to perpetuate the arts. Share the music instead of being greedy with its beauty. It's good for everybody. The band uses tapes to analyze the performance and correct any mistakes in its feel and the fans spread the message to new ears. So it helps the band get bigger and bigger. (Estradasphere 2002)
> It makes me happy when people trade the tapes and get to hear a bunch of interesting music I would never have the time or resources to distribute "legitimately." (Mike Keneally no date)

Pro-taping artists believe that a sense of community is fostered among fans, which benefits them through increased sales of official albums, larger concert attendances, a wider and more loyal fan base, and grassroots promotion. For example, the management of the Dave Matthews Band used Phish.net (an Internet-based fan club) to set up a tape tree and disseminate the band's early demo tapes; this led to a sudden increase in their popularity and wider acclaim (Watson 1997, 129). The band was also able to sell in excess of one million copies of *Live at Red Rocks* using only word-of-mouth publicity (Gordon 1998). Unlike Fripp above, tape/trade friendly artists feel that taping is a part of the concert experience rather than a disruption to it, helping to create, maintain, and expand the fan community:

> Live tapes are a big part of why the Estradasphere are growing so rapidly, and we want to continue to provide as cozy a taping environment for everyone as possible. (Estradasphere 2002)
> This scene [jambands] revolves around live concerts. They help people experience the magic of live music when they can't be at a show. To allow and encourage [trading] is to acknowledge its importance to the jamband culture. (Trafton 2002)
> The Disco Biscuits are aware of how many of you have been turned on to "Bisco" via a tape, CD or MP3 from the web. . . . We feel greatly indebted to the legions of dedicated tapers and traders who have helped spread our music to the world. (Bisco 2002)

Moreover, by encouraging the taping and trading of shows, an artist can reduce the possible market for bootleggers, as the most ardent fans (who form the target market for bootleggers) will already have access to a recording of the show free of charge. Alternatively, artists can create a new revenue stream by recording their shows themselves and making them available to the public through retail, mail order, or Internet distribution methods.

The commercial potential of making archive material available to the public was first demonstrated in 1985 by the Bob Dylan boxed set *Biograph* (Heylin 1995, 406). Like many similar projects since that time, it was heavily weighted towards previously released tracks; hence requiring minimal studio time. Such products command a high retail price and sell to a guaranteed market of existing fans, but may suffer from self-censorship (see Heylin 1995, 389). King Crimson's boxed set *Epitaph*, released in 1997, substantially raised the standard for officially released live archive material. It brought together all the known live recordings of the 1969 lineup, sourcing material from the band's own archives, from commercially available bootlegs, and from fan tapes sent in after a request was made on the band's website. The final CDs took recordings from various sources and edited them together to give the most complete version of a concert with the best possible audio quality. A similar idea for mainstream release is the "official bootleg," often seen as an attempt to subvert or preempt commercial bootleggers (Schwartz 1995). Although seemingly an oxymoron, the term is helpful for consumers, as it suggests that the recording is faithful to the original performance, rather than "cleaned up" in the studio. Some classic examples of official bootlegs are those of Pearl Jam, who released recordings of each date of their 2000 and 2003 tours in retail stores. The success they achieved with this approach is rooted in their extensive fan base and the support that a major label brings to cover production and distribution costs. These are luxuries that are not afforded to many artists. However, the Internet has introduced alternative distribution methods, allowing artists to create new income streams, even with a relatively small fan base.

Internet-based mail-order releases allow anyone in the world to purchase official bootlegs directly from an artist's website, at a quality that cannot be matched by commercial bootleggers. Marillion's Front Row Club[14] offers two membership options for either three or six bimonthly club-only releases. The membership fee is paid upfront so that the band can meet the production costs of the CDs. Members automatically receive each subsequent release of their membership unless they decide to opt out of any particular one. The club also offers access to prior releases, additional optional titles, and runs competitions to name archive CDs. Their inspiration came from the King Crimson Collector's Club, which ran a similar club membership format for a time. The latter club now adopts an ad hoc approach, advertising potential releases through a fan-run discussion group[15] and responding to feedback prior to undertaking any work. The CDs are then made available through the band's online mail-order shop.[16]

Section 2 discussed the various developments in digital storage/compression formats and Internet distribution methods that have been adopted by fans since the 1990s. These are now also beginning to appear on artists' official websites, with some adopting them as an alternative or addition to physical CDs. For example, the Grateful Dead provides a music streaming service in the form of an Internet radio station that narrowcasts live concerts 24 hours a day,[17] while both Phish and Metallica offer sales of their live archive recordings in downloadable mp3 and FLAC formats.[18] Similarly, the jazz guitarist Charlie Hunter makes some of his albums available for download in mp3 and FLAC formats, including three free compilations drawn from his live archive.[19] Should the artist be unable to afford the cost of setting up a download service, there are numerous alternatives: for example, independent artists and labels can make concerts available through iTunes,[20] Sony Connect,[21] or eMusicLive.[22] The latter specializes in independent artists and labels and is particularly interesting because it, rather than the artist, arranges to record concerts at an extensive network of U.S. venues in order to make them available for download from its subscription site. The company also has an on-site retail presence in selected live music venues, where high-quality CDRs of performances that have just finished playing can be almost immediately purchased. Future plans for music fans include "the option to purchase shows digitally at the venues, by loading performances directly onto their digital music player or USB pen drive via a state-of-the-art kiosk" (eMusicLive 2004). Clearly, the outlook for commercial bootleggers is bleak, while the promotional and commercial opportunities for artists are potentially great.

There are, however, some disadvantages to be considered. Firstly, in order to satisfy the urges of fans for complete, unedited recordings of concerts, the artist must cede a certain amount of artistic control, and for some artists this is unacceptable. Secondly, with regard to artists and bands with an extensive archive of material, there are practical contractual limitations, for some have had several recording contracts or numerous members, and it may be difficult to obtain the necessary agreements to proceed. Thirdly, it can be argued that if music fans become accustomed to the availability of music free of charge via the Internet, they may lose their consumerist attitudes, hence harming future sales of officially released live and archive material. Related to this is the fear that official recordings made for sale and digital distribution might find their way onto digital sharing networks such as those described in section 2. However, this chapter has shown that fans will support the artist by buying the official recordings and ceasing to trade their own versions; moreover, fans will actively police their trading networks to ensure that people who trade in these products are excluded from participation. They do this partly because of their respect for the artists and partly out of self-interest, for trading sites can only retain their legality by trading in recordings that have the permission of the copyright holders. A final fear is that the release of live concert recordings during a tour will reduce concert attendances during that tour (Marshall 2001, 201). However, the concert experience remains the ideal for most fans, and no form of recording can match the excitement of the live event itself. Indeed, far from reducing attendance figures, their promotional role may actually increase audience numbers, as has been suggested above.

## Conclusion: A Service-oriented Approach?

Roy Shuker has described bootlegging as "an irritant to record companies" (1998, 32) and an examination of the official websites of major music industry organizations quickly confirms that this is the case, for all forms of nonofficial recording are regarded negatively. Home tapers, commercial bootleggers, and mp3 traders have long been used as scapegoats for the falling revenues of the recording industry (Heylin 1995; Burnett 1996; Marshall 2001), yet not-for-profit traders are not motivated by financial gain but by a love of music. They are not seeking to undermine the official industry but add to it. They are taking control of otherwise unreleased recordings and making them available to a substantial niche market whose needs have rarely been met in the past; in doing so, they demonstrate the active and creative nature of music fandom. Artists who recognize the motivations of traders, and the promotional and commercial potential of the complementary economy that music fans have created, are identifying ways to co-opt the trading networks and demands for their own benefit. As one trader put it, "Artists are realizing money that they wouldn't otherwise, and their fans are getting to hear recordings they wouldn't otherwise. Both sides win" (Interview with AT 2002).

Developments in Internet and communications technology are enabling artists to adopt a service-industry approach that can establish new income streams, maintain and expand their fan base, and undermine the activities of commercial bootleggers. It is likely that as communications technology develops in the future, these income streams will become ever more important to the success of both individual artists and the music industry as a whole. It is therefore a mistake to homogenize and demonize all Internet music traders as audio pirates, for there are significant financial and promotional advantages to be gained by recognizing the motivations and creativity of music fans.

## References to Chapter Eight

Adorno, Theodor W. 1990 [1941]. "On Popular Music." In *On Record: Rock, Pop and the Written Word,* edited by Simon Frith and Andrew Goodwin, 301–14. New York: Pantheon Books.

Adorno, Theodor, and Max Horkheimer. 1993 [1944]. "The Culture Industry: Enlightenment as Mass Deception." In *The Dialectic of Enlightenment.* New York: Continuum.

Attali, Jacques. 1985. *Noise: The Political Economy of Music*, trans. Brian Massumi. Manchester, U.K.: Manchester University Press.

Barthes, Roland. 1977a. "Musica Practica." In *Image—Music—Text*, trans. by S. Heath, 149–54. London: Fontana Paperbacks.

———. 1977b. "The Death of the Author." In *Image—Music—Text*, trans. by S. Heath, 142–48. London: Fontana Paperbacks.

Bauldie, John, and Clint Heylin. 1989. "Bootlegs—25 Under-the-Counter Classics." *Q Magazine* 36, 22–25.

Benjamin, Walter. 1968 [1936]. "The Work of Art in the Age of Mechanical Reproduction." In *Illuminations*, 217–52. New York: Schocken.

Bisco. 2002. Official artist website. Retrieved July 17, 2002, from http://www.discobiscuits.net/

Bourdieu, Pierre. 1977. *Outline of a Theory of Practice*, trans. Richard Nice. Cambridge: Cambridge University Press.

———. 1986. "The Forms of Capital." In *Handbook of Theory and Research for the Sociology of Education*, edited by John Richardson, 241–58. New York: Greenwood Press.

Burnett, Robert. 1996. *The Global Jukebox: The International Music Industry*. London: Routledge.

Chambers, Ian. 1985. *Urban Rhythms: Pop Music and Popular Culture*. Basingstoke: Macmillan.

Christianen, Michael. 1995. "Cycles in Symbol Production? A New Model to Explain Concentration, Diversity and Innovation in the Music Industry." *Popular Music* 14, no. 1: 55–93.

Cooper, Jon, and Daniel. M. Harrison. 2001. "The Social Organization of Audio Piracy on the Internet." *Media, Culture and Society* 23, no. 1: 71–89.

Docker, John. 1994. *Postmodernism and Popular Culture: A Cultural History*. Cambridge: Cambridge University Press.

Duncombe, Stephen. 1997. *Notes from Underground: Zines and the Politics of Alternative Culture*. London: Verso.

eMusicLive. 2004. "About eMusicLive." *eMusicLive.com*. Retrieved May 30, 2004, from http://www.emusic.com/features/emusiclive/about.html

Estradasphere. 2002. Email from the band (author not specified). Received July 18, 2002.

Fiske, John. 1992. "The Cultural Economy of Fandom." In *The Adoring Audience: Fan Culture and Popular Media*, edited by Lisa. A. Lewis, 30–49. London: Routledge.

Flanagan, E. 1994. "Inside the Bootleg Industry." *Musician Magazine* 191:36–49, 94–95.

Fripp, Robert. 1979. "Bootlegging, Royalties and the Moment." *Musician Magazine*. Retrieved May 29, 2004, from the Hot Wacks Press website, http://log.on.ca/hotwacks/zfripp.html

Frith, Simon. 1987. "Towards an Aesthetic of Popular Music." In *Music and Society: The Politics of Composition, Performance and Reception*, edited by Richard Leppert and Susan McClary, 133–49. Cambridge: Cambridge University Press.

Gordon, J. 1998. "Piracy in America: Is the RIAA on Track or Should We Give Them the Boot?" *Pause/Record.com*. Retrieved June 26, 2002, from http://www.pauserecord.com/tapes/RIAA.html

Graham, Gary, Bernard Burnes, Gerard J. Lewis and Janet Langer. 2004. "The Transformation of the Music Industry Supply Chain: A Major Label Perspective." *International Journal of Operations & Production Management* 24, no. 11: 1087–1103.

Hebdige, Dick. 1979. *Subculture: The Meaning of Style*. London: Methuen.

Heylin, Clint. 1995. *The Great White Wonders: A History of Rock Bootlegs*. London: Penguin Books.

Hirsch, Paul. 1990 [1972]. "Processing Fads and Fashions: An Organization-Set Analysis of Cultural Industry Systems." In *On Record: Rock, Pop and the Written Word*, edited by Simon Frith and Andrew Goodwin, 127–39. New York: Pantheon.

Jensen [misspelled Jenson], Joli. 1992. "Fandom as Pathology: The Consequences of Characterisation." In *The Adoring Audience: Fan Culture and Popular Media*, edited by Lisa A. Lewis, 9–29. London: Routledge.

Keith, Michael, and Steve Pile. 1993. "Introduction Part 2: The Place of Politics." In *Place and the Politics of Identity*, edited by Michael Keith and Steve Pile, 22–40. London: Routledge.

Keneally, Mike. N.d. "A Message from Mike." *mktrading.org*. Retrieved May 30, 2004, from http://www.mktrading.org/

Lewis, Lisa A., ed. 1992. *The Adoring Audience: Fan Culture and Popular Media*. London: Routledge.

Leyshon, Andrew. 2001. "Time-Space (and Digital) Compression: Software Formats, Musical Networks, and the Reorganisation of the Music Industry." *Environment and Planning A* 32:49–77.

———. 2003. "Scary Monsters? Software Formats, Peer to Peer Networks, and the Spectre of the Gift." *Environment and Planning D: Society and Space* 21, no. 5: 533–58.

Leyshon, Andrew, Peter Webb, Shaun French, Nigel Thrift, and Louise Crew. 2005. "On the Reproduction of the Musical Economy After the Internet." *Media, Culture & Society* 27: 177–209.

Longhurst, Brian. 1995. *Popular Music and Society*. Cambridge: Polity Press.

Lopes, Paul D. 1992. "Innovation and Diversity in the Popular Music Industry, 1969–1990." *American Sociological Review* 57, no. 1: 56–71.

Marshall, Lee. 2001. "Losing One's Mind: Bootlegging and the Sociology of Copyright." PhD thesis, University of Warwick.

———. 2002. "The History and Future of Bootlegging." In *Looking Back, Looking Ahead: Popular Music Studies 20 Years Later*, edited by Mimi Kärki, Rebecca Leydon, and Henri Terho, 727–35. Turku, Finland: IASPM-Norden.

Meyrowitz, Joseph. 1985. *No Sense of Place: The Impact of Electronic Media on Social Behaviour*. Oxford: Oxford University Press.

Morley, David. 1980. *The "Nationwide" Audience: Structure and Decoding*. London: BFI.

Negus, Keith. 1992. *Producing Pop: Culture and Conflict in the Popular Music Industry*. London: Arnold.

———. 1996. *Popular Music in Theory: An Introduction*. Cambridge: Polity Press.

———. 1999. *Music Genres and Corporate Cultures*. London: Routledge.

Neumann, Mark, and Timothy A. Simpson. 1997. "Smuggled Sound: Bootleg Recording and the Pursuit of Popular Meaning." *Symbolic Interaction* 20, no. 4: 319–41.

Nightliner. 2001. "YesFans.com trading guidelines." August 3, 2001; updated June 2, 2002, and April 9, 2003. *YesFans*. Retrieved May 27, 2004, from http://www.yesfans.com/forum/showthread.php?t=542

Peterson, Richard A., and David. G. Berger. 1990 [1975]. "Cycles in Symbol Production: The Case of Popular Music." In *On Record: Rock, Pop and the Written Word*, edited by Simon Frith and Andrew Goodwin, 140–59. New York: Pantheon.

Phish.com. 2002. "Phish Audio Recording and Transfer Policy." *Phish.com*. Retrieved June 9, 2002, from http://www.phish.com/

RIAA. 2004. "Anti-Piracy." *RIAA.com*. Retrieved July 16, 2004, from http://www.riaa.com/issues/piracy/default.asp

Rothenbuhler, Eric W., and John W. Dimmick. 1982. "Popular Music: Concentration and Diversity in the Industry, 1974–1980." *Journal of Communication* 32, no. 1: 143–49.

Schwartz, David. 1995. "Strange Fixation: Bootleg Sound Recordings Enjoy the Benefits of Improving Technology." Retrieved June 26, 2002, from http://www.law.indiana.edu/fclj/pubs/v47/n03/schwartz.html

Shuker, Roy. 1998. *Key Concepts in Popular Music*. London: Routledge.

Slater, Don. 2000. "Consumption without Scarcity: Exchange and Normativity in an Internet Setting." In *Commercial Cultures: Economies, Practices, Spaces*, edited by Peter Jackson, Michelle Lowe, Daniel Miller, and Frank Mort, 123–42. Oxford: Berg.

Tang, Puay. 1997. "Multimedia Information Products and Services: A Need for 'Cybercops'?" In *The Governance of Cyberspace: Politics, Technology and Global Restructuring*, edited by Brian D. Loader, 190–208. London: Routledge.

Trafton, John. 2002. Email [from the guitarist/vocalist of Strangefolk]. Received July 23, 2002.

Valentine, Gill. 1995. "Creating Transgressive Space: The Music of k.d.lang." *Transactions of the Institute of British Geographers* 20:474–85.

Walser, Robert. 1993. *Running with the Devil: Power, Gender, and Madness in Heavy Metal Music*. Hanover, NH: Wesleyan University Press/University Press of New England.

Watson, Nessim. 1997. "Why We Argue about Virtual Community: A Case Study of the Phish.net Fan Community." In *Virtual Culture: Identity and Communication in Cybersociety*, edited by Steve G. Jones, 102–33. London: Sage.

White, Ron, and Michael White. 2001. *MP3 Underground*. Indianapolis: Que.

CHAPTER NINE

# "Hacking" the iPod: A Look inside Apple's Portable Music Player

### Gabrielle Cosentino

*"Rip, mix and burn. After all it's your music"*
Ad campaign introducing iTunes

*"Don't steal music"*
Sticker on the iPod box

## White Lines and Bottom Lines

New York City, summer 2004. The relative proportion of business suits to stickers protesting the Republican National Convention might vary according to the demographics of each neighborhood, but there is one peculiarly consistent element noticeable across the population of Manhattan: bright white headphone wires linking people's ears to their pockets, purses, and backpacks. These white lines signify the most popular physical embodiment of the digital musical revolution, Apple's iPod.

Since its first introduction on the market in November 2001, the white, 5.6-ounce portable digital music player has gained an iconographic status that few other branded technological devices, with the possible exceptions of Sony's Walkman and PlayStation, have previously attained. The iPod sales figures, about 10 million units sold in the first three and a half years of production, have yet to match the Walkman's, more than 200 million since its first introduction. However, according to an analyst report, the iPod adoption rate is faster than it was for the Sony tape player (Marsal 2004), and the iPod impressive 900% sales growth in 2003, coupled with the four million iPods sold during the 2004 holiday quarter, indicate that Apple's device, which has yet to show its full market potential on a global scale, is something more significant than just a fad.

Media coverage of the iPod, fueled by Apple's notorious marketing savvy, has ranged from columns on tech-forum Slashdot.org to appearances on *Oprah*, from reviews on the *New York Times* to rap music videos, from financial analysts reports to fashion industry catwalks. The imposing sales figures and ubiquitous media coverage have not only made the iPod synonymous with the larger phenomenon of digital music, but might even reflect the birth of a new demographic: the iPod generation.[1] As with similar technologies combining entertainment and fashion, the overall profile of this social segment is for the largest part young, affluent, and urban, thus very profitable for marketing ends. Even traditional institutions such as universities have become aware of the iPod appeal, particularly among youths. In 2004, Duke University gave a free iPod to every new freshman, claiming that it had a significant potential for academic use, on top of being an unbeatable marketing tool to attract new students.

Thus, the iPod seems to have entered popular culture to a degree that adds weight to claims about its revolutionary impact, which is affecting both the consumer electronics and the digital music markets. As with other pop phenomena, language is the domain most receptive to change. The word "iPod" is replacing "Walkman" as a catchall term for "portable audio player," an indication that the power dynamics in the field of consumer electronics, a market long dominated by Sony, are changing. Also, few if any electronic gadgets have been able to develop the same blend of technological and fashion appeal as the iPod, which has become now such a fashion statement that well-known clothes manufacturers are selling garments specifically designed for carrying it (Fried 2004). Another field of significant change is the gender bias of the consumer electronics' market, traditionally male oriented. In February 2004, when Apple introduced the iPod Mini, a smaller version of the iPod available in different colors, nearly as many women as men purchased it, thus indicating that the reach of Apple's digital music player is extending to a larger demographic space.

Patterns of music listening and exchange are also evolving by virtue of the iPod physical portability, technical features and aesthetic flourishes. Users bring their iPods to parties to play music and share their files and playlists. Some even swap their iPods in public places like subways in a practice known as "jacking-in" (Kahney 2003). Professional DJs use it to carry their music collections to live gigs, and in cities like New York and London people set up parties where guests can play their favorite mixes through their iPods.

The spread of digital music, largely fostered by the availability through file-sharing networks of music files in mp3 format, has brought about a deep restructuring of the patterns of music distribution and consumption, both in quantitative and qualitative terms (Alderman 2001). While Napster expanded digital music consumption and distribution beyond the subcultural communities of audiophiles, geeks, and teenagers, it is the iPod that has become the physical embodiment of the same phenomenon. With the wide adoption of a single-branded mp3 player, digital music has taken on a more tangible cultural relevance.

Furthermore, the iPod is part of a larger all-round solution, including the jukebox software application iTunes and the iTunes Music Store (iTMS), that Apple deployed to enter the digital music market. The strong sales figures of the iTMS—200 million songs in its first two years—have proved customers' will to pay for digital music. Such encouraging sales figures could be taken as a sign of reconciliation between music listeners and the music industry, whose relationship for the past few years seemed irreparably compromised by litigation, heated debates, and mutual accusations.

Despite its undeniable success, upon better scrutiny Apple's business solution for digital music is not exempt from controversial elements that have important economic and cultural ramifications. The underlying hypothesis of this research is that Apple has been able to conquer the stagnant digital music market by skillfully walking a fine line between a carefully crafted business plan to sell its hardware and the widely common practice of sharing copyright protected digital content, which in turn creates demand for playback and storage devices. Thanks to a timely business strategy and the leverage of its heavily marketed brand image of cutting-edge company, Apple has persuaded the major record labels to trust the iPod and iTunes formula and make their catalogs available on the iTMS. Apple's music store is in fact the first online service endorsed by the major record labels that does not require a subscription or other forms of long-term engagement, which had fettered previous attempts to sell music online (Alderman 2001). Also, contrarily to previous models, iTMS also works with low digital-rights management (DRM) restrictions.

By drawing an unprecedented level of attention and customers to both iTunes and the iPod, in less than two years Apple has become the strongest player in the distribution of digital music. At the same time, while presenting iTunes as a revolutionary legal solution to digital piracy, Apple has been able to capitalize on the demand for playback and storage devices unfettered by digital-rights management restrictions, which allow for unregulated and often unlawful forms of music distribution.

To weigh such arguments, it might be helpful to consider some figures. As of January 2005, Apple has sold about 10 million iPods, while the iTMS has sold about 200 million; thus, the average iPod user might have about 20 songs on it purchased from the iTMS. Since the store sells individual songs for 99 cents, and albums for a price range of $9.99 to $11.99, very few customers are reasonably expected to be able to fill a 10,000-song capacity device with songs purchased only via iTMS. So one is left to speculate where the other 9,980 songs that can fill the 40-GB version come from, and the proportional split between backup copies of legitimately purchased CDs and, possibly, files unlawfully downloaded from file-sharing systems or other sources. It can be argued, as reported by some news sources (Kahney 2004a), that most iPod owners use it to store, and possibly even share, unlawfully downloaded files. To prevent this possibility, it could be further argued, Apple has set up the iTunes store to provide the iPod with a "legal" skin. Such allegations are further reinforced by the fact that the iTMS, despite being the most popular online music retail service, still does not generate any profit for Apple.[2] It does, however, work as an effective promotional avenue for the iPod. This is particularly interesting because Apple, which is a hardware manufacturer and not a content producer, has been able to gain the trust of the music industry despite the relatively low DRM restrictions enforced by the iPod and iTunes.

However, the main concern of the music industry is the extent to which Apple's and other hardware producers' ambivalent strategy towards intellectual property is affecting consumers' expectations and behaviors. As exemplified by the gap between the high profits generated by the iPod's sales and the low profits of music downloads, the business of digital music has so far proved more profitable for hardware producers than for the recording industry. The response of the entertainment industry, afraid that the expansion of unregulated forms of distribution will soon affect other types of content (i.e., films) has arrived promptly in the shape of a proposal for new legislation. The iPod and other digital portable devices are in fact being targeted by a new draft bill, originally dubbed the Induce Act, that threatens to ban playback devices that do not feature strong DRM protection and thus might "induce" users to infringe copyright (Dean 2004). However, the bill met with widespread hostility both on the part of the computer and the consumer electronics industries, both of which fear its potential chilling effects on technological progress, and its legislative course was stalled. For the future regulation of the still-growing and unpredictable digital music market, legislators will arguably have to acknowledge the fact that the iPod is now an established and profitable standard, and that its commercial success is significantly impacting the distribution and consumption of digital music. As a further example of its emblematic value in the digital music market, the iPod was chosen as a symbol to warn the public of the potential threats posed by the Induce Act (savetheipod.com 2004).

Furthermore, since the iPod is designed to function exclusively with Apple's iTunes digital jukebox, which lets users upload, delete, and organize song and access the online music store, the success of the iPod and iTunes formula is creating the conditions for a market lock-in. This situation has already caused the onset of disputes between Apple and competitors, such as with Real-Networks' attempt to make the songs sold through its online service, Rhapsody, playable on the iPod. Such technical restrictions have prompted critics to evoke Apple's notorious skepticism towards interoperable solutions, a protectionist attitude towards the market that in the past has had major negative effects for the company.

The issues outlined above will be addressed in more detail throughout the sections of this chapter. Specifically, the next section will focus on the development of the iPod within the context of Apple's strategy to enter the market of portable digital players. The design, brand, and marketing solutions that favored the success of the iPod will be observed in the third section. Particular attention will be dedicated to their relation with Apple's history of technological innovations and marketing strategies. The fourth section focuses on the effects that the iPod is exerting on the digital music market, particularly with respect to the role of competitors, regulators and artists.

## Portrait of the iPod as a Brainchild

"Hint: it's not a Mac." This was the teaser on the invitation to a press conference that Apple organized to unveil, in late October 2001, "a breakthrough digital device." According to the rumors (Wilcox 2001), the company had created a portable music player that promised to embody the idea of "digital lifestyle" envisioned by Steve Jobs with the launch of Mac OS X. That device was in fact the iPod, and in retrospect the teaser really hinted at a product that was destined to permanently change the perception of Apple as just a computer manufacturer.

At the time of the iPod introduction—just as Microsoft was lifting the veil on Windows XP—the market of digital portable music players was still in its infancy. Three years before, Diamond Multimedia System opened the market with the Rio PMP 300, 32 megabytes of storage capacity on a removable memory card and a connection to the computer for music download via the standard parallel port. The novelty of the product, coupled with the absence of competitors, accounted for a good market performance—about 400,000 units sold in its first year—but its limited memory and slow music transfer system fettered its wide adoption by the growing number of digital music users (Brown 1998a). Rio was also the target of an unsuccessful lawsuit brought against it by the Recording Industry Association of America (RIAA). At the time of the lawsuit, there was growing anxiety around digital music on the part of the music industry, and anything that dealt with music in mp3 format was considered tantamount to piracy, as eloquently expressed by former RIAA president Hillary Rosen: "We sincerely doubt that there would be a market for the mp3 portable recording devices but for the thousands of illegal songs on the Internet" (Brown 1998b). The lawsuit was brought on the grounds that the Rio mp3 player encouraged music piracy, along the same legal terms of the famous dispute known as the Betamax case, between the Motion Picture Association of America (MPAA) and some of the earliest videocassette recorder manufacturers, including Sony (Vaidyanathan 2003). The terms used by the court to rule against the RIAA lawsuit against the Rio were also similar to the famous Betamax ruling, according to which any technology that allowed for substantial non-infringing use should be considered lawful.

The court order was hailed as an important victory by the hardware and consumer electronics industry, which continued to invest in the production of technology for digital music. However, the entertainment industry and its lobbies did not give up the legal battle to prevent the unregulated flows of digital content. In 2000, as Napster was reaching about 100 million users worldwide and the RIAA, armed with a stronger and more focused legal strategy, successfully filed suit against it for copyright infringement, Creative Labs introduced the Nomad Jukebox, which pushed storage capacity to six gigabytes by virtue of a small hard drive. It was a major improvement in terms of capacity, a quality that appealed to the growing numbers of digital music collectors, but the company lacked the brand and marketing power to really make an impact. Other manufacturers soon followed, including established players in the field of consumer electronics such as Samsung, Casio, and Thomson, as well as new players lured by opportunities of the market. With the expansion of music file sharing inaugurated by Napster and the reluctance of traditional market leaders such as Sony to deal with music formats such as the controversial mp3, the market for digital music seemed to offer unprecedented business opportunities for newcomers. Prior to the iPod, however, no single music player had firmly attained market leadership. Several factors can account for the weak market performance of the digital players, such as consumers' unfamiliarity with digital music, market confusion due to the lack of software and hardware standards, small storage capacity, ineffective user interfaces, poor designs, and ultimately high prices, still considerably higher than for CD players.

At the time of the introduction of its first generation model, the iPod was the portable music player that sported the best ratio between storage capacity and physical space, coupled with an innovative design that was Apple's real signature. However, even for the iPod, the first reactions from the market were not exactly enthusiastic (Fried 2001). Initially marketed at $399, the iPod was the most expensive digital music player on the market, and critics, while acknowledging the beauty of its design and the ingenuity of the interface, ultimately categorized it as a gadget for deep-pocketed Mac lovers.

In March 2003, with the introduction of the smaller, even sleeker, third-generation model, retailing at a slightly cheaper price and featuring higher storage capacity, sales figures for the iPod started to grow. During summer 2003, right after the introduction of the iTMS, the market response started to become very positive. By the end of the year, iPod requests eventually became overwhelming. The third generation iPod was one of the best-selling items during the 2003 Christmas season, with more than 700,000 units sold in the United States alone (Levy 2004).

By early 2004, Apple had become the main player in the field of portable digital audio, with over 60% market share (Walker 2003), an outstanding result for an outsider coming from the computer field. The company's performance looked even more significant when considering its belated approach to the field of digital entertainment, particularly music. Prior to the iPod and iTunes, Apple had never been particularly adept at recognizing the business potential of digital music, largely because of the long-standing trademark dispute with Apple corporation, the Beatles' record label, which prevented it from associating its name to any commercial activity related to music (Smith 2003). Such a hesitant position towards music had significant effects also on the technological choices the company made for its computers. Apple provided its personal computers with CD burners much later than most of its competitors, and the introduction of the iTunes software for storing and organizing music collections on its computers came years after equivalent applications, such as Winamp, had already become widely popular for Windows-based systems (Walker 2003).

So exactly how did Apple, a computer manufacturer that as late as 1997 was on the brink of bankruptcy[3] and for a long time did not express any clear interest in the music business, manage to win over the competitive and uncertain field of digital music, amidst a flurry of high-profile litigations, failed business plans, and technological impasses? Apple is well known for being very protective of the development of its products and business ideas, particularly if successful. Most of the credit for the company's recent renaissance, from the iMac to the iPod, is ascribed to the entrepreneurial skills of Steve Jobs. Jobs is not short on talent for inventing technology that users find enjoyable to own and use. But, as is often the case with business success stories, the "genius" of the entrepreneur is put forth to romanticize and disguise the often bumpy and tentative path of research and development of the whole company, and ultimately to keep competitors at bay from the secrets of its business strategy.

In the wake of the iPod boom, major newspapers such as the *New York Times* and the *Wall Street Journal* investigated the secrets of its success story, to find out how the different parts had been assembled, which company developed the operating system, who gave the crucial design touches, and, most importantly, who envisioned the original business idea. The story that emerges began just a few years ago, around the end of 1999, when the computer world was in the midst of the millennium-bug hysteria and Apple was still mostly focused on video. Apple's most significant technological steps in the field of digital video were the QuickTime video format and the invention, in the mid to late 1980s, of the FireWire protocol, developed for the fast transfer of the large amounts of data required by digital video. In the late 1990s Apple started to add FireWire ports to its personal computer and developed Final Cut Pro, a video-editing software targeted to professionals. In subsequent marketing steps, Apple released iMovie, and then iPhoto, allowing Jobs' grand view of the personal computer as a "hub" for the digital life to materialize (Walker 2003). The last addition was iTunes, introduced in early 2001. The first generation iPod, which connected to computers only via FireWire ports, arrived about six months later. By 2003, with the introduction of the iTMS, Apple had developed a full-fledged solution for digital music, which included a digital music application, an online music store, and a portable music player.

Just as with Apple's overall approach to music, even the iPod was less an inspiration than a gradual assemblage of various inputs, ideas, and parts. More precisely, the iPod was assembled by virtue of hardware and software components coming from six different companies. Apple is very secretive about how the different pieces of the iPod came together, and its public relations division has successfully projected the picture of a "rabbit-out-of-the-hat" product. Aside from the spin, Apple's real strength and main contribution to the project was its ability to coordinate the different partners working on the project. By virtue of an efficient management effort, the development time was reduced to just nine months, from the first concept to the final marketing stage. Apple points out (Walker 2003) that coherence during the development process has been the key to the iPod success, and the secret to efficient technical innovation is the ability to put together the right specialists in the shortest time possible.

In technical terms, the iPod was put together by a team of engineers and designers led by Tony Fadell, who had previously worked for Philips and RealNetworks. Fadell's decision to go to Apple instead of staying at RealNetworks, the strongest player in the field of digital music before Apple stepped in, has been considered a crucial moment in the battle for the digital music market (Markoff 2004). According to Ben Knauss (Kahney 2004b), former senior manager at PortalPlayer, a company that Apple consulted to develop the iPod, Tony Fadell had the original business idea behind the iPod and iTunes, which included both an online distribution service and a portable player. Before coming to Apple, Fadell had unsuccessfully tried to pitch his business proposal to other big consumer electronics companies, including European giant Philips.

The first generation of iPods was based on an operating system licensed from Pixo, a software company founded by a former Apple engineer. Despite Apple's long and successful history of interface development, the tight schedule that had been assigned to the iPod project forced the company to resort to an external support (Yi 2004). Pixo was able to develop the project in a much shorter time because it had already been working on software for cellular phone makers such as Samsung and Nokia. Another company involved in the early development stage was PortalPlayer, a Silicon Valley firm specializing in digital peripherals. PortalPlayer's main field of expertise is the design of hardware and software architectures running on miniaturized hard disks. Most first-generation mp3 players relied on removable memory cards rather than hard disks for music storage because they were too large and heavy to be placed in handheld devices. PortalPlayer's solution was based on a combination of a hard disk and a memory chip, which buffered portions of the data being played, thus reducing the hard disk demand for battery power. Just as with Pixo, PortalPlayer was attractive to Apple because it had already developed the necessary software and hardware solutions, and Apple was in a rush to ship the product before the end of the year. According to Ben Knauss, PortalPlayer's original design accounted for more than half of the finished product. Jobs, however, wanted to add specific features, such as high audio quality, a user-friendly interface, and, above all, Apple's unique design touch. Jobs was personally involved in shaping the device's look and feel, as he previously was with another Apple success story, the iMac. Jobs was mostly concerned with two factors in particular—simplicity and beauty—which had proved crucial to the success of the iMac; the final product had to be extremely simple to use and pleasant to see, use, and "wear." In particular Jobs insisted that the iPod have high storage capacity, excellent audio quality, and a fast and user-friendly interface for retrieving songs through the scroll-wheel.

As mentioned earlier, another crucial factor to the iPod's and iTMS's popularity is the low restrictions enforced through the FairPlay DRM system; Apple's copy-protection technology was built into Quicktime and embedded in the AAC files sold via the iTMS. At first Apple didn't want any DRM and did not request either Pixo or PortalPlayer to implement it in the first-generation models. A DRM system was only added to the second-generation iPods to comply with requirements of the introduction of the iTunes Music Store.

According to the current FairPlay features, the songs downloaded from the iTMS can be burned onto an unlimited number of CDs for personal use, and played on up to five authorized computers. An iTunes playlist containing protected tracks can be copied to CDs up to seven times. Also, FairPlay-protected songs can be downloaded to an unlimited number of iPods. The iPod is engineered to download protected and unprotected songs from any computer with iTunes installed, while the upload function is disabled.

A seductive design, high storage capacity, and low DRM restrictions: these are some of the main features that have made the iPod successful. The next section will focus in detail on how these have been assembled a as part of a precise business and marketing strategy to enter the digital music market.

## The Music Business, Remixed

There is a common thread linking the aesthetic, technical, and marketing components of the iPod's and the iTunes's formula: Apple's ability to straddle profitable, risky business plans and edgy, alternative cultural expressions. Apple acknowledged the drastic change in consumer cultural and economic behaviors brought about by digital technology, and incorporated them into its business strategy. The successful elements of Apple's strategy are a legacy of its experience as an innovative, risk-prone, and brand-oriented company. Since the launch of the first Macintosh computer, Apple's brand has been built on the co-optation of countercultural visual and linguistic signs, to evoke a utopian, liberating, and empowering view of technology, aesthetically translated into an original style of product design.

The most striking quality of the iPod, or its "aura" as a *New York Times* journalist described it (Walker 2003)—echoing Walter Benjamin's (1968) classic definition of artistic quality—stems in fact from its unique design. As the traditional physical support of music (LPs, tapes, or CDs) dissolve into the immaterial, infinitely replicable digital substance of music files, the aura of the work of art moves from the content to the medium—in this case, the playback device. From the elegant cardboard black packaging that stirs childish levels of excitement in even the most blasé customer, to the shiny ivory white of the front cover, the iPod is the embodiment of technological allure. The appeal of the iPod rests in its look as well as in its user-friendly interface. Among its many features, in fact, the one most often cited as the key to the product's seductiveness is the intuitive scroll wheel that allows the user to perform several different functions with just one finger.

Despite the peaks and troughs in the market performance of its products, Apple has always been able to challenge the physical and aesthetic boundaries of technology. Some of Apple's products, such as the colorful and compact iMac, were so successful and widely imitated that they have subsequently become icons of popular culture. More importantly, Apple design solutions have often proved vital for the company's survival. The iMac's successful blend of fashion and technology breathed new life into the Apple brand and prevented, in 1998, the company's share of the desktop computer market from dropping below the dreaded 5% figure.

Apple's experience with the iMac can be considered conducive to the iPod. Both are instances of Apple's emphasis on products that are able to create an emotional and aesthetic resonance with the user. Technology's steady pervasion into daily life has resulted in an increased importance of its function of expressing the user's personality, attitude, and style. Ergonomic and enjoyable devices that users can identify with are able to provide a solution to the growing anxiety about technology, thus countering the dystopian side of technology as embodied by cold and anonymous machines.

Apple's products are thus marketed not merely as high-end and reliable devices but also as expressions of style and personality that can seamlessly blend with the aesthetic and functional environment of the user. Apple has been ahead of its competitors in the computer field at understanding that technological products can be sold as fashion accessories. The basic assumption of brand-oriented companies is that as the core functionalities of products become more standardized across different companies; what now distinguishes a brand is its ability to provide consumers with values and meanings through symbolic and visual choices.

Apple's small share in the personal computer market belies the high ranking of its brand in terms of value,[4] largely thanks the loyalty of its customer base. Since its earliest days, Apple's heavy investments in advertising, design, and product innovation have resulted in a widely recognized and trusted brand. Advertising has always been extremely important to Apple, particularly during the troubled decade of the 1990s. Under the controversial management of former

Pepsi CEO John Sculley, Apple expanded its advertising budget from $15 million to $100 million, partly to the detriment of efficient marketing and product development (Kahney 2002). Despite the disproportionate budget allocation, heavy spending in advertising proved extremely valuable in maintaining customer loyalty and helped to reinforce a unique relationship of trust and identification.[5] John Sculley went so far as to describe Apple as more a marketing company than a computer manufacturer, a risky management attitude that has, however, been credited with helping the brand stay afloat in dire times.

When Steve Jobs returned to Apple as CEO in 1997, he focused more directly on product innovation and sales strategies, while continuing Apple's tradition of robust marketing spending, especially with the $100 million iMac campaign. Apple still spends considerable resources on advertising, an example being the 2002 "Switch" campaign aimed at convincing dissatisfied Windows users to defect to the other side. Conspicuous investments have also been poured on the famous iPod "silhouette" campaign. The advertising campaign, showing black silhouette over monochrome backgrounds, has recently become a hallmark of urban visual landscape, both in the U.S. and across international markets. In the U.K., iPod ads covered bus shelters, the London Underground, and railway stations. Japan was flooded by iPod television ads, while colored iPod silhouette banners hung from the ceilings in Paris's St. Lazare train station. At McGill metro terminal in Montreal, colorful iPod silhouettes were painted onto the turnstiles and stairways (Kasper 2004).

Apple's brand has been one of the essential determinants of the company's survival during the mid-1990s' financial crisis and even for its recent performance with the iMac and iPod (Kahney 2002). The success of the company, it is argued, depends more on the power of the brand than on innovative products. Apple's brand efforts have been targeted at building an emotional brand that creates a strong and intimate relationship with its customers, who are often willing to pay higher prices or overlook product flaws for the sake of the special, unique bond they have with the company. By evoking universal values such as imagination, nonconformity, freedom, and stylishness, Apple presents itself as a company based on the ethos of empowering people through technology, thus pushing the brand-customer relation beyond mere commerce into the realm of representation and identity. Apple's famous "1984" commercial, a retro-futuristic tale of a hero freeing a mass trapped in an Orwellian scenario, carried clear populist undertones and portrayed Apple as a countercultural, rebellious, freethinking company. This branding strategy helped the company to develop an almost ideological affiliation with its customers, based on a shared belief in the democratizing power of technology and communication.

One of the recurring themes in Apple's communications is the tension between alternative and mainstream cultures. Apple has always addressed its customers as an elite of independent freethinkers who don't comply with the homogenizing trends of mass culture. The "Think Different" campaign celebrated historical figures of creative misfits and rebels such as Picasso, Gandhi, John Lennon, and Einstein. Lee Clow, the mind behind the campaign, explained Apple's communication strategy as follows: "The comeback of Harley-Davidson motorcycles was a good model for Apple to emulate. Harley's advertising convinced people that they could feel its renegade spirit even if they were investment bankers rather than Hell's Angels. It rehabilitated a counterculture icon for the baby boomers who had grown up and sold out" (Deutschman 2000).

Apple's brand image of an alternative, edgy company played a crucial role in its move towards digital music. Apple acknowledged the cultural divide that existed between the music industry and digital music users. Apple approached the major record companies with an original business plan aimed at creating a balance between the industry and music listeners, and coupled it with a communication strategy that spoke the language of youth, freedom, and innovation. While keeping one eye on the click-happy peer-to-peer users, Apple was pursuing its main goal, which was to convince the record labels to license their songs to the iTMS. Such ambivalent attitude was epitomized by the controversial "Rip, Mix, Burn" campaign, which infuriated many powerful figures in the entertainment industries, including Disney CEO Michael Eisner (Cohen 2002). Eisner accused Apple of considering piracy its new "killer application" and warned potential buyers that they could engage in theft if they had bought Apple computers.

Apple strategy was grounded in the assumption that users, empowered by technologies such as file-sharing networks, had the upper hand in the transitional phase from analog to digital media, and that they should be approached in cautious and respectful terms instead of being labeled as "thieves." The aggressive approach adopted by the industry towards users of file-sharing networks hasn't proved effective in migrating audiences towards legal solutions, in fact. With the spread of file-sharing technologies, both producers and users of digital content have become very sensitive to the issue of intellectual property, albeit from opposite perspectives. While the industry has sought to maintain absolute control over distribution, users have exploited digital technology to develop new models of distribution, archiving, and content retrieval. Apple realized that to succeed in such a crowded and confusing space, it needed to strike a balance between these conflicting positions.

A crucial aspect of the iPod's success has been its placement within the overall business strategy that Apple has adopted towards the digital music market. This includes the iTunes software, originally available only for Apple computers but expanded to Windows since spring 2004. When Apple entered the market with its strategy, no other company had an integrated business system for digital music comparable to Apple's, which produced and managed the hardware, the software, and the online distribution.

As already pointed out, Apple's success in the digital music market appeared even more striking when its outsider role in the market is considered.

Other large companies were much better positioned in the entertainment field than Apple. However, largely out of the fear of piracy, they were unable to devise a successful business strategy. Probably the most striking example of this failure is Sony, which was the ideal candidate for the leadership in the digital music market since it had the assets both in the field of content and consumer electronics. However, Sony fell into an innovation impasse due, in large part, to a conflict of interests within itself (Rose 2003). Sony's consumer electronic division, interested in selling digital devices for playback and storage, and Sony Music, one of the five major record labels, which has stakes in the distribution of digital content, took completely diverging positions with respect to development and marketing strategies for digital music. Only in December 2004, in a belated attempt to counter Apple's further expansion into digital audio, Sony released the NW-HD3, a portable player capable of mp3 playback (Williams 2004b). Previously, Sony had only released audio players supporting its own proprietary ATRAC format, a strict digital-rights management system that proved rather unappealing for the booming market of digital music users.

It could be argued that one of the reasons for iTunes's popularity is the fact that it was the first service to sell downloadable music à la carte from the catalog of major record labels. The single-choice system, as opposed to the subscription-based models, has proved effective because it catered to the preference models of music consumption established by file-sharing services. Also, the music industry trusted Apple as a reliable candidate to approach potential customers with a viable marketing solution for digital music, particularly with respect to the intellectual property concerns. Steve Jobs was personally involved in the process of acquiring the trust of the recording industry, a daunting endeavor for an executive of a computer manufacturer, given the past discrepancies between the two camps. Jobs qualified for the task by virtue of his strong reputation both in the computer and entertainment industry. Since the early days at the hackers' community of the Homebrew Computer Club with Apple co-founder Steve Wozniak, Jobs has long had good credibility in the computer community, both among grassroots amateurs and industry executives. Thanks to his successful move to computer animation with Pixar, Jobs also developed a strong reputation in the entertainment field. This combination made him the most qualified technology figure to establish the proper terms of agreement with main players of the recording industry.

Jobs presented prototypes of the iTMS project to record labels executives around the country, assuring them of the company's full commitment to the project and of the viability of the business plan. Above all, Jobs guaranteed that Apple would back the project with its full marketing potential, from an ambitious advertising plan to ample promotion through the strategically located and growing chain of Apple retail stores.

Apple believed that the only way to establish a market for digital music was to cater to the needs of the users in the simplest way possible, according to the distribution models initiated by file-sharing services. Apple understood that people buy music to own it, not just to rent it, as offered by other services. Also, Apple's policy towards piracy has been to frame it more as a behavioral rather than a technical issue, and insisted on giving users as much control as possible on the downloaded songs. Apple subscribed to the belief that "on the other side of a lawsuit there is a thriving industry" (Doctorow 2004), and that strict DRM technology would not serve the purpose of preventing copyright infringement. Jobs worked together with industry executives to define the technical and legal conditions that were necessary for the major labels' participation. Jobs initially wanted to sell music without restrictions, but the labels were resolute in blocking his position. He was, however, able to make them compromise on a much lower level of limitations than those granted for any previous online store. After the negotiations, Apple hyped the iPod and iTunes formula as a revolution in the music business with a large-scale advertising campaign.

As of December 2004, the iTMS had distributed more than 200 million songs. Despite some contentions that Apple's online music store doesn't generate profit, the company still intensely promotes and celebrates iTunes's popularity, since the ITMS's bottom line is still arguably to advertise Apple brand in the digital entertainment market, both as hardware producer and as content distributor. This has significant implications in economic terms for the music business, in particular with respect to intellectual property issues. Despite the potentially infringing potential of Apple's solution, the major record labels have nonetheless trusted it as a possible remedy to counter the decline in music sales allegedly caused by file sharing (Borland 2003).

However, it could be argued that in strictly technical terms an mp3 player with 40-gigabyte storage capacity and low DRM restrictions, if used to download songs from different computers and played in private or public venues, could function as a computer connected to a p2p system downloading or distributing mp3 files. One can easily connect the iPod to a friend's computer, download the songs through iTunes or as raw data, and play them back or upload them to the other computer. Once iPod users are allowed to store and play digital files such as mp3s, which don't generally feature DRM, then the devices can be easily used for the unregulated circulation of copyright-protected material. This is currently one of the most frequently heard arguments (McCue 2004) against the low DRM restrictions imposed by the iPod. The technical characteristics of the iPod allow users to easily swap files, carry them around, organize them in personal collections, and play them in public venues.

The iPod's characteristics and the opportunities of music consumption and distribution it allows seem to correspond to the definition of a "democratic medium."[6] Technologies that empower users with alternative forms of interaction, production, and distribution, such as in recent times audio- and videotape recorders (Vaidyanathan 2003), have a history of clashing with the established economic and legal status quo: "Technology that disrupts copyright does so because it simplifies and cheapens creation, reproduction and distribution. The existing copyright businesses exploit inefficiencies in the old production, reproduction and distribution system" (Doctorow 2004).

However, after its first disruptive effects have been absorbed and mitigated by market and political forces, the new technologies tend to reinforce existing power structures or create new ones. In this respect, the iPod is no exception. The characteristics of peer-to-peer file sharing have led to prosecutions for facilitating copyright infringement, while for the iPod they have been exploited for commercial ends. Apple, like many other hardware producers, is arguably profiting from the continuous flows of illegal file sharing. As recently reported (Kanhey 2004a), some are taking this as a sign that the value chain of the digital music market might emphasize the modalities of access to the content, such as distribution services or hardware devices, rather than the actual content.

The characteristics and the fast rise to popularity of Apple's solution for digital music are meeting with contrasting reactions, ranging from the general positive response of customers to the competitors' prompt counter plans to the criticism of music activists. The next sections will focus on how the different players in the digital music business perceive the iPod and iTunes phenomena and how these reactions are in turn affecting Apple itself.

## Apple and the iPod's Complex

During the first quarter of 2004, Apple announced that its profits had almost tripled from the same period the year before (Flynn 2004), largely thanks to the steady growth of iPod sales. For the first time in Apple's history, a noncomputer product sold more units (about 800,000) than all Macintosh computers together, which sold about 750,000. In just three years, Apple managed to shift the focus of its core business from high-end hardware and software to products and services for the entertainment and the consumer electronics market, a move that the company hopes will keep it profitable in the future.

By changing the rules of the game with a mix of technical innovation and marketing, Apple has won over its financially stronger rivals in a highly competitive marketplace. Such a forward move will not be without consequences, both in terms of Apple's own strategy for the future and for the competitors' reaction to it. To a certain extent, the overwhelming success of the iPod has disoriented not only the competitors but also Apple itself, which is now facing the somehow unexpected challenge of maintaining the pole position of the new market born out of the convergence of consumer electronics and digital music distribution.

In 2004 many companies in the field of consumer electronics and computers released portable players to compete with the iPod. None of them still represents a real threat to the iPod, but if the trend of introduction of new products established in 2004 continues in the coming years, Apple will most likely see its share of the portable players' market significantly decrease. Moreover, the iPod's operating margins reached 13% in December 2003 and have fallen an estimated five points since then (Murphy 2004). Also, the iPod's price decrease that followed the introduction of the fourth generation will require Apple to sell 20% more iPods in 2005 to maintain the same profits of 2004. Bigger competitors could eventually overpower Apple, as happened with personal computers, where the company now controls only a thin slice of the market, despite having essentially invented the personal computer and the graphical user interface. The most commonly accepted explanation for Apple's decline during the 1990s is its insistence on confining the Mac operating system to its own hardware products only. Apple's commitment to the production of sophisticated but strictly proprietary product solutions, with a low level of interoperability, has always been its biggest impairment. As Apple should have learned by now, innovation inevitably leads to imitation, and imitators can often overtake the original innovator.

However, the company's response to the iPod's success shows signs that its relationship with the market is still controversial. As more rivals enter the digital music market with innovations at competitive prices, Apple is facing the challenge with a mixed set of reactions, ranging from partnership to open controversy. On the one hand, Apple seems to have learned from past experience, and has signed partnerships to extend the operability of its software and hardware solutions across different platforms, such as with Hewlett-Packard and Motorola. On the other hand, it is fiercely attacking any attempt by competitors to bandwagon on the iPod's boom, as with RealNetworks. The prevailing tendency will ultimately determine whether Apple will be able to maintain leadership in both the market of hardware and software in digital music.

The highly publicized move to make the iPod and iTunes available to Windows users is a sign that the company is trying to avoid being pigeonholed as a manufacturer of strictly proprietary and closed devices. Another important move towards market expansion is the partnership deal signed with Hewlett-Packard, the world's second-largest computer maker (Wong 2004). According to the agreement, HP can sell an iPod model carrying the Hewlett-Packard brand, while shipping HP desktops and laptops with iTunes installed. Such a deal is very favorable to Apple in light of its limited market share in personal computers in the Windows-Intel–dominated computer world.

Also, from the recent introduction of a series of upgraded and new iPod models, Apple seems to be responding to the increasing competition by diversifying its offer. It recently introduced the 60GB Photo iPod, featuring a color LCD screen to browse photographs, and the Shuffle iPod, an even smaller model based on a 512MB flash memory card and sold at a strategic $99 price. Despite introducing a promising multimedia element to the iPod formula, the Photo iPod received mixed reviews because of its high price and technical limitations, above all the lack of camera function, absence of memory card slot, and small screen (Williams 2004a). On the other hand, the Shuffle iPod seems to have the potential of representing a successful addition to the iPod family, much as it was for the iPod mini, for the effective combination of technical features, flash-based memory, small size, shuffle playback functions, and a competitive two-digit price. The Shuffle iPod is also targeted to the flash-based section of the digital music player market, which is currently still larger and more profitable than the hard drive market.

In the coming future, the greatest opportunity for growth for the iPod and iTMS, as well as the strongest competition, might come from the wireless networks and cell-phones market. A wireless enabled iPod—through which users could purchase songs, tune into radio services, and watch live feeds while on the move—might represent a significant advancement both in technical and marketing terms. So far the only tangible sign of Apple's interest in the wireless market is the deal it signed with Motorola, the world's second-largest manufacturer of wireless devices, aimed at making iTMS songs compatible with Motorola phones.

However, the future of the iPod is not being solely shaped by innovations and partnerships. A high-profile dispute with RealNetworks has already cast a gloom of déjà vu over the company. The controversy stems from the technical restrictions imposed on the interoperability of the iPod and iTunes system. As mentioned earlier, currently the only songs sold online that the iPod can play are ITMS songs, and in turn ITMS's songs can only be played on the iPod. In summer 2004, RealNetworks released a new version of its popular RealPlayer software that included an encoding feature called Harmony. Thanks to Harmony, Rhapsody customers can play the downloaded songs on iPods and other portable players. To make this possible, RealNetworks reverse-engineered Apple's own copy-protection system, FairPlay, to encode Rhapsody's songs in a format accepted by the iPod. Apple accused RealNetworks of adopting "the tactics and ethics of a hacker to break into the iPod" (Stein 2004).

Considering Apple's past flirtations with hackers' culture, the statement sounded paradoxical and shed a negative light of protectionist behavior over the company. To Apple's accusations, RealNetworks replied that it was simply giving its customers the choice to play songs bought on its music service on several music players, including the iPod, as well as giving iPod users another source, in addition to iTunes, to get legally downloaded and copy-protected music. Robert Glaser, the chief executive of RealNetworks, which has often been critical of Apple's and iTunes's market lock-in, commented, "Apple is running the risk of following the same path it took in its development of its personal computer" (Stein 2004). Apple's insistence on keeping other portable players out of iTunes by not licensing its FairPlay digital-rights management technology prevents the development of an interoperable music solution, which could prove necessary for the survival of the iTMS as the iPod market leadership decreases.

Apple also threatened to investigate whether RealNetworks's operation violated the Digital Millennium Copyright Act (DMCA). Under the conditions of good market competition, Apple would simply have to choose "whether to make the iPod an open platform, able to work with everyone's music service, or to try to keep it closed, hoping to extract more money," law professor James Boyle argues (2004). However, thanks to the heavily criticized DMCA, interoperability now has a "new legal dimension." The DMCA was supposed to "allow copyright owners to protect their content with digital fences," but it wasn't meant to make interoperability illegal. As further argued by Boyle, technology companies "use the DMCA's broad provisions to make competition in tied services and products illegal" (Boyle 2004).

Another front in legal conflict looming over the future of the iPod comes from the already mentioned Induce Act bill, which would hold companies liable for any technology that would "encourage" people to unlawfully distribute copyrighted materials. Critics argue that the bill would effectively outlaw peer-to-peer networks and hinder the development of new technologies, including devices like the iPod. Critics have strongly criticized the bill by saying that it allows copyright owners to adopt a subjective standard when determining the intent of a technology manufacturer. As feared by hardware producers, the Induce Act would put the entertainment industry in charge of technological innovation, a dreadful scenario for the computer industry as well as for civil rights defendants. As of December 2004, it seems unlikely that the Induce bill will be voted into effect, largely due to a wide campaign to alert the public of its potential chilling effects on technological development.

Also, given Apple's leadership in the field of digital music distribution, a further terrain of confrontation for Apple is the relationship with artists. Music activists' group Downhill Battle launched an Internet campaign criticizing Apple's strategy for digital music. Downhill Battle is accusing Apple's iTMS of sidestepping on the opportunity to free musicians from the unfair business relationships that most of them are forced into by major labels. "Instead of creating a system that gets virtually all of fans' money directly to artists—finally possible with the Internet—iTunes takes a big step backwards. Apple calls the iTMS revolutionary but record companies are using the service to force the same exploitive and unfair business model onto a new medium."[7] While Apple takes a 35% share from every song and every album sold through the iTMS, and record labels receive the other 65%, Downhill Battle activists argue that major label artists receive only 8 to 14 cents per song, depending on their contract. The group thus accuses Apple of giving artists "the exact same deal that artists have always gotten from the big five record companies. Instead of using this new medium to empower musicians and their fans, it helps the record industry cartel perpetuate the exploitation" (Downhillbattle.org 2004). According to their claims, Downhill Battle successfully challenged Apple's use of the phrase "fair for artists" associated with the iTMS, which was in turn later removed from all the promotional material for Apple's music service.

Apple was targeted by another performance of music activism right after the introduction of the limited edition U2 iPod, preloaded with the entire U2 discography. The artist Francis Hwang put on sale on eBay a U2 iPod loaded with several albums from sample music pioneers Negativland. After Apple Computer claimed copyright violations, eBay removed the modified U2 iPod from its auctions. Hwang's intention was to commemorate a court case between Negativland and U2, when U2's record company sued Negativland for sampling a U2 song, in one of the earliest controversies (Negativland 1995) over the now ubiquitous practice of music sampling.

## Conclusions

Apple's bet on digital music as an avenue of development for new business opportunities has so far proved successful. The focus of this research tried to look beyond the iPod's and iTMS's commercial success to unearth more critical issues, such as the co-optation of countercultural practices and symbols for marketing purposes, the unprecedented cross-industry agreements that Apple was able to obtain thanks to its brand appeal, and the instability of the current intellectual property regime.

As recounted in the chapter, Apple has deftly interpreted the conditions necessary to succeed in a time of rapid and disruptive technological change by adjusting its business strategy to the shifting patterns of music consumption and distribution. It has made being a risk-prone and innovation-driven company work to its advantage during a time of transition to new forms of technological and economic arrangements in the field of entertainment and consumer electronics.

Apple's rise to success in digital music has been so fast and overwhelming that the company now faces the paradoxical situation of possessing a quasi-monopolistic control on the market, a position that it reached, however, by exploiting the most controversial aspects of digital and network technology. Apple's market position appears particularly controversial considering that, aside from Apple's effective strategy and the iPod's undisputable technical qualities, a good part of the success of the iPod is due to the wide availability of music in digital content distributed through file-sharing networks and the lax Apple policy towards intellectual property.

The same users of file-sharing networks who were labeled as hackers by the RIAA are now lured by Apple's advertising into becoming iPod's legitimate customers, while their role of providers of a large part of the unlawful content that circulates through network technology is seen as instrumental to the success of the iPod. However, the economic rules that sustain the file-sharing networks are more inspired by practices of the sharing economy (Benkler 2002) or gift economy (see Giesler, this volume), where the subjectivities involved in exchange are more important than the actual product, while Apple's model is forcing the recommodification of digital music, with a peculiar protectionist approach that rules out interoperability across different software or hardware formats.

The company now faces the challenge, for the second time in its history, of maintaining control of a business territory that it has helped to grow. Today's challenge might, however, be greater than that of 20 years ago, when the company helped midwife the desktop computing market. Its position is now complicated not just by the actions of competitors but by the new forms of power seized by users and artists through digital network technologies.

Apple hailed the introduction of the iTMS as the beginning of "the digital music revolution," just as in 1984 they claimed a stake in the computer revolution. Perhaps by now people have grown skeptical of the revolution they are being sold, particularly when they can just freely access it through peer-to-peer file-sharing networks.

## Acknowledgments

The author wishes to thank Siva Vaidyanathan and Sam Howard-Spink for their help and support.

## References to Chapter Nine

Alderman, John. 2001. *Sonic Boom: Napster, Mp3 and the New Pioneers of Music.* Cambridge, MA: Perseus Press.

Benjamin, Walter. 1968. "The Work of Art in the Age of Mechanical Reproduction." In *Illuminations: Essays and Reflections,* edited by Hannah Arendt, 217–52. New York: Shocken.

Benkler, Yochai. 2002. "Coase's Penguin, or Linux and the Nature of the Firm." Retrieved December 14, 2004, from http://www.benkler.org/CoasesPenguin.html

Boyle, James. 2004. "The Apple of Forbidden Knowledge." *Financial Times,* August 12. Retrieved October 5, 2005, from http://news.ft.com/ cms/s/2c04d39e-ec5a-11d8-b35c-00000e2511c8.html

Borland, John. 2003. "Music Industry: Piracy Is Choking Sales." *CNET News,* April 9. Retrieved October 13, 2004, from http://news.com.com/2100–1027–996205.html?tag=fd_top

Brown, Janelle. 1998a. "Blame It on Rio." *Salon.com,* October 29. Retrieved September 7, 2004, from http://archive.salon.com/21st/feature/1998/10/28feature2.html

———. 1998b. "Is Rio Grand?" *Salon.com,* December 9. Retrieved September 7, 2004, from http://archive.salon.com/21st/reviews/1998/12/09review.html

Cohen, Peter. 2002. "Disney Boss Accuses Apple of Fostering Piracy." *MacWorld,* March 1. Retrieved September 17, 2004, from http://www.macworld.com/news/2002/03/01/eisner/

Dean, Katie. 2004. "Copyright Bill to Kill Tech?" *Wired News,* July 22. Retrieved August 22, 2004, from http://www.wired.com/news/print/0,1294,64297,00.html

Deutschman, Alan. 2000. "The Once and Future Steve Jobs." *Salon.com,* October 11. Retrieved September 3, 2004, from http://dir.salon.com/tech/books/ 2000/ 10/11/jobs_excerpt/index.html

Doctorow, Cory. 2004. *Microsoft Research DRM Talk.* June 17. Retrieved August 29, 2004, from http://www.dashes.com/anil/stuff/doctorow-drm-ms.html

Downhillbattle.org. 2004. Available at www.downhillbattle.org.

Flynn, Laurie. 2004. "Profit at Apple Almost Triples on a Sharp Rise in iPod Sales." *New York Times,* April 15. Retrieved September 29, 2004, from http://www. nytimes.com

Fried, Ian. 2001. "Apple's iPod Spurs Mixed Reactions." *CNET News,* October 23. Retrieved August 20, 2004, from http://news.com.com/2100–1040– 274821.html? legacy=cnet

———. 2003. "Will iTunes Make Apple Shine?" *CNET News,* August 16. Retrieved June 20, 2004, from http://news.com.com/Will+iTunes+make+ Apple+shine/2100–1041_3–5092559.html

———. 2004. "Gucci Serves Up Apple iPod à la Mode." *CNET News,* April 20. Retrieved June 12, 2004, from http://news.com.com/2100–1041–5195940.html

Gasser, Bambauer, et al. 2004. "iTunes: How Copyright, Contract, and Technology Shape the Business of Digital Media—A Case Study." Green paper, vol. 1. Retrieved June 2, 2004, from http://cyber.law.harvard.edu/media/itunes

Kahney, Leander. 2002. "Apple: It's All about the Brand." *Wired News,* December 4. Retrieved June 9, 2004, from http://www.wired.com/news/mac/ 0,2125,56677, 00.html

———. 2003. "Feel Free to Jack into My iPod." *Wired News,* November 21. Retrieved July 6, 2004, from http://www.wired.com/news/mac/ 0,2125,61242,00.html?tw= wn_story_related

———. 2004a. "Bull Session with Professor iPod." *Wired News,* February 25. Retrieved August 20, 2004, from http://www.wired.com/news/print/0,1294,62396, 00.html

———. 2004b. "Inside Look at the Birth of the iPod." *Wired News,* July 21. Retrieved July 23, 2004, from http://www.wired.com/news/mac/ 0,2125,64286,00.html

———. 2004c. *The Cult of The Mac.* San Francisco, CA: No Starch Press.

Kawasaki, Guy. 1990. *The Macintosh Way.* Glenview, IL: Scott Foresman.

Kasper, Jade. 2004. "Apple Heats Up World-wide iPod Advertising." *Apple Insider,* March 9. Retrieved July 6, 2004, from www.appleinsider.com/ article.php?id=387

Levy, Steven. 2000. *Insanely Great: The Life and Time of Macintosh, the Computer That Changed Everything.* New York: Penguin Books.

———. 2004. "iPod Nation." *Newsweek/MSNBC News,* December 26. Retrieved July 6, 2004, from http://msnbc.msn.com/id/5457432/site/newsweek/

Linzmayer, Owen. 1999. *Apple Confidential: The Real Story of Apple Computer.* San Francisco, CA: No Starch Press.

Malone, Michael. 1999. *Infinite Loop: How the World's Most Insanely Great Computer Company Went Insane*. New York: Doubleday.

Manuel, Peter. 1994. *Cassette Culture*. Chicago, IL: University of Chicago Press.

Markoff, John. 2004. "Oh, Yeah, He Also Sells Computers." *New York Times*, April 25.

Marsal, Katie. 2004. "iPod Adoption Rate Faster Than Sony Walkman." *Apple Insider*, November 29. Retrieved November 30, 2004, from http://www.appleinsider.com/article.php?id=765

McCue, Andy. 2004. "'iPod Users Are Music Thieves,' Says Ballmer." *Silicon.com*, October 4. Retrieved October 5, 2004, from http://management.silicon.com/itpro/0,39024675,39124642,00.htm

Murphy, Victoria. 2004. "The Song Remains the Same." *Forbes.com*, September 6. Retrieved November 30, 2004, from http://www.forbes.com/home/global/2004/0906/030.html

Negativland. 1995. *Fair Use: The Story of the Letter U & the Numeral 2*. El Cerrito, CA: Seeland.

Rose, Frank. 2003. "The Civil War Inside Sony." *Wired Magazine*, February. Retrieved July 10, 2004, from http://www.wired.com/wired/archive/11.02/sony_pr.html

Savetheipod.com. Retrieved October 14, 2004 from http://www.savetheipod.com

Smith, Tony. 2003. "Beatles Record Label Sues Apple Computer—Again." *Register*, September 12. Retrieved September 10, 2004, from http://www.theregister.co.uk/2003/09/12/beatles_label_sues_apple_again/

Stein, Andrew. 2004. "Apple: RealNetworks Hacked iPod." *CNN Money*, July 29. Retrieved August 3, 2004, from http://money.cnn.com/2004/07/29/technology/apple_real/

Vaidyanathan, Siva. 2003. *Copyrights and Copywrongs: The Rise of Intellectual Property and How It Threatens Creativity*. New York: NYU Press.

———. 2004. *The Anarchist in the Library: How the Clash between Freedom and Control Is Hacking the Real Worlds and Crashing the System*. New York: Basic Books.

Walker, Rob. 2003. "The Guts of the New Machine." *New York Times*, November 11. Retrieved September 6, 2004, from http://www.nytimes.com

Wilcox, Joe. 2001. "Apple to Unveil Digital Music Device." *CNET News*, October 17. Retrieved August 24, 2004, from http://news.com.com/2100–1040–274566.html?legacy=cnet

Williams, Stephen. 2004a. "Apple's Latest Development iPod Photo Seems Unfocused." *LA Times*, November 14. Retrieved December 19, 2004, from http://www.latimes.com/technology/

———. 2004b. "An MP3-capable Walkman Is Set to Challenge iPod." *LA Times*, December 5. Retrieved December 20, 2004, from http://www.latimes.com/technology/

Wong, May. 2004. "HP Deal Is Latest Boost for Apple's iPod." *Information Week*, January 9. Retrieved June 20, 2004, from http://www.informationweek.com/showArticle.jhtml?articleID=17300324

Yi, Matthew. 2004. "Small Startup Pixo Lends a Hand to Apple's iPod." *Salt Lake Tribune*, June 18. Retrieved August 27, 2004, from http://www.sltrib.com/business/ci_23934511

CHAPTER TEN

# The Social Pulse of Telharmonics: Functions of Networked Sound and Interactive Webcasting

## Trace Reddell

> There are times for practical repair work and there are times for huge imaginative excursions into utopia.
>
> —R. Murray Schafer, *The Soundscape*

This chapter concerns recent developments in audio production and performance made possible through digital technologies as sound artists, musicians, and DJs have come to rely on computer networks for some phase of their projects or live shows. In the pages that follow, I describe web-based works, gallery installations, and computer-based media used in live performances and streaming Internet broadcasts. Technologies of sound embed social practice within the media networks of production, collaboration, broadcast, and reception. First, individual performers access a networked database of sound sources and media objects as a way of chronicling associative links among items stored in the material archive. Second, solitary performers collaborate across networks, processing and remixing one another's streaming audio files or sharing virtual instrument interfaces through the Internet. And third, multiple sets of performers and webcasters interact with each other's transmissions, coordinated in a live, globally synchronized event. Over the course of this sequence, I hope to establish some of the ways in which these projects and performances foreground the social function of organized sound in terms of telephonic connectivity.

The following pages also merge a set of historical streams of influence: 19th-century inventor Thaddeus Cahill's "telharmonium," the first networked instrument, a synthesizer that delivered its tones over telephone cables; Vannevar Bush's "memex," a scholarly application for personal, associative indexing and data source management; Mikhail Bakhtin's concept of the "chronotope," a useful way to think about an artistic product as that nexus of space and time which provides a point of transfer between represented imaginary space and lived historical space; Jean Baudrillard's post-May '68 reaction against technology-based, structural theories of media to emphasize instead their social function; the Situationist practice of détournement, a strategy for reprocessing the abundance of the media archive; and turntablism, whereby a device for playing back vinyl records comes to function as a performance medium. How these streams intertwine to yield the various neologisms of the chapter's title and the section headers below makes up the main impulse of what follows.

## The Webmix

The Internet serves as a massive database of sound resources. Content includes everything from corporate broadcast media and blockbuster movie trailers to independent mp3 record labels and web-based art projects. You can find crude fart recordings as easily as audio files derived from genome sequences and astronomical data.[1] File formats and modes of delivery vary almost as much as the content. Audio files may be downloaded directly to your own computer for playback, storage, or editing. Media players stream lengthy prerecorded works or live broadcasts encoded for the web. Still more files are embedded directly into web pages in the form of Quicktime Movies, Flash animations, and Midi files.[2] By default, these formats play within the frame of the HTML browser window itself rather than launching separate and often competing applications. My personal experience of this conglomeration of sound sources blending together into something uniquely musical—what I call a "webmix"—was initially accidental. But the ease of opening multiple browser windows, each potentially playing its own embedded sound source, likely makes such instant audio collages a relatively common occurrence for those with access to a media-rich Internet.[3]

## A Webmix

It might go something like this. You are streaming mp3s from a Shoutcast server in Barcelona through a stand-alone player like Winamp. While checking out the news, you launch a video clip that plays in a separate instance of the RealPlayer application. Both streams manage to share resources on your computer and already the spontaneous mix becomes occasionally cinematic, at other times more like avant-garde electronic music or a segue in a hip-hop track. You decide to go further with this and, digging through your browser's bookmarks, you load up the pages of a couple of your favorite mp3 labels, then start pulling up different files in their own browser windows, each running an embedded instance of Quicktime player. Because in this case you happen to be on an ambient and experimental kick, you come up with sounds that don't feature a lot of competitive rhythm and percussion sequences. Rather, the crackles and pops of the glitch tracks begin to intersect into more complex, though microscopic, beats. The varying layers of synthetic pads and field recordings from the ambient selections hold the flow together. Since each Quicktime player has its own volume control, you can adjust the levels of these portions of your mix. You begin to experiment with manipulating the playback bar to make rough scratches and manual loops. Getting more playful prompts you to dig up Looplab's DJ mixer,[4] an eight-channel sampler programmed in Flash and loaded with electronica and drum-and-bass loops. As you attempt to launch the virtual groovebox, your computer's resources lag. The Quicktime players stutter and skip. RealPlayer cuts out, too, as the streaming media player rebuilds its buffer. There is a pause, a distinctly digital gap, and then everything kicks back in at once, this time accompanied by a fast-paced, heavy bass beat from the Looplab mixer. The shifting layers of the various mp3 sources texture the more prominent beats of the sampler, making the otherwise somewhat canned, overly slick productions of the Looplab mixer sound more gritty and spontaneous, before another conflict among browser windows causes the entire computer to freeze in silence. The webmix features the browser as an interface for improvisation, the border of its spontaneous assemblage marked by the consumption of system resources and computer crashes.

## Practitioners

The process just described is stylized in recent projects from Matt Chiabotti (produced as em.chia) and myself, working under the name of pharmakon.t with the DJ Rabbi collective.[5] Works created using this process have found their way into audiocentric net.art exhibits on the web and been performed live as part of international festivals and in art gallery settings.

Em.chia's "metaxalogical mo(u)rning methods" is a 12-minute webmix included in "The Palimpsest Project" exhibit (2002) at the web-based gallery Stasis_Space.[6] Sonically, "metaxalogical mo(u)rning methods" combines ethereal drones with extended strands of spoken word from charismatic preachers, Yoga instructors, and meditation guides. The overall effect is more poetic than narrative as em.chia forms a rich field of juxtaposition with verbal content that edges the piece toward mysticism and the religious.

Even more of a mystical element has seeped into the work of the DJ Rabbi collective, whose collaborative networked projects treat remixing as an offshoot of holy practice, described on the project's website as a branch of Talmudic performance reading.[7] DJ Rabbi's multimedia projects include remixes of the Ten

Commandments, the Bill of Rights, Julio Cortazar, a DVD remix of Guy Debord's "Society of the Spectacle," and audio projects such as mash-ups of Slayer and Aphex Twin, and remixes of readings by Jorge Luis Borges. In my own material, I have created the persona of the "webspinna," an Internet-only DJ with a virtual record crate full of bookmarked web pages. My audio sets consist of extended musical and beat-driven sequences in a variety of genres, but they lean toward glitchy stutters and hard stops situated within ambient sound-scapes, field recordings, and fragments of spoken word.

The pharmakon.t project contextualizes webmixing as a meditative practice, approaching the collective record as a source for sonic mandalas, revealing otherwise occulted linkages among distinct, often apparently incompatible, data objects. I was interested in positioning my own webmixing work in the context of the DJ Rabbi collective because of the group's emphasis on appropriation, juxtaposition, and remixing as the essential literacies of digital culture. The proliferation of pseudonyms throughout the collaborative project coincides with efforts to question the authority of teachers, religious leaders, politicians, writers, and musicians. For the most part, the DJ Rabbi collective works with materials that are either virtually authorless (the Ten Commandments), collectively authored (the Bill of Rights), or authored by figures like Borges, Cortazar, and Debord, each of whom questioned assumptions about textuality and authorship. Sonically interfacing with popular trends like DJ culture and mash-ups, DJ Rabbi also situates its work at an intersection of issues surrounding copyright and commercial control over broadcast and distribution of music. In all cases, the works of the DJ Rabbi collective suggest that data objects in the store of human experience sustain a meaningful presence not as cultural objects bound by rigid rules for access, use, and interpretation, but only when they are renewed through acts of performative revision.

## The Memex Mixing Desk

The creative persona of em.chia and pharmakon.t spin webs of association across the Internet, documenting episodes of audio-file access in the form of recorded mixes. These documents of multilayered audio trails sonify the output of Vannevar Bush's "memex" (2003). Originally described in 1945, the memex anticipates the personal computer with its combination of automated sorting mechanisms and a pair of desktop projection screens all controlled by a set of indexing levers. The memex desk houses a repository "in which an individual stores all his books, records, and communications, and which is mechanized so that it may be consulted with exceeding speed and flexibility" (Bush 2003, 45). Bush understood the mind to work through an interplay between "the association of thoughts" and "some intricate web of trails" etched into the tissue of the brain (45). The associative habits of thinking had their counterpart in the worlds of academic and scientific publication, where established links among published scholarly content formed larger research categories and experiential contexts. But Bush found the climate of academic research frustrating, feeling that it structurally failed to match the brain's flexibility by prescribing the unnaturally hierarchical file-indexing system of research libraries. Worse still, scholarly dialogues had to extend across the extended lag times of the academic publishing calendar. Bush thought these conditions were counterproductive, hindering the innovation required of the post–WWII scientific researcher by making the sort of associative leaps that should charge a field of scholarly research difficult to manage. Bush sought a device that would allow for modified, personal "associative indexing" systems (45). He argues for three major advantages. First, he desires a device capable of encouraging the brain's formation of new lines of connection. Bush imagined his device an adjunct to memory and an essential tool for the requirements of scholarly research, which consists largely of building "trails of interest through the maze of materials available" (46). Second, Bush hoped that the memex desk might facilitate a reformation of the research industry by allowing for more immediate interaction among a network of scholars. These new memex-using scholars Bush characterized through the heroic imagery of pioneers. "As We May Think" anticipates "a new profession of trail blazers," a growing class of scholars, master memex mixers "who find delight in the task of establishing useful trails through the enormous mass of the common record" (46). Third, Bush envisioned new modes of publication, a prototypical hypertext of encyclopedic works "ready made with a mesh of associative trails running through them, ready to be dropped into the memex and there amplified" (46). The sonic webmixer takes this amplification literally.

The webmixes of em.chia and pharmakon.t turn associative indexing into audio performance, merging the memex with the DJ's mixing desk in order to assemble an improvisational vehicle for the expansion of indexed consciousness into telematic domains.[8]

## Telharmonics

While gliding along the temporary network of media trails and hyperlinks, the web DJ participates in the emergence of spontaneous microstructures. These sonic data designs record a "telharmonic" aesthetic.[9] "Telharmonics" stands for sound-specific telematic arts, the latter Roy Ascott's term for projects utilizing computer-mediated communications networks to link dispersed audiences and information systems: "In a telematic art, meaning is not created by the artist, distributed through the network, and received by the observer. Meaning is the product of interaction between the observer and the system, the content of which is in a state of flux" (Ascott 2003, 233). Though not yet breaking out of the triad of meaning's creation, distribution, and reception that Ascott describes, the webmixer does capture a particular episode of telematic fluctuation, the recording itself often shaped by the ebb and flow of network traffic, processor usage, and wireless access zones. In the telharmonic atmosphere, the webmixer at the controls of a sonified memex mixing desk practices performative audio research, adapting actions that Ascott mostly reserves for gallery installations into modes of daily utility for the sound collector.

The term "telharmonics" pays homage to one of the grandest failures in the history of electronic music: Thaddeus Cahill's early network synthesizer, the telharmonium, which for a brief while around the turn of the previous century transmitted its electric tones over telephone cables to receivers scattered around New York City.[10] Massive dynamos located in the basement of Cahill's New York Electric Music Company generated current at various frequencies, each pitch controlled by a corresponding key on twin keyboards. The telharmonium players mixed multiple wave forms to produce apparently stunning recreations of instrumental voices as well as new, unearthly tones. Without any existent recordings of the instrument and very little remaining documentation, what the telharmonium actually sounded like is left to the imagination. In the only published review of the telharmonium that I have come across—Thomas Commerford Martin's article "The Telharmonium: Electricity's Alliance with Music"—its tones are said to be "of unprecedented clearness, sweetness, and purity" (1906). And yet the quality of the sound itself impresses the reviewer hardly as much as Cahill's unique delivery mechanism. Something like a telephone operator's switching station transmitted the same electric signals to any number of locations at one time. These signals were enjoyed over hand-held telephone receivers, often connected to modified gramophone horns. Even the telharmonium players had to monitor their performances by patching a line back to a local receiver. In Commerford Martin's analysis, Cahill had perfected "a distinct new art that may well be spoken of as telephone's firstborn," a pipe organ that plays not on air but "upon the current," for an audience potentially distributed across all of New York (1906). For Commerford Martin, the "many fundamental and revolutionary ideas embodied in the invention" boil down to a new model of public utility that "gives everybody cheaply, and everywhere, more music than they ever had before":

> Electricity has been the greatest centralizing, unifying force these hundred years, and the "tie that binds" is distinctively made of wire. The art of telharmony pushes one degree further the dominant principle of current-production embodied in the telegraph office, the telephone exchange, the electric-light plant, and the trolley power-house; and it emphasizes just a little bit more the practice of drawing out from the circuit, at the point of consumption, just what is needed for intelligence, communication, illumination, heat, traction, and what not. (1906)

Commerford Martin expresses no doubts that people will be willing to pay for the service. He even sees the service as eclipsing the need for consumers to purchase goods like sheet music and gramophone records. Why bother, when they can enjoy continuous streams of new content, performed by the best keyboard players New York has to offer, over their phone lines and in the comfort of home or favorite dining hall? Subscription-based art, for Commerford Martin, funds the alliance of electricity and music, Cahill's functional-sounding "New York Electric Music Company" suggesting a new model of public utility company that automated civic harmony through the tones of a "beautiful music . . . dispensed everywhere for any one who cares to throw the switch" (1906).

## The Social Pulse of Telharmonics

By drawing the infrastructure of the telephone industry directly into the tasks of musical instrument design, Cahill constructed an aestheticized network architecture that Commerford Martin characterizes in terms of its "telharmony" (1906). The anticipated unity enacted through telharmonic production strikes Commerford Martin as a kind of artistic apotheosis of the functional aspects of a newly networked culture. The scope of the telharmonic effect is at once sonic, aesthetic, and civic. Telharmonic technology begins by "abolishing every musical instrument, from the jew's-harp to the cello," then synthesizes an entire orchestra under the control of a single machine (1906). This movement toward centralized control is counterbalanced by what Commerford Martin enthusiastically calls "a pure democracy of musical electrical waves" (1906). Describing a telharmonic spectrum between poles of centralized control and democratic distribution, Commerford Martin projected that the telharmonium would have several impacts on society. I have already mentioned his brief extrapolation regarding the impact of networked sound on the recording industry. He also thought that the instrument would alter the range of professional opportunities for aspiring musicians. "In the future," he speculates, these young men "will not earn their living by occasional appearances in isolated halls, but as central-station operators, probably in obscurity and seclusion, but charming a whole cityful at the same instant" (1906). Musicians become technicians in telharmonic environments. Commerford Martin thought it no great loss that people might not gather in concert halls to hear some local hack. Rather, he viewed fading traditions and the disenchantment of spaces for communal listening as insignificant in light of the primary advantage gained by the one-to-many dynamic of telharmonic transmission: performances by the best players were available to anyone on the network. Going further into the particular details of Commerford Martin's review is not necessary at this time. Rather, what I want to bring out of Commerford Martin's analysis is his unique synthesis of critical discussions about instrument design, communications networking, and musical production.

Telharmonics provides a way for us to think through the interaction of the artistic, technological, and social impacts of new modes for delivering aesthetic objects and events. Eventually, I will address telharmonics involving communicative interaction among multiple, distributed participants. For now, however, I am concerned with a more basic telematic mode, that between individual artist/performer/participant and the store of media content accessible through a digital audio-filing network. This does not mean that webmixing lacks a communicative exchange. Having exercised a telematic relationship with the data space of networked audio resources, the webmixer returns the telharmonic art object—the recorded webmix—to the network. Releasing the webmix in an Internet-friendly format is an attempt to complete the loop of virtual contact in the telematic embrace that Ascott describes, gifting a new ornamental figure of Internet-based sound back to itself, and so adding another source to another potential mix.

## The Extent of the Database

There are numerous indispensable portals for the web DJ, such as the sound search engine FindSounds, which readily pulls up sound effects and sampled or synthesized instrument voices.[11] The Ubu web archive collects vintage sound poetry, avant-garde performances, radio art, and more.[12] And the Soundtoys project features a frequently updated roster of interactive devices, sound-paintings, and generative compositions.[13] Being networked into computer music culture is its own resource for the webmixer. The Microsound list, for instance, connects composers of quirky digital music around the world through a network of aesthetic discussions, collaborative projects, and press releases devoted to new works and upcoming performances. In "The Resonance of the Cubicle: Laptop Performance in Post-digital Musics," Tad Turner (2003) characterizes the Internet as the most important "cultural catalyst" for the composers and audience of new computer music, two categorical distinctions that the webmixer actually blurs through a kind of performative listening. Turner points to the magnitude of content that can be gathered from the Microsound list alone, which averages 700 posts a month:

> I recently collected 445 website links from three months of Microsound e-mail. Exploring a portion of these links in a single evening enabled me to download 253 compositions, for over eighteen hours of listening. These are not mp3 files that have been "ripped" from commercially offered CDs, but are offered freely by their composers or their representatives. (2003, 84)

Finally, perhaps serving a function analogous to the turntablist's limited releases and white-label rarities, obscure Internet content is particularly prized to the webmixer, such as the now-defunct "TwoFiveSix webPlayer," a Shockwave device that processed HTML tags through a generative music algorithm, thus converting web pages into scores for minimal ambient pieces.

## Information Aesthetics: Access and Process

I have already described the webmix in terms of aesthetics, but it remains to be seen to what extent the telharmonic action of the webmixer involves what Lev Manovich has called the "aesthetics of information access as well as the creation of new media objects that 'aestheticize' information processing" (2001, 217). The "info-aesthetics" of em.chia and my pharmakon.t project bring a turntablist's approach to the web by turning browsers into decks and remediating the DJ's crate of records into a folder of URLs pointing to mp3 files, streaming audio and video clips, interactive works, and animations. The performance of access through the sonified memex mixing desk embodies what Manovich describes as the "new logic" of digital culture, the "selection and combination of preexistent elements" from menus and databases (2001, 135). For Manovich, the DJ is the primary embodiment of this cultural logic. Manovich points out that even while the computerized database altered or eclipsed our understanding of other, somewhat outworn, tropes for material information storage—the library or art gallery—the DJ suddenly becomes a ubiquitous fixture at any hip book signing or opening. The DJ emerges in response to a crisis in the social imaginary, as previous cultural forms begin to lose their relevancy to our current, digitally networked situation. The DJ thus appears to function symptomatically as an iconic form for database cultures coming to grips with the transformations brought on by computerized media and telematic systems. Like the memex-using researcher, the DJ is adapted to associative thinking, performing what Manovich calls a "conceptual transfer" across media sources, documenting trails and links among them. The DJ becomes, in short, a navigational aid.

## Pharmakon.t and the Temporal Status of the Net

In the set of three pharmakon.t recordings released in 2003 on the DJ Rabbi site, at least five sources play at any given time, often for fairly extended periods of time but with rapid sequences of transitions across several layers of files. Because each webmix is a live performance using sources embedded into, or launched directly from, browser windows—and not files downloaded ahead of time—the mix documents the state of sound on the web at a particular time. But more audible registers of telharmonics are products of the unique variables of Internet traffic and desktop sound processing. Running multiple audio players, or even multiple instances of the same application, causes files to compete both for adequate bandwidth and CPU priorities. As multiple audio resources task bandwidth percentages, media players find it harder to maintain their buffers, which are usually around 30 seconds of an audio file preloaded into temporary storage before the player begins transmitting sound. Buffer overruns result in audible skips and disruptions while the software rebuilds its virtual leader of streamed content. Favoring a crude, digital variation of the turntablist's record scratching, my pharmakon.t projects use enough sources to push the limits of buffering and so create harsh, glitchy, minimalist works that bear little resemblance to their source materials. Content delivery is also uniquely shaped by the particular route that information requests and data packets must travel, as well as by packet delays and transmission errors. It is in moments of buffer failure and competing application errors that we hear the data space stutter into shape as an artistic artifact.

## Chronotope

The object of our current info-aesthetics—the webmix—becomes clearer when we turn to Mikhail Bakhtin's concept of the "chronotope" (1981). For Bakhtin, the term emphasizes a form of imaginative organization in, literally, "time-space." In works of art, the imagination of living history temporarily congeals into chronotopic artifacts. Bakhtin's chronotope points to "the intrinsic connectedness of temporal and spatial relationships," which in artistic productions "are fused into one carefully thought-out, concrete whole. Time, as it were, thickens, takes on flesh, becomes artistically visible; likewise, space becomes charged and responsive to the movements of time, plot and history" (1981, 84). I would like to suggest that Bakhtin's chronotope is the aestheticized vehicle for Manovich's conceptual transfer through cultural forms and media. Ultimately acting across very different layers of human experience, the chronotope links the interior space of dreams and symbolic imagination to historical space.

## Em.chia and History

Em.chia's webmix, "metaxalogical mo(u)rning methods," responds to Stasis_Space curator John Kannenberg's call for works that might provide future artists with the first layer of an ongoing palimpsest. The palimpsest is a unique and multilayered document, a manuscript surface that has been used more than once and with the layers of earlier writing only partly erased. The palimpsest situates history across virtual stacks of legibility. Kannenberg turns palimpsest-construction into an intentional aesthetic strategy for networked digital media, as well as a novel approach to gallery exhibition given telematic conditions. Kannenberg proposes multiple projects constructed over time through cycles of erasure and inclusion from previously featured contributions. Sequential generations of web-based artists would rebuild from each other's prior productions, all exclusively accessed through the gallery's website. Though Kannenberg did not provide content restrictions to submissions for the "Palimpsest Project," he notes in the exhibition catalog that some common themes emerged from the foundational layer of submitted works: "a respect for history, the acquisition and storage of knowledge, entropy and the passage of time" (2002). In his own statement for the exhibition catalog, em.chia describes how he explores the distributed environments of the World Wide Web by using the browser as both delivery mechanism and performance instrument. Using an array of browser plug-ins as live DJ tools, and turning directly to the ethereal bitstream of webcasts and embedded sound files for his sources he maps the terrain of the web as a unique space existing only temporarily in the form of connections and referential relationships. (2002)

Em.chia's webmix is the only work in the initial exhibition to treat the Internet itself as the (non)foundation for ongoing artistic explorations of reuse and reinterpretation, constructing what Kannenberg characterizes as "a self-contained history of the world wide web, a starting point for future explorations of internet history" (2002). By throwing the terms of the exhibition back on themselves, em.chia's work suggests that there is no prior, singular layer of creative instigation but rather a distribution of multiple influential sources that combine into new and temporary hybrids through the filter of the artist. The historical charge of the chronotope is thus manufactured, the by-product of a particular act of access. Performance tweaks the chronotope, plays with duration, and meddles with juxtaposition so that patterns of micro-associations form across a portion of the telematic network, intensifying its present manifestation in a set of referential connections while at the same time representing the otherwise impossible-to-imagine totality of the Internet.

## Détourntablism vs. The Media Deconstruction Kit, Part 1

In a 1956 publication of the early Situationist International, Guy Debord and Gil Wolman define détournement in ways that bridge the eras of high modernist collage to those of DJ culture:

Any elements, no matter where they are taken from, can be used to make new combinations. The discoveries of modern poetry regarding the analogical structure of images demonstrate that when two objects are brought together, no matter how far apart their original contexts may be, a relationship is always formed. Restricting oneself to a personal arrangement of words is mere convention. The mutual interference of two worlds of feeling, or the bringing together of two independent expressions, supersedes the original elements and produces a synthetic organization of greater efficacy. (1956)

A combatant form of fragments set against the false cultural totality of what Debord labeled "the society of the spectacle," détournement is a palimpsest-based reworking that treats the media objects of the spectacle as sources for partial erasure and reuse, typically transforming cinema, broadcast television, home movies, newspaper ads, and comic strips into vehicles for propaganda and social theory. In practice, détournement emphasizes appropriation through overdubbing. During the frenzy of mimeographed posters, broadsides and newspapers of May '68, the Situationists let their manifestos and rants occupy the dialog boxes of the Lone Ranger and Tonto or replace the thought balloons of star-crossed lovers from a romance comic. Debord frequently resequenced popular movies, television news coverage, commercials, soft porn, and more, splicing the variety of visual passages into a new piece. These cut up, remixed movies became the anti-spectacular vehicles for Debord's critical and philosophical works, text delivered in voiceover on the film's soundtrack. At this point, I like to splice in turntablism and its digital doubles to get at the performative potential of détournement. Over the past 10 years or so, the live DJ has become almost inseparable from its visual double, the video jockey, or VJ, who typically uses a laptop computer loaded with mixing software and video clips to reprocess much the same kind of footage as Debord. Both DJ and VJ practice a form of live détournement, facilitating sonic and visual detours through the archives of the cultural record. Foregrounding the performative mode of remixing recorded objects, "détourntablism" is about performing Manovichian conceptual transfers across mediating objects, synthesizing chronotopic palimpsests for delivery to, and further mixing by, other memex players. Détourntablism plays with the way in which history enters an ongoing artistic practice and, simultaneously, the art becomes work, a mode of sense-production with a material presence capable of influencing the steady flow of historical time. Situationists linked this critical reprocessing of mass media objects to the practice of political and social resistance. Our webmixing détourntablists follow suit.

## Détourntablism vs. The Media Deconstruction Kit, Part 2

The recent work of Randall Packer and various associates exemplifies the new mode of détourntablism through performances of live digital signal mixing and reprocessing that transform cable news broadcasts into artsy propaganda. In fall 2003, Packer launched his faux branch of government, the U.S. Department of Art and Technology (US-DAT)—and its attendant, grassroots movement, the Experimental Party—to provide a running artistic commentary on American politics.[14] Taking on the corporate control of the mass media, Packer and Wesley Smith's "Media Deconstruction Kit" (MDK) offers détourned news coverage of election year events. Often supplied with recordings of Packer's US-DAT speeches and proclamations, the MDK project sought to expand telematic consciousness through the live reconstruction of networked media channels for delivery over the web in the form of streaming Quicktime movies. The project initially promised a critical contrast to the manufactured diversity of FCC-governed, commercial newscasting. Production of ongoing trails of association across different channels of network news would potentially delve into the common corporate-underwriting of American experience. But as it turned out, the MDK project concentrated solely on the Fox network. The MDK purported "to appropriate with magisterial fearlessness, transforming Fox News into magical images, and bring about the systematic reordering of the senses through the deconstruction of live, broadcast media" (Packer 2004). However, the MDK was subsumed within the partisan politics of network newscasting. With the MDK pitted solely against Fox News, we experience a détourntablist with only one record, an effects processor, and a microphone. This move mistakes the reprocessing of network news broadcasts into glitchy, pixellated abstractions for the provision of a newly politicized discourse that might critique the manufacture of democratic forms and the corporate control of telematic participation. The multi-sourced, associative impulse of the memex-generated chronotope could then utilize conceptual detours into unexpected lines of association as a force for social change. But the MDK is ultimately unable to fulfill its pledge "to swamp the mass media with total illusion" because its productions are intensely partial—even in opposition—to a single channel (Packer 2004). The MDK is absorbed into merely dialectical conflict with one specific, manufactured mediation of an audience's consciousness of the social condition of lived experience. And so the project fails to provide a method for navigating the multitude of spectacular choices that stand between the individual producer and his or her experience of history through ongoing imaginative construction.

## The Internet Download Sound of Galactus Zeit: Communication as Consumption

The MDK is silenced into a state of "mouth-full" consumption, its ironic (re)producers tuned religiously to the same channel as any non-ironic consumer, and to little different effect. The MDK's Fox remixes fail to circulate back to their network of origin but are rather diverted into live performances and web-based movies with little to no chance of confronting either a purportedly "typical" Fox News consumer or the network's representatives. The MDK thus loses its efficacy as a critical communications tool and becomes entrenched in spectacular opposition within a unilateral network of transmitters posing as the entirety of the system of confrontation. In his sobering account of media's tendency to hinder social transformation, 1972's "Requiem for the Media," Jean Baudrillard (2003) discusses the collapse of communication into a closed loop, a systemic failure that he characterizes in terms of information consumption. There is no exchange in consumption, and when communication transforms into the digestion of media objects, social life ceases. Baudrillard contends that media serve a primarily social function, which is the reduction of their living counterparts—every media form is a replacement of a person—to ineffectual, reactive subjects with no means of reciprocal exchange. Without reciprocity in communication, there can be neither antagonism nor ambivalence, only consumption: "The generalized order of consumption is nothing other than that sphere where it is no longer permitted to give, to reimburse, or to exchange, but only to take and to make use of (appropriation, individualized use value)"

(2003, 281). I have treated information consumption as a communicative disorder in a series of networked audio performances at the University of Denver and Denver's Museum of Contemporary Art. In "Internet Download Sound," the search engine becomes an aleatory compositional device for acts of sonic information consumption. Sequences of keywords cued to an event's theme are fed into Internet search engines, where they churn out unpreviewed, frequently very random, audio content that is downloaded throughout the performance and added to the live mix without prior monitoring. Downloaded files and incoming streams are filtered through a granular synthesizer. At first, looping sequences derived from this mixture form abstract sonic textures, cascading sheets of noise, minimal melodic phrases, and short slices of recognizable spoken word. The granular processor then shreds this emerging soundscape into micro-tonal bursts, clicks, and static before silencing them altogether. The challenge in the "Internet Download Sound" series is to remain open to fortuitous accidents of random juxtaposition while using file-processing software that essentially eats away at the performance. This project is performed under the name of Galactus Zeit, drawing on the pop-iconography of Marvel Comics' intergalactic titan, who ranges across the spaceways to sustain his appetite for entire planetary ecosystems. As a meditation on the end of exchange, the hunger of Galactus becomes a metaphor expressing the global telematic network in distress.

At this point, I hope to have established some of the various ways in which an individual artist or performer might fashion a unique telharmonic object or experience out of the networked database of sonic resources. The works of em.chia, my pharmakon.t project, Packer's Media Deconstruction Kit, and the Galactus Zeit shows all adopt live détourntablist strategies for performing network connectivity. Each project highlights the telematic relationship between an individual webmixer and the networked collection of media sources. We are now going to look at a set of works that in some way modify this basic pairing. As communication strategies mingle with media technology systems in new, stylized arrays—and so embody the variety of telharmonic aesthetics taking shape in the chronotopic matrices of information access—they embed social relationships into new cultural forms. In the next three works, automation as well as experiments with new modes of performance, interactive installation, and distribution prompt us to reconsider the social function of consumption, reintroducing the possibility for gifting, exchange, and play within networked collectives.

## Automated Webmixes

In *The Language of New Media*, Lev Manovich explains that one of the principle features brought to media through computerization is "the automation of many operations involved in media creation, manipulation, and access" (2001,

32). Without a doubt, automation appears to be one strand of development along which any given cultural form may emerge, including webmixing. In fact, so pervasive is the role of automatic function in personal computing that it is difficult to imagine any of the previously discussed webmixes taking place without some automated phase of file searching and downloading, playback, and recording. In my own webmixes, I have incorporated such automatic constraints as file buffering and search engine indices as generative devices. But the extent of automation can be more pervasive, with computer programming controlling every phase of the webmixing process, as we will see in the next two projects. First, Peter M. Traub's "Bits and Pieces" (1999) features a self-sustaining, electro-acoustic composition in the form of "a sonic installation for the World Wide Web."[15] Second, Andi Freeman and Jason Skeet's <earshot> (2002) situates webmixing in terms of "hybrid software engineering" and virtual instrument development.[16] Both projects automate the tasks of content gathering, audio-file mixing and processing, and finally, the preparation of new audio files for transmitted output. While similar in their approach to the network of sounds on the web, each work poses distinct consequences that stem from the programming of social function into cultural forms.

## Bits and Pieces

In the thesis accompanying the "Bits and Pieces" installation, Peter Traub claims numerous aesthetic precedents but few technical ones. Traub's project automates the basic strategies of webmixing, removing the entire process away from performance settings and into the virtual space of a self-sufficient installation accessed only through Internet protocols. Traub considers "the use of audio sources from the Web" to be the "primary new concept behind the piece" (1999). Traub's work automatizes the processes of a "search and retrieval" engine, a sample-based synthesizer, and an audio encoder that prepares files for Internet streaming. The "Bits and Pieces" search engine merges the functions of two scripts written in the PERL programming language.[17] These scripts allow Traub's computer to make network connections, download web pages, parse HTML, and download audio files. Using PERL's AutoSearch script, the "Bits and Pieces" search and retrieval process begins with a random selection from a menu of major Internet search engines and an array of generic query terms like "music," "sounds," and "wav files." The search results are gathered into a single web page with a menu of hyperlinks to pages containing their own links to audio files. A PERL subroutine parses this HTML file to extract hyperlinks, download each of these pages, and parse them again for the actual audio files. Files falling within certain size and format limitations are then downloaded into a local folder, converted into a common file format for use in the sound synthesis program, and checked for errors. All files that make their way successfully through this process are exported to a directory from which yet another PERL script—what Traub calls "the sound production script"—randomly selects audio files and loads them into the sound synthesis program, Csound. The Csound script creates a musical score for playing the downloaded files. First, it fragments the audio files into smaller events called "notes." The script then inserts spaces between sequences of notes and records the duration of these gaps into the score. Csound also changes the pitch of particular notes, as well as supplies amplitude envelopes to adjust the attack and decay of notes. The output of this score is saved as a new audio file, which in turn is encoded into the RealAudio format and transferred to a web server. There it joins a queue of the 10 most recent products of the "Bits and Pieces" scripts. Traub situates his installation in the historical and aesthetic contexts of collage and indeterminate art. Especially important are John Cage's spontaneous audio pieces generated through the manipulation of radio volumes and tunings, such as "Imaginary Landscape No. 4" (1951) and "Radio Music" (1956). Again revealing the ubiquitous affiliation between DJ mixing and an emerging digital poetics, the concept behind "Bits and Pieces" apparently evolved while Traub performed a number of experimental DJ sets incorporating Cage's recorded works and techniques, the

> layering further add[ing] to the unpredictability of his works. In "Imaginary Landscape No. 4" and "Radio Music," completely unrelated sounds converge to occur close to each other, creating new and surprising sonic experiences. It is this idea that led me to create processes in "Bits and Pieces" based on randomly selected samples. As the samples are mixed and cut up, they create a sound collage that at times produces meaningful juxtapositions of sonic material. (1999)

But significant differences between Traub's project and Cage's radio compositions reveal a unique info-aesthetic of the automated webmix. Unlike Cage's work, "Bits and Pieces" is specific neither to physical location nor to the timing of specific broadcast events, both key features of the variability of Cage's compositions, in which performance spatialized a unique zone of radio broadcast at a particular time. The audio sources used in "Bits and Pieces" are globally distributed for access at any time. But they are also subject to a different degree of ephemerality than Cage's radio signals. The variability of the web is that of server access, file deletion, file corruption, and other forms of broken linkage. As he accommodates Cage's approach to radio for the telematic network, Traub finds that his interest in collaged forms capable of artistically documenting the web is not unique. He describes his work as a sonic variation of visual web-based collage and cites points of comparison like Amy Alexander's "Multi-Cultural Recycler," essentially a webcam mixer.[18] Drawing on the themes raised by Alexander's work, Traub claims that "Bits and Pieces" circulates similar issues of voyeurism and exhibitionism. He argues that the webmixes created by "Bits and Pieces" are most compelling when derived from the "highly personal aspect of themselves" that some people will commit to the network in the form of digital documentation. Traub writes a couple of years before a blooming of sound-rich sites like mp3 labels of all flavors, the massive collection of files found at the Internet Archive,[19] and audio-blogs such as the beautiful, sonic diary project of Tyler Potts, "52 Songs."[20] And yet even in the late '90s, people routinely sonified themselves on the web by posting links to their own music, other people's music, soundtrack snippets from TV and film, and so forth. Traub's program documents this collective soundscape with an intriguing twist:

> Listeners may hear the ten most recent works in the order that the installation has produced them. Each time a new piece is added, the oldest piece is erased. In this sense, "Bits and Pieces," like most everything else on the Web, is in a constant state of flux. Its pieces, like so much music and art today, are ephemeral. They are not intended to have lasting power, but rather to come into being for a short time, perhaps never to be heard, and finally disappear from history without a trace. (1999)

Automating the manner in which data vanishes, Traub puts information consumption in the service of the unique "ephemerality" of web storage.

## Communication as Monopoly

Periodically passing through stages of content gathering, fragmentation, reconstruction, and erasure, "Bits and Pieces" is one of the loneliest sites on the Internet. I imagine its streams providing a fitting soundtrack for the solitary robot mindlessly wandering the dying space-terrarium in the Bruce Dern vehicle *Silent Running*, an image of programmed tasks accumulating in the cosmic void, with Galactus on the nod. Returning us to Baudrillard's concept of information consumption, Traub locates the death of communicative exchange, what Baudrillard labels the "monopoly of speech. It cannot simply be interrupted, congealed, stockpiled, and redistributed in some corner of the social process" (2003, 281). The information aesthetic of "Bits and Pieces" presents us with the paradoxical tendencies of distributed communication in telematic networks. The installation celebrates a fragmentation of the collective audio archive. Sounds are ripped from context, stripped of file name, and rendered free of their original authorial control. The installation automates control over every active phase of an individual's relationship with recorded sound objects, even their ultimate discarding, which negates the individual's desire to assign aesthetic value to particular webmixes by saving them from erasure and storing them in a growing archive. Instead, registering the vacuum at the heart of Baudrillard's "Requiem," "Bits and Pieces" monopolizes the webmixing impulse through the self-sustaining action of a digital palimpsest, its archive management system an exercise in information consumption that insures the lasting ephemerality of Traub's project.

Traub's "Bits and Pieces" installs the programmatic end of the road for telharmonics. Episodes of fragmentation, remixing, and erasure appear to preclude communicative exchange and response within a space monopolized by a singular script capable of automating every point at which an individual may enjoy a telematic relationship to the cultural store of sound objects on the web. Actually, new possibilities open up once cultural forms such as the webmix begin to generate their automatic doubles. In this case, nothing precludes the output of the automated webmixer from being drawn into an ongoing live mix. We can easily imagine the web page hosting the "Bits and Pieces" installation being incorporated into a webmix—indeed, I have done just that in my own performances. But more compelling would be to consider automation as a way to develop more complex webmixing tools or instruments in their own right. This is precisely the direction in which network sound programmers Andi Freeman and Jason Skeet have taken their own automated webmixer, <earshot>, "a tool that transforms the web into the world's largest sound library" (2002). Beta-stage launches of <earshot> began in the late '90s with an Internet search-and-retrieval script not unlike Traub's own but this time scripted in Java. Freeman and Skeet themselves were the primary users of <earshot> at that time, presenting their webmixes in contexts that appear to have been equal parts experimental audio performance and software demonstration. As the project developed over a four-year period, however, Freeman and Skeet built a complex user interface that now provides numerous points of interaction. A performer uses <earshot> to explore the web for sound files by typing URLs or keywords into the instrument's "Noizeprobe." This sets up a potentially endless chain of searches as the engine follows links between web pages on its own accord. The Noizeprobe downloads the files it finds into <earshot>'s directory, the "Audio Spike." The performer may then manually load up to nine files at a time in the player's "Audio Field." Here, a sequencing blip positions each sound file in a shared field. Moving a blip within the field controls the volume and pitch settings of the corresponding file. Freeman and Skeet call <earshot> "a non-linear composition tool," and their application avoids the tropes of traditional music sequencing software like tempo and time change signatures. Files range freely across the Audio Field, where the graphic representation encourages the creation of "various acoustic spaces according to their relationship to each other" (Freeman and Skeet 2002). Emphasizing the juxtaposition of sound sources in the Audio Field situates <earshot> in the same compositional territory as em.chia's sound map, "a unique space existing only temporarily in the form of connections and referential relationships" (Freeman and Skeet 2002). The latest release of the <earshot> application gives the performer control over many more parameters than spatial positioning, including the looping, muting, reversing, and rewinding of files. Also, <earshot> provides opportunities for chance composition. A single control can cause the functions for file search, download, arrangement, and manipulation to run automatically. The design and programming of such robust webmixing software turns the cultural forms we looked at earlier into what Manovich calls a "cultural interface," a telematic zone "in which computers present and allow us to interact with cultural data" (2001, 70). Following Manovich's trajectory from form to interface, the <earshot> instrument tracks the detour of the webmixer into self-managing software applications at work in the database of networked sounds. As a meditation on erasure and loss, "Bits and Pieces" encodes moments of anxiety over the loss of previous systems for information storage and retrieval. But once developed into a complex instrument, the automatic webmixer scripts modes of practice into computerized interfaces as a way to enhance our ability to access and manipulate media artifacts in their new storage formats. Freeman and Skeet use automation as a way to deepen the imaginative processes embedded in the relationship between individual performer and the sound archive. Cultural interfaces emerge already embedded in cultural practice—in the case of <earshot>, the apparently requisite context of gallery-based DJ sets. The audio archives on the <earshot> website document a series of early software demos, as well as a number of more recent compositions submitted by a small community of <earshot> webmixers. Sets are scored in a minimal notation of URLs, such as the artist Sampler Resistance's "WWWEye," "featuring sounds captured from policescanner.com and jara.demon.co.uk," or Aphasic's "Sound America," with reprocessed "sounds grabbed from soundamerica.com" (Kannenberg 2002). Works by such <earshot> devotees lend credence to Freeman and Skeet's claim that "audio software can be seen as a musical instrument in its own right" (Freeman and Skeet 2002). This simple pronouncement yields surprisingly contentious arguments among producers of digital music, many of whom express a deep discomfort over the ability of complex software to challenge our notions of authorship, originality, and composition. Many traditional concepts of music begin to falter when artists bring user interface design, interactivity, and screen-based editing into the mix.[21] This debate lies beyond the scope of the current work, so I will cut to the chase. Through automation, the compositional interface becomes a space of performance in its own right. In <earshot>, this is a place of telharmonic eventfulness and not a dead-end at all.

## Constellations

The conditions of information access, distribution, reception, and use engrained in our daily relationship to Internet media take an imaginative line of flight when reprocessed as performance rather than an entirely automatic function. Atua Tanaka's "Constellation," a "network music installation," follows simultaneous lines into the gallery, the network, and the cosmos.[22] Premiering in October 1999 during the Experimental Design Festival in Lisbon, Portugal, Tanaka's work provides visitors with a custom webmixing interface installed on several computer kiosks distributed throughout the gallery. The screen depicts an interplanetary arrangement, the user a disembodied vantage floating through outer space. Each of the brightly colored planets that gradually expand into the field of vision embeds a link to a streaming audio file, each one located on a different server on the network. Clicking on a planet launches a contribution from numerous composers of minimal, spatial music, including Shunichiro Okada and Kim Cascone. Works range in length from ten seconds to two minutes. With a planet's size on the screen equating to its volume in the mix, the media interface allows the player to combine multiple audio streams by navigating through the celestial field. The resulting webmix on each computer station is then broadcast into the gallery on its own sound system. So local physical space forms patterns with remote data space through the imaginative figure of outer space:

> The work in this case was not to present the music of one person, but to create a situation—where the sounds of many different artists are heard, piped into context, from general space to specific space. The visitors bring the process to term by creating the mix. (Tanaka 1999)

Tanaka is doing chronotope design here, blurring distinctions "between the actual world as a source of representation and the world represented in the work" (Bakhtin 1981, 253). The resulting chronotope charges the gallery with the force of juxtapositions now operating across very dramatic scales of experience. Using an interface more like a video game than a musical instrument—as well as taking more literally than Freeman and Skeet the emphasis on spatialization as a metaphor for sound mixing—"Constellations" is performed by an audience with little prior experience necessary to begin mixing sound sources. The navigational metaphor is immediately familiar, and the results of such telharmonic flights are almost instantly gratifying. Exhibit patrons become ambience engineers, tracing planetary trails as a way to construct patterns out of the microelements of each computer station as well as from macroelements broadcast into the shared acoustic space. To participate in the creation and maintenance of a shared chronotope fashioned from telharmonic broadcasts is to get a powerful sense of emergence. What emerges is not only an exercise in formal juxtaposition but also a realization of multidimensional polyvocality. Truer to the spirit of the telematic embrace discussed by Roy Ascott, Tanaka's project is "a reflection in sound of human modalities facilitated by the net" (Tanaka 1999). By replicating a simple interface across multiple computers, and by narrowing the scope of available sound resources into a curated set of works by complementary composers of digital music, "Constellations" reveals the collaborative possibilities of many distributed but overlapping telharmonic networks.

## Polycentric Streams

"Constellations" prompts reconsideration of the scale of sound database, the role of interface, and the nature of performance involved in the webmix. Using the computer's formal interface to communicate with others through sonified data clusters, mutual webmixers fashion a kind of cultural chronotope, a shared situation or happening. These collective chronotopes form during the webmixers' immersion into the imaginal field of an exteriorized mediascape, the content and data of which can be directly manipulated, juxtaposed, and rearranged. I am spinning the work of psychologist James Hillman (1975) here into a kind of Jungian media theory that views the telematic network as a vast, technological Dreamtime. Hillman depicts psychological nature as an imaginative landscape "that is no longer single-centered but polycentric" (1975, 24). Hillman suggests ways of thinking about being in imagination—what he calls "a self-sustaining and imagining substrate" of raw psychic images—as a way of thinking about being in media. Being in imagination hardly differs from being in media, after all, for in both images are "the basic givens of psychic life, self-originating, inventive, spontaneous, complete, and organized into archetypal patterns" (1975, xvii). Hillman pushes the term "image" in ways that resist its visual bias and suggest an arrangement of parts, emotions, and experiences into a meaningful construct of multiple senses—in other words, what we have been calling a chronotope. Telharmonics sonify the chronotope and avoid the sublimating aspects of the image altogether. Polycentric personalities achieve distributed modes of expressing, and participating in, manufactured experiences like "Constellations." What I take from Tanaka's work, then, is the possibility for the telematic space of the network to take shape as an imaginary form manifested through the play of multiple participants.

The polycentric-interface design of Tanaka's "Constellations" reinforces collective cultural space through traditions of broadcast technologies and telephony. In the shared gallery space of Tanaka's work, ambience becomes the social responsibility of the participants. The Canadian team of architect Thomas McIntosh and composer Emmanuel Madan—collectively known as [The User]—have likewise found compelling ways to incorporate a telematic network into collectively managed space, this time in the form of a sound-processing device known as "The Silophone." Literally a telharmonic plug-in of immense proportions that reclaimed a Montreal landmark in summer 2000, "The Silophone" blends physical installation design, telematic net.art, architectural preservation, and communication technologies.[23] Located in the city's old port and abandoned in 1996, the repurposed silo has now become famous for its extended reverb. With a telephone and computer both connected to speakers and situated inside the silo, [The User] provides participants with access to this communication system:

> Sounds arrive inside Silo #5 by telephone or Internet. They are then broadcast into the vast concrete grain storage chambers inside the Silo. They are transformed, reverberated, and coloured by the remarkable acoustics of the structure, yielding a stunningly beautiful echo. This sound is captured by microphones and

rebroadcast back to its sender, to other listeners and to a sound installation out-side the building. Anyone may contribute material of their own, filling the instrument with increasingly varied sounds. ([The User] 2000)

Reverb may prove to be the chronotopic effect of choice, featuring the modification and maintenance of spatialized patterns of sound. Space takes shape through the overlapping, intermingling layers of sound, "becomes charged and responsive to the movements of time," as Bakhtin writes (1981, 84). I am inclined to treat "The Silophone" as a telharmonic chronotope gener-ator that, like the acoustically rich space of Tanaka's installation, facilitates the intertwining of telematic networks and shared physical spaces. The apparently closed space of the silo becomes an open zone on the telematic network, a place where potentially anyone can upload sound files or record voice-mail messages. But whereas Tanaka's work stresses the ephemerality of live performance and real-time communication, "The Silophone" is more about the technologies of information storage. In this project, [The User] explores the functioning of chronotopes as vehicles for cultural memory by patching the telematic network back into civic tasks such as landmark preservation and data archiving. But buf-feted by signal-distorting reverberations, cultural memories are actually estranged in telematic conditions, becoming authorless in the face of collective manipulation by the generic user now tasked with the responsibility of social chronotopic management.

We began by considering a number of works in which the webmix desig-nated the creative production of an individual performer drawing on the collec-tive database of sound objects on the Internet. The emerging cultural form of the web DJ was paralleled by developments of automated applications that did the same thing. Automation prompted new modes of net.art sound installation and performance software, as well as new possibilities for interaction and collabora-tive play among multiple networked participants. Tanaka's work is the strongest indicator yet of the possibilities of distributed network performances, while [The User]'s project establishes an important model by which users from multiple locations share the maintenance of a storage server's audio content and so save a civic landmark from disuse and demolition. But even in the imaginatively charged spaces of "Constellations" and "The Silophone," participants experi-ence unilateral telharmonics. In "Constellations," webmixing works according to a broadcast model that automates procedures for importing telematic space into living space. But outer space offers no chance for response. "The Silophone" includes some possibilities for telematic interaction, and yet the reverberating mnemonics of the project distribute communicative gestures across extended periods of time, among participants who are not necessarily using the network to facilitate exchanges in real time.

I now conclude with a quick survey of recent works and events exploring the possibilities of multidirectional, synchronized, networked mixes. A complex social design takes shape through coordinated live streams, networked jam ses-sions, distributed remixes, and massive, international, Internet radio festivals. In all of these cases, the telematic network facilitates interaction with multiple data streams in real-time performance.

## Multitrack Collaboration and Ping Art

Brian Kane's "8-Track" featured interactive webcasting for multiple partici-pants, with continuous real-time performance from April 21 to May 5, 2001, as part of the Boston Cyber Arts Festival.[24] Eight sound artists, DJs, and minimal techno producers from around the world used the Internet to access a basic metronome pulse initially webcast by Kane. Using this clock for synchroniza-tion of tempo, the artists performed along to the metronome, many drawing the pulse stream into their own material directly before modifying it with audio effects. Participants streamed their work back to Kane's studio. There, Kane mixed up to eight channels of incoming audio sources, using the metronomic pulse to synchronize the multiple tracks. The output of Kane's mixer was then webcast on yet another Internet stream. The project website provided a link to the original pulse file, Kane's ongoing real-time mix, a lively chat room allow-ing participants and audience to interact with each other, and guidelines for visitors wanting to transmit their own streams to Kane. Kane describes the proj-ect as "generative, distributed music," sending a data signal around the world in order to use "the Internet as a global digital delay, thus using the net as a musi-cal instrument" (Kane 2001). Kane's description echoes numerous contexts of telharmonics already discussed, going all the way back to Cahill's own efforts to draw telephone lines into instrument design. What distinguishes Kane's own networked instrument from projects like <earshot> and "The Silophone" is his shift away from localized data gathering and modifying points. In <earshot> and "The Silophone," digital content is drawn toward a specific place, altered through the automated webmixer or reverberating interior of the silo, and then streamed back out to the network. The structure of Kane's virtual instrument is polycentric in many ways, incorporating the multiple computer stations of par-ticipating artists and, most significantly, the architecture of the Internet itself. Like all Internet files, audio files and streams are shuttled around from one Internet Protocol (IP) address to another. The Unix command "ping" transmits packets of fragmented data to selected locations on the Internet, then reports back. This command lets you monitor the route that a particular file takes, returning that data to your local point of connection. The route that a packet takes to and from a particular IP address, packet delays, and any number of transmission errors affect a packet's pinging, making it an evocative barometer of the Internet for many artists. For Kane, pinging reveals the various delays as the multiple streaming sources try to make their way back to Kane's studio. Kane thus has an opportunity to create complex polyrhythms out of the simple, pulse-based files. In Pawel Janicki's "Ping Melody" project, performed as recently as November 2004, in Basel, Switzerland, the artist transmits the performance of a solo instrumentalist or singer, digitizes the live signal, packets it up, and pings it out to the Internet as though through an effects box.[25] Janicki uses data derived from the ping command to drive a granular synthesizer and pitch tracker, command variables thus having more to do with Internet traffic than artistic intent. Janicki writes, "Temporary and unique state of all actions of Internet users has an influence on form of music composition" (Janicki 2004). Though defined by data transmission rates, ping-based works are intensely spatial, providing a sonic map of the dataspace. Janicki treats this literally in "Ping Melody," performing against a backdrop of projected maps with geographical markers noting the IP addresses of servers and colorful threads that track the routes of data transfers.

## Atlantic Waves

Visual projection of telharmonic structures provides a means for a local audience to imaginatively perceive the influence of remote forces. This has been the case in several projects discussed so far, including <earshot>, "Constellations," and "Ping Melody." Berlin's Robert Henke suggests that the projection of a software interface offers an entry point at which the audience is drawn into artistic process. Of course, projection only provides an approximate involvement, something that has led Henke to develop musical instrument interfaces for networked collaboration. Henke's "Atlantic Waves" project debuted at Montreal's Mutek 2002 festival as a cross-Atlantic, networked duet between himself, playing in Berlin under the moniker of monolake, and deadbeat (Scott Monteith), who performed in Montreal.[26] Collaborating over the Internet in real time, the performers shared the controls for a sequencer, sampler, and effects unit that Henke built in the Max/MSP programming environment. At the time of the Mutek festival, Henke and Monteith gravitated toward short percussive sounds that could be woven into intricate loops as the duo improvised a set of minimal rhythmic textures. Over the past few years, Henke's software design has moved in two directions, one a robust application for networked collaboration, the other a stripped-down version for public installation. The second variation allows for spontaneous interaction among networked participants at locations around the world. In the notes on his website, Henke describes the intricate intertwining of software interface design and musical composition: the "concept of network performance provides the bridge between club and fine arts, between computer graphics and music, between installation and improvisation" (Henke 2004). It appears that blurring lines between application programming and musical composition in telharmonic systems facilitates linkages among more than cross-Atlantic performers, prompting affiliations across numerous categories for artistic production and reception.

## Radiotopia

Considering polycentric, multidirectional projects such as "8-Track" and "Atlantic Waves," we can begin to imagine a vast proliferation of webmixers working in real time with each other, sharing interfaces of varying complexity, remixing streams on the fly, filtering digital content into a global conglomerate of sound. The Open Air Radiotopia project, part of Ars Electronica 2002, provided such a site of improvisational transmission.[27] Radiotopia consisted of three major components that, like Tanaka's "Constellations," emphasized overlapping layers of networked experience. First, the "online" component consisted of a collective database of uploaded sound files and a networked musical instrument available on the web. Second, the "on air" portion included a dense schedule of international radio productions and streaming audio. And third, the "on site" programming featured numerous live, outdoor performances. In the initial phase of the project, visitors to the Radiotopia website could upload sound files in a number of formats. Participants were encouraged to download these files to their own computers and manipulate them for use in webcasts or for later upload to the database. The project also featured a virtual four-channel webmixer into which a user could easily load files from the database, loop files, and control the basic mix by adjusting each channel's volume. Text on the Radiotopia site stressed multilingual sources, so the resulting mixes leaned toward a variety of human voices with occasional shifting undercurrents of ambient textures, electronic beats, and weird pop and folk songs. Participants had the option of saving their webmixes for upload and possible broadcast over the P.A. system in the Klangpark of Linz, Austria, where the open air events took place over the course of several days. Live performers drew the webmixes as well as the program of international webcasts into their sets—most of them not turntablists or laptop DJs, to my surprise, but guitarists, poets, and small combos. The resulting performances were generally playful, expressing not only the utopic idealism of the event's title but something that Bakhtin characterized as the fundamental force of chronotopic expression. That is, chronotopes—at least, those that were most important to Bakhtin—acted as sources of social repair, restoring "the spatial and temporal material wholeness of the world on a new, more profound and more complex level of development" (1981, 166). We have already seen how the telharmonic networks underpinning installations like "Constellations" and "The Silophone" remind us that our imaginative engagement with the world around us is a shared responsibility, one that we might even go so far as to qualify as the responsibility of response. Response is particularly difficult in the context of commercial mass media, which, according to Baudrillard,

> fabricate non-communication—this is what characterizes them, if one agrees to define communication as an exchange, as a reciprocal space of a speech and a response, and thus of a responsibility. . . . Now, the totality of the existing

architecture of the media founds itself on this latter definition: they are what always prevents response, making all processes of exchange impossible. . . . This is the real abstraction of the media. And the system of social control and power is rooted in it. (2003, 280–81)

Baudrillard offers no chance for an upheaval in this particular mode of monolithic media network, though he did hold out some hope for graffiti artists at work on the streets. He would not likely have seen the computerization of media as a viable route by which communicative response would return to media. In fact, projects like Randall Packer's Media Deconstruction Kit suggest that while it has become easy to grab a transmitted signal off of the television networks, détourn that signal, and then transmit the resulting remix in another media format, there is little value to such a strategy. Despite rhetoric aiming "to swamp the mass media with total illusion" (2004), MDK's detour of commercial newscasts points in the wrong direction. I find myself more inspired by works that shift the entire dynamic away from the established media networks of radio and television, concentrating on productions that take advantage of the relative ease with which one can receive, modify, and transmit Internet content and signals with minimal software running on a single computer. Taking the call-and-response dynamic of Brian Kane's "8-Track," and blending it with the simplified interface design of Robert Henke's "Atlantic Waves" installation, Radiotopia turns webmixing into a way that multiple participants can talk with each other. Here, telharmonics suggest an ideal form of broadcast as communicative exchange enmeshed in the playfulness of music making, where webmixing and multidirectional Internet streaming operate with an immediacy of exchange that points back to early radio, when operators resisted the notion that broadcast should become a unilateral, passive mode of commercial entertainment rather than something that people did as a way to listen across vast geographical distances, dialing their way through a spontaneous mix of the variety of human voices and atmospheric noise. [28] Telharmonics thread throughout the source-fullness of open air.

## The Responsibility of Response

The emergence of a massive chronotopic network for communicative action and reaction "presupposes an upheaval in the entire existing structure of the media," a prerequisite for reviving what Baudrillard calls "the possibility of response" (2003, 281). During such an upheaval, local presence fades, an effect that Marcus Novak has described in terms of the "transarchitecture" of nonlocal space:

What were once centers are now sources. Centrifugal vectors, vectors of dispersal and diaspora propagating spherically, like sound, are everywhere multiplied.

Inevitable collisions of concepts and percepts amplify dispersion into diffraction, as each point of collision becomes a new front, a new contribution to noise. (1996)

Novak is a particularly interesting architect in this context, with a scholarly and artistic investment in bringing sound design into architecture, particularly as a way to deal with the increasing intertwining of physical and virtual spaces, of the local and the nonlocal. Novak's concerns resonate with many of the artists, designers, and producers we have considered here, suggesting that the chronotopic arrangement of telharmonic networks in some way recuperates media's bilateral possibilities. Response is particularly difficult in visual-oriented social arrangements, something with which both Bakhtin and Baudrillard struggled. Bakhtin's chronotope contains a historical force of communicative exchange and play. The chronotope is not so much an image but a sonic arrangement, an expression with the presence of lived experience, where textual energy is a kind of linguistic reverberation rising from the competing rabble of multiple voices that one might overhear in the open air of a marketplace or during carnival festivities. Bakhtin immersed himself in the literary carnival of Rabelais' *Gargantua and Pantagruel*, concluding that Rabelais recorded the once living polyvocality of medieval urban experience. Transcribing the carnivalesque involves a strain against literary conventions and the various forces that regulate what can be said and by whom (that is, the rules defining obscenity, profanity, blasphemy, treason, and so forth). Baudrillard extends this discussion of control and communication into the domains of televised mass media and global communication networks, describing an ultimately fatal conflict between the carnivalesque language wars of the French insurrection of May '68 and the unilateral forces of mass broadcasting. For Baudrillard, the real upheaval of power expressed in those events grew out of a number of multilateral, communicative episodes, like the plastering of walls with micropressed posters and mimeographed handbills, like scribbles of graffiti and détourned billboards and shop fronts, and like the rapid-fire, garbled exchanges over short-band transistor radios. As an alternative to the unilateral modes of official, spectacular communication technologies, these episodes of public speech brought the uncertainties of dialogue back into the real-time flow of personal mediation, where "everything . . . was an *immediate* inscription, given and returned, spoken and answered, mobile in the same space and time, reciprocal and antagonistic" (Baudrillard 2003, 283). Baudrillard's "Requiem" laments the fact that after so much had taken place beyond the frame of a specific, ideological response tailored for incorporation into the mass media stream, a miasma of official televised retrospectives steadily refashioned the experiences of those involved in May '68 into the certainty that something had happened at the expense of the living ambivalence of immediate response.

## Communication as Emergent Phenomena

Events like Radiotopia draw a telharmonic aesthetic into media networks as a strategy for distributing communicative exchanges across massive distances. There is one last step to take, however, which concerns issues of access to the tools of production, communication and participation. In fall 2003, in Barcelona, a collective of network producers known as Platoniq organized their own Open Air Radio festival. They transmitted for several days a variety of international programming over local FM radio and the Internet. But what makes Platoniq our last stop here is the manner in which they contextualized their broadcasts by mixing in additional layers of communication for participants, including workshops and discussion groups covering everything from open source, server-side technologies to the legal aspects of radio production such as copyright and licensing. As the freeform performances of Radiotopia morph into the community outreach aesthetics of Open Air Radio, we find that webmixing has likewise transformed from a cultural form, through a cultural interface, to become something more along the lines of an operative, cultural literacy.

We end up in a telharmonic network of multidirectional broadcasts, participants producing and sustaining "the medium in which opposites are opposed," as well as "the movement and the play that links them among themselves, reverses them, or makes one side cross over into the other" (Derrida 1981, 126–27). The line comes from Derrida, writing in 1968 about the psychedelic undertow of linguistic organizations. The pharmakological slipperiness of this portion of the mix follows the telharmonic transfer into imaginal domains of social organization. "There is not transmitter or receiver on both sides of a message," writes Baudrillard, thinking here about what takes place after media's demise,

> nor, for that matter, is there any longer any "message," any corpus of information to decode univocally under the aegis of a code. The symbolic (of the symbolic exchange relation) consists precisely in breaching the univocality of the "message," in restoring the ambivalence of meaning and in demolishing in the same stroke the agency of the code. (2003, 287)

The repetition of "open air" in the title of both of these massively scaled webcasting events points to this integral ambivalence at the heart of communicative exchange, where content restrictions take a backseat to concern for access to the media through which communication takes shape. This formative event is a telharmonic counterpart to what Sanford Kwinter describes in his *Architectures of Time* as "a class known as 'emergent phenomena'—the product and expression of sudden communicative coherence . . . of converging qualities inexplicably interweaving and unfolding together, even though they may originate at vastly different temporal and phenomenal scales" (2002, 22). At any scale, the webmix functions as a source for imaginative revitalization of our connections to the world, to media, to data, and to each other.

## Open Air

The possibility of response.[29]

## References to Chapter Ten

[The User]. 2000. Silophone: Sonic Inhabitation of Silo # 5. Retrieved April 7, 2005, from http://www.silophone.net.

Ascott, Roy. 2003. "Is There Love in the Telematic Embrace?" In *Telematic Embrace: Visionary Theories of Art, Technology, and Consciousness*, edited by Edward A. Shanken, 232–46. Berkeley: University of California Press.

Bakhtin, M. M. 1981. "Forms of Time and of the Chronotope in the Novel." In *The Dialogic Imagination*, translated by Caryl Emerrson and Michael Holquist, 84–258. Austin: University of Texas Press.

Baudrillard, Jean. 2003. "Requiem for the Media." In *The New Media Reader*, edited by Noah Wardrip-Fruin and Nick Montfort, 277–88. Cambridge, MA: MIT Press.

Bush, Vannevar. 2003. "As We May Think." In *The New Media Reader*, edited by Noah Wardrip-Fruin and Nick Montfort, 35–47. Cambridge, MA: The MIT Press.

Commerford Martin, Thomas. 1906. "The Telharmonium: Electricity's Alliance with Music." *Review of Reviews*. Retrieved April 7, 2005, from http://earlyradio history.us/1906telh.htm

Czitrom, Daniel. 1982. *Media and the American Mind from Morse to McLuhan*. Chapel Hill: University of North Carolina Press.

Debord, Guy, and Gil Wolman. 1956. "A User's Guide to Détournement." *Les Lèvres Nues #8*. Retrieved April 7, 2005, from http://www.bopsecrets.org

Derrida, Jacques. 1981. "Plato's Pharmacy." In *Disseminations*, translated by Barbara Johnson, 61–171. Chicago: University of Chicago Press.

Douglas, Susan. 1987. *Inventing American Broadcasting, 1899–1922*. Baltimore, MD: Johns Hopkins University Press.

Freeman, Andi, and Jason Skeet. 2002. <earshot>. Retrieved April 7, 2005, from http://www.earshot.info.

Gitelman, Lisa. 1999. *Scripts, Grooves, and Writing Machines*. Stanford, CA: Stanford University Press.

Henke, Robert. 2004. *Atlantic Waves*. Retrieved April 7, 2005, from http://www.monolake.de/atlantic.html

Hillman, James. 1975. *Re-Visioning Psychology*. New York: Harper Perennial.

Holmes, Thom. 2002. *Electronic and Experimental Music*. 2nd ed. New York: Routledge.

Janicki, Pawel. 2004. Ping Melody. Retrieved April 7, 2005, from http://wrocenter.pl/projects/ping/index.html

Kane, Brian. 2001. 8 *Track: Experimental Distributed Music*. Retrieved April 7, 2005, from http://www.briankane.net/8track.html

Kannenberg, John. 2002. "Version 1.0 Exhibition Catalog." *The Palimpset Project*. Retrieved April 7, 2005, from http://www.stasisfield.com.

Kwinter, Sanford. 2002. *Architectures of Time: Toward a Theory of the Event in Modernist Cultures*. Cambridge, MA: MIT Press.

Manovich, Lev. 2001. *The Language of New Media*. Cambridge, MA: MIT Press.

Novak, Marcus. 1996. "Trans Terra Form: Liquid Architectures and the Loss of Inscription." *Incorporations*. Retrieved April 7, 2005, from http://www.t0.0r.at/~'krcf/nlonline/nonMarcos.html

Packer, Randall. 2004. "Corporate Control of Media." The Experimental Party. Retrieved April 7, 2005, from http://www.experimentalparty.org

Reddell, Trace. 2003. "Laptopia: The Spatial Poetics of Networked Laptop Performance." *Contemporary Music Review* 22: 11–22.

Schafer, R. Murray. 1994. *The Soundscape: Our Sonic Environment and the Tuning of the World*. Rochester, VT: Destiny Books.

Tanaka, Atua. 1999. *Constellations*. Retrieved April 7, 2005, from http://sensorband.com/atua/constellations

Toop, David. 2004. *Haunted Weather: Music, Silence and Memory*. London: Serpent's Tail.

Traub, Peter. 1999. "Bits & Pieces: A Sonic Installation for the World Wide Web." M.A. thesis, Department of Electro-Acoustic Music, Dartmouth College. Retrieved April 7, 2005, from http://www.fictive.org/~peter/bits/thesis/ intro.html

Turner, Tad. 2003. "The Resonance of the Cubicle: Laptop Performance in Postdigital Musics." *Contemporary Music Review* 22: 81–92.

CHAPTER ELEVEN

# Breaking the Decision Chain: The Fate of Creativity in the Age of Self-Production

## John Ryan and Michael Hughes

> The producer is . . ."the element between the artist and the record company."
> He selects the music and judges the sound. He is the most important person
> from the time the artist enters the studio to the time the session tape is deliv-
> ered to the pressing plant and the marketing people.
>
> (Denisoff 1986, 163)

> To enjoy freedom we have to control ourselves.
> (Virginia Woolf)

### Introduction

What if there was no music industry as we know it? What if there were no oli-
garchical companies with their high-rise buildings, high-paid staffs, worldwide
affiliates, million-dollar marketing campaigns, royalty statements, downloader
prosecutions, copyright protections, and billions in profits?

Of course, there *was* a time when there was no music industry, and what
existed was the creation of music, mostly by community members for themselves and other community members, in face-to-face interactive relationships.
This was folk music in the most authentic sense.

Where there once was community, the technology of music reproduction
(and the industry that grew up to exploit it) created commerce. Where once
music was created by the "folk" for themselves and other "folk," the industry

created "artists," "audiences," and "fans." Thus, the history of the music industry has been a history of separation: production and consumption, performance and reproduction, people and technology. But now, as predicted by Blauner (1964) and his famous inverted U-shaped curve of technology and alienation,[1] and just when it seemed that corporate rationality might swallow all creativity whole, technology has transformed music production and dissemination in ways that might have seemed impossible only a few years ago.

In this new industry, relatively inexpensive, high-quality, small-scale recording hardware and software are driving the professional recording studios to the brink of extinction. And, because of the Internet, for the first time since the advent of rock and roll in the 1950s, the guardians at the gate of recording and distribution, the purveyors of star-making machinery, the major recording companies themselves, are seriously threatened. Music creators are seen as winners because they can circumvent the system in their own form of desktop publishing. Consumers are seen as winners because never before has so much recorded music, from so many places, been available to so many. Whereas technology previously alienated the average person from the music production process, the relationship is now reversed, and technology has returned the means of production to the people, ushering in an era of recording democracy. If you want a voice, you can have one. And the audience votes with the click of a mouse (goodbye, commercial radio—you're next).

So it would appear that much is gained in this digital age. But is anything lost? Technologies carry within them their own logics of production. The hand-wielded hoe predicts the family garden, the plow the farm, and the tractor agribusiness. How has digital production and the Internet changed the production process in the making of music? In the paragraphs below we examine this question with a focus on collaborative production and, in particular, the fate of the music producer in the digital age.

## The Production of Culture

A large body of literature in sociology has shown how artistic production is a collaborative process. For example, in their pioneering work *Canvases and Careers*, White and White (1965) show how French impressionism, rather than springing full-blown from the brushes of aspiring painters, evolved out of an interaction among the painters, dealers, and critics. Similarly, Farrell (2001) offers classic examples of how friendship networks helped sustain creativity in not only French Impressionism but also among the fugitive poets, early psychoanalysts, and other creative groups.

Howard Becker (1982) conceptualizes such systems of collaboration as "art worlds." An art world encompasses the entire supply chain that links a creative idea to the consumer. But it is more than this. It encompasses all of the materials, personnel, technologies, norms, and values involved in creation, distribution, evaluation, and even consumption of artistic works. An art world defines, legitimates, produces, catalogs, critiques, and consumes the product. Art worlds are made up of individuals, technologies, and organizations. They are embedded in a larger normative and legal structure,[2] and they shape both the symbols produced and the audiences for those symbols.

Peterson (1985) has delineated the key components of art worlds oriented toward the manufacture of symbolic products. These are law, technology, industry structure, organizational structure, occupational careers, and market. While in particular places and times, and in particular organizational fields, one or two of these factors may be most salient, always they form a system in which change in one element affects the others and influences the product. For example, the music industry exists in a field containing copyright law, censorship, technologies for music creation, recording, dissemination, and playback, firms competing for a share of a market that are organized in particular ways (e.g., centralized versus decentralized), avenues for creating occupations and careers, producers' beliefs about the audience, and so on. This system is enormously complex, and any one of these factors could be deconstructed into an array of contingencies bewildering to the industry novice and at best only partially understood by even the key players.

Nevertheless, the relationships among the various components of an art world can remain relatively unproblematic until innovations in one part of the system create a disequilibrium that requires adjustment. A good example is what happened when music publishers faced a decline in revenue due to falling sales of sheet music (Ryan 1985). With the advent of radio, sound recordings, and, later, sound motion pictures and television, consumers could hear music without buying the sheet music and playing tunes for themselves. The music publishing industry reacted by winning and institutionalizing rights to the performance of compositions. This new interpretation of copyright prompted the industry to form a performance rights organization, ASCAP, which negotiated and established royalty procedures and agreements with those producing performances through radio, records, movies, and television. Performance rights and ASCAP were resisted in the courts, in the legislative hall, and in the day-to-day dealings of publishers, with night clubs, radio stations, skating rinks, and other establishments where music was used to draw audiences (Ryan 1985). In spite of such resistance, the basic changes remained in place; the structure and culture of music production and distribution had been dramatically and irreversibly changed. Royalties from the performance of music became the publishers' and composers' prime source of income and arguably drove the whole movement to artists recording music they had composed themselves.

There are many other examples of shifts in the six constraints altering the practices and products of music production,[3] but none has been more dramatic and far-reaching than the current digital revolution in music creation and reproduction, coupled with the rise of the Internet as a means of distribution and consumption. In the remainder of this chapter, we briefly outline the historical logic of production in each era of music production. We then show how the digital revolution has altered both the structure of the industry and the logic of production.

## The Popular Music Production Process

In the late 1800s and early 1900s the music industry suffered the high level of turbulence typical of emerging industries. The industry was characterized by patent wars, competing technologies of reproduction and playback, and a variety of visions of how the new technologies of music reproduction could be exploited. At the same time, the process of finding marketable talent and capturing and reproducing marketable sounds was being developed. While multiple models continued to compete, the arrangement that most dominated the industry, and which was later to be typified by the song mills of Tin Pan Alley in New York, lay somewhere between the assembly line and craft-based production. Following the logic of the assembly line, the industry attempted to pass its products through several stages of development before being sold to a market. However, unlike the assembly line, and like craft production, there is great uncertainty in the production process requiring high skill and experienced judgment along the way. The various skills input in the process cannot be codified and built into machinery or performed by unskilled workers. Ryan and Peterson (1982) have termed this mode of production "the product image."

Under this "product image" mode of production, a song that begins with a songwriter and ends up as a recorded product ready for dissemination and sale goes through a "decision chain" of production. The goal of creative personnel at each step is to assess and make changes in the "product" to make it acceptable to personnel at the next stage of production. While Ryan and Peterson focus on the decision chain in country music, a similar process has characterized both pop and rock production to varying degrees throughout most of the life of the industry.

In Ryan and Peterson's study the decision chain process begins with the writing of a song, usually by a professional songwriter. The song then passes to a publisher who may reject the song, accept the song "as is," or edit the song. The publisher then "pitches" the song to a recording artist, an artist's manager, or a producer. At this stage the song is rejected, recorded, or put on hold for the future. During the decision process the song may again be edited in such a way as to suit the "product image" that decision makers have about the nature of the product most likely to be bought by decision makers at the next stage. Perhaps a producer might want the song written in such a way that he or she perceives will be more appealing to a particular artist. Or the manager, the artist, or the producer might alter the song in a way that they believe will be more appealing to radio programmers. Carrying out these directives might be the task of a sound engineer, a producer, and finally, a mixer. Sometimes these roles are embodied in separate individuals, sometimes two or more roles are combined in one person. For example, some producers are also their own engineers and do the final mix as well. Some artists rely heavily on a producer, a manager, or a producer/manager to select songs for them. Other artists write their own compositions and then negotiate with a producer over whether the song will end up as part of the project and in what form. These and other variations in the decision chain coexist within the industry. The key point is that throughout most of the history of the industry, commercially recorded music has been the outcome of a complex collaborative editing process.

Only in the rarest cases—where artists wrote, produced, and mixed their own material, and ran their own record label—have artists been the sole arbiter of what they presented to the public. Among those who have been able at times to operate this way are Stevie Wonder, Prince, Paul Simon, Brian Wilson, Paul McCartney, and Richard Carpenter (Olsen, Verna, and Wolff 1999). However, even in such rare cases, various mediating processes occur. For example, the sound of a recording is influenced by the mastering process over which the artist may have little or no control. More importantly, prior to the availability of Internet distribution, products could be refused by powerful gatekeepers, distributors, and/or radio programmers, thus denying access to the mass audience.

The situation, once considered unusual, where an artist can circumvent the collaborative process linking the creator to the audience by way of a complexly manufactured product, has now been made commonplace by the personal computer and the Internet. Digital technology has made the personal computer into a recording studio, the equivalent of a record or CD pressing plant, as well as a distribution and marketing system (Ryan and Peterson 1993). In its lack of mediation, modern independent music production carries elements of folk production. But what was once produced on the front porch for, at most, a family or neighborhood audience, can now be instantly distributed worldwide and reside for the picking on a myriad of websites. These innovations have greatly expanded the sheer volume of music available, and undoubtedly the variety of music as well. It is clear that what has occurred is a phenomenal democratization of recorded music production, as the mainstream commercial industry is not so much replaced as circumvented by thousands of musicians.

Of course, there are numerous examples in music industry history in which technological shifts have altered the conventions of production. Replacing acoustical horns with electrical microphones in the 1920s made the intimate crooning style possible and allowed singers such as Bing Crosby to become popular (Frith 1986). And multitrack recording, pioneered by Les Paul in the late 1940s, allowed for increasingly complex recordings as the technique was developed and honed through the 1950s and 1960s. While these developments have been widely and justifiably celebrated, perhaps none since the inventions of Edison and Marconi have been as sweeping as the digital revolution. We next focus on the implications of this revolution for one of the key actors in the traditional product chain—the music producer.

## The Music Producer

Like music, film is the result of a complex interweaving of inputs. In this sense there is no single "author" of a film to whom creative credit can be assigned. However, through a complex set of forces in the art world of film, beginning in the 1940s, credit for the creative success or failure of a film was increasingly assigned to the director. As we shall see in the following paragraphs, a similar process of occupational redefinition has occurred in the music industry through the growth and increasing importance of the role of the producer.

From the earliest days of recording, specialized personnel were needed to mediate between the artist, the technology, and the company. The sound engineer occupied a key link in the production chain. The task was to mediate between the musician's live performance and its reproduction. Recorded music production involves a symbiosis between technology and performance. Technology is used to meet the goals of recording, but performers must conform to the demands and limitations of the technology. Indeed, in the early period, the limiting nature of the technology was the dominant issue. It was the engineer's job to alter musical performance so that it could be captured by recording technology of the day. Sound could not be manipulated once recorded, so live sound had to be manipulated before it was recorded. Songs were shortened to fit the two- to three-minute capacity of cylinders. Spoken words worked better than singing. Because some types of singing voices and certain types of instruments recorded better than others, singers and musicians had to alter the way they played or sang so as not to overwhelm the medium. The basic goal was to manipulate the recording process in such a way as to reproduce live sound as accurately as possible with the limits set by the technology.

The role of the sound engineer was usually distinct, performing the task of actually manipulating the machinery of recording. The task of finding artists, picking songs, working with the engineer to determine the overall sound of the recording—in essence, to *produce* the record—fell to the Artists and Repertoire (A&R) person, a role pioneered by Fred Gaisberg for the American Gramophone Company from 1898 to 1939.[4] It was the task of the A&R person to convert the raw material of performance into a product suitable for company needs. Not surprisingly, the A&R person was typically in the employ of a major record company or was an independent owner of a small label.

Record company experiments with electrical amplification in the 1920s, '30s, and '40s solved many of the earlier problems in recording high and low frequencies. Electrical amplification also allowed for creative use of microphones in such a way as to enhance the quality of the performance. Whereas in many ways early recording technology led to recordings that had "less than" live sound, the new electrical amplification allowed for recordings that were "truly live" and on location. Even more importantly, combined with another new technology known as multitracking the possibility existed for recordings that were "more than" live.

The use of magnetic tape recorders for recording began to take hold in the years immediately after World War II. These magnetic tape recorders allowed for the editing of a recording after it had been made, and, by the 1950s, were dominating recording studios. The early tape recorders were closely followed by the advent of multitrack recording in the '50s and '60s. Multitracking created the ability to record performances on multiple channels (strips of the same tape side by side) and synchronize them. These performances did not have to occur at the same time, so it was now possible to, say, record the bass and drums first, then add the other parts later. If there was a problem with any one part, it could be fixed without affecting the others. These innovations made possible much greater control over both performance and recording and created the potential for an enhanced role of the A&R person in the production chain.

From approximately 1950 forward, with the use of tape and then multitracking, more producers began to see themselves, and be seen within the industry, as significant contributors to the *creative* process (as opposed to the sound reproduction process).[5] This new definition was unintentionally enhanced by a restructuring of the industry beginning in the mid-1950s. After its initial period of turmoil, the industry had gravitated toward an oligopolistic structure with production centrally controlled within bureaucratic organizations. At the same time, smaller independent firms, spurred on by the rapid expansion in the 1950s of independent radio stations geared toward the burgeoning teen audience, were able to succeed and thrive in this environment by appealing to the audience on the margins. These labels lived off of blues, rhythm and blues (race), country (hillbilly) music, and jazz. Because of the major record companies' conservative approach to innovation and their general lack of awareness of the power of the teen audience, the smaller independent labels were able to capture the emerging audience for rock and roll (Peterson and Berger 1973).

Contemporaneous with these developments, a larger post–WWII trend toward decentralized and open production systems was gaining currency among U.S. firms. In order to respond to the loss of market share to the independents, major record companies turned toward these new open systems of production (Dowd 2004). The majors began to outsource parts of their operations, including some recording studios and production (Avalon 2002), placing these activities relatively more outside of traditional bureaucratic control.

In this environment a new role evolved: that of the independent producer. Freed from the bureaucracy of the major company, armed with the powerful new recording tool of multitrack recording, and embedded in a baby-boom-inspired era of rapid cultural change and experimentation, the independent producer was now ready to assume a status often equal to, and sometimes exceeding, that of recording artists in the production of popular music. Cunningham describes the then-new status of the producer this way:

> Today, most record producers and engineers operate on a totally independent freelance basis, benefiting from the freedom to work with whom they like, whenever and wherever they prefer. It is a far cry from the early Sixties when the vast majority were dictated by the rules and conditions of their record company employers. (1998, 160)

From the 1950s on, the producer's influence has been an increasingly significant factor in creative production. For example, the Encyclopedia of Record Producers (Olsen, Verna, and Wolff 1999) contains entries on 500 producers who have had an impact on popular music. In pop music, George Martin is often considered to be the prototype of the producer/collaborator and can be compared to some of the great editor/writer and artists/dealer collaborations. In country music it was Owen Bradley and Chet Atkins who pioneered the role in a similar way (Daley 1998), and in jazz, it was Alfred Lion of Blue Note records (Cook 2003). Today, producers who have achieved something akin to artist stature in their own right include Rodney "Darkchild" Jenkins, Jermaine Dupri, Sylvia Massy Shivy, and Walter Afanasieff, to name just a few.

Like Sam Philips, George Martin, and Chet Atkins, these producers are known for their particular sound, their ability to develop artists, and their success in producing commercially successful recordings. They are essentially artistic directors who perform the crucial function of converting creative ideas and musical performances into tangible products suitable for the purposes of commerce. Antoine Hennion (1989) describes the molding of the singer and his or her performance in this way:

> Artistic directors do not willy-nilly accept the singer that they have discovered, with their dreams of glory, their style, their preferred songs, their ideal public. They choose one or two characteristics that they liked from the start and carry them into the studio in the same way as the arranger arrives with one or two ideas about harmonies and orchestration that he or she is ready to modify at the drop of a hat. (409–10)

However, digitalization of music production and distribution, for the first time, allows artists to bypass the standard decision chain and to create a product that is technically sophisticated by contemporary standards without being subjected to the scrutiny, judgments, and editing traditionally provided by producers. Of course, self-production is not required, but it is probably attractive to the most innovative and independent young artists. An irony is that, in most cases, self-production makes large-scale commercial success and star status nearly impossible. Many artists will say that that is not the goal, and others will say that self-production is a necessary first step[6] to becoming recognized by the industry. In either scenario, we know that a key piece of the chain is missing for many of the most creative young artists in the business. But does it matter? We can't say directly, but we can look at examples where we know that producers have helped shape creative output.

## The Artist-Producer Relationship

Alabama native Sam Philips, a former radio engineer and announcer, opened his own recording studio in Memphis in 1950. After recording masters for other labels, including records for B.B. King, Ike Turner, and Howlin' Wolf, and one failed attempt at starting his own label, he started Sun Records in 1952. There, Philips recorded such artists as Carl Perkins, Roy Orbison, Johnny Cash, Jerry Lee Lewis, and Charlie Rich. However, he is best known for discovering Elvis Presley and producing his early recordings, including "That's Alright Mama," "Mystery Train," and "Blue Moon." As Elvis's producer, he hired the musicians (Scotty Moore and Bill Black), selected material, decided when the recording was finished, and created the "rockabilly" sound using sparse instrumentation and his signature rhythmic slapback echo. According to Philips there was no doubt who was in charge in the studio. "I told them, 'Never get too uptight. Just kick things around, come in, and if I say, "No, I don't hear it this time," that doesn't mean that y'all are not right and I am, but I'm the one who's going to make the decision!'" (Buskin 1999, 7).

Philips is credited with not only recognizing Elvis' talent but shaping that talent into a form that could get radio airplay and attract the teen audience. As Philips told one interviewer, "When Elvis came and he performed those first two songs and I was blown away by this guy's talent. By that I don't mean that I heard the finished thing, but I just heard some instinctive things" (Buskin 1999, 6).

If Philips was the prototype, perhaps more than anyone else, George Martin elevated the status of the producer to artist in the production process. In the spring of 1962, Martin, a staff producer for London-based EMI records, entered Abbey Road's Number Three studio where he was to conduct a recording audition for an unknown group called the Beatles. Martin, a former piano and oboe student at the Guildhall School of Music in London, had worked at EMI since 1950 and was best known for his work producing comedy albums for Peter Sellers and the comedy show *Beyond the Fringe*. He became the head of EMI's Parlophone label in 1955. Despite having misgivings about the group's songwriting ability, Martin signed them to an EMI recording contract a few months later. This was the beginning of a now legendary collaboration. Martin's influence included encouraging the firing of original drummer Pete Best and providing arrangements for their early songs. As Martin put it, "I would meet them in the studio to hear a new number. I would perch myself on a high stool, and John and Paul would stand around me with their acoustic guitars and play and sing it.

. . . Then I would make suggestions to improve it and we'd try it again" (Martin and Hornsby 1979, 132).

Martin recalls that the early records were straight forward and required only minimal arranging. However, beginning with the addition of orchestration to the recording of *Yesterday* in 1965, his role expanded. Increasingly Lennon and McCartney relied on Martin to translate many of their ideas through recording techniques and his knowledge of scoring and arranging. Many believe the high point of this collaboration was the *Sgt. Peppers* album, released in 1967. In an often-cited example of Martin's collaboration with the Beatles, it was his job to take a section of the song, *Being for the Benefit of Mr. Kite*, and follow John Lennon's instructions to make the music "swirl up and around" (Martin and Hornsby 1979, 204). Martin did so by taking recordings of Victorian steam organs, dubbing them on to tape, cutting the tapes into foot-long sections, throwing them up in the air, and splicing them back together, and some sections were turned around backwards.

This is just one example of many of Martin's influence on the Beatles' recordings. The release in 1995–1996 of the Beatles Anthology CDs left no doubt that Beatles songs evolved through collaboration in the studio. On the compilation, we hear, for example, the evolution of Strawberry Fields from a gentle acoustic ballad into a very different rock-oriented heavily produced form.

In each of these cases there was a key collaboration between artist and producer that almost certainly altered, and hopefully enhanced, the aesthetic result. Of course, there are undoubtedly as many bad collaborations as there are good ones, but many of these are forever lost in record company archives or destroyed.

While we have focused on popular music production, the literature on artistic creation in general is replete with examples of the critical importance of editing in the production of creative output. In art, there is the relationship between El Greco and his patrons (Mann, Haskell, and Penny 1989); in film, script writers and actors are "edited" by the director who may, in turn, be edited by the film editor (see, for example, Rosenblum and Karen [1979]). And in literature there are the well-known relationships of F. Scott Fitzgerald, Thomas Wolfe, and Ernest Hemingway with editor Maxwell Perkins (Bruccoli and Baughman 2004). In his biography of Perkins, Berg notes that it had been rumored that Wolfe and Perkins had been equal collaborators in producing Wolfe's novels and describes the editor's impact on Thomas Wolfe, "As Wolfe transposed his world into fiction, Perkins had felt it was his responsibility to create certain boundaries of length and form. He said, 'There were practical conventions that Wolfe couldn't stop to think about himself'"(Berg 1997, 7).

In music production, when artists have access to the technology of production and can thus circumvent the complex collaborative process involving sound engineers, sound mixers, and, importantly, producers, they can also avoid being edited in a serious way. In the remainder of this chapter we argue that this technological shift has resulted in a new organization of creative popular music activity, and that a new art world has emerged that provides coherence, structure, and justification for these new organizational forms.

## The New Art World of Pop Music: Self-production

This new system of self-production has not replaced the traditional system of popular music production. Instead, we now have two systems, two art worlds, existing side by side: the traditional system and the new system of self-production. We are not arguing that self-production is new or that artists have never had independent access to music production technology. As we indicated above, "authentic" folk music is "self-produced." But in order for folk music to get into the marketplace, successful practitioners have almost always engaged the traditional system of production. Also, for most of the history of recorded music, there have been independent recording studios run as businesses that would record the works of aspiring musicians for a fee. But using these services required the significant burdens of going into a studio that may be far from one's home and paying high fees for each recording session. In addition, while home recording has been widely available since the 1980s, until very recently, this form of music production was better characterized as a hobby than an art world. Without sophisticated technology, the potential of a high-quality product was completely missing.

The most important factor in the emergence of this new art world of self-production is the cost, and thus the availability of, sophisticated technologies. In the past, considerable investments were required before an artist was allowed access to the technology. To make the investment worthwhile, artists had to be perceived to have "talent," and they had to be willing to enter into a cooperative relationship with a producer.

In the new world of affordable technology, ownership of and/or access to the means of production of popular music is widely available, and barriers to access and acquisition are so low that anyone who wants to can use sophisticated production technology to produce and distribute his or her own music. Most of this equipment, and nearly all of this access, is available through the computers that are in the homes and offices of nearly every middle-class American. In addition, an infrastructure is emerging for the exploitation of this technology.

As the technology of music production became increasingly accessible, independent avenues of promotion, distribution, and sales also evolved. The fifth edition of *The Indie Bible* (Wimble 2004), a resource publication for independent musicians, lists over 400 websites where independent musicians can upload music for distribution, covering over thirty genres from pop to rock to hip-hop, from women in music to reggae, from ambient to noise to space rock. Each site provides free or paid access to recordings made by anywhere from a few dozen to hundreds of artists. Today it is not uncommon for bands to write their own material, self-produce a recording in a home studio, and upload the songs to one of these sites. Typically these sites allow for samples of audio files and full downloads for a monthly or yearly fee. The idea is that subscribers to the service will then be captivated by the music samples and be willing download the whole CD for a larger fee. Sometimes site viewers are allowed to rate or even review the music they listen to.

The most comprehensive of these sites also allow the artists to post bios, photos, tour dates, and other promotional material. Artists can pay more to be a "Featured Artist." Being a "featured artist" means that a number of techniques are employed to draw attention to a particular artist on the site.[7] As one site boasts, "It has been demonstrated on this site, and others like eBay, that highlighted artists generate the most traffic" (http://www.auralgasms.com/). Other premium services for which artists pay include "feature article" slots, which can either be professionally written or self-composed, and banner advertisements.

There are other services available online that in some ways mirror the traditional industry. For example, an artist can send off his or her home-produced CD and have it critiqued for a fee. Other sites will develop a professional marketing campaign, also for a fee. Still others claim that they serve the traditional A&R function for the industry, providing sites where recording companies can browse for talent.

Taken together, these Internet-based services make up an art world that resembles the traditional mainstream industry. All of the pieces of the decision chain appear to be there. Some of the sites even have their own Internet radio stations just like the mainstream industry has broadcast stations.[8] However, there is a critical difference and that difference has to do with power.

A close examination of these Internet services reveals that in almost every case they are hired services and the power lies with the artist who is paying the fee and not with a set of editors or potential editors who have hired or contracted with the artist. The traditional power situation of the beginning artist has thus been reversed. In the traditional system, there are many more artists than available slots for recording and promotion. The recording company's greater relative power came from the fact that they controlled both the infrastructure and the technique needed to record, disseminate, and promote commercial products.

Focusing specifically on the role of the producer, under the traditional model the artist needed the expertise of the producer and at the same time the producer acted as gatekeeper. In the case of the Beatles, they needed producer George Martin because without him they literally would not have been able to record. And they needed to take his suggestions seriously because without his approval it would not have been possible to move further through the decision chain. Of course, in pop music it is not possible to predict the outcome of paths not explored, but it is interesting to speculate what might have happened to the Beatles' career if George Martin had been a paid consultant to the group, not a power-wielding producer, when he advised them to replace drummer Pete Best or made suggestions regarding songs and arrangements.

The potential ramifications of the new art world of self-production go considerably beyond what might happen to a single artist or group. As we have indicated, domination of music production by the traditional system required creative artists to submit to a complex editing process controlled by producers. Though such relationships were by necessity cooperative, artists were not always happy or satisfied with either the relationships they had with producers or with the musical products generated. If we assume that highly creative artists are among those least likely to want to conform to the vision of others, it is reasonable to expect that the most creative of young artists would avoid the fetters of the traditional producer-centered production process and gravitate instead toward a decentralized artist-centered system of self-production. Without an industry to edit the sheer number of artistic products, this self-production system overwhelms the audience with product. Undoubtedly, the vast majority of products of even very creative artists are never discovered by most buyers, and certainly not at an audience level sufficient to sustain a full-blown career. At the same time, the ease of production means that artists use up their material much more quickly. It is not uncommon for artists to have several CDs while their reputation remains, at best, at the local level.

Meanwhile, if we are correct, more compliant artists, and probably in many cases less creative artists, will gravitate toward, and find a comfortable home in, the traditional system organized around producers. In this complex collaborative system, judgments and expertise of professional producers, engineers, and marketers of popular music carry significant weight. An important demand of this system is that the creativity of the artist must be made to fit the requirements of the traditional decision chain. In this system, creativity is not lost, but it is trimmed or limited so that it does not undermine the marketability of the product. How innovative and influential the final product is depends in part on the raw creativity the artist brings to the system. Our argument is that in the system of bifurcated art worlds—self-production and traditional—the freedom allowed by self-production siphons off the most creative artists into a system of production that generates products that are unlikely to reach a mass audience, are unlikely to receive critical acclaim, and ultimately unlikely to be influential or to have lasting value. At the same time, less-creative artists, who are willing to submit to manipulation by the music industry, are left to produce a large body of popular music even more vacuous than has been the case in the past.

In summary, if we assume, based on classic examples of artist/editor collaborations across a variety of media, that in many cases the editing process is critical to artistic development, then the art world of self-producing digital recording appears to be detrimental to artistic creation. The new freedom of the recording artist is widely celebrated and justifiably so. Access to relatively cheap, high-quality recording equipment is for musicians what readily available canvas and paint are to painters—the opportunity to create a lasting performance. However, we have tried to argue that this freedom comes with several costs. Those costs include the loss of the opportunity to hone creativity in the context of the professional artist/editor relationship, the potential for creative products to disappear under the sheer volume of recorded material produced, and the depletion of the quality of creative inputs into the mainstream of popular music. Whether these costs are fully compensated by the emerging world of self-production remains to be seen.

## References to Chapter Eleven

Avalon, Moses. 2002. *Confessions of a Record Producer*. San Francisco: Backbeat Books.

Becker, Howard S. 1982. *Art Worlds*. Berkeley: University of California Press.

Berg, A. Scott. 1997. *Max Perkins: Editor of Genius*. New York: Riverhead Books.

Blauner, Robert. 1964. *Alienation and Freedom*. Chicago: University of Chicago Press.

Bruccoli, Matthew J., and Judith S. Baughman. 2004. *The Sons of Maxwell Perkins: Letters of F. Scott Fitzgerald, Ernest Hemingway, Thomas Wolfe, and Their Editor*. Columbia: University of South Carolina Press.

Buskin, Richard. 1999. *Inside Tracks*. New York: Avon Books.

Cook, Richard. 2003. *Blue Note Records: A Biography*. Boston: Justin, Charles.

Cunningham, Mark. 1998. *Good Vibrations: A History of Record Production*. London: Sanctuary.

Daley, Dan. 1998. *Nashville's Unwritten Rules*. Woodstock, NY: Overlook Press.

Denisoff, R. Serge. 1986. *Tarnished Gold: The Record Industry Revisited*. New Brunswick: Transaction Books.

Dowd, Timothy J. 2004. "Concentration and Diversity Revisited: Production Logics and the U.S. Mainstream Recording Market, 1940—1990." *Social Forces* 82 (4):1411–56.

Farrell, Michael P. 2001. *Collaborative Circles: Friendship Dynamics & Creative Work*. Chicago: University of Chicago Press.

Frith, Simon. 1986. "Art versus Technology: The Strange Case of Popular Music." *Media, Culture and Society* 8:259–78.

Hennion, Antoine. 1989. "An Intermediary between Production and Consumption: The Producer of Popular Music." *Science, Technology and Human Values* 14:400–424.

Mann, Richard G., Francis Haskell, and Nicholas Penny. 1989. *El Greco and His Patrons: Three Major Projects*. Cambridge: Cambridge University Press.

Martin, George, and Jeremy Hornsby. 1979. *All You Need Is Ears*. New York: St. Martin's Press.

Moore, Jerrold Northrop. 1999. *Sound Revolutions: A Biography of Fred Gaisberg, Founding Father of Commercial Sound Recording*. London: Sanctuary.

Olsen, Eric, Paul Verna, and Carlo Wolff. 1999. "The Encyclopedia of Record Producers." New York: Watson-Guptill.

Peterson, Richard A. 1985. "Six Constraints on the Production of Literary Works." *Poetics: International Review for the Theory of Literature* 14:45–67.

Peterson, Richard A., and N. Anand. 2004. "The Production of Culture Perspective." *Annual Review of Sociology* 30:311–34.

Peterson, Richard A., and David Berger. 1973. "Cycles in Symbol Production." *American Sociological Review* 40:158–73.

Peterson, Richard A., and John Ryan. 1983. "Success, Failure and Anomie in Arts and Crafts Work: Breaking in to Commercial Country Music Songwriting." In *Research in the Sociology of Work*, vol. 2, edited by I. H. Simpson and R. L. Simpson, 301–24. Greenwich: JAI Press.

Rosenblum, Ralph, and Robert Karen. 1979. *When the Shooting Stops . . . The Cutting Begins: A Film Editor's Story*. New York: Viking Press.

Ryan, John. 1985. *The Production of Culture in the Music Industry: The ASCAP-BMI Controversy*. Lanham, MD: University Press of America.

Ryan, John, and Richard A. Peterson. 1982. "The Product Image: The Fate of Creativity in Country Music Songwriting." In *Individuals in Mass Media Organizations: Creativity and Constraint*, vol. 10, *Sage Annual Reviews of Communication Research*, edited by J. S. Ettema and C. D. Whitney, 11–32. Beverly Hills, CA: Sage.

———. 1993. "Occupational and Organizational Consequences of the Digital Revolution in Music Making." In *Current Research on Occupations and Professions*, vol. 8, edited by M. Cantor and C. Zollars, 173–201. Greenwich: JAI Press.

White, Harrison H., and Cynthia A White. 1965. *Canvases and Careers: Institutional Change in the French Painting World*. New York: Wiley.

Wimble, David. 2004. *The Indie Bible*. Ottawa: Big Meteor.

# On the Future of Music

## Jonathan Sterne

Though it is possible to point to articles that address the role of the Internet and music production, circulation, and consumption (e.g., Jones 2000; Jorda 1999; McCourt and Burkart 2003), *Cybersounds* offers us an unprecedented opportunity to reflect on music on the Internet and the state of scholarship about music on the Internet. *Cybersounds* situates music as an important site for Internet culture—as something that attracts people to particular online sites or conditions their modes of online practice. Even as it elevates the Internet as an important social site for understanding musical culture, the book's contributors collectively deflate the sense that the Internet is a "special case" of social relations. When approached with an ethnographic curiosity, we find many of the same characteristics in online "communities" as ethnographers have been finding in musical subcultures for years. Genre-savvy breakcore producers mock outsiders but welcome and even console persistent newbies. New Model Army fans argue amongst themselves—and with the band—about the meaning of fandom. Progressive rock fans develop their own ethics for illegal file sharing. DJ Dangermouse uses Internet distribution to circulate an illegal product that would be stopped in its tracks if it were released as a compact disc. As these examples from the collection suggest, music culture is not a "purely" online culture. It systematically violates the "online/offline" distinction upon which much Internet ethnography is still based. This much is obvious when we talk about fans of bands or genres who meet on bulletin boards to discuss their experiences and the meaning of their fandom. But even the Internet-based compositions discussed in Trace Reddell's chapter have the exact same status as any other musical sound when they exit the computer in headphones or speakers: they are no more or less "virtual" than the sounds that come out of a computer when the user pops in a compact disc. Thus, the online ethnography of music cultures offers us one useful way to think about the role of the Internet in people's everyday lives, rather than a space apart or a special case of culture. Some of the chapters in the book are also quite harmonious with other work on cyberculture. There's a good bit of "grist for the mill" for people interested in the construction of online identity and authenticity, or for people interested in the ongoing debates around file sharing and media ownership.

The most radical theme in *Cybersounds* is an emerging debate around the status and future of musical creativity. "Future of music" questions have tended to revolve around the intellectual property debates and matters of industry control over professional musicians or musicians who aspire to make their living as musicians (see http://www.futureofmusic.org). While intellectual property remains a crucial political question, to say that it is *the* question for the future of music assumes that music should first be understood as a profession and an industry, and only later as a social practice. While questions concerning the nature of creativity have long haunted music scholars, they are relatively rare in Internet studies, even in discussions of net art. *Cybersounds* is at its most urgent and innovative when the authors ask us to consider questions about the changing nature of creativity (whether corporate or individual), the status of collaboration in music production and listening, and the relationship between amateurism and professionalism. Tied up with these questions are long-standing debates around what counts as creativity in modern capitalism; how to think about and value acts of production, circulation, and consumption; and of course the specter of the recording industry, which at once nourishes and shuts down creative energy at all points in the circuit of culture.

As a subject of study, musical creativity has undergone tremendous shifts in the past few decades. Though the model of the romantic genius is still alive and well, it has been challenged by a variety of critical approaches that highlight the social and collaborative nature of music making. The most engaging work has come from a group of ethnomusicologists who see creativity as a socially dispersed quality that exists in the spaces among performers and audiences. Because he uses the "lone genius" model as a straw figure, Christopher Small's classic *Music-Society-Education* states the stakes clearly: the aesthetic ideal of gifted individuals who produce singular artistic works is rooted in a peculiar Western worldview. For Small, the "lone genius" ideal is essentially authoritarian and antidemocratic. Small casts the "lone genius" model as a building block of modern music education, which treats education as "preparation for life rather than part of life" (Small 1977, 209), and where musical pedagogy is tied to scientific rationality and class mobility. Despite its centrality to Western musical culture, Small views the figure of the compositional genius as a pathetic character. I quote at length to give a flavor of Small's tone and argument:

The great dilemma of our musical culture today is the position of the composer, who is an isolated figure, cut off from the vast majority of the community, sending out his messages into the void and wondering if anyone is listening, condemned always to speak to an essentially passive audience, with whom the closest relationship he can hope to achieve is that of producer to paying customers at a concert. He has not even the satisfaction of feeling that he is doing something that the community values; most composers have to fight hard even to have their music heard, and if a plague were to carry off every composer listed in John Vinton's *Twentieth-Century Music Dictionary* I very much doubt if the majority of the community would even notice their absence.

That this need not necessarily be so is clear from our cursory examination of other musical cultures, as well as that of eighteenth-century New England, where all are free to participate in the work of creation (not everyone wants to, but that is another matter) and the composer is a valued and necessary member of the community. From the point of view of individual virtuosity, speaking technologically these are all 'low energy' cultures. The position of the 'professional,' in so far as he exists at all, is that of leader, of pacemaker, of mentor, rather than of producer and his work is intimately bound up with the community of which he is so important a member. (Small 1977, 217).

Although Small's book is just under 30 years old as I write, it does seem to call out from another era, another paradigm. Small is obviously writing about Western art music, so-called classical music, which is produced and enjoyed by a relative minority of people. Small's unreconstructed utopianism, normative language, and use of the male pronoun date him stylistically and his idealization of African culture and of 18th-century New England have both been widely noted and criticized by others. Yet the passage—and the book as a whole—are a fascinating read against musical practices that emerge with digital media.

Small's critique of big technology and idealization of "low-energy" cultures comes from Ivan Illich, specifically Illich's book *Energy and Equity* (1974), which argued that once energy consumption exceeds a certain per capita level in a society, inevitable inequities will follow in the form of a necessary division of labor. It is a provocative and terrifying environmental hypothesis, but it also operates within the paradigm of "big" technology that reigned in the 1960 and 1970s. Certainly an Illichian today could point out that digital technologies also are predicated on a monstrous division of labor and waste that cement world inequalities (Fuentes and Ehrenreich 1998; Puckett et al. 2002). And yet at the level of musical practice, which is the plane upon which Small wants to operate, one needs only to follow digital recording technologies a short distance to find some of the erosion of the professional ethos for which Small calls.

Since we are talking about music and technology, let us turn to one of the most "technologized" roles in music today for an example. Consider the fate of the professional recording engineer and the so-called professional studio. It is now cliché to note that it costs a fraction of what it once did to get into recording. It is cheaper than ever to self-release a CD. A musician or group of musicians with about US$2,000 (depending on genre and creativity, it can be done with even less money) can put together a passable digital home studio (either based around a computer or a standalone all-in-one "digital audio workstation"), complete with microphones and cables, that has considerably more technical capacity than a low-level professional studio would have had even two decades ago (though they will still need to spend more money or find a benefactor to release the CD). Of course, such a person would still need to learn the skills of recording, but as with music, the skills of a recording engineer improve most with routine practice.

Three major studios closed in the winter of 2005: Cello Studios in Los Angeles, Muscle Shoals Sound Studio in Sheffield, Alabama, and the Hit Factory in New York City. All three closures were greeted by laments in the music industry press and mainstream outlets like *Rolling Stone* and the *New York Times*, which claimed that these closures marked the end of an era and possibly the decline of the "recording" section of the music industry. All three studios were based on an old business model of recording, where record labels paid well over a thousand dollars a day to a major facility for a band to essentially "move in" for months at a time. Studios like these are struggling, and the genre itself may well be in decline, as is suggested by *The Mixerman Diaries* (2004), a parody written from an anonymous recording engineer's point of view that chronicles his travails as he works on an ill-fated big-budget project.

To use another concept from Ivan Illich, professional studios used to hold a "radical monopoly" on the recording of music: "I speak about radical monopoly when one industrial production process exercises an exclusive control over the satisfaction of a pressing need, and excludes nonindustrial activities from competition" (Illich 1973, 52). As a byproduct of a new sphere of industrial competition, we are witnessing a moment when that radical monopoly of the professional recording studio is deteriorating. There are now many, many ways to get your music recorded.

To state it in plainer language, Larry Crane, editor of the independent recording magazine *Tape Op*, writes that "the business model of 'we have the technology needed to make records—you don't' is gone. This model allowed many studios to charge whatever prices they could" (Crane 2005, 82). Today, smaller and mid-level studios adapt by becoming educational facilities that hold recording workshops and work with home recordists who want to spend a few hours or a few days in a professional facility to do what they can't at home, rather than spending a few weeks or months in a facility to do an entire album. As Crane points out, the old big studios would lose money on such arrangements whereas smaller operations can adapt. For him, the so-called crisis of professional recording is not a crisis at all:

In terms of studios, it seems that smaller, versatile and community-oriented types might be more apt to survive. We can lament the loss of historic rooms like Cello/Western, a place that should rightly become a museum if it doesn't keep functioning as a studio, but just as the government's funding of the sinking airline business makes me nervous, I don't see why a studio should just stay open because we are afraid of change. For me, the loss of Hit Factory is different than that of Cello. I had the opportunity to tour this gigantic facility a few years back. A more boring, soulless place for making records I cannot imagine. (Crane 2005, 81)

Crane's column reads to me like a distant echo of Small's hope for the future of music. Crane's ideal professional engineer is not far from Small's role for the composer: a leader, a pacemaker, a mentor, whose work is intimately bound up with his or her community. The political continuity is interesting because here, the ideal is decoupled from Small's adaptation of the Illichian "low-energy" norm. In other words, we don't need to wait for the end of modern capitalism in order to begin noting and effecting changes in musical culture. To use an old cultural studies standby, music, creativity, and industry are *articulated* phenomena: they have no "necessary" connection with one another; rather their connections are forged through social practice (Grossberg 1992; Hall 1986).

It is tempting to put Small and Crane in dialogue with Jacques Attali, whose *Noise: The Political Economy of Music* (1985), was first published in French in the same year as *Music-Society-Education*. *Noise* famously ends on a utopian note, calling for a coming age of "composition": "doing solely for the sake of doing, without trying artificially to recreate the old codes in order to reinsert communication into them. Inventing new codes, inventing the message at the same time as the language. Playing for one's own pleasure, which alone can create the condition for new communication" (134). Later, Attali calls composition "participation in collective play, in an ongoing quest for new, immediate communication, without ritual and always unstable" (141). Attali writes about elite musics, but his language evokes images similar to Small's: music as a dispersed activity; a musical world where music creation and enjoyment is a collective enterprise, rather than one located in the solitary individual. One could imagine a heady mix of Attali's romanticism with a 1990s style of cyberutopianism to argue that digital recording heralds the new age of composition.

That is why some caveats about amateurism and location are in order here. We should not get too excited about the liberating power or leading edge of digital technologies, because the line between professional and amateur has long been blurred in actual practice. The move into the textualized world of online musical practice may have led us to rediscover something old, rather than to discover something new. Academics have tended to focus on those spheres of musical practice closest to their own habitus, leading to many considerations of high art, or the segments of popular culture most likely to appeal to cultural studies scholars, when in fact a much wider range of musical practice already exists once we look outside the world of professional musicians and dedicated fans. As George Lipsitz puts it in his introduction to the very interesting book *My Music* (a compilation of 41 interviews with residents of Buffalo, New York), "music as a social experience is broader and more complex than the musical activities encompassed by social institutions concerned with music" (Lipsitz in Crafts, Cavicchi, and Keil 1993, xiii). To that I would add that musical experience is broader and more complex than the sites which academics are disposed to study would lead us to believe. Rob Drew's artful ethnography of karaoke takes this thread a step further by mounting a persuasive defense of amateur singing and amateur musical performance. He points out that the disappearance of the amateur is largely a myth:

> Though we're surrounded by music nearly everywhere, many of us see musical creation not as an everyday form of communication but as an occult affair marked off by concert stages and studio walls. It's become a platitude of cultural history that Americans don't make music anymore—that, over the past century and a half, amateur and regional forms of music and leisure have been superceded by mediated, commercial forms. The case is easily overstated. Plenty of music is being made out there, much of it aided by the very technologies that are commonly blamed for killing music making. The parlor piano has given way to the Casio keyboard, hip-hop and dance musicians have turned cutting and mixing into an artful mode of performance, and pretty much every town has its complement of rock and pop bands that slog it out on the local bar circuit. Yet much of this musical activity is hidden from view. (Drew 2001, 13)

When it does get noticed, Drew points out, local music is treated by reporters, scholars, and sometimes the musicians themselves as "something to get *beyond*" (Drew 2001, 13, emphasis in original). His point is well-taken. Amateur, paraprofessional, and everyday forms of music making tend not to be as valorized in scholarship about music and culture. So when we hail the proliferation of cheap digital technologies for music making, we need to be careful to note that this represents the expansion of an already-present condition into the realm of engineering, rather than a revolution in contemporary musical culture writ large.

Additionally, as musical cultures vary around the world, we need to be careful to mark the place of digital technology in an expansively "globalized" musical culture that nevertheless always has particularly local manifestations. Drew is careful to contrast American attitudes toward public singing with stories of more casual attitudes toward karaoke in Hong Kong and several Japanese towns. His point is that the resistance to public singing which so conditions karaoke practice in the United States is not a universal phenomenon. This point can be expanded to other realms of musical practice, including the recording studio itself. In what is probably the first full-length ethnographic study of a recording studio, Louise Meintjes' study of Downtown Studios in Johannesburg, South Africa, meticulously documents the power struggles over sounds, studio knowledge, the boundaries of the studio itself, and technology in the studio. In parts, Meintjes' tale is similar to other stories we have heard: as digital recording technologies proliferated, "small studios with facility to produce competitive sound quality mushroomed in backyards, garages, offices, flats and houses" (Meintjes 2003, 78). Her attention to the iconography of space travel in studio design also rings familiar to anyone who has spent time in a large North American studio. But in Downtown Studios, perhaps the biggest studio in South Africa, the equipment also signifies a certain level of internationality: "simply by owning an SSL [a brand of mixing board, what Meintjes calls the 'Mercedes Benz 560EL of the studio world'], Downtown indexes the internationally competitive quality of its technicians and the elevated positioning of the studio within the hierarchy of the domestic recording industry" (Meintjes 2003, 82). Meintjes casts other signal processing equipment in the same light: "the multinationals are wired into the studio system. They name their indelible presence—Lexicon, Roland, Yamaha, Korg, Technics, Amcron—on the face of their products" (Meintjes 2003, 87). The point here (perhaps obvious to any ethnographer) is that like all technologies, digital technologies mean different things in different places. So again, any desire to hail the proliferation of digital recording technology as the herald of a new formation in musical practice needs to be tempered by the knowledge that while such a formation may have international reach, its various endpoints will not register in an identical fashion.

All this is to say that new things like digital audio may lead us to attend again to old things, like amateurism and the locally differentiated meaning of global technologies. Indeed, digital audio signals very contradictory developments. While cheap (relatively speaking) digital audio production has damaged big studios' radical monopoly over the recording of music, it has not deindustrialized music. The 1990s saw a boom in magazines dedicated to music equipment as sales of recording equipment soared. The shift from analog to digital technology has allowed the manufacturers of musical instruments to subject them to the much more rapid product cycles of computing equipment (see Sterne forthcoming; Théberge 1997, 242–57). Similarly, the final stages of production, such as mastering, are still heavily professionalized. Mastering engineers used to cut the master copies of records, making sure that the needle didn't jump the groove. Today, they put the final polish on recorded mixes and set levels among songs on albums before they go to CD production plants for mass replication. While anyone *could* do this, the fact is that there are still only a handful of mastering engineers who handle the vast majority of recorded music that people hear. In other words, the aesthetics of recorded music are still very much subject to industrial control even if the making of recorded music is more dispersed than ever.

If that's not enough, the rise of the home studio has also in some ways buttressed the ideology of the lone musical genius. After all, a single person can now theoretically control the creation of an entire oeuvre of music at every step from conceptualization to small-scale replication. As John Ryan and Michael Hughes point out, musical collaboration is in some ways more optional than ever before, and there may well be an aesthetic cost to people "going it alone" in musical creation. Yet it is interesting to read their essay alongside Trace Reddell's ideas about using the world wide web as a musical source, Andrew Whelan's study of amateur musicians who listen to and critique one another, and Andre Pinard and Sean Jacobs' documentation of a transnational hip-hop scene. The list could go on. *Cybersounds* outlines the initial contours of a debate I hope to see flourish in the coming years concerning the future of musical creativity and the role of digital technologies in that future.

Music scenes are as vital as ever around the world, and as several chapters of *Cybersounds* demonstrate, their online presence allows musicians and listeners who might otherwise toil alone to find one another and collaborate. Indeed, those of us interested in the study of music and media technologies must now include the Internet in our research, because not only is it a space where music technology is discussed, it is also *itself* a set of technologies for musical practice in a wide range of genres and cultures. Changes in industry structure and technological design have occasioned a mild democratization of the tools for musical communication. We thus stand at an exciting juncture, where musical practice could follow and become more democratic, or it could be recuperated back into some new radical monopoly. Perhaps, dear reader, you would like a prediction. But I will instead end by turning the question around to you: how do you want musical practice to change, and what will you do to see those changes through?

## Acknowledgment

Many thanks to Carrie Rentschler for her reading and commentary on this essay.

## References to the Afterword

Attali, Jacques. 1985. *Noise: The Political Economy of Music*. Translated by B. Massumi. Minneapolis: University of Minnesota Press.

Crafts, Susan, Daniel Cavicchi, and Charles Keil. 1993. *My Music: Explorations of Music in Daily Life*. Middletown: Wesleyan University Press.

Crane, Larry. 2005. "It's the End of the World as We Know It (and I Feel Fine)." *Tape Op* (March/April): 82–91.

Drew, Robert. 2001. *Karaoke Nights: An Ethnographic Rhapsody*. New York: AltaMira.

Fuentes, Annette, and Barbara Ehrenreich. 1998. *Women in the Global Factory*. New York: Hushion House.

Grossberg, Lawrence. 1992. *We Gotta Get Out of This Place: Popular Conservatism and Postmodern Culture*. New York: Routledge.

Hall, Stuart. 1986. "On Postmodernism and Articulation: An Interview with Stuart Hall." *Journal of Communication Inquiry* 10:45–60.

Illich, Ivan. 1973. *Tools for Conviviality*. New York: Harper & Row.

———. 1974. *Energy and Equity*. London: Calder & Boyars.

Jones, Steve. 2000. "Music and the Internet." *Popular Music* 19:217–30.

Jorda, S. 1999. "Faust Music On Line (FMOL): An Approach to Real-Time Collective Composition on the Internet." *Leonardo Music Journal* 9:5–12.

McCourt, Tom, and Patrick Burkart. 2003. "When Creators, Corporations and Consumers Collide: Napster and the Development of On-Line Music Distribution." *Media, Culture & Society* 25:333–50.

Meintjes, Louise. 2003. *Sound of Africa!: Making Music Zulu in a South African Studio*. Durham, NC: Duke University Press.

Mixerman. 2004. *The Daily Adventures of Mixerman*. New York: MixermanMultimedia.

Puckett, Jim, et al. 2002. *Exporting Harm: The High Tech Trashing of Asia*. San Jose, CA: Silicon Valley Toxics Coalition.

Small, Christopher. 1977. *Music-Society-Education*. London: John Calder.

Sterne, Jonathan. Forthcoming. "What's Digital in Digital Music?" In *Digital Media: Transformations in Human Communication*, edited by P. Messaris and L. Humphreys. New York: Peter Lang.

Théberge, Paul. 1997. *Any Sound You Can Imagine: Making Music/Consuming Technology*. Hanover, NH: Wesleyan University Press.

 NOTES

1.    An example of common emerging language on university websites comes from UNLV:

The University has recently received a large number of formal complaints regarding use of the University's network to download or upload copyrighted materials, including copyrighted videos, music, software and written material. The University is required to take these complaints very seriously, and to take steps to address any infringing activity. Failure to do so can potentially result in liability for the University itself. Additionally, any person using his or her University on-line access privileges to engage in the down-loading, uploading, or other unauthorized distribution of copyrighted materials is poten-tially at risk of becoming the target of a legal action for copyright infringement, in addition to any University imposed sanctions.

The Campus Housing copyright policy states, Residents shall not violate the legal protection provided by copyrights, licenses, or other legal means. They shall not make copies of any licensed or copyrighted computer program found on any Campus Housing or other UNLV computer or storage device. They shall not share with others: messages, information, or data that is private, licensed, proprietary, or covered by non-disclosure agreements. This includes but is not limited to video, music, software or any written material that you have not obtained permission to distribute.

When the University receives a complaint that implicates a student, sanctions may include immediate referral to UNLV Student Judicial Affairs for disciplinary action under the UNLV Student Code of Conduct. Disciplinary sanctions imposed can include a requirement that the infringing material be removed and not further distributed, ter-mination of on-line access privileges, educational projects, probation or others. Addi-tional complaints may result in even more serious sanctions.

If you are currently using software that allows you to download or share material over the internet, only items you have permission to share may be shared or the sharing function must be disabled. Anytime peer to peer software is installed or updated it needs to be checked to make sure sharing functions are disabled for items you do not have per-mission to distribute.

2.    It is important to note that not only music is impacted by the changes with the DMCA; consider Boucher's (2002) concern regarding libraries: "A time may soon come when what is available for free on library shelves will only be available on a pay-per-use basis. It would be a simple matter for a copyright owner to impose a requirement that a

small fee be paid each time a digital book or video documentary is accessed by a library patron. Even the student who wants even the most basic access to only a portion of the book to write a term paper would have to pay to avoid committing a crime."

3.    For full discussion of fair use, see, for instance, Patry (1995).

## NOTES TO CHAPTER TWO

1.    All informants' names were changed in order to guarantee confidentiality. Informants' permission for direct quoting in this article was sought, resulting in informants' unanimous agreement.

2.    Testimony of Shawn Fanning, founder, Napster, Inc., before the Senate Judiciary Committee, Provo, Utah, October 9, 2000.

3.    http://news.com.com/2100–1023–234092.html?legacy=cnet

4.    http://www.campchaos.com/show.php?iID=232

5.    http://www.reuters.com/newsArticle.jhtml?type=musicNews&storyID=6384899

## NOTES TO CHAPTER THREE

1.    The origins of the term "bedroom producer" are unclear, but it is commonly used to denote the ideal-typical amateur electronic musician, whose musical activity and social "scene" has been made possible by the combination of Internet communication and increasingly affordable and sophisticated music production software.

2.    I have deliberately omitted the name of the p2p network in question, out of respect for the privacy of its users.

3.    Wikipedia (n.d.). *Breakcore*. Retrieved July 8, 2004, from http://en.wikipedia.org/wiki/Breakcore; IDM is "intelligence dance music."

4.    Section V 63(1)(b) of the Criminal Justice and Public Order Act refers to "sounds wholly or predominantly characterised by a succession of repetitive beats." Under the Act, police were given powers to stop unlicensed "gatherings" at which such "sounds" were played. This extraordinary piece of legislation was "one of the most direct interventions in popular culture by a British government in the twentieth century" (Gilbert and Pearson 1999, 151).

5.    "DJ /rupture," personal correspondence, February 20, 2003.

6.    Of course, music fans are well aware of this fine line. In Dublin, for instance, there is a freely circulated 'zine called *Anorak*, the title of which reclaims the local pejorative term for "music nerds."

7.    I am grateful to Barbara Bradby for this point.

8.    This dialectical relationship is rendered explicit in the 2004 movie *Mean Girls*, with the character of the "mathlete" Kevin G, whose business card reads "Math Enthusiast/Bad-Ass MC" (Dir. Mark S. Walters, Paramount Pictures).

9.    Exchanges are reproduced exactly as they occurred online. An ellipsis (" . . .") indicates where material of a personal or extraneous nature has been removed from the text. Some names have been changed in accordance with the wishes of the participants in question. In some instances, for the sake of brevity I have cited a question but omitted the response; I hope that the regularity with which such questions are asked goes some way towards showing that they are also answered.

10.    The "amen," a classic and ubiquitous breakbeat, originates in The Winstons' "Amen Brother," recorded in 1966.

11. Some users render their names with letters replaced by numerals of similar appearance, for instance, using "4" for "A," "3" for "E," or "1" for "L." Thus Fas3r3d's name is in all probability pronounced "Phasered."

12. Soundforge and Fruity Loops are two popular music programs for editing and composing/sequencing respectively.

13. "AntiCorporate Manifeso," personal communication, July 31, 2003.

14. "Dnb" is an acronym for "drum and bass," a wide umbrella term of which ragga jungle and breakcore could be considered subsets.

15. "m-loc," ragga jungle room, September 20, 2003.

16. How to define a "sample" is a topic of ongoing debate. For present purposes, a sample is a segment of or "quotation" from an earlier audio recording, extracted from its original context, usually so as to be redeployed in a "new" composition.

17. "D/1" or simply "dl" is an acronym for "download."

18. "VBR" is an acronym for "variable bit rate," referring to the quality of the compressed audio.

19. "Bong-Ra," personal correspondence, February 18, 2003.

20. By "southern Hemi demi," mic_mainstream means a "southern hemisphere demo."

## NOTES TO CHAPTER FOUR

1. We requested responses to a series of questions that Dan Petruzzi, webmaster of Okayplayer.com, posted on the message boards. All the quotes in this chapter that reference the message boards resulted from this posting by Petruzzi.

2. Do You Want More?!!!??! (Geffen Records, 1995) and Illadelph Halflife (Geffen Records, 1996).

3. The term *conscious* within the hip-hop community connotes lyrical content that strives to inject reflexive and critical discourse into the mainstream hip-hop environment, an environment that is characterized as hypercommercial, standardized, and materialistic.

4. According to John Perry Barlow, a fellow at Harvard's Berkman Center for Internet and Society, "[Okayplayer] knew that what they were producing was the production of a community" (quoted in Wiltz 2000).

5. These include the message boards "okayartist discussion," "general discussion," "the lesson," "reviews," "freestyle board," "okaysports," "okayactivist," and "high tech." For this study, we focused mainly on general discussion, okayartist, and okayactivist.

6. PBS later recorded some tracks with the American hip-hop pioneer KRS One for their album *New-York Paris Dakar* (Africa Fete, 1997).

7. "Rumba kali" was derived from an old Tanzanian rap song and meant "being broke" in Swahili, the regional language in East Africa.

8. The convention took place over four days in Newark, New Jersey, on the campus of Rutgers University. For more information, see the conference website, http://www.hiphop-convention.org/.

## NOTES TO CHAPTER FIVE

1. Prophets of da City (POC) is a pioneer rap group from Cape Town, South Africa. In the early '90s, POC and Black Noise were instrumental in developing Cape

Town's hip-hop scene. Much of their creative work was geared toward engaging critically with the discourses as well as multiple and fractured realities of apartheid.

2.    Mzwakhe Mbuli is a spoken word artist who often performed at political rallies such as those organized by the now-defunct antiapartheid organization, the United Democratic Front (UDF), during the '80s in South Africa. Mbuli served a jail sentence after being implicated in alleged armed robbery charges. He was released in 2004.

3.    The original version of Napster facilitated peer-to-peer file sharing in a decentralized manner, whereas the new, co-opted version of Napster turns the service into a centralized and conventional retail operation. We thus see a shift from active cooperation and exchange between music fans to a situation where music fans engage in financial transactions with a vendor of music.

## Notes to Chapter Six

1.    See Lawrence Lessig's *The Future of Ideas: The Fate of the Commons in a Connected World* (2002) and Robert McChesney's *Rich Media, Poor Democracy: Communication's Politics in Dubious Times* (1999) for detailed accounts of U.S. policymaking and the private sphere shift that the Internet took.

2.    Titles are usually mash-ups themselves, the mixing of the name of the artists that were used as well as the songs that were used. For example, the U.K.'s Go Home Productions' mash-up of legendary funk-soulsters Sly and the Family Stone plus contemporary R&B songstress Beyoncé Knowles plus '80s girl band The Bangles plus hip-hop group N.E.R.D. is called "Sly Beyoncé Walks Like a Nerd."

## Notes to Chapter Eight

1.    The RIAA (2004) defines unauthorized reproduction of both released and unreleased studio recordings as *pirate recordings*. A pirate recording that consists predominantly of previously unreleased music is often known, somewhat confusingly, as a bootleg among the public at large. A pirate recording that duplicates the audio content and packaging of an officially released product (hence is seeking to pass off as an official product) is known as a *counterfeit*.

2.    For example, the Tape Trader Network (http://www.tapetradernetwork.com/), run by Steve and David Zimmerman.

3.    MP3 (Motion Picture Expert Group Audio Layer 3) was originally developed by the International Organization for Standards, which sought to establish a set of standard protocols for the emergent Interactive Television industry (see Leyshon 2001).

4.    For a fuller history of the early years of SugarMegs, see http://www.sugarmegs.org/.

5.    SHN was developed by Tony Robinson of SoftSound Ltd. and is available under a noncommercial license; FLAC was developed by an informal team led by Josh Coalson (for further details see http://wiki.etree.org or http://www.furthurnet.org/). The FLAC format is also now supported by a number of portable and in-car media players, as well as by several PC-based media players.

6.    Available at http://www.etree.org/index.html.

7.    The data integrity check allows users to verify that the compressed files have been downloaded successfully and without corruption. This is important because a track will be completely ruined if even a single byte is out of place.

8.     BitTorrent was originally authored by Bram Cohen, and FurthurNet by Jamie Addessi; however, as both are Open Source programs, they are under constant development by a number of programmers (see http://bitconjurer.org/BitTorrent/ or http://www.furthurnet.com/).

9.     They also publish lists of trade-friendly artists (see section 4), together with evidence such as official statements or interview material to confirm that they are so.

10.    Some artists have formalized this license; examples and details of terms will be discussed further in section 4.

11.    At the time of writing, the Tadream discussion list is hosted by Yahoo.com (see http://groups.yahoo.com/). Full details of the Tangerine Tree and Tangerine Leaves releases can be found at, among others, http://www.blackaxis.co.uk/tdtree/index.htm (run by Matthew Sawyer in England) and http://www.feldoncentral.com/tdtree/artwork.html (run by Morgan Feldman in the U.S.). The project as a whole is organized and coordinated by Heiko Heerssen in Germany.

12.    Similar projects include the Progressive Rock Remaster Project (see http://from1fan2allothers.com/) and a variety of projects run by Genesis fans (see http://www.genesis-movement.co.uk/).

13.    The Internet Archive (http://www.archive.org/) is a public nonprofit "Internet library" that contains a range of cultural artifacts available in digital formats. The audio section of the collection incorporates the LMA, the content of which is provided by members of the etree.org trading community in SHN, FLAC, mp3, and Ogg Vorbis formats.

14.    The Marillion Front Row Club homepage is http://www.marillion.com/frontrow/join.html.

15.    http://www.krimson.news.com/.

16.    http://www.disciplineglobalmobile.com/order/.

17.    http://gdradio.com/.

18.    http://www.livephish.com; http://www.livemetallica.com.

19.    http://www.charliehunter.com.

20.    Apple's iTunes service (www.apple.com/itunes/store/) has grown rapidly since its launch in April 2003. It has since created a proprietary lossless format called Apple Lossless in competition with the nonproprietary FLAC and SHN formats in use among traders. This shows that Apple recognizes the importance that audio fidelity has among a substantial market share of music fans.

21.    Sony Connect (http://www.connect.com/) was launched in May 2004 as an attempt by Sony to regain its former position as a personal electronics leader. The site uses Sony's ATRAC, ATRAC3 and ATRAC3plus (Adaptive TRansform Acoustic Coding) codecs, which are supported by Sony's Mini Disc player/recorders (http://www.sony.net/Products/ATRAC3). These codecs are, like mp3, "lossy."

22.    http://www.emusic.com/features/emusiclive/index.html

## Notes to Chapter Nine

1.     From a survey personally conducted in May 2004 on 100 participants of online forums of two websites, ipodlounge.com and macobserver.com, dedicated to Apple and the iPod, 60% of the iPod owners interviewed were between 18 and 35 years old, and 30% under 18. PC users accounted for 65%. In terms of frequency of use, 70% of the users

responded used the iPod every single day. As far as the key feature of the iPod, the majority indicated its storage capacity, while 40% mentioned both the Apple brand or the design. When asked what was the original source of the digital music that their iPod contained, the majority responded "backup of regularly purchased music," while 35% answered "digital music bought via the iTunes store," and only 20% indicated files downloaded from file-sharing programs. The survey also requested comments on how the iPod had changed the users' way of listening to music. In general, it was mostly emphasized that with the iPod music had permeated users' lives to an unprecedented extent, thus creating the condition of a very intimate, ubiquitous relation with the device.

2.	After iTunes became available on Windows, Apple senior vice president Phil Schiller stated in an interview, "The iPod makes money. The iTunes Music Store doesn't. Using software to drive hardware sales is a typical strategy for Apple, so it might accept moderate losses from the store to recover a net profit with device sales. In addition, inasmuch as Apple can require use of iTunes and Apple's Quicktime to play Fair-Play files, Apple can increase the value of its brand by associating Apple with all uses of digital music" (Gasser et al. [2004]. See also Fried [2003]).

3.	For a comprehensive account of Apple history, see Malone (1999); see also Levy (2000) and Linzmayer (1999).

4.	In 2004 Apple Computer gained 24% in brand value and went from number 50 to 43 of the most valuable global brands chart (http://www.businessweek.com and http://www.interbrand.com).

5.	For a comprehensive investigation on the cult-like relationship between Apple and its users, see Kahney (2004c).

6.	"New media tend to be decentralized in ownership, control, and consumption patterns; they offer greater potential for consumer input and interaction, and heighten the user's control over the form of consumption and over the relation to media sender. More important, they constitute a challenge to the one-way, monopolistic, homogenizing tendencies of the old media" (Manuel 1994, 2).

7.	http://www.downhillbattle.org/itunes/

## Notes to Chapter Ten

1.	For instance, http://farts.netcarver.com/creations.htm; http://algoart.com/music.htm; and http://www.heliotown.com/Spectrographs_introduction.html (retrieved April 7, 2005).

2.	Midi stands for Musical Instrument Digital Interface. In 1984, Midi provided an important step toward open platform communication in the computer music industry. Midi provides an interface through which synthesizers and other gear from different companies may be linked together for control by a common source, such as a keyboard or sequencer. Midi data files record note values such as pitch, volume, and duration, which can then be fed into a variety of sound-generating sources. The soundcards of most personal computers include a patch of synthetic voices that are triggered by Midi files.

3.	In November 2002, a posting popped up on the Microsound mailing list of one member's discovery:

I want to thank Tu Mp3 and ubu.com for posting those links just when they did. I went to the Tu-m site and started listening to one of the 'soundtracks.' (It showed up as a quicktime audio bar . . . not sure if it's supposed to do that or if the quicktime I recently installed has hijacked my mime settings.) I switched back to the menu and clicked on a different piece, but forgot to stop the first one (they were in different windows.) My browser dutifully played the second piece right over the first one. Well, that pricked up my ears. I started adding more and more files to the 'mix,' revelling in the noisy glory. I use Mozilla and the tabbed browsing really came in handy: I didn't have to open as many windows. Well, I soon decided I was wasting my time and really should get back to reading my emails. Lo and behold, my next email had the link to ubu.com, where I quickly found the 'sound' page. . . . I quickly picked a name at random from the pop-up list and then clicked on a sound file. The overlapping mess of Tu-m files that I had started was still going, so my microsound collage was suddenly blessed with some strange Italian mouth noises (I think it was Giacomo Balla). Somehow I'd managed to pick stuff that all worked relatively well together and the results were sublime. (BJM, email posted to microsound@hypereal.org, November 18, 2002)

4.  http://www.looplabs.com (retrieved April 7, 2005).

5.  DJ Rabbi is Mark Amerika, Marcos Bastos, Giselle Beiguelman, Chad Mossholder, and Rick Silva. Information and works may be found at http://www.djrabbi.com (retrieved April 7, 2005).

6.  http://www.stasisfield.com (retrieved April 7, 2005).

7.  http://www.djrabbi.com/about (retrieved April 7, 2005).

8.  Roy Ascott derives the term from the work of Nora and Minc "to designate computer-mediated communications networking involving telephone, cable, and satellite links between geographically dispersed individuals and institutions that are interfaced to data-processing systems, remote sensing devices, and capacious data storage banks" 2003, 232). See "Is There Love in the Telematic Embrace?" (1990), reprinted in *Telematic Embrace: Visionary Theories of Art, Technology, and Consciousness.*

9.  I have written about the spatial poetics of the telharmonic system in "Laptopia: The Spatial Poetics of Networked Laptop Performance," published in *Contemporary Music Review* 22, part 4.

10.  See Thom Holmes' *Electronic and Experimental Music*, 2nd ed., pp. 44–52. Also see the section on Cahill at the website "Electronic Musical Instrument 1870–1990," retrieved April 7, 2005, from http://www.obsolete.com/120_years/

11.  http://www.findsounds.com (retrieved April 7, 2005).

12.  http://www.ubuweb.com (retrieved April 7, 2005).

13.  http://www.soundtoys.net (retrieved April 7, 2005).

14.  http://www.usdat.us and http://www.experimentalparty.org (retrieved April 7, 2005).

15.  http://www.fictive.org/~peter/bits/ (retrieved April 7, 2005).

16.  http://www.earshot.info/ (retrieved April 7, 2005).

17.  PERL stands for Practical Extraction and Reporting Language.

18.  http://recycler.plagiarist.org (retrieved April 7, 2005).

19.  http://www.archive.org (retrieved April 7, 2005).

20.  http://www.tylerpotts.com/52songs.html (retrieved April 7, 2005).

21.  See David Toop's account of Markus Popp's "Oval Process" software in *Haunted Weather: Music, Silence and Memory*, 181–82, 200–201.

22.  http://sensorband.com/atau/constellations/ (retrieved April 7, 2005).

23.	http://www.silophone.net/index.html (retrieved April 7, 2005).
24.	http://www.briankane.net/8track.html (retrieved April 7, 2005).
25.	http://wrocenter.pl/projects/ping/index.html (retrieved April 7, 2005).
26.	http://www.monolake.de/atlantic.html (retrieved April 7, 2005).
27.	http://www.aec.at/radiotopia/ (retrieved April 7, 2005).
28.	See Lisa Gitelman's account of parallels between radio and Internet cultures during their early phases of development in her *Scripts, Grooves, and Writing Machines,* 227–28. Also see Daniel Czitrom's *Media and the American Mind from Morse to McLuhan* and Susan Douglas, *Inventing American Broadcasting, 1899–1922.*
29.	Please see http://www.du.edu/~treddell/telharmonics/ for pictures, audio clips, and links to web-based projects.

## Notes to Chapter Eleven

1.	For Blauner, the relationship between the technology of production and alienation could be charted on a graph by means of an inverted U-curve. It was at its height in the assembly-line industries of the early 20th century. But as technology moved beyond the assembly line to more automated systems, the remaining workers were liberated from mundane jobs by the technology.

2.	This is not to imply normative consensus. Artistic creations often are meant to challenge the prevailing normative structures of production, content, and consumption. So, for example, hip-hop music has been in part a challenge to conventional notions of melody and musicianship. Similarly, the legal challenge to file sharing is an example of consumption as contested legal terrain.

3.	For a comprehensive review of the production of culture literature, see Peterson and Anand (2004).

4.	Gaisberg was a sound engineer but is credited with recognizing the potential for recorded music and actively developing talented singers. He is perhaps best known for his work with Caruso (see Moore [1999]).

5.	Beatles producer George Martin sees the advent of stereo recording as being another factor in the changing role of the producer. He put it this way: "During the whole period—before and even after the Beatles arrived—the record producer was basically an organizer. Of course, he could make decisions about what should be put on a record, and he could advise artists on how to best put over their performances. But it was the advent of stereo recording which truly made him what he has become today—a creative person in his own right" (Martin and Hornsby 1979, 104).

6.	In their study of country music songwriters, Peterson and Ryan (1983) observed an anti-industry attitude among some songwriters who had not yet broken in. However, for many writers this attitude dissipated when actual commercial success was achieved.

7.	These techniques include special icons accompanying the artists' name, bold type, and a special location on the navigation bar.

8.	The actual audience of many of these stations is undoubtedly quite small, perhaps primarily limited to artists who are expecting to hear their own material. One station we listened to gives a running total of how many listeners are online. Over several hours the highest number of listeners never exceeded 15.

# List of Contributors

**Chris Anderton** is a PhD candidate in the Department of Geography at University of Wales Swansea. He is currently co-editor of the annual periodical *Swansea Geographer* and a member of the International Association for the Study of Popular Music (U.K. and Ireland). His current research project investigates the history, characteristics, representation and reception of U.K. music festivals. Other research interests include music fandom as it relates to fan creativity and notions of community; contested notions of musical authenticity and genre hybridity; and the impacts of digitization and the Internet on models of business organization. He received a BSc Hons (First) (2001) in geography at the University of Wales Swansea, and an MBA (Dist.) (2002) in music industries from the Institute of Popular Music, University of Liverpool.

**Michael D. Ayers** is a visiting professor at the Manhattan College Department of Sociology in the Bronx, New York. He is the co-editor of *Cyberactivism: Online Activism in Theory and Practice*. His current research interests include the sociology of culture in relation to media, music, and art; social and cultural movements; and cyberspace and cyberculture. He has received degrees in sociology from Virginia Tech and the New School for Social Research. Michael is a contributing music critic for *Billboard.com*, *Giant* and the *Village Voice* and has had essays published by *McSweeneys*, *Stop Smiling Online*, and *Metro New York*.

**Elizabeth A. Buchanan**, PhD, is Assistant Professor and Co-Director of the Center for Information Policy Research at the School of Information Studies, University of Wisconsin-Milwaukee. Her research interests revolve around information ethics, intellectual freedom, virtual research ethics, and online education. Elizabeth's recent work appears in such journals as *Journal of Information Ethics* and *Ethics and Information Technology*, as well as many anthologies. She is the editor of the 2003 compilation, *Readings in Virtual Research Ethics*.

**Gabriele Cosentino** is a PhD student in the Department of Culture and Communication at New York University. His current research interests include the role of media in democratic politics, grassroots and alternative media, and intellectual property reform movements. He holds a Laurea degree in communication from the University of Bologna, Italy. He is part of d-i-n-a, a network of artists and researchers developing events and projects in the field of art, technology, and activism.

**Kathy Doherty** is Senior Lecturer in Communication Studies at Sheffield Hallam University. Her current research interests are in feminist and discursive psychologies, including projects on accounting practices for sexual violence; fashion, gender and identity; and online fan communities. She is coauthor (with Irina Anderson) of *Accounting for Rape* (Routledge, forthcoming) and has also published research on accounts for sectarian violence, psychotherapy talk, identity and enterprise culture and on issues of methodology and epistemology in psychology. She received a BSc (Hons) in psychology in 1992 from the University of Sheffield followed by a PhD in social psychology in 2000. She is co-editor (with Simeon Yates) of *Discourse Analysis Online* (www.shu.ac.uk/daol).

**Markus Giesler** (PhD, MBA, MEcon) is an Assistant Professor of Marketing at York University's Schulich School of Business, where he teaches classes in marketing management and entertainment marketing. He also has extensive entertainment industry experience having produced over 300 records for major record labels. An anthropologist by training, Markus's research explores entertainment and leisure consumption at the intersection between marketing, culture, and technology. He has written and published articles on file sharing, consumer emancipation, conspiracy consumption, consumer lifestyles, and post-copyright entertainment culture. Markus can be reached at http://www.markus-giesler.com.

**Adam Haupt** lectures in the Centre for Film & Media Studies at the University of Cape Town. He has also lectured at the University of the Western Cape and the University of Stellenbosch as well as Peninsula and Cape Technikon. Haupt has freelanced for *Mail & Guardian*, *SL* magazine, and *Y* magazine, and has been involved in e-commerce ventures as an editor and copywriter. He has published in the field of black South African youth culture and his PhD research explores debates about global capitalism, technology, and intellectual property as well as youth culture.

**Michael Hughes**, Professor of Sociology, received his PhD in sociology from Vanderbilt University in 1979 and has been at Virginia Polytechnic Institute and State University since then. He is currently the editor of the *Journal of Health and Social Behavior*, the medical sociology journal published by the American Sociological Association. His research interests in mental health/illness, racial attitudes, ethnic and racial identity, and patterns of cultural choice have resulted in more than 60 articles in professional journals. With Carolyn J. Kroehler, he is author of *Sociology: The Core* (7th ed., McGraw-Hill, 2005).

**Sean Jacobs** is a researcher and journalist based in New York City. Born in South Africa, where he worked as a political researcher, he holds a PhD in politics from the University of London (2004). In 2004 he was festival director of Ten Years of Freedom: Films from the New South Africa staged in New York City. He has held fellowships at Harvard University (1998), the New School for Social Research (2001), and New York University (2003–2004). He is the co-editor of *Shifting Shelves: Post-Apartheid Essays on Mass Media, Culture and Identity* (Kwela 2004).

**Daragh O'Reilly** is a PhD candidate in the School of Cultural Studies at Sheffield Hallam University, U.K., as well as a lecturer in marketing at Leeds University Business School, U.K. His current research interests include the relationship between business and culture, the marketing and consumption of popular music (doctoral research), and product placement in the movies. He contributed a chapter on the marketing of popular music to *Arts Marketing*, an edited collection published by Elsevier (2004). He received a BA (1975) in modern languages and literature from Trinity College, Dublin, Ireland, and an MBA (1990) from Bradford University School of Management, U.K.

**André Vladimir Pinard** is a PhD candidate in the Sociology Department at the New School for Social Research in New York. His fields of interest include sociology of culture, sociology of race, and ethnography. André is also a budding photographer.

**Trace Reddell** works at the intersections of audio and multimedia production, digital networking, media theory, literary criticism, and the history and philosophy of drug culture. He currently teaches and directs the graduate program in digital media studies at the University of Denver. Recent works include a contribution to the Stasisfield CD, *The Audible Still-Life*, and the soundtrack for the DVD, "Society of the Spectacle (A Digital Remix)," which continues to screen internationally at galleries and media art and film festivals. Publications include articles in *Leonardo Music Journal* and *Contemporary Music Review*. Trace edits the "music/sound/noise" portion of the Electronic Book Review (http://www.

electronicbookreview.com). More information may be found at his website, http://www.du.edu/~treddell.

**John Ryan** is Professor and Chair of the Sociology Department at Virginia Tech. He is coauthor of *Media and Society: The Production of Culture in the Mass Media* (Allyn & Bacon, 2000) and has written extensively on the music industry and arts production. Current research interests include the digital transformation of the music industry, and the role of culture consumption in peer networks.

**Jonathan Sterne** teaches in the Department of Art History and Communication Studies at McGill University. He is author of *The Audible Past: Cultural Origins of Sound Reproduction* (Duke, 2003) and many essays on media, technologies, and the politics of culture. He is also a member of the production team for *Bad Subjects: Political Education for Everyday Life* (http://badsubjects. org), the longest-running publication on the Internet.

**Andrew Whelan** is a PhD candidate in the Sociology Department of Trinity College, Dublin. He received a Dip. H.E. (1997) in sociology from Ruskin College, Oxford, and a BA (2001) in politics, philosophy and economics from Somerville College, Oxford. His current research interests include authenticity and identity in electronic music, the social circulation of musical commodities, and the interaction between technology and creativity in musical subcultures.

# Index

General Editor: *Steve Jones*

**Digital Formations** is an essential source for critical, high-quality books on digital technologies and modern life. Volumes in the series break new ground by emphasizing multiple methodological and theoretical approaches to deeply probe the formation and reformation of lived experience as it is refracted through digital interaction. **Digital Formations** pushes forward our understanding of the intersections—and corresponding implications—between the digital technologies and everyday life. The series emphasizes critical studies in the context of emergent and existing digital technologies.

Other recent titles include:

Leslie Shade
  *Gender and Community in the Social
  Construction of the Internet*

John T. Waisanen
  *Thinking Geometrically*

Mia Consalvo & Susanna Paasonen
  *Women and Everyday Uses of the Internet*

Dennis Waskul
  *Self-Games and Body-Play*

David Myers
  *The Nature of Computer Games*

Robert Hassan
  *The Chronoscopic Society*

M. Johns, S. Chen, & G. Hall
  *Online Social Research*

C. Kaha Waite
  *Mediation and the Communication
  Matrix*

Jenny Sunden
  *Material Virtualities*

Helen Nissenbaum & Monroe Price
  *Academy and the Internet*

To order other books in this series please contact our Customer Service Department:
(800) 770-LANG (within the US)
(212) 647-7706 (outside the US)
(212) 647-7707 FAX

To find out more about the series or browse a full list of titles, please visit our website:
WWW.PETERLANGUSA.COM